EUGENE
MEYER

EUGENE
MEYER

MERLO J. PUSEY

Alfred · A · Knopf / 1974

NEW YORK

LIBRARY OF CONGRESS CATALOGING IN PUBLICATION DATA
PUSEY, MERLO JOHN, DATE   EUGENE MEYER.
INCLUDES BIBLIOGRAPHICAL REFERENCES.
1.   MEYER, EUGENE, 1875–1959.   I.   TITLE.
HG172.M5P87   332'.092'4 [B]   74-7174
ISBN 0-394-47897-5

TO

Katharine Meyer Graham

WHO CARRIES THE TORCH

HER FATHER LIT

MY WANT IS THE RIGHT RESULT FOR THE WORLD.
—*Eugene Meyer in a letter to Louis Wehle, May 6, 1919*

CONTENTS

CONTENTS

ILLUSTRATIONS

ILLUSTRATIONS

Washington's newspaper publishers at a 1937 Community Chest luncheon.

*Meyer visiting the Post composing room on the fifth anniversary of his
publishing venture.*

Meyer and Lord Halifax in a London air raid shelter, September 1941.

A happy family reunion during World War II.

Meyer and his grandson Vincent Homolka, about 1945.

*The Famine Emergency Committee meeting at the White House,
March 1, 1946.*

ILLUSTRATIONS FOLLOWING PAGE 336:

A photograph of Agnes Meyer used on her lecture tours.

Meyer and his great friend, the photographer Edward Steichen.

A Herblock cartoon while Meyer was president of the World Bank.

*Truman parade in Washington, November 5, 1948, after his upset election
victory.*

Meyer and Winston Churchill.

Meyer celebrates a Washington Post *anniversary with a group of employees.*

A family gathering on Eugene Meyer's 75th birthday.

The executive staff of the Post in January 1951.

*Meyer is made an honorary member of the International Printing Press-
man's Union.*

At his desk in the Washington Post *building.*

*The final purchase of the Times-Herald: a joyous occasion for the Meyers
and Grahams.*

Meyer displays the first edition of the Washington Post and Times-Herald.

*Philip L. Graham explaining the Meyers' stock gift to the paper's em-
ployees, June 19, 1955.*

The Meyers in his study at Mount Kisco.

F O R E W O R D

THIS BOOK RELIES HEAVILY UPON THE BIOGRAPHICAL DATA assembled under Eugene Meyer's supervision in the last years of his life. On the basis of interviews with Meyer and much additional research, Sidney Hyman wrote an exhaustive eight-volume manuscript that was never completed. In dealing with the period of the great depression, he had the assistance of Bray Hammond of the Federal Reserve System. The major events of Meyer's life are also outlined in a series of interviews he gave to Dean Albertson of Columbia University's Oral History Research Office in 1952. These sources have been invaluable in writing the present volume.

I have also had free access to the Meyer Papers relating to all phases of his career, to family correspondence, and to dozens of his friends, associates, and co-workers. Members of the family, especially Katharine Meyer Graham and Elizabeth Meyer Lorentz, have been enormously helpful. The personal diaries of Agnes E. Meyer and her unpublished manuscript entitled "Life as Chance and Destiny" also proved to be valuable sources, along with her autobiography, *Out of These Roots*.

It was my privilege to be a member of the staff of the re-created *Washington Post* throughout the quarter century when Eugene Meyer directed its policy as publisher or indirectly guided its course as chairman of the board. Though well aware of his special qualities as a journalist and a public figure, I have tried to tell his story as an objective observer, conscious of human foibles as well as dedication and genius. My sole aim has been accurate portrayal of a fabulous character.

M. J. P.

EUGENE MEYER

1 /

Youth in San Francisco

"TELL ME," THE BEAMING FATHER EXCLAIMED WHEN HE WAS told that the child he had been waiting for was indeed a son, "is he intelligent-looking?"

The father was Marc Eugene Meyer, French-Jewish immigrant from Strasbourg who had settled in the frontier town of Los Angeles. What he seemed to be pondering was whether this squalling infant would grow up to be a worthy successor to himself. But he could also have been worrying about the economic calamity that had hit the area. The collapse of a real estate boom in Los Angeles had coincided with the downward sweep of a more general speculative orgy. Every bank in California was closed, and specie had disappeared from circulation. Certainly the stricken community was in need of wiser management of its booms and busts.

This first son of Eugene and Harriet Newmark Meyer was delivered on Halloween 1875 while the panic was in full swing. There is no indication that it left any mark upon him, but in point of fact he would develop unusual skill in coping with panics on a national scale. He would reap great wealth from the financial twisters of his day. He would add much to human know-how about meeting economic emergencies, and his skill as a troubleshooter would take him into high governmental positions in the hours of national need. As a capstone to his career, he would rescue a dying newspaper from the toils of depression and make it a great institution.

In those dark days of October 1875, however, the rejoicing over his birth was family-oriented. The child was named Eugene Isaac Meyer after his father (who had never used the name Marc) and his grandfather. It was taken for granted that he would follow in the footsteps of his French-Jewish ancestors. At an early age young Eugene was steeped in this tradition and kept under pressure to prepare himself for the position he would one day inherit. The fact that he had three older sisters, Rosalie, Elise Hortense, and Florence, did not alter his special

3

status in the family. As the first-born son, he would be responsible for perpetuating the Meyer name and business enterprises.

Not much is known of young Eugene's early years in Los Angeles, but it is clear that his parents were worried about the meager education and health care the town could offer their growing family. At the age of five Eugene was taken to San Francisco for treatment of a throat ailment (apparently tonsillitis) because he could not speak above a whisper. Three years later Eugene Senior was invited to take charge of the London, Paris & American Bank in San Francisco, and he welcomed the opportunity to give his family a wider horizon. San Francisco was then a city of 225,000 people. Meyer sold his mercantile business in Los Angeles, and the family moved to the Golden Gate area on the first day of 1884.

Eugene Junior's first memorable experience in San Francisco was not, however, precisely what his father had in mind. The white starched Eton collar that the boy's mother required him to wear to school, despite his protests that no one else in his class wore one, made him a conspicuous mark for a ritual that was practiced on the playground. The older boys put younger ones into a circle and forced them to fight bare-knuckled until one had a bloody nose. When the ring closed around Eugene for the first time, he suffered a pounding by a bigger lad because his nose would not bleed. Finely wrought and arrow-straight, his nose may have looked fragile but extraordinarily tough cartilage prevented it from bleeding, and his self-esteem prevented him from begging for mercy.

The toughening Eugene got from subsequent encounters stood him in good stead when the family moved to Alameda. Two more daughters, Ruth and Aline, and two more sons, Walter and Edgar, had been added to the Meyer family, and, with the birth of her eighth child, Harriet's health had been shattered. The doctors prescribed rest and sunshine, and fog-free Alameda seemed the best place in the Bay Area to find it. The family took a house on Encenal Avenue. Eugene had scarcely enrolled in the Alameda grammar school when he clashed with a bully who ruled the playground. The tussle was short and violent. To the surprise of everyone, including Eugene, it left the young dictator in the dust, and Eugene was hailed as a liberator. Almost in a flash he became the swaggering chieftain of a little gang that worshipped physical prowess.

His new prestige was gratifying, but it led to trouble both at school and at home. He became the leader of classroom mischief, so much so that he was automatically whacked on the knuckles with a ruler when another student fired a spitball at the teacher. Eugene's protests were so voluble that the teacher took him into the hall for a talk. "Even if you didn't fire that spitball," she said at last, "you've done enough I haven't caught you at to justify the whack." That left the young troublemaker without a comeback.

At home his pranks were a source of turmoil. He led the younger children in open revolt against the housekeeper. They walked on tiptoe near the room where their mother was trying to rest, but elsewhere the house was a bedlam. In later years Eugene would explain this phase of his youth by saying: "I was just a bad boy, and I was unable to behave in an orderly way—making too much noise, chasing the girls around, teasing them, pulling their hair."[1] Eugene Senior decided to take drastic measures. He asked his eldest daughter Rosalie (Ro in the family) to drop out of school and manage the household until her mother was well again. Ro was only sixteen, but she readily consented and racked her brain for means of taming her wild brother. When lecturing and scolding failed, she bought a cat-o'-nine-tails, but Eugene tripped her as she chased him with the whip, and she fell flat.

The obstreperous lad did, however, respect the authority of his father and continued on generally good terms with him. His father took him horseback riding and paid a trainer to give him riding lessons. As they went clattering down the main avenue of Alameda, Eugene Junior let his imagination run as wild as his actions had been doing. He thought of himself as a crown prince riding beside the reigning monarch on a tour of the realm that one day would be his. As his ambition soared he was certain that his horsemanship was just as good as the reigning monarch's and perhaps a little better. In his exuberance he made the colossal blunder of expressing these ideas to Ro.

The harried sister seemed to ignore this psychological pole-vaulting at the time, but young Eugene had created a trap for himself. The next time he provoked Ro, she snapped: "No more horseback riding for you. Father will listen to me when I tell him it's giving you a swelled head."[2] Fearing loss of his treasured pastime, the young hellion asked for terms. "Read this," Ro commanded as she handed him a statement she had carefully prepared for the occasion, "and sign on the dotted line." It was a solemn compact committing him to proper behavior at the table, faithful performance of household chores, adherence to a schedule for going to bed and getting up, escort service for his younger sisters, and general obedience to Ro's orders without fuss and nonsense—all in return for continuation of his riding privilege. The more he protested the more he

[1] Dean Albertson's interviews with Eugene Meyer, p. 17.
[2] Sidney Hyman's manuscript, "Life of Eugene Meyer," Part 1, p. 60.

convinced Ro that she had found his Achilles' heel at last. Eugene signed. It was a complete capitulation, but it greatly enhanced the respect he had for his sister throughout his life.

Rosalie's role as substitute mother was intended to be temporary, but Harriet managed to rise from her bed and resume her activities for only uncertain intervals. So Ro was to continue the heroic assignment until her own marriage at the age of twenty-three. Meanwhile the family returned to San Francisco; Harriet had gained little from the Alameda sunshine; commuting had proved burdensome to Eugene Senior; and the family had missed its San Francisco friends. They took a large house in the 1700 block of Pine Street. Here Eugene Junior faced the problem of finding a new set of friends for the third time in three years.

Life was further complicated by an accident. While Eugene was catcher in a baseball game, his usual position, he was knocked down by a swinging bat and cut his eyebrow on a stone. Following the folklore of the day, his companions sought to stem the flow of blood with cobwebs from a nearby stable. The boy went home with the flesh around his eye turning black and blue and his face a mess of blood and cobwebs. His father was horrified. A washing disclosed that the injury was not serious but the consequences were. "No more baseball for you," the distressed father said. "Your mother is sick. We can't have things like this to worry about." That prohibition was especially cruel because Eugene had already been forbidden to indulge in such "dangerous sports" as football and sailing on Lake Merritt.

Shortly after this event Harriet and Ro went to Europe for six months seeking doctors who would know how to cure "nervous dyspepsia." In their absence a housekeeper looked after the children. The return of his mother and sister about Christmas-time in 1886 brought Eugene another experience that strained his relations with his father. With school recessed for the holidays, he played all day away from home. When he returned about four in the afternoon, the family was frantic because Eugene Senior had decided to meet Harriet and Ro at a junction in Nevada and to take Eugene Junior with him. He had telephoned to have the boy ready to catch the train at five, but no one had been able to find him. When the returning youngster was informed of this furor and rushed upstairs to report to his father, he was greeted by a slap in the face.

"Where were you?" the impatient parent cried. "Why doesn't anybody know where you are?"[3]

The blow was the more mortifying because it was the first time that Eugene had felt the sting of his father's hand in anger. Though he

[3] Albertson interviews, p. 18.

6

wanted to strike back, he dared not; he could only scramble into some fresh clothes and pack a few things for the journey. They caught the train with a few minutes to spare, and then it was evident that the father was chagrined by what he had done. There was no apology, but he made special efforts to see that his son was comfortable. Young Eugene remained disconsolate, pressing his face against the train window as the light of an early winter evening faded. Resentment filled his mind through a sleepless night in the Pullman berth.

Morning at the Nevada junction brought a drastic shift in his emotions. The pair detrained amid a tribe of Apache Indians that was being shifted after United States troops had suppressed an uprising. To young Eugene, who now felt guilty because of the harsh thoughts he had harbored against his father, the scene appeared to have the makings of a scalping party, with himself as the victim. As fear gripped him, he took his father's hand and begged forgiveness for the heartache he had caused. In his own relief at this reconciliation, the father talked of his pride in his son and said that he lived and worked with his future in mind. The boy did not feel secure, however, until he was reunited with his mother and Ro and they were safely on the train for home. He would never again feel a blow from his father, but the humiliation of that one resort to physical punishment would continue to color their relations.

There was never any doubt about who ruled the Meyer family. Eugene Senior was a consistent example of character and determination, though not lacking in kindliness. His dark hair (except for one white lock), his full moustache and short beard covering only his chin, his straight nose and deep-set eyes made him a striking figure. He carried himself with a dignity that was enhanced by his long, double-breasted coat, wing collar, and bow tie. Born in Strasbourg of French-Jewish parents on January 26, 1842, he never lost his French accent and he managed to preserve some of the grace of the Old World even on the California frontier.

He migrated to America after the death of his father, Isaac Meyer, who had been educated as a rabbi and served as secretary of the Jewish Consistory. The Meyers had lived in Alsace for many generations. Eugene's grandfather, Jacob Meyer, had been a member of the Congress of Jewish Notables convoked by Napoleon I for the consideration of Jewish rights, and the Emperor had made him an officer in the Legion of Honor. After Isaac's death his wife, Sephora Loeb Meyer, tried to support her family by selling white flour to Jews for their Sabbath bread, but it was necessary for the children to leave school and take jobs. Eugene's two sisters, Ernestine and Amelie, found work in dry-goods stores; his brother Constant became a monitor in a training school for silversmiths. At the age of fourteen, Eugene left his studies at the Gymnase Protestant and took a job with "L. and N. Blum," a firm that had a store in Donaldson-ville, Mississippi, in addition to its small business in Strasbourg.

The tales Eugene heard from the Blum brothers about America had convinced him that he should see for himself what it had to offer. When Nathan Blum planned a business trip to Donaldsonville, he offered to take his young bookkeeper with him. Sephora Meyer reluctantly gave her consent on condition that her son would keep away from the yellow fever areas. Since this meant that he could not go to Donaldsonville or New Orleans, his interest shifted to California, which the French press was picturing as a land of romance and adventure.

Blum and Meyer sailed from Le Havre in September 1859 on the steamship *Vanderbilt*. The young adventurer chose to keep out of debt by going third class for $110. He slept in the foul air and grime of the hold amid boxes of merchandise and subsisted largely on food taken with him, but travel was only a means to an end. After waiting two weeks in New York, he caught a steamer for Panama, crossed the Isthmus on the narrow-gauge railroad, and continued on to San Francisco.

Here the seventeen-year-old immigrant began a totally new experience. His feeling of being lost in a strange new world was relieved somewhat when he went to see Alexandre Weill of the firm of Lazard Frères, carrying a letter of introduction given him by Alexandre Lazard in Paris. Weill found his fellow countryman a place to live, and Simon Lazard, sensing that the newcomer was a youth of good habits and serious purpose, gave him a temporary job in his flourishing export-import business to make sure that he would not be sucked into the gambling dens or the gold craze that was stirring that raw western town.

Lazard later found the young man a job with Smiley, Yerkes & Voizin, a new auction house. Although Eugene began as a clerk and porter at $50 a month, he managed to make and save $1,500 in a year by picking up bargains at the auctions and selling them at a profit. In 1861 he decided to go to Los Angeles, where Solomon Lazard, a cousin of Simon's, was said to need a clerk in his store. Arriving by stagecoach, he was so disappointed that he wanted to leave within forty-eight hours. His description of that "one-mule town," with its three or four thousand inhabitants, mostly foreigners, seemed to justify his reaction:

There were only four brick houses in the place. The other build-ings were built for the most part of adobe with roofs covered with pitch that would crack and in winter allow the rain to leak in. The town had no paved streets and no sewers; the water supply both for

drinking and irrigation came from ditches or "sanchas." The hotels
at the time were the Bella Union and the Lafayette. There was a
morning paper called "The Los Angeles Star." Surrounding the town
were large cattle ranches but few or no orange orchards. Stages,
which took three or four days to make the trip, ran to San Francisco
three times a week.[4]

Yet the young Frenchman took a job as a clerk and bookkeeper in the
S. & A. Lazard general store on Alameda Street. He lived in a back room
of the store and often slept on the counter with his gun in order to protect
the merchandise. In his spare time he learned Spanish so that he could
communicate with the many Basque sheepmen who patronized the store.
As his reputation for sobriety and reliability spread, some of his new
friends began leaving money with him because there were no banks.
Eugene kept a safe in his room and a double-barreled shotgun on the wall.
One day a Basque came in and said a friend had bet him $20 that he could
not get back the $50,000 he had deposited with Meyer. The neophyte
banker counted out $50,000 in gold coin, and the Basque staggered off with
it and won his bet.

After three years in Los Angeles, Meyer entered into partnership with
Solomon Lazard to operate a department store which came to be known
as The City of Paris. Lazard provided most of the money, and Meyer ran
the business and did most of the work. Ten years later Eugene and his
brother Constant took over the business. Meanwhile Eugene also became
agent for some of his San Francisco friends in lending money in the Los
Angeles area. He became a director of the Farmers and Merchants
National Bank; he was an organizer of the Los Angeles Social Club;
armed with two derringers and bowie knife (still prized relics in the
Meyer family), he helped to maintain law and order as a member of the
Vigilance Committee. For some years he was also consular agent of France
in Los Angeles.

The marriage of Eugene Meyer and Harriet Newmark took place on
November 20, 1867, with the bride's father, Joseph Newmark, performing
the ceremony.[5] Rabbi Newmark had migrated from Germany in 1824;
after founding the Elm Street Synagogue in New York, he had lived in
many parts of the United States before making his way to Los Angeles.
His wife Rosa, a native of London, had joined him there after sailing
around Cape Horn when Harriet was less than two years old. Harriet was

4 Eugene Meyer's journal, p. 12.

5 Harris Newmark, *Sixty Years in Southern California, 1853–1913* (New York:
Knickerbocker Press; 1926), p. 290.

the Newmarks' youngest daughter and was only sixteen at the time of her marriage.

Though the wedding itself was a happy occasion, it brought the participants a grim reminder of the violence of the frontier. While Rabbi Newmark intoned the ancient Hebrew marriage prayers at the Bella Union Hotel, mourners on the floor below were keening over the body of a man slain a few hours earlier in a gun battle. Eugene and Harriet began their married life in a typical adobe house, but a few years later they built a comfortable home on Fort Street, now Broadway. In later years the younger Eugene would find much amusement in pointing out the spot in downtown Los Angeles where his father used to keep a cow, and the father would lament that if he had merely kept the lots he once owned in Los Angeles he would be worth five times what he had earned in a lifetime of toil.

Harriet proved to be a charming companion and an affectionate mother. She was short and petite, with a kind and pretty face. Her hair was customarily pulled back from her ears into a bun, and on social occasions she wore the fancy lace dresses that were characteristic of the period. Although she managed her household well and had unusual nursing skills, she lacked Eugene's stamina, and her illness, which later developed into diabetes, was a serious problem for the entire family.

The Meyers belonged to a reformed Jewish congregation, but religion was not a major factor in their lives. In San Francisco young Eugene was sent to a class for the study of Jewish history, Hebrew, and the meaning of rituals, and was scheduled for confirmation along with other youths. But when he was told to go to the altar and repeat the credo, declaring "a perfect faith" in each tenet, he declined. "I believe some of these things," he explained, "but I don't believe them all with *perfect* faith." Thinking it indecent to lie in a holy place, he played hookey on confirmation day. There was momentary trouble at home when he nevertheless received his confirmation certificate by mail, with regrets that illness had kept him away from the ceremony. "But you weren't ill," his father remonstrated. "I never said I was," Eugene replied. "I just didn't show up." As the lad explained his difficulty with the credo and his unwillingness to lie, his father's critical tone mellowed into a smile. The incident was indicative of the younger Eugene's lifelong attitude toward the faith of his fathers. Though his moral concepts and many traits of his character were closely related to the Old Testament and he did not regard himself as being irreligious, he never joined a congregation.

The lack of a "perfect faith" did not mean that Eugene was ashamed of his Jewish ancestors. On the contrary, he was proud of the part his people had played in the history of Europe. Even then his uncle Zadoc Kahn, who had married Eugene Senior's eldest sister Ernestine, was Grand Rabbi of France. In the family and in the synagogue Jewishness could be cherished, but the youngster was loath to have it become a dividing line between him and his associates of different faiths. Eugene Senior had become a United States citizen, and his eldest son felt primarily American.

His sense of oneness with all people was deeply offended when the boys at school taunted him as a "sheeney." The sting was not diminished by the fact that they also called others among them "Polacks," "Micks," "Bohunks," "Wops," or "Chinks." Eugene was somewhat resentful because his father had not warned him of the blind prejudices he would encounter, but he knew that he would have to make his own adjustment to the world around him. Deep within him a resolution began to take shape— he would prove that a Jew could be as honorable and as successful as anybody.

By way of extending his useful skills, Eugene was permitted to join the junior class at the Olympic Athletic Club, where he was introduced to the French foil and took boxing lessons from James J. Corbett, then on his way to the heavyweight boxing championship of the world. The elder Meyer was pleased to provide this instruction for his son—even a gentleman should know how to defend himself. But Meyer, the dignified banker, was shocked by a newspaper picture of his son fighting another boy with the publicity-seeking trainer looking on. When a similar offense to his sense of propriety occurred, Meyer put a stop to the publicity. The boxing lessons too were soon to be discontinued, but not before young Eugene's reputation as a pupil of "Gentleman Jim" Corbett's had given him new stature among his peers.

School offered little challenge to the energetic youngster, and he coasted along without doing his homework. Reading at home, however, was not regarded as work. Eugene was fascinated by the novels of Scott, Dickens, Hugo, Dumas, and Bulwer-Lytton, and made a practice of reading in bed when he was supposed to be sleeping. His citation for one of three medals for academic excellence when he finished grammar school came as a complete surprise. Eugene went home and boasted to his father that he had emerged third in his class.

"Why weren't you first?" the father demanded.

"Well," Eugene retorted defensively, "only one could be first. Why isn't third place good enough?"

"The world is full of people who stand third," the elder Meyer came back, "and they don't amount to much. If you were a blockhead, I'd say:

'All right, God has given me a son who is a blockhead, and I should be grateful if he at least knows enough to tie his shoes without a nurse to help him.' But you are not a blockhead. You simply don't stretch yourself except when I bear down on you."

The deflated youngster promised to work harder when he entered high school in the fall. High school would be a special challenge because his father had originally insisted that he be educated in France after the grammar grades, and Eugene had won his argument for an "American" education only with great effort. Yet he continued to breeze through course after course at the Lowell High School with little effort. His confession in later years was: "I just worked mischief, that's all—nothing very ruinous, just raising hell and playing tricks."[6]

In his senior year Eugene was spurred by a rule that allowed the upper ten pupils in the class to enter the University of California without examinations. His father provided a second spur. "I've made arrangements with Professor Henry Senger of the German department of the University of California," he said, "to have you come in to see him every Monday, Wednesday, and Friday from four-thirty to six."

"What for?" Eugene asked with obvious irritation. "I don't need a tutor if that's what you had in mind. I'm one of the first ten."

"I know," the father replied with finality, "but you don't work enough to suit me. You came out third in your grammar class. Do you call it progress to drop from third to tenth? Professor Senger will teach you how to work."

Despite his misgivings, Eugene soon discovered that the tutoring was a delightful experience. Professor Senger was a highly trained and intelligent German pedagogue. "We shall proceed," he said, "as if you know nothing about Greek, Latin, ancient history, or mathematics." Drawing his fingers across the boy's head, he added, "I wipe the slate clean. Let us now see if we can discover a few things worth writing on it." His technique was to open new worlds of intellectual interest, and Eugene was soon participating in the sport with great enthusiasm. Pursuit of knowledge the Senger way was fascinating. Not content to translate classical Greek and Latin into English and English into Greek and Latin, Eugene canvassed the fruit stores in the area until he found a vendor who subscribed to a Greek newspaper. Thereafter he bought one piece of fruit each day in exchange for the right to read the Greek paper in the back of the store.

When the graduating ceremony was held in the Odd Fellows Hall in May 1892, Eugene was not first in his class, but he was close to it. Far more

---

[6] Albertson interviews, p. 12.

important, he had discovered the excitement of working on projects that are near to one's heart. Eugene would never forget the great debt he owed to Professor Senger. Many years later, on learning that Senger's position at Berkeley was endangered because of the anti-German hysteria that swept the nation in World War I, both Eugene and his father would rally their San Francisco friends in defense of the professor.

The experience with Professor Senger also seemed to give Eugene a new appreciation of his father. The senior Meyer was sometimes brusque and lacking in sympathy for youthful ideas and yearnings, but he had the best interests of his children at heart. His business affairs and private books were always in good order. He kept his eldest son fully informed about the estate he would someday have to manage, and he met the problems of life with courage, good judgment, and resourcefulness. Eugene paid his father a high compliment a few years later when a French woman who had corresponded extensively with his father remarked to him, "Your father writes very clearly."

"Well, that isn't very difficult," he replied to the surprised matron. "What is really troublesome is to think clearly." That was the major attribute he ascribed to his father.

As the children grew toward maturity, the Meyer home became a center of social life. Eugene Senior was well-to-do and he wanted his daughters to appear to good advantage, whether it was a children's party for Ruth and Aline or a gala ball for Ro, Elise, and Florence. Ro was a striking beauty, and all the others were attractive. The bevy of well-favored females brought to the home swarms of boys and young men, and those of marrying age came under close scrutiny. The doting father made it his business to find out how their minds worked and what their economic prospects were.

The younger sons in the family were never as close to their father as was Eugene. Walter, the middle son, though generous and gifted in some respects, lacked Eugene's natural aggressiveness and Edgar's especially lovable traits. Ground between upper and nether stones, he seemed unable to find a comfortable niche for himself in the family. Edgar, the last-born, was a gay and sweet-tempered lad. He made a place for himself wherever he was, although, separated from his father by a gap of forty-two years and seven older children, he came to look upon his eldest brother, nine years his senior, as protector, confidant, and counselor.

The necessary breadth of parental concern in a family of eight was never permitted to diminish the status of the first-born son. Only he could take his father's place. Eugene was introduced to the financial journals of New York, London, Berlin, Frankfurt, and Vienna to which his father subscribed. From these and his home environment he picked up a working knowledge of French and some German. The San Francisco newspapers kept him aware of local events, and his father consistently drew attention to stories of significance in the business world, especially the scandals involving the "utility crowd" which he hoped his son would avoid as if it were a plague.

Important letters from Meyer's business associates overseas were shown to Eugene, and he was likely to be cross-examined as to their meaning. When the father was involved in a lawsuit—there was much controversy over poorly surveyed federal land grants to the Lazard interests for their upkeep of military roads in California and Oregon—the son was given the legal brief to read and was excused from school to attend the trial if it promised to be informative.

Adult entertainment in the Meyer home was often geared to an educational purpose. Because of Harriet's semi-invalidism, these affairs tended to be for men only. While they sometimes played cards, politics and high finance usually proved more interesting. Young Eugene was expected to be present on these occasions and to keep his ears open and his mouth shut, except for an occasional apt comment or humorous thrust. The international banker would not have the son he was grooming appear oafish before a group of men who well understood the father-son tradition and who occupied positions in which they could greatly help or hinder budding careers.

Despite the restrictions, Eugene was delighted to mingle with his father's friends. Among them was Raphael Weill, who was to be a founder of the Bohemian Club and builder of San Francisco's celebrated White House department store. Another favorite guest was the Democratic United States Senator from California, Stephen White, who was also the elder Meyer's personal lawyer. White was known as the "silver-tongued orator," not only because of his eloquence, but also because he stood for free coinage of silver. Since Meyer was a sound-currency man or "Gold Democrat" who greatly admired President Grover Cleveland, he clashed sharply with White on the emotion-charged monetary issues of the day. Yet their friendship remained warm, and instead of fearing that his son would be corrupted by White's "radicalism," Meyer permitted the young man to disregard all bedtime regulations when the orator was present.

The most memorable event in the Meyer family in this period was Rosalie's marriage to Sigmund Stern on October 3, 1892. The ceremony took place in the Meyers' lavishly furnished parlor under a canopy of flowers in a spacious lace-curtained bay window, with a picture of Uncle Zadoc Kahn, Grand Rabbi of France, pinned to one of the curtains. The setting was a far cry from that which had characterized the marriage of Eugene Meyer and Harriet Newmark a generation before in the adobe village of Los Angeles. The Meyers were now enjoying affluence in the gilded Victorian age, and Ro was marrying a nephew of Levi Strauss, who had gone to San Francisco in 1850 intending to pan for gold and instead had struck gold in a different fashion by converting the heavy canvas he had brought with him into pants—the famed "Levi's" that were to make his name a common noun in many lands. As he never married, Levi Strauss had trained his sister's sons, Sigmund, Abraham, and Jacob Stern, to manage and ultimately inherit his business. With Ro married to Sigmund and with the second Meyer daughter, Elise, virtually engaged to Abraham, the high hopes of Eugene Senior for his family appeared to be materializing in a most gratifying fashion.

2 /

College in Three Years

EUGENE'S DESIRE FOR AN "AMERICAN" EDUCATION LED TO WIDE discussion in the family as to where he should go to college. Meyer often heard the fathers of young men at Harvard complain that they spent too much money without learning anything "useful." Yale seemed much too interested in champion athletic teams. Columbia University was in the bacchanalian city of New York. In the San Francisco area, Leland Stanford University was only one year old. The University of California was thus chosen by a logical process of elimination. Meyer was pleased because his son could commute to the campus and would still be at least partly under the parental thumb. Eugene wanted to retain contact with many friends and to avoid an entrance examination.

The young man had heard from students who called on his older sisters that college was just a happy round of shaking dice, playing poker, and drinking beer. Eager to conform to the accepted pattern, Eugene spent most of his freshman year in pursuit of these diversions. It was possible for him to do so because, thanks to Professor Senger, he was already familiar with much of what the freshman courses had to offer. Since he was still forbidden to play baseball or football, he made poker his specialty, which led to an embarrassing confrontation with his father. A classmate who owed him a poker debt mailed the money to his home in a letter addressed to "Eugene Meyer." The elder Meyer opened it and put his son through a sharp cross-examination. The son wriggled without disclosing his gambling activities and thereafter added "Jr." to his name.

Some of the professors made an impression on him, including Bernard Moses in economics and George Richardson in Latin. There were some serious-minded students: Frank Norris, the future novelist, and Milton H. Esberg, who was to be a lifelong friend. For the most part, however, Eugene's companions were the rowdies in the class. He was one of the freshman gang that put a giant "96" made of white paper on the hillside behind the college. When it was raided by sophomores, individual fights ensued and the outnumbered sophs were tied up one by one until their picture could be taken in this humiliating position with the smirking frosh in the background. Eugene's exclusion from the fraternities—no Jew was admitted in those days—irritated him, but it didn't interfere with his year of revelry. All in all, he liked the University of California.

While Eugene was wasting his freshman year, his father—indeed, the entire country—was undergoing an economic crisis. Despite the election of Grover Cleveland as President in 1892, on a platform promising repeal of the Sherman silver coinage act, the policy of monetary debasement was running its course. European creditors cut off loans that had provided some elasticity to the American money supply. Large quantities of American railroad bonds held by frightened Europeans were sold. Hoarding became widespread, and the drying up of credit caused a collapse of agriculture with consequent repercussions in industry.

The storm struck while Meyer was wrestling with a momentous personal problem. Alexandre Weill and the Lazards of Paris had offered him a partnership in Lazard Frères in New York. Though the financial inducements were attractive, and Meyer, at fifty, was still in the prime of life, he was loath to uproot his family. California was home to all of them. In the end, he nevertheless decided to make the move in the belief that the New York position would enable him to advance the interests of all his children and to make a more secure berth for Eugene.

New York seemed to belong to a far-off world apart, and to reach it by means of the crude and poorly coordinated railroads of the early nineties was something of an ordeal. The Meyer family had lost the steadying hand of Ro, who was now married and soon to have a child of her own. She remained in San Francisco, where she was to become an eminent civic and cultural leader. With Harriet long since a bystander in family affairs, Meyer organized his seven children who would make the trip into squads: the girls under command of Elise; the boys directed by Eugene. Each commander could enforce discipline by any means short of a firing squad, and any differences between them were to be ironed out when they reported to the supreme commander at breakfast, lunch, and supper.

In this way the family endured the long ride to Chicago—four days and four nights—in May 1893. Despite the dust from the new, untreated roadbeds, the scarcity of good food, and the tiresome transfers between trains, the trip made a lasting impression upon seventeen-year-old Eugene. For the first time he saw America. The land in which he lived was an unbelievably vast continent with obviously rich resources. He was fascinated by a new thought. This magnificent expanse of prairies, grain fields, forests, rivers, and towns was a legacy that belonged to all the people of the nation and to him personally because he was a part of the nation. A land so potentially fruitful must hold boundless opportunities, and he could really be somebody. It all seemed for the first time to minimize the importance of the position his father was so meticulously preparing for him.

Arriving in Chicago, the family stayed a week so that Harriet could rest, Meyer could tend to a business matter, and the children could go to the Columbian Exposition. So Eugene got another assist, despite the gaudy carnivals at the fair, in visualizing the future of America. Then a train ride of twenty-four hours took the Meyers to New York where they settled down temporarily in the Savoy Hotel.

New York further stimulated the seventeen-year-old's imagination. Then a city of more than 3,400,000 inhabitants, it was far bigger than any man-made thing he had ever seen. Eugene promptly wrote his sister Ro about "three hotels with a luxury of furnishings and magnificence of interiors unsurpassed anywhere, towering story on story over nearby princely private dwellings of marble." Yet to a transplanted Californian accustomed to foliage, light, and space, these New York showplaces "were jarring in ensemble as they lined a noisy, dirty square, with but a few trees and no grass to relieve the eye or to break the heat thrown up by the pavement."

Eugene's exploration of the city also took him to the Lower East Side with its depressing sweatshops, tenements, pushcarts, and shabby markets. Italians, East Balkans, and Jews from Russia, Poland, and Lithuania jostled one another in their struggles for a bare existence. Eugene was shocked by the misery that was everywhere apparent. Why were these Jews so different? Here was an appalling problem that would need attention, but just now there were many other problems closer to home. His father had plunged immediately into the work awaiting him at Lazard Frères, and the young scion was assigned to the chores of office boy. At the same time he was on exhibition as the heir apparent to his father's position in a great international banking house. In everything he did, he was told, he must prove himself a worthy carrier of his father's hopes.

His new world proved to be very intriguing. Even a messenger could see the wheels of a fascinating system go round. Lazard's of New York held a key position in the communications network which involved the United States Treasury, the big city and interior banks, and the banks in many European cities. Eugene would race up the stairs to a visitors' gallery in the Stock Exchange, whenever possible, and spend a few minutes watching the swirl of men and paper on the floor below. Sometimes he would pause within the swarm of speculators and free-lance brokers who operated on the Curb outside the Stock Exchange. The Curb had more color—since garish hats or blazers aided identification—more expertise, more fever, more headaches, and wider fluctuations in stock prices. Eugene listened to many tales about men who had been ruined in the recent panic and about others who had survived. What made the difference? Why had some escaped? The eager messenger plied his elders with questions, but the answers seemed strangely unsatisfying. His father often used the word "system" in describing the choices that could be made, but it seemed very elusive. Was there really a "system" that could make success or failure in this world of Wall Street less a matter of accident? Eugene made himself a promise that he would "look into this," but it would have to be later on.

In the new setting, continuation of Eugene's studies seemed almost an afterthought. Only three weeks before classes were to begin, he decided to try to enter Yale, which would have the advantage of taking him away from home. To his pleased surprise, he found that his father had changed his mind about Yale. One of the Lazard partners had sent his son there, and the son of another was to register as a freshman that fall. So Eugene wrote for a recommendation from Martin Kellogg, president of the University of California, and began cramming for the Yale entrance test. The response he got from Berkeley gave him credit for only "fairly acceptable work in his studies," but affirmed that he "maintained an unblemished character." While worrying about this halting recommendation, he tried to master a subject called "mechanics" and managed to survive the examination.

Eugene was pleased by his first view of the New Haven Green. "Its plain and gently sloping surface," he wrote his father, "its elms methodically arranged in shady avenues, the clean well-kept walks that intersect it, the quiet simplicity and lack of pretension combined with immutable evidence of cultivation, all seem to reflect the spirit of New England people." But Yale in 1893 was not a congenial atmosphere for a newcomer from the raw and scarcely civilized West, especially when that newcomer happened to be the son of a Jewish immigrant. Because of his late registration, Eugene lived some distance off campus, sharing a room in a boarding house with the freshman son of his father's partner. He also went automatically into the fourth division—a sort of cellar that transferring students shared with known blockheads.

The chagrin of being at the bottom of the heap aroused Eugene's competitive instincts. His glimpse of the business world had also given him a new incentive to prepare himself well for what lay ahead. If he could not now buckle down to consistent study, he told himself, he had better get a job and stop wasting his father's hard-earned money. The result was that he signed up for twenty-one credit hours instead of the prescribed fifteen, adding German, French, and political economy to the routine load. His daily schedule included an early breakfast at the Commons, chapel at 8:15 a.m., morning classes, lunch at the Commons, afternoon classes, study in his room or at the library, an hour of exercise in the gymnasium, dinner at the Commons, and more study in his room, often well into the night.

The hard-working sophomore wrote to his sister Ro in California: "I often feel so lonely, and so often want to talk to you about the things going on in my mind, that if I wrote to you everything, all the forests would be denuded to provide the paper pulp for the stationery I would need." But loneliness could be turned into an asset. At the end of his first year at Yale his down-to-business attitude had won him a place in Phi Beta Kappa without so much as an application for the honor. Suddenly he was lifted from the cellar to the top echelon of his class. This dramatic shift in his status was the more important because it lent support to another plan that had been taking shape in his mind. With what appeared to some Yale professors as rash temerity, this untamed Californian was devising a bold scheme to skip his junior year and graduate in 1895 instead of 1896.

The first step in Eugene's unorthodox campaign was to win the support of William Lyon Phelps, his faculty adviser. Phelps was then a new instructor in English, but the sparkle and warm human qualities that would endear him to successive generations of Yale students were already in evidence. His friendship and helpfulness had been an oasis in the social desert Eugene had found at Yale. But this did not mean he could accomplish the impossible. Phelps's response was that similar requests from two other students—one aiming to be a teacher and the other a minister—had just been rejected.

Eugene argued with great pertinacity that his case was different. He intended to be a banker; when he left Yale he would be going to Europe for postgraduate work, and he did not want to be an "old man" at the beginning of his career. "Will you let me write the petition and will you then look at it?" he pleaded. Phelps agreed to that much without giving the young man any further encouragement.

Meyer drafted his petition as if his life depended on it. Noting that he would have seven extra credit hours at the end of the 1894 spring term, he proposed to spend the summer earning eight additional credits in logic, ethics, psychology, Spanish, and the history of English literature, taking "such examinations in September as may be necessary." Finally, he argued, he had not changed his course in any way in order to skip a year, and there need not be any concern about ruining his health from overwork. His health was the best, and "if the work should prove too heavy a strain—which I do not anticipate—I should at once give up the idea."

After an anxious wait, Eugene was notified by his adviser on June 22, 1894, that the faculty had given its consent "on account of your experience outside the academic world, and also the excellence of your work at Yale the past year." Eugene was elated, and his father scarcely less so. At last the boy was proving himself worthy to step into his father's shoes. All family claims upon his time were shelved, and Eugene spent the summer in concentrated study.

Since he already knew Greek, Latin, and French, the first-year Spanish course was easy. For help in English literature, he turned to Herbert L. Towle, who had recently passed the course with excellent marks. Towle wanted him to slow down and savor the elegance of literature, but Eugene could not slow down. What gave him the greatest trouble was the course called "Logic, Ethics and Psychology." The text was a very abstract and somewhat woolly volume by Professor George T. Ladd, head of the department. Eugene found it difficult to get beyond the first paragraph which concluded: ". . . we define psychology as *the science which describes and explains the phenomena of consciousness, as such.*"

"What the devil does he mean by 'as such'?" Eugene asked. Having gone to New Haven for ten days of cramming on the book, he hired a tutor and decided to digest sixty pages of the six-hundred page text per day. But the tutor bowed out, and at the end of his ten days Eugene was still lost in the fog. If the Ladd text offered the best analysis of the human mind and the nervous system, he concluded, then psychology must be the greatest unplowed field for human study. "If I didn't have to be a damn banker," he said to himself, "I'd like to take it up."[1] Here was the beginning of his lifelong interest in psychology and psychiatry.

In his direct encounter with Professor Ladd for the examination young Meyer decided to play a sort of verbal poker. Ladd asked questions Eugene did not understand. He gave answers which he thought the professor did not understand, but one bluffer's respect for another seemed to carry him through. At least he passed the examination, and, having sailed through his other tests, was granted senior status.

To the sophomore who had suddenly become a senior, Yale turned a pleasanter countenance. Eugene shared a nice room in Lawrence Hall on the campus with a member of Zeta Psi. Though he was still excluded

[1] Dean Albertson's interviews with Eugene Meyer, p. 31.

from the fraternities, his membership in Phi Beta Kappa led to friendships with some of the more brilliant students. Among these were Francis Burton Harrison, who was to become governor general of the Philippines; Cornelius Vanderbilt, Jr., a future general in World War I; George Dwight Kellogg, valedictorian of the class of '95, who was to head the classical department at Union College; and Albert Galloway Keller, who would eventually hold William Graham Sumner's chair at Yale. Eugene also found the intellectual fare more to his liking. Steeped though it was in traditionalism and the rigidities of the classical curriculum, Yale did allow its seniors some opportunity for reflection and classroom discussion. An essay that Eugene wrote for his class in modern European history on the future of French-German relations shows a considerable grasp of the forces that were then moving the world.

The highlight of his senior year was Professor Sumner's course in social science. Eugene was one of half a dozen who pressed around the lectern after class to ask questions and test the professor's wit. Powerful but bent in frame, with a stern face deeply creased by time, the great man expounded his laissez-faire philosophy with both humor and patience. His concern for the preservation of individual liberty struck a responsive chord in Eugene, and the latter did not flinch from the Sumner thesis that liberty could best be preserved by free competition in which the fit would survive and the weak would fall by the wayside. Of course this would lead to industrial strife, but strife was a sign of "vigor in a society." To give free rein to the constructive forces of competition, Sumner opposed monopolies, labor unions, tariffs, and governmental "tinkering" with the monetary system.

Subsequent events would deal harshly with the Sumner thesis, and Meyer would help to dethrone it as national policy. In 1895, however, Eugene carried away the wisdom of the granite-faced economist as the most significant contribution of Yale to his education.

Because of skipping a year, Eugene was one of the "babies" of the class that graduated in June 1895, being four months shy of his twentieth birthday. Nevertheless, he graduated with honors and stood nineteenth in a class of 250. His senior year had been easy compared to the load he had carried as a sophomore, but there was no doubt in his mind as to the most valuable lesson he had learned: Work was the key to all success. As Meyer looked back at his Yale years in later life, he was convinced that many of his classmates were hurt more than they were helped by their college experience. Sent there chiefly to mingle with "the sons of the right people," they "learned false standards of how best to get along in life and bad habits in a variety of directions."[2] That is one reason why he would urge his brother Edgar to go to Cornell.

Yet he retained a warm spot in his heart for Yale as an institution. He would consistently attend class reunions and come to know his fellow classmen far better than he knew them in 1895. Yale would bestow upon him all the honors available to its sons, and he in turn would become a generous benefactor. All this sentiment would remain tinged with regret, however, that the great institution at New Haven was not better prepared in the nineties to train eager young minds who were looking toward the new century.

Before resuming his education in Europe, Eugene returned to Lazard Frères for a brief period as a $12-a-week clerk and substitute bookkeeper. Then he was off for Paris in April 1896, and received a hearty welcome by Alexandre Weill and many other friends of his father's. There was a jarring experience, however, when he visited his Aunt Ernestine and her husband, Zadoc Kahn, the Grand Rabbi of France. The rabbi was deeply involved in the national furor resulting from the imprisonment of Captain Alfred Dreyfus, a Jew, at Devil's Island, on trumped-up charges of treason. While the Kahns, with other guests, were celebrating Eugene's arrival, they were aroused by a tumult in the street. An anti-Dreyfus mob was shouting, "Down with the Jews." That outburst of prejudice in a city he had always regarded as the cradle of liberty intensified Eugene's interest in the Dreyfus scandal as it continued to rock the French government for another decade, and when at last Dreyfus was exonerated, with the help of Eugene's uncle, the outcome would profoundly enhance his confidence in the ultimate triumph of truth.

For several months Eugene worked in a Frankfurt bank, lived with a German family, and spent his free time bicycling in the beautiful Rhine Valley. After a brief stay in Hamburg, he then went to Berlin, where his time was divided between the Dresdener Bank, the theaters, and the University of Berlin. His chief interest at the university was a course taught by a German economist named Wagner who seemed to contradict almost everything that Eugene had learned from Sumner at Yale. As an Alsatian, Eugene was supposed to hate everything German, but he found the Germans pleasant and decided to quit disliking them.

The peripatetic young banker-student was still in Berlin when he reached his twenty-first birthday on October 31, 1896. In a letter of congratulations his father asked what should be done with Eugene's "no-

[2] Eugene Meyer to Deane W. Malott, May 12, 1955.

smoking fund" which then totaled, with interest, about $800. Meyer had promised his son $100 if he did not smoke until he was eighteen, and had then said that he would add $500 more if Eugene did not smoke until he was twenty-one. Proud to have a little capital of his own, the new man in the family asked his father to invest the money in Northern Pacific common stock. It was his first plunge into the stock market—a move that was ultimately to bring him great fortune.

In January 1897, Eugene shifted to London, where he worked with Lazard Brothers and then for a stock exchange brokerage firm. Though he attended lectures, operas, and theaters and made a point of acquainting himself with Toynbee Hall in the slums of Whitechapel, he found London less interesting than Berlin. As spring came, he went to Paris for a stint in the main offices of Lazard Frères, which resulted in a flattering offer from Alexandre Weill. If Eugene would settle in London and devote himself to building up Lazard's business there, Weill said, he would be made head of a major London branch after a few years of seasoning. The banker also intimated that an attractive daughter in the Lazard family was available.

Gratified though he was by such an offer at the age of twenty-two, Eugene concluded that his prospects in his homeland were no less alluring. "Besides," he said to Weill, "Europe looks to me like an armed camp. I think you're going to have war here, and I'd rather live in a country that won't be involved in that war."[3] In 1897 no one dreamed of the United States being drawn into Europe's wars.

So the European adventure came to an end on a note of high confidence on the part of the adventurer in himself and in his country. Eugene joined his father and mother, his sister Ro and her family, his brother Walter, and other members of the tribe who had spent the summer in Europe, for a happy reunion aboard a French steamer which took them to New York. At last he felt prepared to settle down to a career, for which he had had ideal preparation. Yet a tinge of regret remained. Eugene knew that he would never again be as free as he had been in his year and a half abroad. His youth was over.

[3] Sidney Hyman's manuscript, "Life of Eugene Meyer," Part I, pp. 180–1.

3 /

Breaking the Tradition

THE RESUMPTION OF WORK IN THE NEW YORK OFFICES OF Lazard Frères proved to be a let-down. Once more Eugene became a $12-a-week clerk, with about forty persons in the hierarchy above him and none below. Although his salary was raised to $25 a week within six months and later doubled again, he felt that there was no recognition of the experience he had gained in Europe. Nor was there any possibility of vaulting out of the cellar, as he had done at Yale, to a responsible position.

Eugene's father hoped that his son would ultimately become a leader of the firm, but there was no evidence at the time that the young man was being groomed for anything. On the contrary, he was expected to take his place in the bureaucracy of the firm and await his turn. Meanwhile there was a good deal of friction. Eugene's immediate superior was George Blumenthal, who was soon to marry the third daughter in the Meyer family, Florence. Blumenthal was recognized as one of the best foreign exhange bankers in New York. J. P. Morgan, E. H. Harriman, and many other eminent men in the financial world made frequent use of his talents. But he had an abrasive personality and seemed to find satisfaction in making life miserable for those around him. Eugene deferred to Blumenthal's greater experience and sought to learn from him as they worked together in the securities end of the business, but his ego and quick temper were as sparks to Blumenthal's combustibility.

A substantial part of the business under Blumenthal's supervision was the buying of securities in European markets for resale the next morning in the United States. Losses could result from miscalculations or from some unforeseen disturbing event during the night, but profits could also be substantial. One transaction initiated and carried through by young Meyer, involving Southern Pacific Railroad bonds, gave Lazard Frères a profit of $100,000 and brought him a $2,000 Christmas bonus in 1897.

The bright spot in the firm was its bookkeeping department presided over by a genial Ulsterman, James W. Hoban, a graduate of the University of Dublin. Taking a special interest in Eugene, Hoban would stay after hours to teach the young man all there was to know about keeping books. A prodigious worker, he was accurate in every detail and could ride either a panic or a boom with unflagging self-assurance. Eugene was so pleased by Hoban's performance that when he set up his own firm Hoban would be the first man he would hire and their association would continue through forty-six years.

The young bank clerk began studying law in his after-office hours but dropped it out of boredom with both the teachers and students. Remembering London's Toynbee Hall, he then went to the Lower East Side one night a week to work in a boys' club and managed sand-lot baseball on Sundays. In his first glimpse of the Lower East Side in 1893 Eugene had been appalled by the degradation of the Jews from eastern Europe. Now he took a more sophisticated view. These wild youngsters who had been uprooted and driven to the United States by anti-Semitism were reacting as many other oppressed people had done. Their problems were complicated by the fact that they were repudiating their parents who could not speak English. Recognizing Eugene's interest in how the other half lived, Mary Kingsbury Simkhovitch asked him to be a director of Greenwich House and Lillian D. Wald induced him to furnish money for a settlement house nurse.

After two years of relatively uneventful work for Lazard Frères, Eugene took a trip to Canada with Max Lazard, son of one of his father's French partners. Carrying a letter of introduction from the ambassador of France to the archbishop of Quebec, they met many interesting people and then tramped the north shore of the St. Lawrence River, took a steamer up the Saguenay and then canoes through northeastern Quebec. Even with the help of two French-Canadian guides and two Indians, the trip proved very taxing. Their food supplies ran low, the nights were bitter cold in spite of the stove which was part of their equipment, and the portages over tangled and little-used trails with heavy loads were too much for an unhardened clerk from Wall Street. Eugene returned to New York burning with fever; the doctors found he had typhoid, double pneumonia, and pleurisy.

A grim fight for life ensued, and it often appeared that Eugene would lose it. The family was in a state of alarm, and everything that the senior Meyer had been planning for since the birth of his first son seemed to hang in the balance. Due to the starvation diet then prescribed in the treat-ment of typhoid fever, Eugene lost sixty pounds. When his fever was broken and his temperature remained normal for three weeks, his mother took him to Lakewood to complete his recuperation, but another onset of the disease put him in bed again for several weeks. His tough constitution ultimately pulled him through, but a year elapsed before his health was fully restored.

Through his long convalescence Eugene spent a great deal of time reading and thinking about his future. Among the books that interested him was *The Map of Life* by William Edward Hartpole Lecky, suggesting that a man's life should be planned as a single whole in which each stage would be a prologue to the stage that followed. Eugene turned his attention to a map of life for himself. His first twenty years had already been given to what he characterized generally as "school." The next two decades, from age twenty to forty, would be given to growth, expansion, and experimentation—learning from life and the correction of his mistakes. During this period he would earn a "competence," marry (preferably at about twenty-eight if he could afford it), and start a family. The third period, from forty to sixty, would be a time for delivery—performance— on the basis of all that had gone before. If feasible, it should be devoted to public service. In any event, he would try to be independent by his fiftieth birthday so that he could render ten years of public service before retiring at sixty. The remaining years of life would be a time "to grow old gracefully" and to help the younger generation.

The idea of giving part of his life to public service had taken firm root in Eugene's mind when he was at Yale. His father had advised him to keep out of politics, but the son took a more serious view of the citizen's role in a democratic country. Arthur Twining Hadley, later president of Yale, had developed the thesis that a principal function of a university was to train young men for public service. Eugene was so taken with the idea that he would create a public-service fund at Yale which he would ultimately raise to $250,000. Beyond this, he was strongly motivated to give of his own time and talents to some public cause.

There was no doubt in Eugene's mind that sixty was the right age to retire: old men in high places were a roadblock to bright young men with new ideas. This was all too evident at Lazard Frères, where many of the men who had advanced to good positions on the basis of seniority had neither imagination nor courage and were too lazy to investigate anything outside of the routine. Even his own father, who had recently passed the threescore mark, was worrying excessively over trivial things. "If he keeps it up," Eugene said to himself, "he'll worry himself into an early grave. It's time for him to retire." The young man's fixation on retirement at sixty was thus an indirect rebuke to all the old men who were standing in his way.

His map of life had another clouded area. Nearly five years of his second phase had elapsed—the phase in which he was to acquire a family and a "competence"—and he was a long way from having either. Social opportunities were not wanting. Many invitations came his way from French-Jewish and German-Jewish families in New York who had marriageable daughters with a dowry. His sisters seemed to be constantly making potential matches for him among their friends. Several of these girls aroused his interest briefly, and Irène Untermeyer, a gifted daughter of attorney Samuel Untermeyer, did so for several years. But how could he support a wife and family on the $200 a month he was earning? The fact that his father was well-to-do did not essentially change matters; the elder Meyer had no thought of blunting the urge of economic necessity by subsidizing his sons.

Pressed by his immediate ambitions and his concern about the future, Eugene began to ask himself if Lazard Frères was not a blind alley. Aside from the fact that it was dominated by older men who were likely to occupy the top positions for a long time, he questioned whether the firm could hold its place in the sphere of international finance without drastic changes in its orientation. Its business was chiefly the financing of imports and exports. Eugene reasoned that the big trust companies which had more funds available at lower costs would cut seriously into this business, unless Lazard's locked itself into the fast-developing industrial economy of the United States, without hindrance from the mother firm in Paris; but his fears made no impression on his superiors.

Another source of concern was the sybaritic living of the Lazard heirs in Paris. Eugene had great respect for his father's associates in the firm, but their sons seemed to be chiefly interested in girls and horse racing. Yet these were the men who would someday control the firm. At that time the Paris partners were firmly in the saddle; they had the capital and the name; in some measure they seemed to share the general European attitude of the time that, financially and commercially, America was a colony to be exploited. The three New York partners owned only a 45 percent interest in the firm, and the dominant French partners had a right to break up the combination on the expiration of three-to-five-year contracts. In joint transactions the Paris branch could thus load on charges for meager services, and the New York partners would have to go along or jeopardize renewal of their contracts.

The elder Meyer had long accepted a secondary role because the Paris partners were his dear friends, and he did not want to fight with them. George Blumenthal had furious rows with them when he felt the New York office was being exploited, but he had not succeeded in bringing about any fundamental changes. Eugene reasoned that he might spend his best years trying to get a satisfactory deal from Lazard Frères and then possibly find himself cast out in middle age if he did not knuckle under to the Paris office. "If I'm going to be free," he finally said to himself, "I may have to get out. If I'm going to get out, it's better to get out now and start at the bottom on the ladder."[1]

Several times during his convalescence Eugene screwed up enough courage to let his father know the trend of his thinking. Meyer treated the disclosure as a product of mental depression resulting from his son's long, critical illness. Eugene would regain his reason along with his physical strength; so the father urged patience, and the son acquiesced to the extent of going back to work in the early fall of 1900; but patience did not mean inaction.

Eugene's best hope stemmed from the fact that he had $5,000. The $600 nonsmoking fund he had received from his father in 1896, plus interest, had been wisely invested in Northern Pacific common, and a few savings had further swelled his net worth. As the presidential campaign of 1900 warmed up, the young banker saw a chance to parlay his modest savings into enough capital to give him a start in the business world. The campaign turned into a rerun of the previous contest between President McKinley and William Jennings Bryan, with stock prices again marking time because of the uncertainty over the monetary issue, despite the continued rise in company earnings. Eugene concluded, as he had done four years earlier, that McKinley would win and that stock prices would then rise in response to the improved earnings and the outlook for continued prosperity. Without disclosing his plan to anyone, he sold his stock and used part of the proceeds to buy gold bonds as insurance against a possible Bryan victory. With most of his $5,000 he bought options giving him the right to buy 1,000 shares of the best railroad stocks at specified prices after the election.

The morning after McKinley was reelected, Eugene cashed in his gold bonds and bought more option contracts. The anticipated boom brought a spectacular rise in the prices of the stocks covered by his options. In January 1901, he sold his option contracts for $50,000, a tenfold increase in his capital. The sum was precisely the amount he needed to buy a seat on the New York Stock Exchange then being offered for sale by the executors of an estate.

With this favorable turn of events, Eugene faced his father for a show-down. It was an excruciating experience. Despite their numerous differences, the son had a deep and abiding love for his father. He was painfully aware that his decision would hit the older man with the impact

---

[1] Dean Albertson's interviews with Eugene Meyer, p. 74.

of a sledgehammer—that a lifetime of toil in his behalf would seem to be rejected and that his father would not be able to understand such seeming ingratitude. Yet he must live his own life. The young man approached his father at home and said as unemotionally as he could: "I've made up my mind to leave Lazard's."

"You're not serious!" the incredulous father exclaimed.

"I'm very serious."

"But you can't leave. I've worked all my life to make a position for you in the firm. You know I've had you in mind in everything I've done. What sort of ungrateful son are you?"

"Don't think I'm ungrateful. You've done everything a father could do for his son, and a good deal more besides. I owe everything to you—my education, my training in business, my values, my life itself. But now you've done enough. You can't deny me the one thing you had."

"I've denied you nothing."

"You've denied me the spur of necessity to make my own way in life. I've got to stand on my own, or be crippled for life. With the background you've given me, I feel confident that I can make good."

"But why should you leave Lazard's? Have you gone crazy? There isn't another young man in this city who wouldn't sell his soul for your connections and your prospects in a great international banking house."

As remembered in later years, the discussion then went into the specific reasons for Eugene's decision: the anticipated evolution of international finance, the advancing age of the partners in Paris, and their resistance to change. Finally the dejected father asked: "What would you do if you left the firm right now?"

"I really don't know," the son replied with complete candor. "The only thing I'm clear about is that I want to buy a seat on the Stock Exchange. Then I'll look around a bit and see what comes."

"I won't give you the money for a seat!"

"I don't need your money. I have enough to buy the seat."

"Are you foolish enough to think you can buy a seat with your $5,000?"

"I have $50,000, not $5,000."

"Where did you get it?"

"I earned it."

"Earned it? You've been speculating behind my back. How many times have I warned you against speculating!"

"No, I haven't been speculating."

Apparently realizing how weak this denial was, Eugene proceeded to give his father a full account of how he had parlayed his $800 nonsmoking fund into enough to buy a seat on New York's big board. But the elder

Meyer remained unreconciled. A vital part of his world seemed to be crumbling. There followed a long series of maneuvers in which leading members of the firm tried to change the young rebel's mind. Alexandre Weill, patriarch of the Paris branch, offered Eugene a small partnership interest in the New York office, but it would have been taken out of his father's share. Soon afterward Weill came to New York because it appeared that Eugene's defection might be contagious. Although ostensibly seeking a heart-to-heart talk with the young man, Weill, a man of small stature, indulged in his usual habit of sitting in a swivel chair extended to its maximum height so that he could look down on whomever he was talking to. "It's symbolic," Eugene mused. " 'Paris' looks down on everything except 'Paris.' " The effect was to undercut Weill's repetition of his 1897 offer that Eugene build up a strong Lazard Frères branch in London.

When Eugene's resignation became final, his father also decided to leave. Though he was only sixty, he felt there was no further purpose in remaining in the firm. George Blumenthal also joined in the exodus, although he was to return a few years later when Paris belatedly accepted the changes sought by the Meyer clan. Blumenthal would make his return contingent upon an open door for Eugene if he also wanted to go back, but he would again decline. For the elder Meyer it was the end of his business career. At first the family was worried about his ability to shift from a life of toil to a life of ease, but he rode horseback in Central Park, played cards at his club, kept books on his private affairs, and often went to Eugene's office to see what was going on. Since he was to live to a ripe eighty-three, his retirement was ultimately accepted as a blessing in disguise. While the smart of Eugene's unorthodox behavior was keenly felt, the discomfiture of his father was a powerful incentive for the son to demonstrate that he had taken the right course.

4 /

Experimental Years

THE FIRST MOVE OF THE CONFIDENT YOUNG MAN WHO TURNED his back on Lazard Frères was to fall into a Wall Street sinkhole. Having spent his entire capital for a seat on the New York Stock Exchange, he had no funds to start a brokerage house, to buy a share in an existing firm, or even to rent and furnish an office. His father could have lent him the funds he needed, but Meyer made it plain that he had no intention of bailing out a son who threw away his opportunities so recklessly; and Eugene, having proclaimed his independence, was in no position to beg for parental generosity. The easiest way out of his dilemma was to affiliate himself with a brokerage house, and he picked one about which he knew virtually nothing.

The floor of the Exchange, which Eugene had previously seen only from the gallery, proved to be an exciting place. Here he rubbed shoulders with the masters of capital, the plungers, the penny-ante players, the bigots, the wise and the unwise. It was a thrill to be executing his own orders in this great, yet wild and seemingly unpredictable marketplace. Here he encountered Bernard Baruch, who was destined to become a close friend, and many other operators whose fortunes were to mount to fabulous heights or to be wiped out.

Eugene was conscious of the special advantages he brought to his new occupation. Most of the brokers on the floor knew only the New York financial scene. The young newcomer had been schooled in the fine points of foreign exchange, arbitrage, and the differences in interest rates in New York and the capitals of Europe. He was especially attuned to the time differential which made it possible for a New York broker to begin his day with knowledge of what had already happened in the markets of Europe. By the time New York went to work, Meyer had already cabled buy-and-sell orders to his correspondents in Europe and planned his actions on the New York Exchange in the light of reports from London and Paris.

Yet all his special training and worldly know-how did not save him from the commonest blunder on Wall Street—affiliation with a bucket shop.

The nature of the firm had not been immediately plain to him because he was serving his own clients, and they were not sucked into the account-juggling and dexterous manipulations by which the firm made its profits. But this scarcely diminished Eugene's disgust with his new associates and with himself, when the truth became apparent.

"You owed it to me," he complained bitterly to the head of the firm, "to tell me what kind of bucket-shop operation I was being asked to join."

"It was *you* who asked to join us," was the comeback. "This is not Lazard's. If you don't like it here, no one is going to beg you to stay."

Meyer's humiliation was the more acute because his walk-out from the bucket shop came only a few weeks after his resignation from Lazard's. Instead of enhancing his position, he had fallen on his face. What would his father say? Who could have confidence in a young man who had thrown away an assured future in a great financial firm and walked blindly into a Wall Street shearing operation? Seeking comfort and moral support, Eugene wired his sister Ro in San Francisco. An immediate reply expressed surprise but no sense of shock: "We feel as you do, that if the situation you faced was intolerable you were wise to break free of it without a second's delay. Don't torment yourself with fears of what other people think. Any setback you may have with your clients will be outweighed by the gains of a lifetime."

Ro's understanding telegram eased Eugene's ordeal of facing his father. At first the young man's confession unloosed all the pent-up anger that his father was still nursing over Eugene's foolishness in leaving Lazard's. Then for the first time since that painful incident the older man began to soften. "Well," he said, "even if something seems to have gone wrong with your head, I suppose I should be thankful that your heart still knows the difference between right and wrong."

From that point on, Meyer assumed a more helpful attitude. On the following Sunday when the Meyers assembled for their customary dinner together, George Blumenthal began to haze Eugene about the bucket-shop affair. "George," Meyer rebuked him, "we can all do without your mockery. There is no need to humiliate *my* son any more. He has learned a lesson the hard way, and there is nothing to be gained by grinding his face into the dust." The family patriarch then declared that he intended to use Eugene as the broker for his own stock market operations and that he would recommend his services to friends. If George counted himself a member of the family, he added, he would do the same. Blumenthal not only followed the suggestion; he also lent Eugene $50,000, which the latter repaid within a few months after having used it to accumulate a tidy surplus of debt-free capital.

Before Eugene had fully regained confidence in himself, he was caught in the mad, swirling torrents of the 1901 panic resulting from the "Northern Pacific Corner." The giants of Wall Street had unloosed chaos by their historic struggle for control of the Northern Pacific Railroad. Edward H. Harriman, who dominated the Union Pacific, Illinois Central, and Southern Pacific, had attempted to round out his railway empire by acquiring the Chicago, Burlington and Quincy. But John Pierpont Morgan, the greatest financier of the day, had thwarted Harriman by making the Burlington line a subsidiary of his Northern Pacific Railroad, acting in alliance with James J. Hill of the Great Northern. Harriman had then struck back with a direct assault on Morgan's Northern Pacific. In cooperation with James Stillman, president of the National City Bank, and other financiers, he had secretly authorized Jacob H. Schiff of Kuhn, Loeb and Company to buy up Northern Pacific shares. If he could thus seize control of the Northern Pacific, the Burlington would fall automatically into his domain, and he would dominate rail service in a vast area reaching from San Francisco to Chicago and from Winnipeg to New Orleans.

Schiff's skillful buying campaign had caused no alarm because the Morgan forces had expected the price of Northern Pacific shares to rise as a result of the Burlington acquisition. Even some of Morgan's allies took advantage of the higher prices to sell their Northern Pacific stock to Schiff, secretly buying for Morgan's rival. The great Wall Street czar himself was giving little attention to his railroad system because he was deeply involved in organizing the United States Steel Corporation, which was to be the biggest industrial complex in the world. It was Hill who finally smelled trouble in the mounting Northern Pacific transactions on the New York Stock Exchange and rushed from Seattle to Wall Street by special train to investigate. By this time, however, Schiff had acquired 370,000 shares of Northern Pacific common and 420,000 shares of preferred stock for the Harriman interests, making a majority of the two classes of stock taken together.

In a direct confrontation with Schiff, Hill confirmed his suspicions of a raid, and Morgan's partners cabled him in Italy for authority to buy at least 150,000 shares of Northern Pacific at any price. Morgan readily agreed, well knowing the vulnerability of his position since he and Hill together held only about 260,000 of the 800,000 shares of common stock outstanding.

Meanwhile, Harriman, who was ill at home, began to worry about a weakness in his position. Although he held a majority of the common and preferred stock, taken together, his common shares alone fell short of a majority, and the Northern Pacific directors could, if they chose, retire the preferred stock. His concern about this Achilles' heel caused him to place an order with Kuhn, Loeb to buy an additional 40,000 shares of Northern Pacific common on Saturday morning, May 4. Harriman assumed that his order had been carried out during the day, but the Kuhn, Loeb partner who had taken the order felt that it was necessary to check with Schiff. When Schiff was finally located at Sabbath services in a synagogue, he held up the order on the ground that Harriman was being too cautious —that it was not necessary to pay the excessive prices at which the stock was then selling. On Monday morning Harriman discovered to his dismay that he did not have the stock he had ordered; so he plunged into a wild scramble to acquire the additional shares at the very moment that the Morgan-Hill forces unleashed their blitz to establish a majority position of their own.

After two days of fierce bidding, the price of Northern Pacific common had risen from $110 to nearly $150. The Morgan-Hill forces had acquired more than a majority of the common stock and seemed for a time to be satisfied. Harriman and his allies, still holding a majority of the two classes of stock combined, concluded that they could take over the Northern Pacific by electing a new board of directors. With both of the contending giants thus feeling some security, they stopped buying, and speculators, seeing that the price of Northern Pacific was far above its intrinsic value, began selling it short with the expectation of being able to buy the shares they would need for later delivery at much lower prices.

But the war was not over. Resumption of Morgan's and Harriman's competitive buying on Wednesday pushed prices still higher, and the shorts were thrown into panic. As Northern Pacific skyrocketed, very little of it could be bought at any price. Unable to borrow in the suddenly tightened money market, the shorts found it necessary to dump other stocks on the market to finance their desperate efforts to buy some of the Northern Pacific shares that were essential to save them from ruin. Pandemonium thus ran its course. Meyer saw a block of 300 shares of Northern Pacific sell at $1,000 a share while many other good securities were being dumped at a fraction of their value. Probably half of the Wall Street brokerage firms were technically insolvent. The seething mass of humanity on the floor of the Exchange went from screaming and jostling to kicking, clawing, and gouging.

Though Meyer was battered by the raging storm, he was not among the economic victims. His rule never to sell short and to discourage his

clients from resort to this tricky device had saved him from the trap that
so many others had fallen into. Instead of moving with the panic, he
decided at the end of the third day to move against it. The frenzy over
Northern Pacific could be broken as soon as shares from Europe could be
poured into the New York market, he said, and even before that could
happen the financial community would probably end the panic by some
collective action. The time had come, he told his father, to start buying
the good securities that were being sacrificed. The elder Meyer was skeptical, but Eugene went ahead anyway. Deluged with orders, he put the
"buy" slips, including his own, on top of the "sell" slips as the panic went
into its fourth day. His tactic could have been ruinous if it had miscarried,
but before the day was over, fifteen banks had formed a syndicate to ease
the money crisis and the Morgan and Harriman interests agreed to let the
shorts who had sold them Northern Pacific stock settle at $150 a share.
The storm blew over as suddenly as it had arisen.

Meyer thus emerged from his first Wall Street tornado in a greatly
strengthened position. Not only had he been substantially enriched by his
purchases of stock while the selling fever was still raging; he had also
swung handsome profits to some clients, including his father and George
Blumenthal, who had decided to join in his operations at the last moment.
Far more important was the psychological lift that accrued to the young
broker. Taunts about his leaving Lazard Frères and aligning himself with
a bucket shop suddenly ceased or lost their sting. In the convulsion that
had seized Wall Street he had seen the professionals as well as the novices
lunge and stampede as if they were frightened cattle, while he as a newcomer had behaved with cool deliberation and unerring judgment. With
a flush of self-confidence, Eugene concluded that he had little to fear
from any future test of wills on Wall Street. At home he had greatly
enhanced his standing in the eyes of his father. Though he would continue
to hear reproaches from time to time about abandoning Lazard's, he was
increasingly entrusted with the management of the elder Meyer's financial
affairs, and he would quadruple his father's wealth.

In "the Street" Meyer's performance won him new respect—and new
clients. The most tangible evidence of his enhanced prestige was an offer
of a partnership in the brokerage firm of Bernard Baruch. It was a flattering gesture from a man of great charm who was somewhat older than
Eugene, then twenty-six. Even so, Eugene declined with thanks. Baruch's
reputation was that of a highly successful speculator; young Meyer liked
to think of himself as an investor and felt it desirable to avoid any close
contact with the more speculative spheres. Nevertheless, the incident led

to a close personal friendship between the two men, and this in turn would lead to their association in both business ventures and public service.

For weeks after it was over, the panic was the subject of postmortems in the Waldorf Bar, where Bet-a-Million Gates, James Keane, Diamond Jim Brady, and their crowd met regularly after the Stock Exchange closed. In the lively talk about those who had been mauled and those who had emerged unscathed, the story of the "kid broker" who had coolly reaped a harvest out of the general calamity was told and retold. On the occasions when Meyer dropped in at the Waldorf Bar, he found himself an object of unusual interest. His new popularity did not, however, induce him to become a "regular" at the Waldorf. He did not wish to be identified with the plungers who gave the place its tone and color or to be exposed to the tipsters who swarmed through the bar.

Sometimes, however, the Waldorf Bar gatherings could be useful. A broker much older than Eugene made a practice of badgering him on the floor of the Exchange. Their differences reached a climax in a hot argument about the future prospects of a certain stock. Meyer was so irritated that he laid a trap for his tormentor. Waiting several hours so that the Waldorf Bar would be crowded, he walked in with the expectation that the exasperating broker would renew the feud. He did so, and the bluster went on until Eugene proposed a rather complicated bet that would run for six months. A two-point rise or fall of the stock in question would entail a pay-off of $1,000, with the pay-off mounting with each additional point of change, up or down, to $2,000, $4,000, $8,000, $16,000, and so forth. Having left himself no easy escape from this "put-up-or-shut-up" challenge, the blustering broker accepted it.

At the end of two months the broker was asking to be let off the hook; by the third month he was begging for mercy, but all he could get from Meyer was an invitation to discuss the matter at the Waldorf Bar. Before an amused crowd the terms of the bet were rehearsed.

"The way things are going," Eugene said, "I could ruin you financially two months from now. If you should welch on the bet, your credit would be ruined. Now I don't want to take all your money or to ruin your credit. What I want is a promise that you will never again try to bully men of my age who are minding their own business on the floor of the Exchange. If you make that promise to me, I am ready to settle the bet on equitable terms. You are to pay me one-half the difference between what it cost to buy the five hundred shares four months ago and what it costs to buy the same amount right now. I figure that comes to $8,000." The humiliated broker bowed to the inescapable, and, as far as Meyer could observe, was never thereafter troublesome on the floor of the Exchange. The "kid broker" had demonstrated that he was not a person to be trifled with.

Nevertheless, he continued to be frustrated by some older men. Meyer concluded from the amount of work the George A. Fuller Construction Company was doing in New York that it had possibilities for growth and learned that Henry Morgenthau Senior was floating an over-the-counter stock issue for the company. The Morgenthaus were neighbors of the Meyers in Elberon, New Jersey, where both had summer homes. So Eugene called on Morgenthau and asked for an option to buy part of the Fuller stock to place with some of his clients. Morgenthau assented; the stock was readily sold. With this success to recommend him, Eugene went back to Morgenthau and said he thought he had earned a right to manage a new operation then taking shape incident to listing the Fuller shares on the New York Stock Exchange.

"Not so fast, not so fast!" Morgenthau replied.

"Why not so fast?"

"Because you are still a young fellow, and a young fellow should get the crumbs."

"And what should the older fellows get?"

"The cake."

"As a matter of justice," Meyer persisted, "or as a matter of age?"

"As a matter of power."

"What is power?"

"The ability to say no to you," Morgenthau answered with finality, "and make it stick."

Morgenthau gave general command of the Fuller stock to the Hall-garten brokerage and banking house, but he saw to it that Meyer was given an opportunity to create a market for the stock. It proved to be something more than a crumb, for the stock climbed rapidly under the stimulus of New York's building boom and the bull market in Wall Street.

Optimism was still strong and stock prices were soaring to heights never before reached when Meyer discovered an ominous portent. On January 7, 1902, he read a small item in a newspaper to the effect that the State of Minnesota had filed suit against the Northern Securities Company, charging that it was an illegal combination in restraint of trade. Northern Securities was the holding company created by the Morgan, Hill, and Harriman railroad interests as a means of resolving their contest which had created the panic of 1901. In the wake of that disruptive and costly episode the contending magnates had entered into a cooperative understanding for the operation of their rail systems. The holding company was set up to take over Morgan's Northern Pacific and Hill's Great Northern Railroad, with Harriman surrendering his Northern Pacific stock for a comparable interest in the new $400-million corporate giant. If this settlement of the railroad war should be upset in the courts, another donnybrook on Wall Street could be anticipated.

Meyer had noticed the news item from St. Paul only because of the habit he had picked up from his father of reading the fine print, especially in regard to lawsuits. He reasoned that most of the brokers in Wall Street, who seemed to feel that nothing of importance ever happened west of the Hudson River, would miss the item at first. Yet the impact would ultimately be felt, because rail stocks then dominated the big board and the fate of a $400-million corporation would affect the economic climate in general. The next morning after he had read the item he sold every stock he owned and deposited the cash, amounting to half a million dollars.

When many stocks continued to make gains, Eugene wondered if he had been overcautious. But a general retreat developed after the federal government brought suit against the Northern Securities Company in March, and the merger was ultimately to be dissolved by a famous five-four decision of the United States Supreme Court. That decision would not come, however, until 1904. Meanwhile the foresighted "kid broker" had a half a million dollars and didn't know what to do with it.

Meyer's search for a sound investment outside the stock market led him back to Henry Morgenthau. That capitalist who wanted to keep the cake for older men, especially himself, had organized a trust company that held bonds and mortgages representing real estate. Meyer reasoned that real estate ought to be more stable at that period than stocks and that Morgenthau himself was a tower of financial strength. He invested his half million in the stock of Morgenthau's trust company. It was soon evident, however, that the forces causing prices to sag in Wall Street were also reducing construction activity and depressing real estate prices, which meant a decline in the Morgenthau stock. Meyer decided to bail out but not before he had lost half of his capital. While licking his wounds, he drew a moral to guide his future conduct: "When things generally look bad, don't have a pet."

The experience was unnerving beyond the loss of money. Meyer faced the fact that his judgment, while excellent in some instances, had been painfully uneven. Was there not some way by which he could introduce an element of science into his operations? He was not satisfied to live at the mercy of impulse and chance. Nor could he visualize himself routinely earning commissions by the purchase and sale of stocks for clients. What he dreamed of was a major role in the creation of new enterprises for which he could underwrite stock issues, but this would take large amounts of capital and more reliable judgment than he had demonstrated to date.

For a time Meyer devoted himself to recouping his losses by unremitting toil, but he remained dissatisfied. In February 1904 he took his first vacation since he had left Lazard's for the special purpose of reviewing his activities and trying to devise a better approach to his goals. Finding a retreat at Palm Beach, Florida, he cogitated a few days and then wrote a memorandum to himself entitled "Plan for Developing a Business." Its chief points were: "Get in with the best people" in the very beginning; interest yourself in "securities you can know"; "introduce system and order for the better and more economical conduct of the business"; direct the organization along constructive lines, avoiding the destructive so far as possible; plan and build as if for all time." The key idea was to know what he was doing.

Meyer returned to New York determined to improve the means by which he kept himself informed. Here is the genesis of his statistical approach to stock market operations that would lead to great wealth and to high public responsibilities. In the same period he read a book by Senator Theodore E. Burton: *Financial Crises and Periods of Industrial and Commercial Depression,* which analyzed the causes of booms and busts. The effect was to stimulate Meyer's own thinking about broad economic movements and to strengthen his conviction that research into company operations, industrial conditions, and economic trends would pay big dividends.

The best man to assist in developing this new type of investment banking firm, Meyer concluded, was Lyman B. Kendall. As a former head of the United States Geological Survey, Kendall had an exceptional fund of knowledge about the geography, natural resources, climatic conditions, transportation facilities, crops, and industries of the entire country. After leaving the government, he had gone to New York as a consultant on mining properties and then concluded that he could do better in Wall Street. Meyer had met him there in mid-1903, and their mutual interests led to a close friendship. On his return from Florida, Meyer outlined his plan to Kendall and offered him a place in the new company he intended to form. Kendall seemed fascinated by the idea, and his initial reluctance to join the firm was overcome when Meyer offered him a salary of $20,000 a year plus an interest in the profits of the firm and complete freedom in summertime. With this settled, the new brokerage and investment banking house of Eugene Meyer, Jr., and Company was formally launched.

The recruiting of statisticians proved more difficult. Believing that men working for the financial press had many of the skills that would be required, Meyer obtained a list of promising financial reporters from two of his friends: Melville Stone, manager of the Associated Press, and Clarence Barron of *Barron's Weekly*, who would later found the *Wall Street Journal*. But the first reporters he hired were disappointing and did not stay long. Meyer was an exacting taskmaster with a sharp tongue. One of these men tried to reply to a tongue-lashing for some gaffe by saying: "But, Mr. Meyer, I thought—"

"If that is what you do when you think," Meyer cut in, "stop thinking."

In time Meyer did find a newsman who seemed to have all the qualities he had been seeking: Charles Boynton, general superintendent of the Associated Press. Boynton had often called at Meyer's office; he seemed to sense that something novel was afoot there and was pleased to become a part of it when the offer came. The morning he reported for duty he got a surprising order. "For the next year," Meyer told him, "you are to do nothing except learn." Boynton took the exasperating order in stride and became an invaluable member of the firm. When he left six years later to strike out on his own, his place was taken by George W. Batson over the vigorous protest of Clarence Barron, who accused Meyer of "stealing my best men."

Another stalwart in the firm was Eugene's youngest brother Edgar, who held a degree in engineering from Cornell University. His training, alert mind, and amiable disposition made him the ideal associate for Eugene. Edgar was made a partner in the firm in 1908 when Kendall withdrew. Eugene's mother begged him to take Walter into his firm, but he refused because of friction between them.

At first the research department of Eugene Meyer, Jr., and Company concentrated on the railroads. In those days very little information could be obtained from the Interstate Commerce Commission. Investors were in the dark as to how the railroads handled their financing, what they spent on maintenance, and whether they were being looted to maintain an attractive dividend policy. Meyer and Kendall set out to fill this informational vacuum. Their elaborate charts and statistical tables began to tell many stories about the relative soundness of the American railroads. The Chicago, Milwaukee, and St. Paul, for example, was paying big dividends and its stock was bringing high prices when it was spending only $40 a car for maintenance. Harriman's Southern Pacific was paying no dividend but spending $150 a car on maintenance. One was headed for receivership, the other for profitable future operation.

Though there was a good deal of scoffing at Meyer's "scientific" methods, his storehouse of accurate facts gave a ring of authority to his conclusions and created new demands for his services. One of the first to see promise in Meyer's technique was Henry Evans, president of the Continental Life Insurance Company. The insurance business had been shaken to its foundations by scandals which led to the famous investigation by Charles E. Hughes. Having survived that rigorous housecleaning in good standing, Evans was about to launch the Fidelity-Phenix Fire Insurance Company, which would also be a pioneer investment trust company; he reached eagerly for the respectability of "scientific" investments.

Meyer was gratified when Evans asked him to take stock in the new company, to be a director and help organize the remainder of the board, and then to be chairman of Fidelity-Phenix's finance committee. Since Evans was close to several eminent financiers in the Morgan crowd, it was a high compliment to a young man of twenty-eight. Though he privately felt puffed up to be a director of a big company for the first time, Eugene publicly took it in stride as if there was nothing whatever unusual about it. His first step was to bring the statistical resources of his own firm to bear on the investment program of the new company.

The privilege Meyer had of bringing his special knowledge of investments to the attention of various bank presidents who were also members of the Fidelity-Phenix board proved to be a mixed blessing. His judgment was often challenged, and hot arguments ensued. The banker members— some as old as his father—were not easily swayed from their more traditional views, and Eugene, despite his youth, had the tenacity of a tiger. However reserved, considerate, playfully ironic, or sensitive to personal feelings he might be among his intellectual friends, his sharp tongue wagged with little restraint in a business debate. Resentment was plainly evident, but there was no revolt, and the investments of Fidelity-Phenix generally followed the Meyer pattern.

The result was enrichment of the company, with consequent increases in the value of its stock. Evans soon began using Meyer to guide the investments of the Continental company, and the bankers who had fought him in the finance committee sought his counsel in selecting investments for their banks. Stubborn, outspoken, and brash though he might be, Meyer was establishing a reputation for knowing what he said he knew when he talked about investment values.

In one instance Meyer made himself a thorn in the side of a railroad president who had been comfortably coasting on public ignorance. His firm's research brought to light the fact that the Pittsburgh, Chicago, Cincinnati, and St. Louis Railroad—"the Panhandle"—was making rapid gains in business and earnings, but the dividend on its preferred stock had not been increased, and it paid no dividend on its common stock. Sensing an opportunity for substantial gains, Meyer bought some of the common stock and advised his clients to do likewise. A year passed, however, and nothing happened.

Meyer then made a more intensive study of the Panhandle, giving his whole time to it for three weeks before the annual stockholders' meeting in 1906. He concluded that inside directors of the parent Pennsylvania Railroad were milking the Panhandle for their own benefit. Armed with an arsenal of facts, Meyer and his friend Paul Herzog called on James McCrea, soon to be president of the Pennsylvania Lines, and then went to the stockholders' meeting and raised a series of embarrassing questions. Why did the Panhandle's annual report carry no details on spending for maintenance? Why did the Panhandle spend from 50 to 100 percent more on certain maintenance items than the Baltimore and Ohio, although McCrea controlled both roads? Why did not the Panhandle issue more bonds to cover part of its development costs?

To the latter question McCrea replied that he could not issue bonds because the preferred stock was selling below par. "If you paid the preferred stockholders the 5 percent dividend they are entitled to, and paid a decent dividend of say 3 percent on the common," Meyer came back, "the preferred stock would go above par and you could easily market a bond issue for improving the road." As the argument went on, Meyer offered to guarantee responsible underwriters for a $15-million bond issue if his conditions were met.

"I haven't asked you down here to finance the Panhandle Railroad."

"No, but I have a right to answer your arguments."

"Who would underwrite the bonds?"

"Your own bankers—Speyer and Company! I have talked to them at length, and they agree with my argument. Did you ever talk to them with *your* argument?"

"No."

"So I learned from them. *Will* you talk to them?"

"Well, there may be something in what you say. . . . We are going to make a business inspection trip, and we will invite you to go with us."

"I don't want a free ride. I just want you to do what's right and sensible."

The Panhandle soon began paying dividends on its common stock, increased its preferred dividend, and floated a $15-million bond issue. Meyer and his clients reaped their reward and his reputation was hoisted a few notches higher.

About the same time Meyer encountered for the first time an eminent railroad man of very different caliber. From youth he had looked upon

Edward H. Harriman as the greatest figure on the American industrial scene. Far from being a robber baron, Harriman was a builder who improved every property that he acquired—a Napoleonic sort of man with foresight as well as courage and great generalship. The facts that the Meyer firm turned up in its investigations of the Harriman railroad empire seemed to confirm this view of the man. He was reconstructing the bankrupt Union Pacific, which he had taken over in 1898, and would apply the same technique to the Southern Pacific. Earnings had dramatically increased under his management, but dividends lagged because of the vast amounts that Harriman was plowing back into improvements. Having opened a secret window upon what was happening, Meyer invested heavily in Union Pacific and then Southern Pacific (for himself as well as his clients) with great confidence that dividends and stock prices would someday catch up with the physical improvements that were being made.

The harvest came in 1906, when Harriman and his board of directors increased the dividends on Southern Pacific stock from 4 to 5 percent and on Union Pacific stock from 6 to 10 percent. The effect was sensational. At last Wall Street woke up to the fact that a supposed sleeper was in fact an industrial giant. The belated discovery touched off the "Harriman boom" in which big and little investors alike rushed in to buy securities that were following the Union Pacific skyward. The denouement of this frenzy is another story. The significant point here is that Meyer, who had previously made his first million, now began to count his profits in multiples of that figure.

5 /

A Compassionate Journey

THE MOUNTING GOOD FORTUNE OF THE MEYERS IN NEW YORK was suddenly thrown into eclipse when disaster threatened their kinfolk in the old home town of San Francisco. In the spring of 1906 that city was rudely shaken by an earthquake, and fire threatened to obliterate what the quake itself had left standing. As reports of the catastrophe reached New York, the Meyers reacted as if their own city were burning; two of the Meyer daughters, Rosalie and Elise, were still living in San Francisco with their husbands and children. With telephone communications knocked out and with the telegraph lines hopelessly clogged, there was no way of knowing whether they were alive or dead.

News from the stricken city continued to worsen. Of its 500,000 inhabitants nearly one-third were homeless. The firefighters were dynamiting buildings in a desperate effort to confine the conflagration, but it continued to sweep on. City Hall and the Hall of Justice were wrecked, landmarks of the business district and the city's newspaper plants were in ashes along with the hotels and theaters. With members of the family caught in this kind of peril, there could be only one reaction from the Meyers in New York. However vehemently they might quarrel and go their separate ways in ordinary circumstances, they had a powerful tradition of pulling together in an emergency. Eugene concluded that it was his responsibility to rush to the side of his sisters.

At first he tried to hitch a ride on the special train that was to take E. H. Harriman on a relief mission of the Bay Area, but it left before the magnate could be reached. With a twinge of envy toward his hero who could operate in such a grand manner, Meyer boarded the New York Central with a light traveling bag, a money belt around his waist, and a pistol. Remembering his father's experiences as a vigilante captain in pioneer Los Angeles and the reports of looting in stricken San Francisco, the transplanted Californian decided to be prepared for any eventuality.

In Chicago, Eugene went to a broker's office to chat with a friend while he waited for the afternoon train. As they talked, a stock quotation on the board caught his eye, and he put in an order at what seemed an appealing price. At train time he sold what he had bought and took his $2,500 profit in cash on the assumption that it would be a handy supplement to the $30,000 in his money belt. When the Overland Limited reached Ogden, Utah, Eugene joined all the other passengers in a stampede to the telegraph office to see if there was any message for a person of his name, but he found only the chaos of 60,000 messages awaiting transmission. At Sacramento there was better luck. A telegram from New York informed him that his sisters and their families had survived and were in Fair Oaks (later Atherton), near Palo Alto. Ro had gotten a letter through to an aunt in Los Angeles who in turn had wired the Meyers in New York.

With a feeling of great relief, Eugene went on to Oakland and caught a ride by automobile to San Jose, where he telephoned to Ro. "I knew you would come," she said. An emotional reunion followed when Ro drove up in her Pope Toledo, said to have been the first limousine in San Francisco. It was a long way from the cat-o'-nine-tails days. Ro was now a "wonderful sister."

Sigmund and Rosalie Stern had been asleep at home when the earthquake struck. Their solidly built house was not damaged, except by falling plaster and collapsed chimneys, but the family enterprise, Levi Strauss and Company, was destroyed by the fire. As soon as it was evident that the city was on fire, Ro had taken command of the family's safety measures. Her eleven-year-old daughter Elise had been confined to the safety of the Pope Toledo, parked in the open. Her sister Elise, wife of Abraham Stern, had been ordered to come with all her household and valuables to Ro's home so that they could face an uncertain future together. She was also to bring the valuable paintings from the home of Jacob Stern, a brother of Sigmund and Abraham, who was in Europe. When they were all assembled, including nurses, cooks, butlers, maids, and other servants, the two merged households numbered twenty-eight. They had stayed all night and day, camping on the ground at Ro's, except for trips to a lookout point at Buena Vista where they could see the fiery agony of the city and hear the dynamite explosions. On the second day, however, hot winds from the fire a few blocks away had driven them to the Presidio. The wealthy Sterns in their Pope Toledo, towing a pony cart (Elise with the paintings under her arm), joined a stream of humanity out of Chinatown. On the third day they had moved on to the safety of Golden Gate Park, and a turn in the wind had helped to bring the fire under control. Because of the damaged roofs at home, the Stern families had decided to continue on to Fair Oaks, where one of the summer cottages they had rented proved to be still usable.

After hearing how well Ro had guided her enlarged family through the disaster, Eugene felt rather useless. What could he do, except perhaps help to restore the morale of his loved ones? In pursuit of this objective he insisted on sleeping on the second floor of Ro's cottage, while the refugees from the earthquake slept in the garden. A tremor during the night shook the house and reduced his posture of courage to plain foolishness. Ro put her head in the doorway leading to the second floor and shouted at him as if he were once again a troublesome ten-year-old: "Eugene! Stop your nonsense and come down here immediately. We have prepared a bed for you out in the garden." Eugene hastened down, and his pretense that he did it to relieve his sister's mind seemed to convince no one, not even himself.

The next morning it became evident that he *could* be useful, but in quite a different way. There was little food in the cottage because cash was scarce and nothing could be bought without it. The New Yorker with the money belt thus became a sort of ambulatory bank for his family and friends.

His first trip into San Francisco to look for his father's friends was a depressing experience. Thousands of people were poking around in the charred rubble. Three-quarters of the charming city he had known thirteen years before lay in ruins. In returning for the first time, moreover, Meyer was suddenly conscious that he was a nobody here. Despite his comparative youth, he could not avoid dwelling upon the contrast between himself and Harriman. He (Eugene) had created nothing and had developed only one talent—making money on the stock market—a talent that seemed rather futile and meaningless just then; the great railroad entrepreneur commanded an empire, and, having sped personally to the scene, he had placed all the resources of that empire at the disposal of the ruined city. After listening to many community leaders expound on how and when and by whom the city should be rebuilt, the imperious man of action took his turn: "I have only one thing to add to what has already been said. Stop talking and get to work!" San Francisco responded, and the herculean reconstruction efforts that Harriman directed were soon in evidence.

As Meyer roamed through the ruins, he was struck by many stark monuments to individual heroism and dogged human resistance to nature's rampage: a church still intact because its minister had climbed to the bell tower and hacked down a blazing cross and adjoining timbers; fishermen's cottages saved by blankets soaked in wine; the United States mint containing $220 million, still erect in a wilderness of ashes because forty men had remained behind its iron shutters in perilous heat to wet down sills and sashes.

The bank that the older Meyer had directed before he left San Francisco had been completely obliterated. Eugene succeeded, however, in finding the president of the institution and listened to his tale of woe. The bank would be expected to open within ten days, and people would be asking for their money. "What can we do?" the president asked. "There will be a run on the bank and, to make matters worse, we've been abandoned by our friends in New York." He had telegraphed Lazard Frères for a loan of $2.5 million to be remitted through the San Francisco mint and had received no reply.

Eugene tried to convince the despondent president that he had not been abandoned by his friends in New York; the telegraphic bottleneck at Ogden had made communications impossible. "When the telegram finally gets through," he said, "you will be getting all the money you need. If Lazard Frères doesn't come through for you," he added, "everyone in my family will—and that includes me, if you are interested." The banker seemed to be worried because George Blumenthal, who had returned to Lazard's, was now its head. "You know what George is like," he said. "He is a hard one."

"Not *that* hard," Meyer answered.

At the end of the conversation Meyer told the despairing banker that he thought he knew a way to get the message through to New York. Taking a ferry to Oakland, where Harriman's private train was serving as his headquarters, Eugene identified himself as the brother-in-law of George Blumenthal and asked to see the rail magnate on important business. Within minutes he was ushered into the presence of the man who, more than any other, had aroused his profound admiration. As he explained his mission, he sensed that two penetrating eyes were examining him swiftly but thoroughly. Although the so-called Colossus of Roads was short, slight, wiry, and dark-complexioned, his face radiated determination and self-confidence.

Desperately eager to make a good impression, Meyer explained that his mission might seem insignificant compared to the great projects Harriman was directing, yet it had an importance all its own. Repeating his conversation with the bank president, he said that relief of the banker's anxiety was an important factor in restoring the financial stability of the city and asked if he could use the Southern Pacific telegraph wires to get through to New York. Harriman readily assented, and promised to have an answer the following morning.

The response from New York was waiting when Eugene called at the Harriman car at 10 a.m. The $2.5 million loan would be granted as requested. Meyer expressed profound thanks, and Harriman responded that he should feel free to use the Southern Pacific wire for any messages that might contribute to the revival of San Francisco. Word of that offer was spread around, and for nearly two weeks Meyer acted as a courier between the stricken city and the Harriman car. These shuttle operations were the more gratifying because they gave him many opportunities to talk with Harriman and to observe his style.

As thinking shifted from disaster to rebuilding, Meyer surveyed the resources available. California had plenty of timber, and labor was abundant, but there was no ready supply of nails in the West. Eugene thereupon ordered a shipload of nails for San Francisco from New York, cabling by way of Yokohama because of the congested telegraph lines.

After two weeks in the Bay Area Meyer took a train for Santa Barbara to see some oil wells prior to returning home by way of Los Angeles. A fellow passenger, Isaac Liebes, had described these wells, during the trip to San Francisco, as a great investment opportunity. Meyer found the wells capped because there was neither a refinery nor a pipeline in the area, but after listening to glib sales talk he invested $250,000 in the venture on the spot and helped to raise $2.5 million to build a refinery after he had returned to New York. The company had a contract to sell its oil to a Japanese steamship line, but when the capped wells were opened they produced only salt water. Worse still, the price of oil had suddenly increased and it appeared that the company might have to spend $9 million for oil to satisfy the contract if specific performance should be demanded. Under California law Meyer faced a possible loss of $1.5 million. When the Japanese mercifully canceled the contract and Meyer's loss was reduced to his initial $250,000, he hailed that turn of events as if it were comparable to the turning of the wind that had saved remnants of San Francisco.

Eugene's confession of his blunder to his father revived an old refrain: "It's too bad you didn't consult me. I could have told you that California corporations are liable pro-rata." Soon there was another confession and a similar response. Alfred Cook, who had married Eugene's sister Ruth, joined him in forming a syndicate that acquired an island in the Sacramento River with the object of growing three crops a year (celery and early vegetables) in its rich alluvial soil. Despite the installation of protective dikes, floods ruined the crops, and even the installation of pumps failed to rescue the experiment the second year. When Eugene bailed out and made his confession, there was a variation of the familiar theme.

"I could have spared you a lot of grief," his father said. "You see, I once owned that same island. I had the same idea you had about the three crops a year. I did all the things you did, and failed just as you did, and got rid of it just as you did."

Obviously the scientific method of making investments that Meyer had so painstakingly developed did not save him when he reverted to mere impulse. With the experience of the earthquake, the salt-water wells, and the Sacramento island behind him, the enterprising Wall Street operator returned to a more familiar habitat.

6 /

Riding the Panic of 1907

HARRIMAN'S RETURN TO NEW YORK FROM THE SAN FRANCISCO disaster served to qualify Meyer's previously unbounded admiration of the man. The rail magnate got approval from his board to raise the Southern Pacific dividend and nearly double the Union Pacific dividend about 11 a.m. on August 16, 1906, but the public announcement was delayed until 10 a.m. the next day. As previously noted, the effect of the increase was to touch off the "Harriman boom"—almost a riot of speculation not merely in Union Pacific stock but across the board. Even before the public announcement was made, Harriman was widely accused of withholding the good news so that he and other insiders could make a fortune by buying the stock before its inevitable advance began.

Harriman's explanation of the delayed announcement was that the board wished to inform several leading directors who were absent from the meeting before its action was made public. But the secret leaked, and the announcement was then timed to coincide with the opening of the New York Stock Exchange the following day to avoid an unfair advantage to the London stock market. Meyer concluded at the time, and later research would affirm his judgment, that this explanation was correct in its main details and that Harriman had not bought any stock during the twenty-three-hour delay. As Harriman would later tell the Interstate Commerce Commission, he had been buying Union Pacific stock ever since 1898, whenever it was cheap, in anticipation that the dividend would some-day be increased. There was no occasion for him to plunge in at the last minute after the increase had become a *fait accompli*. It was easy for Meyer to accept this view because he himself had been following a similar course since 1904.

In subsequent years Meyer had an opportunity to study the incident from original sources because the Harriman papers were removed to his office after the magnate's death to enable George Batson of the Meyer staff to write a Harriman biography. It was a comfort to know that this towering figure had not stooped to a stock-jobbing trick and was not guilty of the chicanery attributed to him. Yet that did not entirely dispose of the matter. Meyer saw in the incident a reaffirmation of the age-old truth that a man in a position of great responsibility must not only take the right course but also avoid appearances that might arouse suspicion. In his own operations he would try to improve on Harriman.

Meanwhile he was getting richer by the hour. The Harriman boom pushed stock prices to unprecedented levels, especially the stocks in which Meyer had invested most heavily. By November 1906 he was alarmed by the extent and persistence of the speculative fever. Having exhausted their local sources of capital, American speculators were tapping the financial resources of Europe by means of "clean bills"—so called because they represented an advance of European funds against stocks held in New York without involving any commercial operation. Used for regular economic purposes, "clean bills" were an indispensable tool of finance, but in late 1906 London alone had provided nearly a billion dollars in excess of normal American borrowing, and it had been poured into the swirling Wall Street cauldron. Europe would not long continue to risk its capital so recklessly. Remembering the economic blight that had fallen upon the United States when Europe cut off its credit in 1893, when he was only a youth, Meyer began to prepare for another crisis.

His course of action was influenced in some measure by a tragedy. The only child of his sister Florence and George Blumenthal, a six-year-old boy of much promise to whom Eugene had become especially attached in his role of bachelor uncle, was stricken with typhoid fever on a steamer bringing him and his mother home from Paris. In the frantic effort to save the child after he reached New York, Eugene wore himself out by his vigil at the bedside, in addition to his long office hours. After the lad died of peritonitis, both his mother and his uncle were ill and distraught; Eugene decided to seek recuperation on the Italian Riviera. He sold a substantial portion of his stocks and urged his clients to take a similar course in preparation for the approaching storm.

Meyer's attempts to apply this policy to the holdings of the Fidelity-Phenix Fire Insurance Company, in his capacity as chairman of its finance committee, met stiff resistance from Henry Evans. On advice from J. P. Morgan and George Perkins, Evans argued that there were still more "points" to be had in the market. Meyer replied, with characteristic bluntness, that if the president of the company intended to reach for a few more points while economic clouds were threatening, he would sell all his Fidelity-Phenix stock, except for the few shares required to qualify as a director. He wanted to remain a director, he said, for the sole purpose of holding his friend Evans personally responsible for the consequences of his policy. The threat brought Evans around not only in regard to the company's holdings but also in the disposition of his own stock. Apparently he harbored no resentment from the incident, for years later he gave Meyer broad discretionary power to sell any stock he was holding for Evans "and to make any purchase you may deem wise for my account." To this he added, "I have absolute confidence in your judgment."[1]

While Meyer was in Europe, some events he had not foreseen contributed to a Wall Street turn-around. The Interstate Commerce Commission moved against unlawful rebates to shippers; the government gave several twists to its antitrust thumb-screw; and *The New York Times* carried a dispatch to the effect that President Theodore Roosevelt intended to "break" E. H. Harriman as an example to other railroad magnates. Added to mounting fears that stock prices had reached unsustainable heights, these straws in the wind signaled a slide and then a cave-in on March 14, 1907. Union Pacific, which had led the boom, dropped twenty-five points in a single day.

Before returning home in March, Meyer visited the financial circles of Paris and London where, in more propitious times, he had been placing American securities. As he collected figures on the swollen American bank borrowings in Europe, he listened to repeated threats to shut off the flow of funds and to demand repayment of loans previously made. The danger of a money famine was still very real. Back in his office, Meyer reported his findings and told his staff that a very conservative policy was still in order. Charles Boynton dissented. "You were right last fall," he said, "but my friends think it has now been cleaned up." Though Meyer agreed that margin speculation had been cleaned up, he insisted that investment in real estate had also gone to extremes and that the market would not be on a sound footing until that had been cleaned up also.

"I wish you would come down and see Frank A. Vanderlip," Boynton persisted. Vanderlip was then vice-president (later president) of the National City Bank, New York's largest, and was widely accepted as spokesman for the financial community. He was full of optimism and confident that the time to resume buying stocks had arrived. Contrary to his usual custom, Meyer listened to the exposition with feigned respect for the great banker's views. To all outward appearances, Vanderlip had made a convert.

"Well, what do you say?" Boynton inquired as the two returned to their offices.

[1] Henry Evans to Eugene Meyer, June 13, 1911.

"If that's the best he can say for the situation," Meyer responded, "it's worse than I thought. I'm going to stay in the cyclone cellar until the fundamentals are better."[2]

Although Meyer was somewhat more optimistic in June, he rushed back to the cyclone cellar when he received a demand for immediate payment of funds he owed in London. Complying immediately, he cabled friends in London to ask the meaning of the peremptory demand. The Bank of England, he was informed, had quietly decided to stop rediscounting the "clean bills" of American borrowers in British financial institutions because of the abuse of this line of credit for speculation. This caused those institutions to make demands on New York banks, which in turn would put pressure on interior banks. A critical credit squeeze was in the making. Meyer was the more fearful of the consequences because he knew that American crops had not been harvested and that a great many debtors would therefore not be in a position to meet immediate demands upon them. Acting before the tightening of the credit strings in London was generally known, Meyer paid all his own debts in New York, refused to borrow money for anyone, and advised all his clients to prepare for a cruncher. As an extraordinary precaution, he stashed in his vault an "emergency ration" of $80,000 in cash.

The climax was not long in coming. By late August credit was so tight that New York could not sell its bonds. Stock prices hit new lows in October, and rumors spread that major banks were in trouble. The Mercantile National Bank was reorganized in a desperate effort to save it. A run on the Knickerbocker Trust Company forced it to close on October 23 with $56 million in demands against it. Almost everyone was scared; credit in New York virtually disappeared.

Secretary of the Treasury George B. Cortelyou met with J. P. Morgan, James Stillman, George F. Baker, and other financiers. The outcome was an announcement that the government would deposit $25 million in the national banks as a stabilization measure. Nevertheless, fear-stricken crowds besieged the Trust Company of America and several other banks. Three important trust companies went under before Morgan and other bankers cooled the panic by means of a $25 million emergency fund to support the weaker banks.

Meanwhile pandemonium reached a new peak on the Stock Exchange. Banks were demanding repayment of loans to brokers, and in the wild scramble to meet these demands stocks were dumped for what they would bring. Even so, there were few buyers. The price of call money bounded

---

[2] Dean Albertson's interviews with Eugene Meyer, p. 87.

upward to unbelievable heights, and one day there was none to be had at any price. A partner of C. D. Barney and Company, a respected brokerage house with many wealthy clients, clutched Meyer's arm on the floor of the Exchange and wailed that his firm and its clients alike, however rich in stocks, had no cash whatever and could not borrow any, even with government bonds as security. Remembering the $80,000 emergency fund in his vault, Meyer offered to lend it to his fellow broker and asked what the call rate was.

"Eighty percent per annum," the broker answered.

"Well," Meyer responded, "I wouldn't take that even for overnight. It is incredibly high."

"On the contrary," the frantic broker said, "I would be very grateful for a loan at any interest rate."

Tears of gratitude welled up in the broker's eyes as Meyer produced the money. By two o'clock that afternoon the call money rate had gone to 100 percent.

With desperation still sweeping the Exchange and prices in a state of collapse, Meyer placed orders for $1 million worth of stocks, without having the money to pay for them. Some of his friends thought he was courting ruin—that he had abandoned his own rules of prudent investment. Actually, he was following the basic principle behind all his Wall Street operations—to run against the mob at precisely the right moment. This technique had succeeded in the panic of 1901. Now he reasoned that the money famine was so acute that the bankers would have to agree to the use of clearing-house certificates, a sort of fiat currency. In that event money would be plentiful, and he could borrow whatever he needed. If they did not provide this essential relief, the stock market could not possibly open the next day, and therefore he would not have to pay immediately for the stock he had bought.

The bankers did authorize clearing-house certificates, and Meyer went immediately to a broker who handled bank loans on the floor of the Stock Exchange.

"I want to borrow a million dollars," he said.

"What!" exclaimed the broker. "You mean you are sticking your head into the lion's jaws? You're about the only one who has been out of the lion's jaws for the last few weeks. Have you gone crazy?"

"You may not know it," Meyer retorted cheerfully, "but the war is over."[3]

There were times when it appeared that Meyer's plunge might prove

[3] Sidney Hyman's manuscript, "Life of Eugene Meyer," Part II, p. 309.

to have been premature. In the following week call money again fluctuated wildly, business was prostrate, and confidence was as limp as an empty bag. Even more worrisome were the rumors that the Tennessee Coal and Iron Company might collapse, taking with it a large brokerage firm which held $5 million of the company's stock as collateral, and sending perilous tremors through various other brokerage houses. This peril was averted, however, when the United States Steel Company decided to buy the T.C.&I., and Elbert H. Gary and Henry C. Frick convinced President Roosevelt that, in order to stem the still-threatening tide of panic, he should not press antitrust charges.[4] Roosevelt acquiesced apparently because he was being assailed for having touched off the crisis and because he was genuinely worried by the economic abyss into which the country had fallen.

When the emergency had passed, the House of Morgan and the United States Steel Company were accused of having deliberately caused the panic as part of a scheme to acquire Tennesee Coal and Iron at their own price. Meyer did not accept that view. Years later when James W. Gerard subscribed to the conspiracy theory in a book he had written, Meyer challenged the thesis and reiterated his belief that the primary cause was the secret action of the Bank of England in shutting off the flow of credit that had been supporting the speculation in Wall Street.[5] Morgan may have taken advantage of the panic, but he did not cause it. Meyer felt that any astute financier could have seen the panic coming, as he had done, and his eyes had not been focused on the House of Morgan.

The difference between causing a panic and taking advantage of it when it came was vital to him because he too had profited mightily from the economic trauma of 1907. This did not mean that he had helped to bring about a disaster that would line his own pockets. On the contrary, he had exerted his influence, meager though it was, against the speculative rampage and then against the excesses of the shakeout. Had a majority of the operators in Wall Street followed his example, the crisis might well have been avoided. For the moment, however, the chief significance of his performance was personal. His practice of getting out of the market during cyclones of speculation and of then reentering in force when the heedless had been laid low could no longer be dismissed as a manifestation of good luck. At the still youthful age of thirty-two he had a technique that

[4] William Henry Harbaugh, *Power and Responsibility, The Life and Times of Theodore Roosevelt* (New York: Farrar, Straus and Cudahy; 1961), p. 314.

[5] Eugene Meyer to James W. Gerard, June 28, 1951.

could lead to inestimable wealth, if shrewdly applied—and if he cared to give his life to money-making. But techniques are seldom a controlling influence in life, and this would be peculiarly true in the case of Eugene Meyer.

7 /

Broadening Horizons

THE ECONOMIC STAGNATION THAT FOLLOWED THE PANIC OF 1907 had one redeeming feature as far as Eugene Meyer was concerned: it afforded him more time for the pursuit of personal interests outside the business sphere. There was more opportunity to meet friends at the Lotos Club—among them, Melville Stone, Clarence Barron, and J. Hartley Manners, the dramatist who was soon to be made famous by his *Peg O' My Heart*. Meyer still lived with his parents on Seventy-second Street near Central Park. His friends outside the family's social circle were in the professions or the arts. His fellow brokers held no interest for him in leisure hours because their horizons were too narrow, and he talked shop only with his partners and clients.

Having begun a collection of Dürer and Whistler etchings, American literary manuscripts, and Lincolniana, Meyer often browsed in the shop of George S. Hellman, poet, author, and collector. Hellman mentioned an artist who was trying to dispose of a painting of merit for only $400 and asked if Meyer would like to see it. A meeting was arranged at the artist's studio; Meyer bought the painting and struck up a friendship with a rare character—Gutzon Borglum. From the cataract of words that fell from Borglum's lips, Meyer learned that he was also a sculptor, that his work had been praised by Auguste Rodin, and that he was obsessed by the idea that the greatness of a hero could be properly depicted only by colossal statues. Even then Borglum was working on a six-ton block of stone from which he would carve a huge head of Lincoln. Almost before he realized it, Meyer was drawn into this project.

He placed his Lincolniana at the disposal of Borglum and began regular visits to the studio to see how the work was progressing. Once he asked Borglum what he was going to do with his masterpiece. The sculptor hoped someone might buy it; he had to make a living. Several days later Meyer suggested that the best place for the head would be a public building in Washington and that if the price were reasonable he would buy it and give it to the federal government. Borglum replied that the government did not accept artistic gifts from private persons. But suppose an exception could be made, Meyer came back, what would the price be? The sculptor put the price at $8,500, and his newfound friend agreed to pay it if the authorities in Washington would accept the striking likeness of Lincoln that was emerging.

When the statue was finished, Borglum wrote President Roosevelt to ask if it could be shown in the White House on Lincoln's birthday, 1908. The President acquiesced and, having lived with the solemn countenance of the Great Emancipator for a few weeks, pronounced it "a really remarkable work" and asked Borglum what would be done with it. The sculptor replied that a personal friend in New York stood ready to buy it and present it to the government if the procedural obstacles could be lifted. T.R. then suggested that the head should rest permanently in the Capitol and asked Borglum to bring his friend to the White House.

Strange as it may seem, this mission took Meyer to Washington for the first time in his life. The occasion rekindled his interest in political affairs as may be seen from the following paragraph of a letter he wrote to his sister Ro:

> If I have a criticism to make of Mr. Roosevelt, it is not that he wishes to use the arm of government to protect the individual against the strong-arm concentration of private economic force. It is that he has not yet worked through the problem of how the nation can gain the benefits of low-cost goods through larger units of production, without suffering the social and political evils of bigness as well. I have also come to feel that in his denunciations of the "malefactors of great wealth" he has not even begun to deal with the greatest malefactor of all. I have in mind a political order that has neglected to provide the nation with a monetary mechanism that can prevent the kind of panics we have lately experienced. I should like myself to come to grips with these questions. But I have no doubt that they will still be with us by the time I am in a position to leave business behind me, and follow through on my long-standing plan for some sort of direct participation in the management of governmental affairs.

The meeting at the White House was a routine affair, with T.R. in an exuberant mood. He called in Senator Winthrop Murray Crane, who said the best procedure would be for him to take Meyer and Borglum to see Senator Redfield Proctor, chairman of the Joint Committee on the Library. "Bully," said T.R. as he again assured his guests of his great interest in their project. Proctor's first concern was that his committee had never seen the sculpture. Would it be possible to have the Lincoln head shipped to the Capitol? Borglum said that it was at the Walters Gallery in Baltimore but he could make and send a plaster cast. The replica was flawless; the committee was pleased; and Congress passed a joint resolution on May 11 accepting the gift. Roosevelt expressed his delight to Borglum, and to Meyer he wrote: "As President, I want to thank you most heartily for your generous gift. It is a fine thing and the nation is your debtor. I should have been more than sorry if that splendid head of Lincoln had not come to the Capitol."

When the text of the resolution was sent to Meyer, he was pleasantly surprised to note that, by its terms, the Lincoln head was to adorn the rotunda of the Capitol. But he was embarrassed to read in the same resolution that his name as donor was to be carved in the pedestal. That requirement, he said, had neither relevance nor good taste. In a note to Senator Proctor he asked that his name be eliminated and that only the names of the subject and the sculptor appear on the pedestal, but Proctor replied that there was no point in disputing the terms of a resolution that both houses had approved and in any event Congress had more pressing business. Occasionally this disregard of his wishes would rise to haunt the donor. After Borglum had carved his great figures at Mount Rushmore, the *Rapid City Journal* said the Lincoln head had had its origin in Eugene Meyer's "lust for publicity." But Mrs. Borglum replied to the *Journal* that this was "wholly untrue and a gross libel on Mr. Meyer." Regret over the accidental parading of his role as donor did not, however, undo the continued satisfaction he derived from having presented to the nation a magnificent image of its greatest President. In his Washington years he would often be touched to see tourists and schoolchildren fall silent as they approached the majesty of that marble face.

Meyer's artistic interests led to another encounter that would have much more far-reaching consequences in his life. Returning from a visit to his sister Florence, who was ill, he drove down Fifth Avenue and decided to drop in at the American Art Galleries on Twenty-third Street to see a collection of Japanese prints. It was Lincoln's birthday, 1908. At an intersection he saw a lawyer friend, Edgar J. Kohler, looking frail and dejected, and he suggested they go to the art gallery together.

As they entered the gallery they met two other friends coming down the stairs. "When you get through looking at the art," the male member of the duo said, "there's a very nice-looking girl up there." Though he was a bachelor at thirty-two, Eugene gave no further thought to the remark until Kohler, having spied a young lady as they viewed the exhibit, nudged him and said: "That must be the girl." Turning to look, Eugene assented: "She is very attractive."

Agnes Elizabeth Ernst, with her golden hair, blue eyes, finely molded features, and lithe figure, was indeed a striking incarnation of feminine charm. She was wearing a gray tweed suit and a cap of squirrel fur trimmed by an eagle's feather—the compliment of an admirer. Her air of vigor also had a special appeal to Meyer whose experience at home had caused him to associate women with invalidism. Beyond this, the girl seemed to glow with self-assurance—a hint of both egotism and independence in her nature. As Eugene watched her, she suddenly became, in his mind, the embodiment of the qualities he had been seeking in a wife.

"That's the girl I'm going to marry!" he announced to his startled companion.[1]

"Are you serious?" Kohler asked.

"Never more so."

"Then you'd better speak to her or you'll never see her again."

"I don't think she would like that," Meyer said, having observed that a male friend was with her, although they were not viewing the artwork together. "We'll meet her again somewhere—you or I. If you meet her, you introduce her to me, and if I meet her, I'll introduce her to you."[2]

Only a week had passed when Kohler called Meyer at the office and asked: "What do you think happened?"

"You met that girl."

"Damn you, I did."

Kohler went on to explain that he had been invited to a ball by a Barnard College graduate, that the Prince Danilo who danced the "Merry Widow Waltz" during the amateur performance turned out to be a girl, that when she reappeared in an evening gown he had recognized her as the girl they had seen at the art gallery, that he had introduced himself and told her about the agreement with his friend. Kohler added that he was going to give a luncheon to which Meyer and the young woman would be invited.

The luncheon was pleasant but not a climactic event. It established the fact that Eugene Meyer and Agnes Ernst had many interests in common but also diverse obligations and ambitions that were taking them in different directions. Eugene was enchanted and eager to know her better. Agnes found his company very pleasant, but she had no thought of being

[1] Sidney Hyman's manuscript, "Life of Eugene Meyer," Part II, p. 325.
[2] Dean Albertson's interviews with Eugene Meyer, p. 108.

bound down by "serious interest in this new friend or any other."[3] Her fondest yearning was centered in Paris where she hoped to go for a year and a half of postgraduate study at the Sorbonne.

Eugene saw her frequently in the months following the strange triangular luncheon, but it was all too evident that he had formidable competition. Most of what he learned about her pleased him. She was working as a reporter for the *New York Sun*, not only supporting herself but also helping her parents. What he did not learn at the time was that Agnes, disillusioned by her father's "Bohemian ways" and failure to support his family, had decided to escape from an unhappy home life.[4] No hint of this was evident in her gay conversation or her air of self-confidence. Having worked her way through Barnard College, she was determined to paddle her own canoe. Nor was she dazzled by Eugene's success on Wall Street. On the contrary, she was soon to be reproaching him for the price he paid for it.

No less pleasing were her exuberance, wide range of interests, and spontaneous humor. Her zest for life set her apart from most of the daughters-with-a-dowry Eugene had encountered. Though her intellectual interests seemed more masculine than feminine, her beauty served to restore the balance, and her wit rounded out a rare personality. At a dinner party when a man chided her for being too puritanical and then asked, "What would *you* do if I tried to make love to you?" she was overheard to reply, with a mock-holy twist: "I'd be a good Christian and turn the other cheek." And when her unrestrained denunciation of a particular work of art brought a reminder of the biblical injunction, "Judge not, that ye be not judged," she exclaimed: "But I'm not judging. I'm damning." Friends accustomed to her impulsiveness, sparkle, and irrepressible nature had nicknamed her "Gloria."

According to Agnes's own account, four months of intensive courtship culminated in a proposal of marriage by "forceful, rich and reckless" Eugene Meyer and its rejection by "forceful, impoverished and reckless" Agnes Ernst.[5] Not even Lochinvar could have diverted her from her intention to study in Paris. It was a bold proclamation of independence that was to set the tone of her future relationship with Eugene.

Two days before her departure on August 4, 1908, Agnes acknowledged to Eugene that her friend Nancy N. had decided not to go because she could not afford it. "How much do you have for this expedition?" he

[3] Agnes E. Meyer, *Out of These Roots, The Autobiography of an American Woman* (Boston: Little, Brown and Company; 1953), p. 72.

[4] *Ibid*, p. 73.

[5] Agnes E. Meyer's unpublished manuscript, "Life as Chance and Destiny," p. 112.

62

asked. Agnes said she had $500, apparently not confessing that even that had been borrowed from a friend. Eugene laughed despite his admiration for her independence. "How long do you think that will last?" "Oh, six months at least," she said, "but I shall earn more by doing interviews for the *Sun*."[6] To relieve his anxiety about Agnes going on her adventure alone, Eugene offered to lend Nancy $500, as coming from an anonymous friend who did not care whether or not she repaid it, and she readily accepted.

Letters were exchanged after Agnes arrived in Paris, and by autumn the bereft suitor was looking for an excuse to visit her. As it turned out, no excuse was necessary: a new business venture required his presence in London, and his father became seriously ill in Carlsbad (now Karlovy Vary, Czechoslovakia). The cables that reached Eugene were alarming. The elder Meyer, who had taken his wife to the health resort at Carlsbad, had developed erysipelas blood poisoning after a pedicure. Abscesses on his leg led to a series of operations, and he was alternately reported as on the mend and as dying.

Eugene was deeply concerned because illness seemed to be dogging the Meyer family. Aside from his mother's chronic ailments, Ro had been a semi-invalid for nearly seven years, Florence was still bedridden from the shock of losing her son, and Walter had been snatched from the very jaws of death in 1907 when Eugene had directed the attending physicians to use an untried discovery in blood transfusions. Eugene Senior, then in his sixty-eighth year, had seemed to be the only one who escaped the ravages of disease. In recent years his children had taken to calling him "Governor," an honorific title which conveyed something of their veneration now that the ties of parental control had been relaxed. Driven by dread of losing this tower of strength in the family, Eugene rushed to his father's side.

The "Governor" had been moved to a new hospital in Komotau (now Chomutov) near Carlsbad; he had undergone twenty-five operations for leg abscesses, and his doctors felt that the worst was over. At Eugene's request, Agnes Ernst had sent him an American nurse from Paris, and his youngest son Edgar was soon to arrive. After a week at his father's bedside, Eugene felt free to attend to his other business, and he hastened to Paris.

Agnes introduced him to the gay, stimulating world of the Sorbonne. He took her into a totally different atmosphere—the financial and governmental circles of Paris. In between there were trips to nearby châteaux and cathedrals, lunches at swank hotels, and kisses for the ardent suitor "in front of the concierge's door while Nancy was waiting on the stairs."[7]

[6] Agnes E. Meyer, *Out of These Roots*, p. 73.
[7] Agnes E. Meyer to Eugene Meyer, June 15, 1914.

Eugene won high favor with Agnes's Latin Quarter friends by taking "flocks" of them to "feasts" at the Tour d'Argent, which none of them could otherwise afford. Agnes admitted that her friends "adored him," but her own emotions were not so easily defined.

Meyer also went to London where he had some important engagements. On the day before his departure he called on Henry Oppenheimer, a banker whom he had known for a decade, and sought his advice. The doctors in Komotau, he said, were treating his father by merely cutting open the abscesses and were not doing anything about the blood where the infection was. Did the banker know any specialist in London who might be helpful? The banker recalled that a vaccine specialist, Sir Almroth Wright, had cured a friend of severe carbuncles. Sir Almroth proved to be in Cologne but, through a series of telegrams sent from his London office, he agreed to meet Meyer there the next day at midnight. Appearing at the Cologne railway station in a white tie and a little unsteady from wine, Sir Almroth said he could not himself go to Komotau because of a lecture he must give at a medical convention but his assistant, a Dr. Matthews, could make the trip. Meyer got Dr. Matthews out of his hotel bed and took him in tow.

Although the elder Meyer's condition had not worsened since Eugene had previously seen him, the English doctor said vaccine should be administered at once. The attending German doctor refused to give his consent on the ground that the patient was on the mend and that any change of treatment might cause a setback. At Eugene's request, however, Dr. Matthews was allowed to make the vaccine and leave it to be administered by the attending doctor in case there should be a turn for the worse. Eugene then returned to London to tie some loose ends in a refinancing arrangement; he was leaving his hotel for another tryst with Agnes Ernst in Paris when he heard a page calling his name. A telegram from Edgar said that their father was in grave danger; the infection had spread to his whole body and nothing was being done to stop it.

Meyer continued on to Paris and then telephoned his banker friend in London and asked him to induce Sir Almroth to go to Komotau and administer the vaccine his assistant had made. Oppenheimer called back and reported that Sir Almroth would not go; he had a very demanding and lucrative practice; his fee for such a trip would be £1,000—then equivalent to $5,000, a figure designed to discourage any further demand upon him. Meyer was furious.

"Please phone Sir Almroth again," he said to Oppenheimer, "and tell him this for me. My father's money is not at stake. Nor is mine. My father's life is at stake. Tell him that I don't care how much he charges if he will only go."[8]

Sir Almroth went, and within three weeks the elder Meyer was able to sail for home. Though his scarred leg would continue to trouble him, despite skin grafting, he was to live for another fifteen years, and he often remarked that he owed his escape from the grave to the devotion and stubbornness of his eldest son. The effect of the experience on Eugene was not confined to the new note of tenderness in his relationship to his father; he became a passionate advocate of medical research. Soon after his return home he joined the board of directors of New York's Mount Sinai Hospital and helped to provide funds for its research work. Later he would underwrite Mount Sinai research teams who went to plague-infested Mexico and Serbia to administer anticholera vaccine on a mass scale. When Sir Almroth extended his inoculating department in London, Meyer contributed £100 to it annually.

One other interest outside the business world claimed some of Meyer's time in the last years of his bachelorhood. He wanted an attractive place in the country where he could spend weekends and holidays free from the bustle, congestion, and heat of New York. Whenever he had time, he drove the back roads of Westchester County, Long Island, the Connecticut shore, and New Jersey looking for a place to buy. In this way he discovered an ideal spot near Mount Kisco—a farm on rolling terrain interlaced with woods high above Lake Byram. Since the owner declined to sell, Eugene consoled himself by buying a place at Pound Ridge in Westchester County with timber, a brook, and an apple orchard. Then he took an attractive place at Roslyn on Long Island in payment for a bad debt and dreamed of building a house there because it was closer to New York. Meanwhile, the owner at Mount Kisco changed his mind; Meyer bought the place, and the high cliffs on Byram Lake again became a focal point of his planning for the future.

In Paris, Agnes encountered new experiences of a very different sort. Eugene had taken her to visit Rodin, the famous French sculptor, at his house and studios at Meudon, and Agnes, enchanted by the Maestro, accepted numerous invitations to visit him after Eugene had returned home. One day the sculptor, who was noted for his amorousness, sent his new disciple a long telegram almost commanding her presence in his *"jardin enfleuri."* Scenting danger, Agnes consulted her friend Edward J. Steichen, who told her flatly: "You can't possibly go."

[8] Hyman manuscript, Part II, p. 351.

The two argued for an hour, with Agnes insisting that if she did not go she would lose her great teacher. Though passionately in love with the artistic atmosphere she found in Paris, Agnes was coolly aloof to the sexual promiscuity that she had encountered for the first time. Clinging to "an ideal of purity and perfection,"[9] she was repelled by any suggestion of "casual sexual experiments." But she had great confidence in her ability to manage any situation. Failing to dissuade her from going, Steichen admonished as she went out of the door: "Be sure to wear your longest hatpin."

Rodin's coachman driving an ancient barouche met Agnes as she arrived at Meudon, and the Maestro himself was waiting at his door. Through a garden of flowering trees, he escorted her to a cozy room at the back of his most remote studio and locked the door. As he began to murmur his affection, there was loud pounding on the door. "Get away," he shouted. "But Monsieur Clemenceau is calling," the servant outside yelled. "Tell him to go to the devil," the sculptor replied, "I'm busy."

The exchange magnified Agnes's sense of alarm. As Rodin seated himself in a comfortable armchair and drew her to him, she seized his powerful hands and fell on her knees before him. With fear and admiration struggling for control of her face and her voice, she pleaded in French: "Dear friend, you cannot imagine what you mean to me. You are the greatest artist, the greatest teacher I have ever known. Dear, dear friend, there are many men in the world. There is only one Rodin. I don't wish to lose him."[10]

Agnes thought she saw tears in the old man's eyes and a look of relief on his big, expressive face. Here was a woman who was different—who loved him for his art and shrank from his physical embraces. Surprised and intrigued, Rodin reverted to the role of genius and teacher. Thereafter he invited Agnes to Meudon when he had distinguished guests; he took her to the Louvre for discussions of art; he spent seemingly endless hours demonstrating his techniques and talking about the essence of beauty. When she left Paris, he gave her one of his most superb drawings and sent her fascinating illustrated letters while she was studying art in Italy. The adventurous girl from New York had not only won the devoted friendship of a great sculptor; she had demonstrated that she had a way with men and that art-inspired romance need not degenerate into sexual license.

---

[9] Agnes E. Meyer's "Life as Chance and Destiny," p. 124.
[10] *Ibid.*, p. 131.

8 /

Astride Copper Mountain

THE FIRST FAVORABLE ITEM THAT CAME INTO VIEW AS EUGENE Meyer, Jr., and Company scanned the desolate economic horizon of 1908 was a notice that the International Harvester Company would list its shares on the New York Stock Exchange. Believing that the Chicago-based company was sound and that its $10-million issue of stock would help to get investment buying back on the track, Meyer sent Charles Boynton to ask George Perkins of the House of Morgan if he would need any help in marketing the Harvester shares and if he would care to talk to Meyer. The answers to both questions were affirmative, and a conference was arranged.

It developed that the House of Morgan would welcome help because its soundings had indicated it would be difficult to make a market for the stock in New York. Black pessimism still hung over the entire economy, and Wall Street traditionally ignored any enterprise based on the interior of the country. Harvester's position was complicated, moreover, by the fact that it had had to defer payment of $25 million it owed to a bank until farmers could pay their debts in the fall. After Meyer and Lyman Kendall had probed into the company's records, however, they agreed to buy $6 million of the new stock issue and took an option to place the remaining $4 million within a reasonable period.

For a time it appeared that Meyer's post-panic optimism had betrayed him. In taking most of the Harvester issue on his own shoulders, he had counted heavily on sales in Europe through the excellent contacts he had established, but the Dutch-born agent he had sent to place the stock in France and Germany made little progress. Thinking the man's limited experience might be the cause, Meyer was contemplating a trip to Europe so that he could lend a hand, when other demands upon him became urgent.

The Boston Consolidated Mining Company, a subsidiary of a British copper mining concern, had locked horns with the Guggenheims' Utah

Copper Company over ore deposits they both owned at Bingham, Utah, about twenty miles southwest of Salt Lake City. Boston Consolidated owned the top of the mountain and Utah Copper the lower portion. They were trying to work out a merger so that the property could be developed in a sensible fashion, but the negotiations had gotten nowhere. Feeling that they needed an American on their side of the table who could "stand up to the Guggenheims," the British interests had asked George Blumenthal to recommend someone for the spot, and he had suggested Meyer.

Copper had intrigued the ambitious young financier for some years, but he had avoided any direct connection with the industry because of its strife and volatility. Now he took a hasty look at the possibilities at Bingham, changed his mind, bought a large bloc of Boston Consolidated stock, and was elected to its board of directors. His partner Kendall, after making an investigation, had carefully avoided any expression of judgment about the *quality* of the ore. In part, therefore, Meyer's action was impulsive, and for a time it appeared that he might have walked into another trap.

Boston Consolidated had not developed its property enough to prove that it had substantial copper deposits. Its meager output, moreover, could be refined only by the special process that Utah Copper had developed for handling low-grade ore. Poor management and the collapse of copper prices in the panic of 1907 had further worsened the plight of Boston Consolidated. Its bond issue of $1,500,000 fell due in 1908, and new capital had to be raised if there was to be any further development of the mine. The Guggenheim interests were obviously waiting for their faltering competitor to topple.

The outlook was so bleak that the parent British company began to balk. The necessary new capital, the London directors said, would have to be raised in the United States. The American directors were quite willing to dump the whole burden on "the strong man" who had been added to the board of directors with that in mind. Meyer dug himself in deeper by raising the essential working capital and then began to worry about whether the parent company, at its annual meeting of stockholders in September, would authorize new bonds to replace the $1.5-million issue falling due in October. Obviously he had to attend that meeting in London.

The disillusioned British directors unloosed all their pent-up anger upon the hapless new American director as if he were personally responsible, not only for Boston Consolidated's troubles, but also for "the American peril" then causing so much excitement in the old world. "It's your company—not my company," Meyer reminded them, "and the mismanagement is yours, not mine." He urged them to send over a manager who knew something about engineering. As for the refinancing, Meyer's argument that the British interests should take one half of the new bonds met with stiff resistance. "All right," he said at the stockholders' meeting, "if you don't want to stand behind the bond issue on a share-and-share-alike basis, I'll get it done." To his astonishment, this brought down on his head an accusation that he was trying to deny the English people their right to invest in and prosper from the American subsidiary. Meyer had not deliberately borrowed Tom Sawyer's technique for getting his fence whitewashed, but he was greatly relieved by the belated agreement of the British interests to do their share.

Back in New York, Meyer had no difficulty in disposing of the American share of the new bonds. Wall Street had recovered from its jitters, but Boston Consolidated's troubles were not over. An excess of iron in the ore prevented the refining process from working economically. It looked as if receivership and sale for a song to Utah Copper were not far down the road. The subject came up one night when Meyer and his friend William Boyce Thompson, both tipsy, were indulging in their customary raillery at the Lotos Club.

"Bill, the Guggenheim crowd think they have this Boston Consolidated business ripe for a plucking. Well, they don't. The law of gravity is on our side, not theirs. We have the top of the mountain. They have the bottom. And you can't mine the bottom without the top—unless you are in the landslide business."

"So?"

"So, why don't you and I jointly buy a fifty-one percent ownership in Boston Consolidated for the sole privilege of closing the damn thing down and paying the taxes on it. Then let's sit tight and wait for the Guggenheim crowd to come to *us* with a proposition *we* will turn down. They've got to come to *us*, or else they will never be able to work *their* mine."

Thompson found this shrewd turning of the tables against the Guggenheims much to his liking. Together he and Meyer quietly bought up Boston Consolidated securities from both British and American holders who were delighted to unload them. By the time they had 40 percent ownership, Thompson, no longer able to contain his amusement, let the Guggenheims know about the trap that had been laid for them. Meyer was furious about this premature leak, but he cooled quickly when Daniel Guggenheim, head of the clan, called at his office and invited him uptown for consultation. Before the two emerged from a cab at the Guggenheim headquarters they had agreed to combine Boston Consolidated and Utah Copper, with Meyer a director of the enlarged company and a member of its finance committee.

Once more, the young financier had turned a brush with disaster into a fabulous opportunity. The great Utah copper mine, then believed to have a life expectancy of about twenty years, was to produce 550 million pounds of copper a year during World War II and to continue on into the indefinite future, with enormous enrichment of its owners. Meyer's favorable connection with the industry also led to the financing of a number of other big copper projects and to additional directorships in other companies. He was soon to become a key figure in the copper industry.

In a brief period Meyer had thus succeeded in aligning himself with two of the most powerful financial empires in New York—the House of Morgan and the seven Guggenheim brothers. Yet it was not a matter of an ambitious young man hitching his wagon to famous chariots for free rides. Meyer had been welcomed into association with the Morgans and the Guggenheims because they saw in him a valuable ally.

Despite the significance of a working relationship with the House of Morgan, there were times when it seemed a doubtful blessing. In trying to dispose of the International Harvester stock, Meyer discovered that the name Morgan was anathema among many financiers in Paris and London. "Had not Morgan put together the United States Steel Corporation with a capitalization of $1.4 billion of which at least one-half turned out to be water?" he was asked. Many European investors assumed that the offering of International Harvester stock was similarly watered.

The European disenchantment spread far beyond any particular stock or institution. In the financial and social circles in which he moved during his 1908 trip, Meyer heard repeated references to the growing "American peril." The larger role of the United States in international affairs during the presidency of Theodore Roosevelt, the building of the Panama Canal, and the round-the-world cruise of the United States fleet, combined with the expanding American industrial power and a succession of booms and panics, had brought an awareness of power in the New World that Europe had long thought of as its hinterland. European investors did not like what they saw, and, even though many of their fears were grossly exaggerated, Meyer concluded that he could no longer rely upon mere trust in himself as a lone operator.

Within the range of his interests and his knowledge, he sought to counter the raging hostility. Some of the water in United States Steel had been squeezed out, he argued, and it was being further reduced by withholding earnings to build an immense plant at Gary, Indiana. As business revived and this plant came into production, along with improved facilities elsewhere, he said, the corporation's earnings would sharply increase and capitalization per ton of production would be reduced. He was full of confidence that a new period of substantial growth was in progress in the wake of the panic.

As he thus labored to clear a path for his International Harvester shares, Meyer suddenly realized that he was grappling with a side issue. A flash of insight told him that the key to a better market for American stocks in Europe—and Wall Street, too, for that matter—was more precise knowledge about the companies behind the stocks, starting with that Gargantua, United States Steel. Investors and even financiers were floundering in the dark; fears and prejudices were filling the vacuum that had previously spawned gullible hopes, and the only reliable cure was facts and more facts—an analysis that would go to the very heart of the great corporation and its prospects as a business enterprise.

Actually, this was the idea on which Meyer had built his business, but the probings of his staff up to this time had been largely confined to the companies he was especially interested in. Now he saw an opportunity to strike at the very center of the information vacuum. If he could succeed in this, International Harvester would take care of itself and his young investment firm would attain a new dimension of service to investors. On his return to New York, Meyer put his brother Edgar and Lyman Kendall to work on the project, insisting that they dig far below the top layers of available facts. The report should show what the earnings of United States Steel would be (a) with a low level of production and relatively low prices; (b) with slightly higher production and price levels; and (c) with full production and fairly high prices. The findings in each of these situations should then be related to the financial strength of the corporation, to its costs of production relative to its capitalization, and to the prospective value of its shares. The report was to be precise, comprehensive, and lucid—a worthy sample of the service his firm could offer.

Published in 1909, with 60,000 copies in English and 5,000 in French, the report on U.S. Steel had an excellent reception. *Barron's Weekly* led the financial press in hailing it as a tour de force and said it would create a new standard by which all circulars issued by Wall Street investment houses would be judged. For the first time a spotlight had been turned on the country's industrial giant with accuracy, fairness, and understanding of its inward workings and its relationship to the economy as a whole.

The outcome was highly favorable both to U.S. Steel and to the Meyer firm. The price of Steel stock rose dramatically in line with the earnings that the circular had projected. Orders to buy stock flowed in large volume into Meyer's office from Europe as well as the United States. In the wake of this demand Meyer also disposed of the International Harvester stock he held, picked up the remaining shares under option to him and sold those too. Promoters of new business ventures inundated Meyer with requests for help, and security issues floated by his firm were oversubscribed as soon as he laid the facts on the line.

In the House of Morgan, Meyer's standing underwent a sudden transformation. Instead of having to seek an audience by indirect means, he was hailed when he walked into the place almost as a conquering hero. Even the great financial czar himself sent for Meyer. Without mentioning the occasion when Meyer had been introduced by his father fourteen years previously, the magnate said: "Your steel circular is the best study of the kind I have ever seen produced on Wall Street. My secretary has an order to keep it on my desk every day. It keeps on telling me things about the U.S. Steel Corporation I never knew precisely."[1]

Morgan's compliment seemed sincere enough, but it did not mean that Meyer had been accepted into the circle of the great financier's favorites. About the same time he warned one of his partners, Harry P. Davison, to "watch out for that fellow Meyer, because if you don't he'll end up having all the money on Wall Street." It was this attitude that seemed to dominate Morgan's future thinking about Eugene Meyer.

The steel circular brought Meyer attention from another source. The art dealer Joseph Duveen, who made a specialty of selling masterpieces at exorbitant prices to men who were building fortunes on Wall Street, came to Meyer with a scheme that would assure him immortality in the realm of the arts. Amused by the man's snob appeal, which had apparently lured Morgan and other multimillionaires into spending fortunes for arty prestige, Meyer decided to play a game with him. Pretending to be taken in by the visions of a hallowed place beside the masters, he agreed to Duveen's grandiose proposition tentatively, subject to further discussion, but the discussion went on and on until the supersalesman could no longer avoid the conclusion that Meyer was pulling his leg. Duveen left, and that was the end of the scheme.

In the years immediately ahead, copper—not steel—would loom largest in Meyer's operations. In addition to his interest in Utah Copper, he would invest heavily in Anaconda and Braden. He would become deeply involved in financing two other big companies—Chile Copper and Inspiration Copper. In the case of Chile Copper, Meyer's firm would under-

---

[1] Sidney Hyman's manuscript, "Life of Eugene Meyer," Part II, p. 359.

write two bond issues totaling $50 million on the basis of his independent engineering studies after financing had been refused by Morgan and Kuhn, Loeb. By 1915 Meyer's position astride the copper industry would be such that an optimistic forecast by him would appear to spark a boom in copper stocks. Questioned about his role, he would declare that he was not a Chanticleer who believed that his crow caused the sun to rise,[2] but there would be disagreement on that point because of his major role in the industry.

At no time, however, did he confine his interests to any one industrial field. Despite his initial disillusioning experience with oil, he helped finance Mid-Continental Petroleum Products in the prewar era, and this time the gush consisted of oil instead of salt water. He even financed new generating facilities and transmission lines for the Montana Electric Power and Light Company so as to provide more power for Anaconda Copper, taking precautions to conceal this operation from his father, who regarded all public utilities as corrupt. But this was his only venture into the utilities field. ". . . if my father hears about this," Meyer confessed in a letter to his brother-in-law, Sigmund Stern, "he will unhesitatingly hurl more lightning bolts at my head than all the electricity the utility company could generate."

The energetic young tycoon was keeping the whole of industrial America within his range of vision. Still in his middle thirties, he was well advanced toward realization of the dream that had taken root in his mind on his first transcontinental trip. But there were many clouds on the horizon, and one of them reflected his difficulty in getting along with people. His solidifying habit of success exacerbated his tendency toward cocksureness and flashes of anger. A series of irritations led his brother-in-law, Alfred A. Cook, who was also his attorney, to explode when Meyer patronizingly informed him by letter that information about a brokerage firm, which Cook had requested, could not be properly committed to writing. Cook's sizzling reply: "I see that impudence still abides with you. I am disappointed. . . . I thought . . . time would work a reduction of an abnormal cranial enlargement—the existence of which was quite explicable. . . . I suppose it was most foolish of me to entertain the hope that the leopard would change some of his spots, however much they might need changing."

Meyer had plenty of reminders that the conquest of self was no less important than the mastery of economic forces.

[2] *Boston News Bureau*, November 2, 1915.

9 /

'Round-the-World Honeymoon

IN HIS AFFAIRS OF THE HEART THE YOUNG FINANCIER HAD MADE little progress. Though he was still in love with Agnes Ernst, she had shown no disposition to center her affection on any one of the men who continued to flock around her. Eugene had visited her in Europe in both 1908 and 1909; they had exchanged many letters and each continued to be intrigued by the other; but this did not change the compelling drives which took them in different directions.

To him, "the *Sun* girl," as she was called by many friends, was a challenge worthy of his best efforts. Tall, statuesque, and beautiful, she would be a wife to be proud of. She was at home in the larger world of intellectual ferment and artistic ideas that held his interest. Eugene had cast aside the occupational mold that his father had so carefully prepared for him at Lazard Frères in order to attain a larger sphere of operations. Now, in seeking a wife, he again tried to break out of the narrow French-Jewish circle to which his parents belonged. He had found some objection to every eligible girl in that group. Agnes was different; she moved in the wide American stream. Her parents were natives of Hanover, and her father came from a long line of Lutheran ministers, her paternal grandfather having been clergyman to the last king of Hanover. Born in New York City in 1887, she had grown up in Pelham Heights. Her experience abroad had sharpened her literary ability and artistic taste, and enhanced her feminine charm. A wife with these qualities could be a passport to a broader, fuller life.

Yet one ingredient of romance was missing; Agnes evaded the question of love. Some of her letters had been sharply critical. With characteristic frankness, she had once written him: "I must try to teach you to stop fighting everything that crosses your path. It would be excusable if you were a bee that puts its whole purpose into a sting. But you were meant to be a human being. Why not be one?" Rebukes of this kind were

74

tempered, however, by her obvious pleasure in his company and by the many interests they shared. Agnes cared enough to write him long letters and to importune her mother (Lucy Schmidt Ernst) to invite Eugene to dinner. Her letters were little essays by a girl in love with life and with herself but not in love with any particular man. In later life Meyer would show some of these letters to a friend with the comment: "Very intelligent letters, aren't they? But there is no love in them."[1]

Eugene had much to offer in marriage, in addition to his wealth. Though only five feet and nine inches tall, he was erect and well proportioned. His clean-shaven face and rimless pince-nez suggested refinement, and the twinkle in his deep brown eyes betokened humor and kindliness, despite the hard-boiled quality that was evident in his nose and chin. Integrity and reliability were deeply etched into his nature. As his sister Ro once wrote to Agnes, "There is a strength in Eugene that compels all his sisters and brothers to turn to him in times of indecision or trouble, and he has never failed us."

Strength and integrity had not, however, swept Agnes off her feet. After Eugene's second visit with her in Paris she remained sufficiently noncommittal that he "kind of dropped her" from his thinking. By autumn his interest was absorbed in another alluring project: a trip around the world. For some months he had been seeking an opportune time for more extended travel, as all his trips abroad up to that time had been confined to western Europe. President Taft supplied an appropriate occasion for suspended business operations by getting his administration into an appalling mess.

Having contributed $25,000 to the 1908 Republican campaign, Meyer had had high hopes for the Taft regime when it first came into power. The judicious-minded Taft could give the country a welcome respite from the flamboyant tactics of Theodore Roosevelt. But Taft had allowed the standpatters in the Senate to run roughshod over him on the tariff and seemed to bungle every issue. Meyer concluded that the President would come under heavy attack and that the bullish march in Wall Street could not last. Trouble was also brewing in the railroad industry because of the hostility toward labor's demand for wage increases and recognition of the unions. After surveying both of these situations carefully, Meyer turned most of his assets into cash in preparation for turbulent weather. While waiting for the storm to pass, he would make a leisurely jaunt to the Orient. "The Far East," he explained to one friend, "is a sleeping giant, just waking up. I should like to see him turn over on his side before he gets up."

[1] Author's interview with Sidney Hyman, June 4, 1971.

One day near Christmas there was a familiar voice on the telephone. Agnes had returned home after spending some time in Germany, Austria, and Italy. Once more there were pleasant dates and animated talk about Paris, New York, and many other things. It was soon evident that Agnes was again involved in an emotional conflict with her father, which caused her to regret that she had ever left Paris. Frederick H. Ernst was a misfit lawyer who preferred to think of himself as a writer. His failure to sell his dramas and other manuscripts and his general pattern of self-indulgence and irresponsibility had left his family in a miasma of poverty and debt. Agnes's relationship with him had evolved from adoration in her childhood to contempt and rebellion. She would describe it in her autobiography as "an exaggerated burning shame" that haunted her throughout her young womanhood. She could find peace only by getting away from the family, as she had done when she went to Europe.

Now that she was back in New York, the logical escape for her was marriage, but this idea led to another area of turmoil. Three men were expecting her to marry them, or hoping that she would. One was an adoring slave, sensitive but physically unattractive, who had long pursued her as the most enchanting female alive. Another was handsome Alfred von Heymel, a "brilliant, cultivated, undisciplined and utterly charming aristocrat" whom she had visited in Munich. It was he who had designed the gray-squirrel hat with the eagle feather—softness and daring combined— that she had worn on the day Eugene had first seen her. Eugene's courtship was less intensive than that of the other two, and they combined their hostility toward him because of his wealth. Agnes was torn between her much older relationships to her "devoted artist friends" and her "far greater confidence in Eugene Meyer's character and personality."[2] As she lunched with Eugene in the old Waldorf-Astoria late in January 1910, she confided in him that she might have to return to Paris in order to straighten out her inner confusion.

"I have decided to get away for a bit myself," Eugene said casually. "I'm going to take a trip around the world, starting next month."

"Why? How long are you going to be away?"

"Oh, at least six months."

Agnes felt as if the ground were caving beneath her. In the misery and frustration that confronted her at home, Eugene had been a source of understanding and at least an anchor to hope. Now he was about to

[2] Agnes E. Meyer, *Out of These Roots, The Autobiography of an American Woman* (Boston: Little Brown and Company; 1953), p. 95.

disappear from the scene without waiting around for her to make up her mind. The thought was unbearable. For a few minutes she sat in desolate silence and then heard her voice saying, as if it were scarcely a conscious decision, "I'm going with you."[3]

"Yes, I know that," he replied simply. "I have your tickets."

"Well," she gasped as the implications of her decision began to bear in upon her, "then I must go to the telephone and cancel a two o'clock appointment." At the time she did not acknowledge that she had been about to leave him for a date with another man. On her return to the table he asked in the calm, matter-of-fact tone that had prevailed throughout the proposal and acceptance, "How soon can you get ready to go?"

"Lincoln's birthday is two weeks off," she replied. "Let's celebrate it by getting married."

As recorded by both the principals, the exchange was an affirmation of mutual need rather than a declaration of love. Agnes would later explain her decision in her autobiography in these words:

> Incredible as it may seem, it had never occurred to me until I became engaged to Eugene that it would have been impossible for me to marry anyone who was not well-to-do. For the only dowry I had to bring a husband were my father's debts and my own. The fact that I could confess to Eugene the perpetual nightmare of my relationship to my father was a release from deep inner tensions. It gave me the sharpest realization that I was no longer alone in the world and the added blessing that henceforth I would be free of a crushing burden of debt. Let no one undervalue the importance of economic independence.

No doubt both realized that a marriage contracted under these circumstances would be subjected to extraordinary strains. Some friends freely predicted that the marriage could not last more than six months. Eugene once reported that Agnes's mother "was very shocked that she should have chosen a heathen."[4] One of Agnes's suitors exclaimed when she broke the news to him: "My God! You're not going to marry that madman Eugene Meyer? Why he's already lost more money on Wall Street than the rest of us expect to make in a lifetime." One of Agnes's admirers begged her to wait until she could think about the whole matter more clearly. It was true, he said, that Eugene had a "strong character,"

3 *Ibid.*
4 Eugene Meyer to Dr. Marion E. Kenworthy, February 10, 1958.

but that only guaranteed clashes with her indomitable will. There was also an age difference; he was thirty-four and she twenty-three. Eugene himself was not blind to the hazards. He broke the well-kept secret of his marriage on the day before the wedding with this explanation to Melville Stone:

> I am going to marry tomorrow Miss Agnes Ernst, the young lady whom you met at a dinner I gave at the Beaux Arts about a year and one-half ago. You spoke of her at that time as a "charming creature." I find her all of that and even more. After having watched the troubled seas of matrimony with an observant eye for many years I am going to embark for the voyage.

The voyage might be stormy, but both the principals must have foreseen that it would also be extraordinarily interesting and fruitful.

The wedding took place at 4 p.m. on February 12, 1910, precisely two years from the day when Eugene had first seen her at the American Art Galleries and announced his intention of marrying her before they had been introduced. The Reverend John Schiller, pastor of the Trinity Lutheran Church, performed the ceremony at the Ernst home, 1370 Prospect Avenue, the Bronx, with only members of the two families present. Agnes's choice of a Lutheran wedding in keeping with the Ernst family's strong religious ties had met with no opposition from Eugene, who had quietly dropped the Jewish affiliation of his youth. His parents may have felt some disappointment that he was not marrying within his own ethnic group, but there was no indication of this. At Eugene's age, they were probably happy to see him married to *any* promising girl, and, with Eugene successfully managing his father's affairs as well as his own, they were scarcely in a position to offer their advice in any circumstances.

The New York Times printed half a column about the wedding, emphasizing the surprise element and announcing that the couple had already left on their trip around the world.[5] Actually, they had gone to Eugene's farm at Mount Kisco to spend their first week together.

Then came a trip to Washington where a new friend of Eugene's, Postmaster General Frank H. Hitchcock, smoothed the way for them. The highlight was Mrs. Herbert Wadsworth's gala ball, which gave both the bride and groom their first introduction to Washington society. It was fascinating to meet Cabinet members, justices of the Supreme Court, and many other high officials, but Eugene felt a little uneasy when he concluded that he was the only Jew present. The thought brought a new appreciation of Agnes as he observed her circulating among officials and

[5] *The New York Times*, February 14, 1910.

society matrons with assurance and grace. Though only twenty-three, she was a wife who could be relied upon to do her part well in any social setting.

Less to his liking was a farewell gathering at the Plaza Hotel in New York when they returned to pick up their trunks. All Agnes's beaux came to say good-bye and refused to leave. One brought her a gold vanity case inscribed "Sic Transit Gloria." Despite his eagerness to complete their last-minute preparations, Eugene finally invited all the visitors to lunch, and when his parents came in to wish the couple bon voyage they found him at one end of a long table, with Agnes at the other end, and both sides lined by disconsolate males.

Whether or not the parting was painful for Agnes, she was soon entranced by a totally new experience. Eugene had brought from Europe a courier valet whom he had used on his trips there and provided a maid for his bride, who had been traveling third class in Europe. The four boarded a private car, *The Constitution*, which was routed over many railroad systems by special arrangement so as to take in the Grand Canyon of the Colorado and other points of scenic interest. In Montana a call on "Big Bill" Thompson, Eugene's partner in the copper-mountain episode, took an amusing turn. As the honeymooners were leaving, Mrs. Thompson fixed her gaze with embarrassing intensity on the string of matched pearls Agnes was wearing—her wedding present from Eugene. Unable to restrain her envy, she exclaimed: "Bill, do you see those pearls? What are you going to do about it?"

In San Francisco there was a week of social gaiety with Eugene's sisters and their circle of friends, in striking contrast to his previous visit just after the earthquake and fire. The resourceful Ro also put them in touch with a trained nurse, Margaret Powell, who was hired to take the place of the unsatisfactory maid they had brought from New York. "Powelly," as she came to be known, accompanied them on the rest of the honeymoon and would remain with the Meyers for sixteen years, becoming, in many respects, the real mother of their children.

Honolulu provided another week of traditional honeymooning before the larger adventure in the Orient began. The financier was in sharp competition with the reporter in soaking up information about the new lands they visited. On the long voyage to Yokohama, Eugene delved into a two-volume work by Japanese authors on the history, constitution, laws, defense system, industry, and agriculture of Japan. Intensive observations followed in Yokohama, Tokyo, Kyoto, Osaka, and Nara for a period of seven weeks. Visits to art collections, flower gardens, religious temples, and theaters were interspersed with exchanges of information in banking and industrial circles. Eugene carried a letter of introduction to James Russell Kennedy of the Associated Press, who opened many doors to them.

When Kennedy took the newlyweds to a garden party for the emperor of Japan, Agnes described him as "a fat, elderly gentleman with a pigeon-toed walk . . . and a very hideous fat face." Eugene was curious as to why this man who was venerated as a god should be wearing red trousers that did not fit. Standing in a crowd about 150 feet away from the emperor, Eugene whispered to his host: "Why can't he get a better fit?" "Because," Kennedy replied, "the tailor to the emperor can't get any closer to his body than we are."

Most of the questions asked ran to more profound depths. Near the end of their stay in Japan, the Meyers presented a letter of introduction they had obtained in San Francisco to Marquis Shigenobu Okuma, editor of the Japanese book they had been reading, in the hope of being invited to view his famous garden. The response was an invitation to take tea with him in addition to visiting the garden. Okuma, a handsome intellectual who had founded the first women's college in Tokyo, had lost a leg when a bomb was thrown into his carriage as a protest against his progressive ideas and friendship for the West. In the course of an extended conversation, Meyer asked why travelers from the West did not see the things in which the Orient was superior and adapt them to the Occident. In some areas in which the West had pioneered, the Japanese were great copiers. Why did not the process work in reverse? Okuma was evasive; the conversation turned to other subjects; but ultimately Meyer came back to his question by saying that he had not understood the answer, although he did not wish to press the matter if his host preferred not to reply. Thus cornered, Okuma responded: "It's easier to adapt the material things than the spiritual things." Meyer came away from that tea thinking the West had much to learn from the East.

The visit to Korea was depressing, especially in Pusan, where "there was nothing but mud huts" and treeless land. Korea was under a protectorate and was soon to be annexed by Japan. The Meyers watched a Japanese shopkeeper, as if by way of illustrating the Koreans' plight, empty a pail of dirty water over the head of a dignified Korean in an immaculate long white gown as he walked down the street.

Peking, too, gave them the impression of a sea of mud huts beside awe-inspiring tombs and palaces of departed dynasties. As a relief from the degradation of the Chinese people and the crude plumbing in the hotels, they visited the Winter Palace and dined with Prince de Berne, secretary of the French Legation, who had the Prince D'Orleans, pretender to the

Spanish throne, as his guest of honor. En route to Hankow by rail, in the company of the American minister, they abandoned plans to stop at a river resort because of an uprising. Sun Yat-sen had begun his drive toward "nationalism, democracy and socialism" for the Chinese people. The sleeping giant was indeed waking up, but there was not enough time to wait for him to turn over on his side.

In Hankow, Eugene visited a pig-iron plant. Then came, as Agnes reported on a card to her mother, "three of the most delightful days in the Far East. On board the 'Kiang-Yu' we sailed 600 miles down the Yangtse Kaing with cool breezes blowing, perfect comfort on the boat, interesting stopping places now and then, and lovely country to look at from the boat-deck whenever we were not too lazy to do so." Shanghai proved to be memorable chiefly because of the time spent with Admiral Roger Welles, commander of two American cruisers there, and his charming wife, who became fast friends of the Meyers.

At Shanghai the travelers gave up their original plan to return home by way of Java, India, and the Middle East because of the intense heat at that time of year. Instead they journeyed to Dairen, Mukden (where they visited the Ming tombs), Harbin, Vladivostok, and then to Moscow on the Trans-Siberian Railroad. A comfort crisis threatened because Eugene could not get first-class accommodations, but he induced the officials to transfer the one passenger booked for the second-class car and thus had a private car for the entire ten-day trip across Siberia. Moscow afforded another round of sightseeing and fine restaurants; yet the most striking sight of all was its human misery. As in the Far East, poverty and ignorance seemed endemic. Eugene summed it up by saying that Russia was 250 years behind western Europe and America. His premonition that the "political and social structures" of the country could "not survive the industrializing process" was expressed in a letter to Kennedy: "Meanwhile, the clerks who are running things in the name of the Czar seem to kick all hard facts out of the door, only to have the facts come flying back through the window, for another kick out of the front door—and so on around again. . . . But sooner or later, someone is going to break something more than his leg in this kicking game."

Long before their journey ended, the newlyweds were satiated. Their laughter, sense of exhilaration, and excitement in the discovery of new customs and new beauty gave way to weariness and irritations. For Agnes the first major intrusion of grief into the honeymoon came in Korea when Eugene received a letter from a wealthy brother-in-law saying that her father had approached him to borrow money. Having paid all Frederick

Ernst's debts before leaving New York, Eugene merely regretted that he had not anticipated this latest call for help, but Agnes was deeply humiliated and burst into "an uncontrollable flood of tears." The long degeneration of the once-glorified image of her father was a torture that even Eugene's generosity could not assuage. Meyer would continue his financial aid to Ernst until he died in 1913.

The long train ride over the Siberian prairies brought a still more withering experience. Eugene was preoccupied with a financial problem that he did not discuss. Agnes was nauseated and supersensitive because she was pregnant—a probable blight on many of the dreams she was still harboring. As they lunched together in their private car, something she said unloosed a lightning bolt of anger from Eugene that she had never before witnessed. Stunned and miserable, Agnes retreated to her compartment and locked the door. For hours she lay nursing her wounded spirit and brooding—she had married a man whom she did not know, and "happiness with such a man was impossible."

Writing about the incident many years later, Agnes would attribute her "neurotic overreaction" to the fact that she was "a spoiled child, lacking any sound basis of common sense."[6] She had been surrounded by men who assured her that she was perfection itself. Eugene's unmerciful deflation of her ego did not provoke her to rebellion (divorce was abhorrent in her code of values), but it did alter the relationship between them. Agnes had discovered what Eugene's business associates well knew—that he had a hot temper that could flare up without the slightest warning. As the years passed, Agnes would learn to live with this mercurial temperament, although she "never ceased to tremble when Eugene unleashed the fires of his wrath" against her.[7]

The business problem that was worrying Eugene was chaos in the copper industry. While still in Shanghai, he had received a cable from Edgar about a copper war that had broken out in the United States. As early as May 10, George W. Batson of the Meyer firm had advised Eugene to cut his trip short because his presence in New York "might mean one or two million dollars to you." At first Eugene dismissed the worries of his home office. Though he had kept his copper stocks, he had no debts and felt rather comfortable about the economic storm at home, which he had anticipated. "All wars so far followed by peace," he cabled Edgar.

As he continued to receive alarming reports from New York, however,

---

[6] Agnes E. Meyer's unpublished manuscript, "Life as Chance and Destiny," p. 169.
[7] *Ibid.*, p. 170.

it began to dawn upon him that he might be the only person who could bring about peace. The Guggenheims and the Anaconda Copper Company were fighting a price and production war, with each apparently determined to destroy the other. With 400 million pounds of surplus copper in sight, with demand flattened by the Taft depression and prices in collapse, the struggle could easily be pushed to a point where it would mean disaster for himself and many others. Meyer was the only figure of any stature with a foot in both camps; in addition to being allied with the Guggenheims, he was a director and banker for Inspiration Copper, in which Anaconda had large interests. But even he seemed to have only a remote chance of bringing about a compromise because the hostile factions would not speak to one another.

As the Trans-Siberian train crept over the seemingly endless prairies, the copper war became the dominant interest on Eugene's horizon. Moscow temporarily brought him back into his honeymoon mood, but, knowing that the copper kings would be summering in Europe as usual, he took time out to wire Edgar for information on where they could be reached. He was ready, as he wrote to James Kennedy, "to usurp the Rooseveltian role and be a peacemaker between the warring sides."

The solution that Meyer came up with was a 7.5 percent reduction in the output of copper on both sides to bring production more nearly into line with demand. No price-fixing was involved. It was the kind of sensible adjustment to the prevailing economic climate that the companies would have made individually if they had not been locked in a lethal struggle. The big question was whether they would listen to reason. By the time the Meyers reached Berlin a reply from Edgar reported that John D. Ryan, the head of Anaconda, was also in Berlin. At first Meyer's talk of settling differences brought only explosive protestations from Ryan that he preferred ruin to any further dealings with the Guggenheims. "They wanted a fight to the finish," he said. "They are getting it."

"John, I'm not asking you to sit in the same room with the Guggenheims," Meyer pleaded. "All I'm asking you to do is to listen to my formula and say yes or no on the point of whether you think it is fair and sensible."

When Ryan acknowledged that the terms of the Meyer plan were "fair and sensible," the peacemaker further asked, "I can count on your meaning that?" Ryan again assented.

Meyer then hastened to Vichy where the Guggenheims were fuming against Ryan. Once more he put his question and got an affirmative answer. Would the principals now go one step further and confirm the understanding to one another? The Guggenheims refused to go to Berlin and Ryan would not go to Vichy, but they finally agreed to meet in the neutral city of Paris. One key figure was missing, however—C. M. McNeil, president of Utah Copper. The Guggenheims said it would be impossible to find him because he was motoring in Switzerland with a girlfriend and had left instructions that his bliss was not to be interrupted by anything. Knowing that McNeil was addicted to luxury, Meyer secured a list of the fifty largest first-class hotels in Switzerland and sent McNeil identical telegrams at each of them at a cost of $75. The missing executive responded and was summoned to Paris immediately.

As the instigator of the peace move, Meyer presided over the meeting in Paris, and a settlement was reached on the basis of his recommendations. No documents were signed, and there was no price-fixing. A cutback in production was "understood," but, apparently with an eye on the antitrust laws, Meyer insisted that "there wasn't any real fixed percentage. It was just agreed that all the managements had been acting like damn fools. Everybody had their feelings assuaged and used a little common sense."[8]

The peacemaker was asked to bring the Rothschilds' Rio Tonto mine into the understanding, and Meyer went to London for that purpose. At first the Rothschilds insisted that the agreement be reduced to writing. "You're not going to get anything in writing," Meyer said. "Besides," he added, trying to look serious, "we are accustomed in America to dealing with honorable men who honor their agreements." The Rothschilds agreed to go along on the basis of Meyer's personal assurance that the understanding would be respected.

Whether or not the "understanding" dented the Sherman Act, or later interpretations of it, the end of the copper war won wide acclaim in the industry. Meyer had substantially enhanced his reputation as a businessman of initiative, common sense, and ability to get things done even among quarreling giants. In London he talked over the ludicrous aspects of the affair with A. Chester Beatty, a great engineer who had developed Utah Copper and was then living in England. Beatty introduced his partner—Herbert Hoover—and, as he and Meyer clasped hands, each seemed to take the measure of the other. Yet neither could have dreamed at the time that their fates would be "interlocked at an awesome moment of American history."[9]

Probably no one was more relieved by the termination of the copper

[8] Dean Albertson's interviews with Eugene Meyer, p. 125.
[9] Sidney Hyman's manuscript, "Life of Eugene Meyer," Part III, p. 20.

war than Agnes. Eugene might now revert to his role as groom on a wedding trip. But despite his neglect of her, he had won new respect in the eyes of his wife. She now saw that in his own sphere he was as skilled an artist as any she knew in the world of letters where she felt most at home. "My wife loves mountain climbing," he would say in later years, "especially to the point where she can look down on everyone—except me." It was a proper exception, for the irritation that she would often feel did not undercut her admiration for the man she had married.

The honeymoon was scarcely back on the track, however, when Eugene dropped in to see his old friends at Lazard's of London. Fully aware of his feat in settling the copper war, they greeted him warmly and asked if he would like to see an experiment in which they were financially involved— an experiment to determine whether a "mineral flotation" process developed in Australia to refine lead and zinc ores could be applied to copper. Before the question had been fully phrased Meyer was on his feet to go. In a London basement, engineers were crushing low-grade copper ore that was usually regarded as waste and mixing it with a special kind of oil so that small oil bubbles would bring particles of ore to the surface to form a mineral froth that could be ladled out to capture a high-grade copper residue. Meyer was fascinated. If this method could be successfully applied to large-scale mining operations, such as Utah Copper, it would enormously increase the metal recovered. With the refining methods then in use, a copper mine had to yield an average of about fifty-five pounds of copper per ton of raw material to be commercially profitable and 68 percent of the copper content had to be captured in the refining process. Mineral flotation held the promise of profitable operation if the copper averaged only eighteen pounds per ton of raw material, with the capture of 90 percent of the copper content. Meyer was so excited about the possibilities of the new method that he bought a substantial bloc of stock in the English-owned mineral flotation company and obtained a concession for use of the process in America through a licensing and royalty agreement. The deal was fully wrapped up before he and Agnes returned to Paris and then sailed for home on August 9, 1910.

Paris was a fitting climax to the wedding trip, for they spent most of their time buying paintings and *objets d'art* for their home-to-be. With the help of Edward Steichen, they put aside the advice of conventional-minded collectors at home and bought some elegant Cézannes and Picassos at a time when Paul Cézanne was still considered a freak in the artistic world and Pablo Picasso had just begun to invent cubism.

After six months of travel the couple settled down in a home on Fifty-first Street, directly opposite St. Patrick's Cathedral. The marriage had already lasted longer than some of Agnes's friends had thought possible. But Eugene's preoccupation with business and his wife's basic uncertainty about herself would be intensified in their home environment. The end of the honeymoon was by no means the end of the drama.

10 /

Flirtation with

the Motor Industry

SOME DIFFICULT YEARS FOLLOWED THE LUSH MEYER HONEY-moon. Eugene discovered that his enthusiasm for the mineral flotation process was not shared on this side of the Atlantic. He set up an American corporation to license use of the process, and centered his first sales effort on the Utah Copper Company, of which he was a director. Engineers for the great open-cut mine had no interest in experimenting with an untried method. Meyer's argument that the yield could be further improved was dismissed as special pleading from one who stood to profit from the proposed change.

At first the door was also closed against the new process by the Braden mine in Chile which Meyer had helped to organize and for which he had also underwritten three bond issues totaling $4 million. The Guggen-heims held a sufficient interest in Braden to veto the flotation process, and this policy persisted even though all the borings showed so high an iron content in the ore that the copper could not be reclaimed by the method then in use. Meyer felt a special obligation to do something because he had used Bernard Baruch to place some of the Braden bonds, and Baruch and his clients had relied solely on Meyer's word that they were good. So Meyer agreed to underwrite the cost of an experiment with the flotation process. His outlay proved to be only $50,000, and the result was to make Braden one of the great copper mines of the world, with profits that would be counted in hundreds of millions of dollars during the next half century. Mineral flotation soon came into universal use in the copper industry, and was also widely adapted to American lead and zinc, to the great enrich-ment of Meyer's licensing company.

Utah Copper could not hold out against the trend, but instead of acknowledging its error of judgment in rejecting mineral flotation, it pirated the process. An employee of the mineral flotation company in London was reported to have made the technique available to Utah Copper and certain lead and zinc producers. Meyer brought suit, despite the fact that, as a director of Utah Copper, he was a defendant as well as plaintiff. The unlicensed users of the process were compelled to take out licenses, and they eventually paid between $8 million and $10 million in royalties to the mineral flotation company.

Meyer's long absence during the first part of 1910 had not weakened the confidence of the financial community in him. Within days after his return a Morgan partner asked if he would interest himself in $17 million worth of Atchison, Topeka and Sante Fe bonds that had been left on its hands from a $45-million issue. After investigating their soundness, Meyer bought part of the bonds, took an option on the remainder, issued a circular, and readily sold the bonds to banks and trust and insurance companies. Apparently Meyer's statistical analysis of investments inspired more confidence than the Morgan name.

Kuhn, Loeb and Company asked Meyer if he could sell $11 million in leftover Chesapeake and Ohio Railroad bonds. In this instance he sold the bonds to the Rockefeller Foundation and John D. Rockefeller personally, Kuhn, Loeb's own clients. The outcome should have brought great satisfaction, for the young financier had not only given both of the great investment banking houses a lesson in enterprise; he had also fulfilled a long-standing dream that he might become involved in railroad financing. "Yet, somehow," he wrote to his sister Ro, "the excitement has gone out of these matters." It seemed increasingly obvious that railroading had had its day and would not be the industrial romance of the future.

The plight of the railroads was further underlined by a visit Meyer made to the White House. The government had denied the carriers rate increases to match the sharply advancing wage scales, without so much as a hearing. After failing to get the President's ear through any of several friends, Meyer asked for an appointment with him through Postmaster General Hitchcock. Arriving at the White House at the hour fixed, he was met by the President's secretary, Charles D. Norton, who said that Taft was golfing.

"I thought I had an appointment," Meyer said.

"I thought I'd see you first," Norton replied, "to find out what it was about."

Meyer explained the purpose of his visit, and Norton insisted that the President would not touch a problem of that kind because it would involve a lot of work and the President preferred golf. Meyer left feeling sorry for

the country, the railroads, and even the President because of the dis-
loyalty of his secretary. Certainly, with this attitude in Washington, the
railroads were no longer good investments. The young financier was
already looking elsewhere, as he had written to Ro: "The new world of
the automobile is only now beginning its march in earnest, and I mean
to fall in step with it."

The motor car industry, however, could be a bog hole as well as a
bonanza. In turning to this erupting field of enterprise, Meyer seemed to
revert to his former impulsiveness before his firm had worked out its
statistical investigating process. Perhaps that was the only road that could
be traveled into the prevailing chaos. Henry Ford had begun to revolution-
ize American manufacturing methods by mass production of his "Tin
Lizzie" for the multitudes, and William Crapo Durant had organized the
General Motors Company in 1908, but these were the only two relatively
stable centers in a wilderness of motor car companies that were numbered
in the hundreds. Most of them sold stock to gullible investors but never
got around to producing a motor car.

George W. Perkins baited the hook that took Meyer into this quag-
mire shortly before his wedding trip. Recalling all of Meyer's triumphs
on Wall Street and the good work he had done for the House of Morgan,
Perkins outlined an opportunity for Meyer to do for a struggling new
motor company what Harriman had done for the bankrupt Union Pacific
Railroad. Perkins and other Morgan partners had invested heavily in the
enterprise called the United States Motor Company. The family of utility
magnate Nicholas Brady was the largest single stockholder. The company
had many different models and an especially good car, Perkins said, in the
Maxwell, which had a self-starter and the first "detachable rims." Brady
also owned a patent on steel wheels. The management had been poor and
the sales methods faulty, but these were being improved. What the company still needed, Perkins said, was a strong man on its board of directors
to keep the enterprise moving in the right direction. Would Meyer buy
into the enterprise with the object of becoming that strong man? If so, he
could count on the backing of Perkins and all the other Morgan partners.

The Perkins offer came at a moment when Meyer was in a receptive
mood. Having purchased and driven several different cars, he felt he knew
a good deal about automobiles. His ambition to be on the ground floor of
what would undoubtedly be a great new industry had further under-
pinning from his youngest brother, now a partner in the firm. Edgar held
a degree in mechanical engineering from Cornell; his research into gas
engines had produced a new theory as to the velocity of flame propagation;
he had designed an electrically illuminated taillight and sold the patent

to General Motors. Eugene felt that an association of the firm with the motor industry would give Edgar a chance to spread his wings in his own field. For these various reasons he bought heavily into the venture while he was selling other stocks because he did not like the looks of the economic and political weather.

It was soon evident, however, that the United States Motor Company was in trouble. That rival to GM had been organized in 1910 with authorized capital of $30 million. Its chief promoter was Benjamin Briscoe, head of the Briscoe-Maxwell Company, who had grandiose plans to seize leadership in the automotive industry. But the company's working capital was soon exhausted. Its nine plants were haphazardly scattered in six different states, and their demands mounted perilously. Cars were sold through an expensive system of branch offices which took in used cars for which there was no market. Meyer's sensitive nose smelled chicanery, and a quiet investigation showed that the treasurer of the company had once been jailed for fraud and embezzlement. The suspicious director demanded an independent audit of the treasurer's report, but Price, Waterhouse and Company could find no irregularities, thus putting Meyer in the doghouse because of his suspicions.

In December 1911, Meyer and F. M. Peters induced the company to hire Orrin S. Goan to eliminate the inefficiency and waste in its operations. Goan found that enormous losses had been concealed, that interfactory shipments were out of balance by $400,000, that the company had no need for a large truck factory it had built, that many employees were collecting salaries for doing nothing. The company had attempted to "do all the automobile business in sight, and in every size and grade of car, including even trucks and taxicabs,"[1] without having the resources or the management for such an undertaking. About the same time Meyer insisted on a new study of the company's financial condition by Ernst and Ernst, which showed it to be insolvent. That finding was especially embarrassing because Meyer had previously agreed to head a syndicate that would underwrite an issue of $6 million in bonds convertible into stock.[2] With the true condition of the company thus brought to light, Meyer insisted that the syndicate itself would have to absorb the bonds and that the company would have to be put into receivership, reorganized, and given a new infusion of capital. The collapse came in August 1912. A committee set up to effect the reorganization included George W. Davison, Charles H.

---

[1] Goan's report to Meyer, May 17, 1912, in the Meyer Papers.
[2] Lawrence H. Seltzer: A Financial History of the American Automobile Industry (Boston: Hougton Mifflin; 1928), p. 38.

Sabin, Benjamin Strong, Jr., Albert H. Wiggin, James C. Brady, and Eugene Meyer, Jr. They transformed the United States Motor Company into the Maxwell Motor Company, raised $3 million of fresh capital, and purchased the Flanders Motor Company in order to get Walter E. Flanders as a new manager.

The reincarnation did not, however, end either the company's troubles or its internal squabbling. Meyer was soon at odds with Flanders, who continued what he (Meyer) regarded as the disastrous Brady policies. On several occasions Meyer complained bitterly about the company's false advertising. Efforts to oust Flanders proved to be futile because he had a five-year contract and a majority of the directors stood by him. Meyer was thus left in a serious predicament. With a dangerously high portion of his liquid assets committed to Maxwell, he was not in control; his heavy investments in copper had not yet begun to pay off, and, with the stock market in the doldrums, he could sell other securities only with heavy losses. The Morgan partners who had promised to back him in this venture were unloading their own stock. For the first time since he had become a major Wall Street operator, Meyer was embarrassingly squeezed. He was tempted to pull out and let the company take its own course, but many of his clients had bought Maxwell stock and banks had made loans to the company on his recommendations. He would not leave them to sink in deeper.

By way of retrenching while the squeeze was on, the Meyers (they now had two daughters, Florence and Elizabeth) moved, from the elegant house at Seventieth Street and Park Avenue which they had bought from Senator Root, to the St. Regis Hotel. This was not, of course, a confession of poverty. Their apartment ran the entire length of the hotel, and among their neighbors were such conspicuously solvent citizens as Daniel Guggenheim and William B. Thompson. Nevertheless, the move was sufficient to feed rumors in Wall Street that Meyer was in a bind. Some denizens of the Street seemed to find special delight in embellishing stories to the effect that the boy wonder who had successfully ridden the previous panics had managed to go broke all by himself. It was no disgrace, they said, for a Wall Streeter to go broke in a general deluge. But what of the prodigy who falls into a trap of his own making in calm weather?

Some of Meyer's enemies decided to lend a helping hand to the forces that were embarrassing him. By concerted action they could drive his stocks down and thus teach the arrogant upstart a salutary lesson. Meyer caught wind of the plan and the day it was to be executed. As he left for his office that morning, he warned Agnes not to call him on the telephone to ask how things were going lest some innocent phrase be overheard and contribute to his undoing. When the stock market opened, he was personally on the floor, a practice he had not followed for years. It seemed to confirm the conclusion of the cabal that he was in deep trouble as they moved in for the kill. To their amazement, however, Meyer began not to sell but to buy substantial quantities of all the stocks he was interested in, including Maxwell Motors.

For an hour or more he kept up a steady flow of buying as if he anticipated a sharp turn in the market, and such a turn did materialize. The hostile banking and brokerage houses, apparently concluding that they had underestimated Meyer's resources, fell into line as sheep behind their shepherd. When the buying became general, Meyer left the floor confident that it would continue. The timorous Wall Streeters who had planned a wake thus allowed themselves to be drawn into a triumphal march for the intended victim. Meyer never did tell them that, as he was furiously buying that morning, several of his own brokers were quietly selling what he bought in case his maneuver did not work. But it worked admirably. Courage to move alone against the instinct of the herd had saved him from possible bankruptcy.

The squeeze from his involvement with the motor industry was not so easily managed, however, within the Meyer family. When the clan assembled for its customary Sunday dinner at the home of Eugene Senior, he couldn't avoid replaying the old refrain—if his eldest son had stayed with Lazard Frères he would not have been trapped by his "double-crossing Wall Street friends." George Blumenthal, then back at the Lazard helm in New York, joined in the badgering. Agnes too came under siege from her in-laws, who begged her to tell her husband that he must be more cautious now that he was a married man. Her response was that she had not married Eugene for his money and that just now he needed their confidence rather than their criticism. When the sniping continued, Agnes's anger flared openly. "Now listen to me," she said, in a tone not customarily heard from a woman in a Meyer household, "Eugene knows more about finance than all of you put together. And I'm glad he's not as conservative as you are, for if he were, I wouldn't have married him."

The outlook for Maxwell improved somewhat after the dramatic 1912 showdown on the floor of the Stock Exchange. Meyer emerged from that test of wills owning nearly 50 percent of the Maxwell common stock—not enough to fire Flanders but enough to force the installation of a new vice-president and general manager—Orlando F. Weber, a tough-minded industrial engineer who understood mass production and distribution. Despite his flaring temper and occasional rudeness, this self-taught giant won Meyer's confidence, and the two were to be associated for many years.

Weber soon had the Maxwell company operating much more successfully, but Flanders then concluded that he could get along without Weber and tried to make him resign. Fully aware of Weber's temper, Meyer feared that he might be provoked into a sudden resignation and therefore exacted a promise from him that he would never resign for any reason without consulting his sponsor. The affairs of the company thus rocked along for some years with neither side satisfied by its schizophrenia.

Meanwhile Meyer began to look elsewhere in the automobile industry. The General Motors Corporation seemed to offer more hope for the future than did Maxwell. By 1910 the combine was turning out 21 percent of the cars made in the United States, but because of its enormous borrowings, control of the company had passed from William C. Durant to a syndicate of investment bankers. Durant was struggling to get the reins back into his hands and was putting together the Chevrolet company as a means to that end when Meyer called on him late in 1914.

Not knowing that the Chevrolet venture had any direct relationship to GM, Meyer said that he had reason to believe that Durant needed additional funds to develop the Chevrolet and that he would be glad to buy Durant's General Motors stock, with a premium of $2 a share above the highest going price, making an offer of nearly $4 million for Durant's 40,000 shares.

"No, sir," Durant replied. "I won't sell you my General Motors shares. I'll do something better. I'll lend you my 40,000 shares . . . for use as security on which you can borrow money to buy 40,000 shares for yourself. Together, we would have 80,000 shares out of a total of 150,000. Then, when the voting trust expires in 1915, you and I will kick the goddamned stinking bankers out of General Motors and run the company the way it ought to be run."

Meyer was flabbergasted. The two men scarcely knew one another. Yet Durant seemed to be making an offer of partnership that was generous to the point of being reckless. "Are you serious?" Meyer asked, as he struggled to retain his composure.

"Absolutely!" Durant exclaimed. "Let me take you to the vault where I keep the stock and we can get started on this business right away."

"Mr. Durant," Meyer responded, "I appreciate your very generous proposal. But I don't think you have fully understood my purpose. I came here to buy *from* you, not *with* you. Good day, sir."[3]

There is a strong temptation to list this incident as one of the foremost missed opportunities in American industrial history. Perhaps it was. It should not be casually assumed, however, that Meyer's abrupt answer to

[3] Sidney Hyman's manuscript, "Life of Eugene Meyer," Part III, p. 89.

Durant's amazing gesture shattered his own dream of directing an industrial empire. Durant had lost control of General Motors because of his impetuous practice of buying automobile companies without regard for intrinsic values, and he never really regained it. Meyer's experience with Maxwell doubtless warned him against any impulsive attachment to a comet that seemed to be burning itself out. Yet 40,000 shares of General Motors stock, if he had purchased it and held it, along with the stock dividends, through all the subsequent splits, would have been worth $373 million in 1950 and $2 billion in 1972.

No such caution was evident in Meyer's dreaming of a fortune from gold mining about the same time. He and Bernard Baruch underwrote the sale of 400,000 shares of stock in the Alaska Juneau gold mine, and Meyer became the largest shareholder, with more than 111,000 shares. Engineers had estimated that the mine would produce ore valued at $80 million, and there was talk of Alaska Juneau becoming one of the world's great gold mines. It was fated to become, instead, a symbol of false hopes. Sold at $10 a share in 1915, the stock fell to less than $1 when the mine fizzled. In 1934 Franklin Roosevelt's boost in the price of gold would give Alaska Juneau a miraculous revival, with the stock rising as high as $30 a share, but that only meant a longer fall when the collapse came.

Meyer continued to search for ways and means of stimulating Maxwell sales. When a survey showed that 75 percent of all cars were bought under the influence of women, he conceived the idea of hitching a sales campaign to the growing women's suffrage movement. The Maxwell, with its self-starter and demountable rims, should have a special appeal to women. With the approval of the Maxwell board, he set up a committee of suffragettes headed by Crystal Eastman Benedict, sister of Max Eastman, who brought into the promotion venture such nationally known suffragettes as Carrie Chapman Catt, Alice Carpenter, and Inez Mulhod Boissevain, a famous beauty of the day. Through his suffragette friends Meyer also succeeded in getting Mary Pickford, the widely idolized moving picture star, into the Maxwell's New York retail outlet for extensive pictures with the car on the one day when she was not under contract barring such commercialization of her pulchritude.

Meanwhile Flanders and the Bradys continued to tighten the thumbscrews on Orlando Weber. Unable to fire Weber or rewrite his contract, Flanders progressively limited the range of the general manager's activities. With the Meyer faction thus impotent, Flanders raised the price of the Maxwell by $40, putting it at a competitive disadvantage; returned to the old distribution system that Weber had abolished; and ordered use of the wire wheel, in which the Bradys had large interests.

As involvement of the United States in the European war began to seem inevitable, Meyer met privately with Nicholas Brady and expressed fear that Maxwell, a producer of pleasure cars only, might not survive the war unless drastic measures were taken. His first suggestion was that Flanders be replaced by any one of several commanding figures in the automobile industry who were available. Brady refused. Meyer soon returned with another proposal—that Maxwell be merged with the Nash Motor Company, which was producing trucks that would doubtless be in great demand during wartime. Meyer had interested the Nash people in the proposed merger, but again Brady refused. A similar attempt to marry the Maxwell and the Studebaker was no more successful. In December 1916, Meyer tried to induce the Maxwell executive committee to authorize an impartial study of the firm's financial and production status by three outside engineers, but the controlling faction remained adamant.

Thus frustrated at every turn, Meyer resigned on December 17, 1916, complaining not only that his wishes had been systematically disregarded but also that many decisions had been made behind his back at "social gatherings" in the Brady home to which he was not invited. He offered his stock to the Bradys at a price to be mutually agreed upon. When the Bradys declined, he waited for two days before starting to sell his stock on the Exchange. Meanwhile he notified all the bankers who had lent money to Maxwell partly on his recommendation that he considered the current policies of the company unsound.

It is not surprising, therefore, that his attempt to sell his stock turned into a bear race. Heavy selling from other sources at the same time drove the price down to about·half of what it had been when his resignation had been announced. Meyer faced heavy losses, which he could have absorbed, but he was loath to give the Bradys the satisfaction of taking him to the cleaners in addition to forcing him out of the Maxwell company. As the price slid to $40 a share, Meyer stopped selling and sent one of his men onto the floor to buy all the Maxwell stock that anyone wanted to sell. The result was a sharp turnabout in the price trend. The canny antitrend operator then "played possum" until the price recovered. Ultimately he sold his stock with substantial profits.

The Maxwell, which had once rivaled Ford with an output of about 75,000 cars a year, went to the doom that Meyer had feared. The company's plant facilities were ultimately taken over by the Chrysler Corporation. This was not a cause for gloating on the part of Eugene Meyer. He liked the automobile business, and even his departure from Maxwell and his rejection of the proffered partnership in General Motors did not entirely sever his connection with it.

In March 1915, Meyer had been asked to finance an auto body manufacturer in Massachusetts, and Weber had suggested that he should first visit the Fisher Body Company in Detroit, which was preeminent in this field. Meyer spent a Saturday and Sunday with Fred J. Fisher, head of the enterprise, and his brothers, who gave the visitor access to their plants and records and fully answered his searching questions. On Sunday, Meyer was invited to dine with the Fisher clan and observed that even the men who were running the business looked to their mother for guidance. "After I saw her in action as a trainer and teacher of men," Meyer said in later years, "I was ready . . . to bet my last nickel on the sons raised by this mother."

The Fishers made clear that they were planning to expand their plants because only 10 percent of the bodies they were then furnishing to Ford, Maxwell, Studebaker, and some other companies were closed, and they expected a vast expansion in the closed-body business. As Meyer prepared to leave, Fred Fisher asked him if he was going ahead with the financing in Massachusetts. "No," Meyer replied, "I wouldn't care to finance a competitor of yours. But if you ever need any money, I'll be glad to finance you."

A year later the Fishers approached Hallgarten and Company for help in raising $5 million through a preferred stock issue and mentioned Meyer as one who was interested. Meyer was delighted to join Hallgarten in underwriting the issue on an equal basis. Because of a strong sinking fund which promised to retire the stock in a few years, the issue sold readily even though it was the first stock offering of an auto body company. At Meyer's suggestion the shares were listed on the New York Stock Exchange, and he then urged the Fishers to list also their common stock. At first they balked at this, as they wanted to keep most of the common stock in the family. Finally they agreed to sell one-eighth of their 200,000 shares of common stock at $25 a share, but at this point Hallgarten balked. Common stock of an auto body company, with no sinking fund behind it, was deemed entirely too hazardous. Meyer thereupon agreed to take over the 12,500 shares that had been allotted to Hallgarten, paying them a generous and unasked profit of $10 a share "just to keep them happy." He then had 25,000 shares of Fisher Body common to sell to the public and discovered that no one would buy as much as ten cents worth because of mounting fears that the United States would be drawn into World War I. After distributing some of the stock to friends and members of his family, Meyer continued to hold 22,000 shares.

"I suppose," he said to Fred Fisher, "this makes me the eighth Fisher boy. How do you feel about my being in your family?"

"All seven of your brothers are delighted," Fisher said.

Meyer too was delighted, for he had full confidence that seven able and hard-working brothers, acting under the watchful eye of a remarkable mother, in an industry of great promise, were certain to succeed. Among the friends obtaining Fisher Body stock from Meyer was George Kellogg, a classics professor who had been valedictorian of Yale's graduating class in 1895. For many years Meyer had managed Kellogg's small savings and had built up a tidy supplement to his income. Now he bought 100 shares of Fisher Body common for Kellogg's account at a cost of $2,000. When Meyer closed out his business and could no longer manage the accounts of his friends, he gave Kellogg some parting advice. The Fisher Company, he wrote, is absolutely sound. " . . . regardless of what anyone tells you, hang on to this stock. You can sell anything else, including your soul, but don't sell this Fisher Body stock."

Some years later, after Fisher Body had grown enormously and tied itself into General Motors, the two men met at a Yale class reunion, and Meyer asked his friend if he still had the Fisher Body shares. Kellogg sheepishly confessed that he did not; a broker had persuaded him to sell the stock because it was not paying dividends. Meyer held his peace. "I know what you are thinking," Kellogg then continued. "I have worked out the arithmetic . . ."

"And what figure did you arrive at?"

". . . I would now have a return of around $230,000 on the $2,000 investment you made for me in Fisher stock."

"That's about right," Meyer agreed. To console his friend, he then told him how the highly respected Hallgarten investment banking firm had given up its 12,500 shares of Fisher Body common and how he himself had passed up the opportunity to become one of the two largest stockholders in General Motors.

"I feel a little better," Kellogg said.

"Good," Meyer answered. "Now let's join our classmates for another session of lying about how smart we all have become since leaving Yale."

Actually, however, Meyer's faith in the Fisher family had put millions into his pocket. His flirtation with the automobile industry had not made him a Harriman, but it had broadened his experience and helped to prepare him for the next big venture that would come his way.

11 /

The Meyers at Home

THE EARLY YEARS OF EUGENE MEYER'S CAREER HAD SEEMED to bring him one triumph after another; the years following his marriage evened the score with problems, misfortune, and tragedy. At the beginning of 1912 his brother Walter was battling a protracted case of typhoid, and the family was mourning the death of his brother-in-law, Abraham Stern, in San Francisco. Then on April 14 came the cruelest blow of Eugene's lifetime when the White Star liner *Titanic*, on her maiden voyage across the Atlantic, crashed into an iceberg and sank. On board were Edgar Meyer and his wife Leila.

As in the case of the San Francisco earthquake and fire, the family rallied to sustain one another in the dark hours that followed the collision. Hopes rose when Ro wired from California a wild report that all the passengers had been transferred to the *Carpathia*, which had reached the scene of the wreck. But the absence of any reliable news was more conducive to despair. From the first word of the disaster, Eugene feared the worst because he knew that the gentle and generous Edgar, with his penchant for helping other people, would be among the last to leave the sinking ship. On April 16 the family learned that Leila was safe aboard the *Carpathia*. At first she had refused to leave Edgar, but he later compelled her to get into a lifeboat because they had an infant child. After helping to launch the last boat to leave the doomed vessel, he was seen running toward the stern, the only part of the *Titanic* still above water at the time.

Nine days after the tragedy Eugene wrote to Ro:

Mother had a very bad day on Sunday but was better yesterday, quieter and calmer, although in her heart of hearts I feel she still keeps up a little hope—some way from somewhere—Edgar may come back to us. Father, of course, accepts the situation, and knows exactly how it is. I hope the body will be recovered only on account of Mother.

Even that small comfort was denied them. The youngest, gayest, and most lovable member of the family had simply vanished into the sea, and only hallowed memories and gnawing sorrow remained. The tragedy was the more galling because of the belief that the fatal collision "was clearly and unquestionably a case of criminal negligence."[1] There was a great outpouring of sympathy from friends and business associates, but only Eugene himself could appreciate the full magnitude of his loss. Because of Edgar's youth (he was only twenty-eight at the time of the tragedy), Eugene had been more of a father than a brother to him. Yet Edgar had become a good right arm in the Meyer firm and was the only true business partner Eugene ever had. Between them was a tacit understanding that Edgar would someday inherit the business they were building when Eugene made his exit for a tour of public service. In later years the bereft brother would express his high regard for Edgar by setting up a scholarship in his honor at Cornell.

The sense of loss was magnified when George W. Batson, another young man of great promise in the Meyer firm, died of meningitis following a mastoid operation. Fate seemed to be on a rampage. Meanwhile business was in the doldrums. The Balkan wars, with the ever-present threat of spreading to a wider theater, were a disturbing factor. In the United States the preliminaries of a three-cornered race for the presidency, in which Taft and Theodore Roosevelt would split the Republicans asunder and Woodrow Wilson would romp to a Democratic victory for the first time since Cleveland, left business in a wait-and-see mood. Wall Street was generally hostile toward T.R. and at the same time worried about what Wilson might do. Yet the disillusionment with Taft was profound. It was not a happy outlook from the business and banking points of view.

Meyer's strong Republican moorings kept him in the Taft camp as the lesser of three risks. He accepted the widespread belief of the period that in general a Republican administration meant good business and a Democratic one bad business. During the campaign his brother Walter, a graduate of the Harvard Law School, introduced him to a doughty champion of the Progressive cause—Felix Frankfurter. Sparks flew when Eugene and Felix talked politics, thus fixing the pattern for what was to be an extended but nevertheless prickly friendship.

After the Wilson administration was settled in Washington, Meyer saw in it at least one favorable omen. The new President had promised reforms reaching into many phases of American life, and this atmosphere should be conducive to changes in Wall Street also. Ever since he had

[1] Eugene Meyer to Albert and Leonard Seligman, April 19, 1912.

innocently associated himself with a bucket shop at the beginning of his career, Meyer had been eager to strike a blow at malpractices in the sale of stock. In February 1913, he was elected to the board of governors of the New York Stock Exchange and gladly embraced the opportunity to work for the reforms he had long talked about. His personal letter to J. B. Mabon, president of the Stock Exchange, accompanying his formal acceptance of a place on the board, was a clear call for action:

> The Stock Exchange has opposed everything and anything that has thus far been suggested to remedy known abuses. It has not come forward with any constructive suggestions of its own, though the very large number of catch-penny propositions that have been put over the public through the medium of the Exchange has impaired public confidence in the institution. The public is demanding that "something be done." We cannot blindly resist this demand.

In Meyer's view only the federal and state governments could adequately supervise the way corporations were organized and securities were floated. But the Stock Exchange, he insisted, had a duty to work with the authorities in designing a supervisory mechanism, and it should "take after itself with a big stick . . . to remedy abuses of its own making in areas where it is fully competent to act."

At the first meeting of the board of governors he attended, however, Meyer found himself resisting a proposed disciplinary measure. The listing committee headed by Clarence Day, Sr., who was soon to be memorialized by his son, Clarence, Jr., in *Life with Father*, had recommended that a stock be de-listed on the ground that the issuing company, known as "Goldfields," had failed to comply with its contract with the Exchange. Meyer listened to the report and the subsequent discussion with mounting concern. Though the listing committee was obviously trying to protect the public interest and an officer of "Goldfields" had technically violated a requirement of the Exchange, there was no evidence that the stockholders knew anything about it. At the risk of offending his friend Day, Meyer said that to act without information on this point would confirm the demagogic view that the Stock Exchange was a high-handed institution. All interests would be better served, he added, by notifying the "Goldfields" stockholders that one of their officers was violating their contract with the Exchange; the stock could then be de-listed if they did not comply within sixty days.

Flinty and formidable though he might be, the elder Day began nodding his head as soon as he caught the drift of Meyer's comments. "Gentlemen," he said, "would you repeat with me a slightly amended version of the Declaration of Independence: 'We hold Meyer's truths to be self-evident.' " All the governors agreed, and, with Meyer a member of the listing committee, the less arbitrary procedure became the rule for all de-listing cases in the future.

Encouraged by this minor achievement, Meyer sought much broader reforms. Governor William Sulzer of New York was fulminating against the Stock Exchange as a gigantic gambling institution, and Wall Street was responding in terms of defensive bombast. Meyer tried to cut through the fog of words by inducing the board of governors to create a special committee that would conduct public hearings, with highly qualified witnesses, "on all the questions involved in the incorporation, organization, promotion, capitalization and flotation of securities." A second committee would cooperate with public authorities "in bringing about the adoption of uniform measures for the greater protection of the investing public . . ." Following months of debate, the board of governors approved both projects on November 26, 1913. Meyer became the chairman of a five-man committee to conduct the educational hearings and a member of a ten-man committee that went to Albany to seek the needed legislative reforms. Nothing came of these efforts, however, because the appeal was directed to Albany instead of Washington, and the growing international crisis soon overshadowed all lesser issues. Tighter control of the securities business had to wait until the stock market crash of 1929 and the subsequent great depression made it imperative.

The year 1913 brought the darkest days of Meyer's business career. Details of what happened are lacking because of his inclination to conceal mistakes of judgment, but an intimate friend, Edward J. Steichen, remembered walking the streets of New York with him all night "the day he went broke."[2] Letters exchanged within the family also make it clear that he was caught with overextended holdings at a time when the stock market was in the doldrums. His stock in the American Cotton Oil and Inspiration Copper companies could not be sold at fair prices in the market even though they continued to have intrinsic value. Meyer was in the position of having to dump a substantial volume of stock with critical losses unless he could borrow enough to carry him through the crisis.

In desperation he cabled his brother-in-law George Blumenthal who was in Baden-Baden, Germany. Apparently there was a mix-up in the cables. Blumenthal later claimed that the message he received contained an "information mistake of $1,300,000 in your position."[3] In any event, Blumenthal did not respond with the urgency the situation demanded.

[2] Author's interview with Edward J. Steichen, May 7, 1971.
[3] George Blumenthal to Eugene Meyer, August 20, 1913.

Meyer weathered the storm with the help of other relatives, although he sustained substantial losses. Blumenthal did get around to offering a loan, with Inspiration Copper stock as collateral, but by that time the emergency had passed. The result was to intensify the bitterness between the Meyers and Blumenthal. Animosity flared openly despite agreement on both sides that "the family peace should be preserved." Agnes wrote George a scorching letter on August 20, 1913, including this paragraph:

> I had always felt one thing about you preeminently, that you. were the sort of person on whom one could rely in an emergency of any sort. When this emergency came all that I could understand from this side was that my feeling about you was wrong. That, however, would have been merely a disappointment. But what at the time aroused anger in me was the effect of your discouraged tele- grams. Eugene needed nothing at that period as much as he needed belief and the confidence that he got from everyone over here was almost undermined by your clearly and repeatedly expressed doubts. ... if I who had to counteract your attitude day after day, was bitter against you, it was not only forgiveable, it was the only natural way for me to feel.

That Eugene was seriously shaken by the experience is also made clear by a letter he wrote to his sister Florie (Mrs. Blumenthal) suggesting that people would not care much for his advice in the future. To this, Blumenthal replied: "Get that idea out of your head. As for me I believe that your judgment in the future will be a great deal better than in the past few years. Quick, great success warps the judgment of most anybody and makes people too sure of themselves; once they see that they can be wrong all their good sense comes back again into full play." But neither this seasoned observation nor the soothing words of confidence and love Eugene received from Florie closed the widened breach between the two families.

Agnes met the turn in the family fortunes with magnificent aplomb, trying to be gay and insisting that they keep their social engagements even at "the very worst point." Some members of the family chided her for this seeming insensitivity to her husband's financial woes, but she replied with maturity beyond her years that there was no reason to be "unhappy" because "we had been unfortunate."

The cohesiveness with which Eugene and Agnes met financial ad- versity was not always evident in other aspects of their married life. After the honeymoon was over, they had tended to go their separate ways. Both were preoccupied by interests to which they had become strongly attached before marriage. Eugene almost buried himself in his work. There was little time for leisure or the enjoyment of life together.

Agnes, who described herself as "an unruly, self-centered, freedom-loving creature," found her new duties taxing. She had to manage a house, direct a big staff of servants, and be polite to Eugene's innumerable friends. The birth of her first child came as a shock. "What a horror!" Agnes exclaimed. When at last the ordeal was over, a nurse brought her, not a pretty pink-and-white darling such as she had seen in prams on the street, but a "wretched-looking object, made even more hideous by abrasions on her poor little temples by the forceps." Agnes groaned to her faithful Powelly: "Take her away." But the infant was hungry. The distressed mother's account of the incident continues: "This limp object attacked my bursting breasts with a force that bloodied the nipples and caused more excruciating pain which never abated. Obviously I had not been well prepared for the ordeal of motherhood. Emerging after weeks of horror, my only compensation was to look at myself in the mirror and realize with surprise and delight that the slender figure to which I was accustomed, had returned. . . . I became a conscientious but scarcely a loving mother."[4]

Determined not to let baby Florence or any other demand of domesticity crush her personality, Agnes spent much of her time at "a little hole in the wall" at 291 Fifth Avenue that served as Edward Steichen's studio and as a gathering place for artists, poets, revolutionaries, and others concerned about "the artistic aridity of New York." The projects launched at "291" became such an obsession that she methodically dumped all the calling cards that accumulated in her absence into the wastebasket without looking at them, and she repeatedly forgot her baby until overflowing breasts caused her to rush home conscience-stricken because she knew that the child would be screaming with hunger and Powelly would be frantically walking the floor with it.[5]

During her first labor Agnes had repeatedly asked her obstetrician, Dr. Edwin Craigin: "Why on earth does any woman have a second child?" But she bore a second daughter, Elizabeth, in February 1913, without much change of attitude. When the child was a year old, Agnes began to dream of revisiting her beloved haunts in Europe where she might once more find the exhilaration she had known before marriage had complicated her life. At first there was talk of husband and wife taking a relaxed holiday together, but Eugene smelled the approach of war and concluded

[4] Agnes E. Meyer's unpublished manuscript, "Life as Chance and Destiny," p. 172.
[5] Agnes E. Meyer: *Out of These Roots, The Autobiography of an American Woman* (Boston: Little Brown; 1953), p. 103.

that it would be unwise for him to leave New York. Business was always interfering with their life together. Agnes felt that Eugene's whole existence had been devoted to work, while hers had been devoted to living, and she would not go over to his world. "Terribly restless and dissatisfied," she worked only to forget herself. There were moments when she felt "as if the life within me were dying from lack of nourishment and what that nourishment could be I did not know."[6] Concerned about the widening gulf between them, Eugene agreed that she should go to Europe alone. It would give her an opportunity to gain fresh vigor and strength, to think about her relationship to her family, and to write to him—the inference being that an exchange of letters from opposite sides of an ocean might be a better means of communicating some thoughts than face-to-face conversation.

Agnes sailed aboard the *Vaterland* in May 1914. Her qualms were evident. Before the voyage began she wrote a note to "Dear old honey-bunch" asking why he had left so long before the boat sailed. As the vessel neared Southampton, she was concerned about not having received a wireless message from him. On May 29, she wrote:

> I have already decided that I shall never again go away without you. . . . A whole mixture of emotions is pulling me in every direction. Are you thinking of me lovingly in spite of the fact that I have temporarily deserted you? This is a revolutionary age even for marital relationship and I hope that you will not cease having confidence in me and loving me when I have a period of thinking things out. It only means that my feeling for you will be clearer and therefore finer.

At home with only the children and servants, Eugene was obviously unhappy. He wrote to his friend J. R. Kennedy in Tokyo that brokers in New York were having rough sledding, Europe was in deep trouble, and Agnes had "deserted" him for "a little vacation, rest and pleasure." His letter continues:

> Alas, this is a world of woe! Only when I retire to Seven Springs Farm and take a walk in my nice, old hemlock wood and look at the iris and peonies—which are in full bloom—and contemplate the first blushing tints of red which are beginning to adorn my strawberries, do I begin to believe that there is some consolation somehow—somewhere.

[6] Agnes E. Meyer to Eugene Meyer, June 25, 1914.

The nostalgia that Agnes had felt on the boat quickly evaporated as soon as she returned to her old haunts. She wrote to Eugene from Berlin:

> Since getting off the boat my old travel fever has returned. Every minute seems absorbing and wonderful.
> I love you and my babies very much. Do not forget me.

She was soon sucked into the fascinating world of Chinese art. Dr. Otto Kümmel, a great connoisseur of Oriental art, showed her his collection kept under lock and key and also took her to Jacobi's, where she saw masterpieces that she was sure would live with her forever. Then came Alfred Walter von Heymel, the Leipzig publisher whom she had rejected to marry Eugene. Agnes wrote to "Dear Euge" on June 4, 1914, saying in regard to von Heymel: "He called for me as soon as he got to town and took me to his charming apartment for tea. Don't be shocked; it was as full of domestics and as proper as any ménage." The letter continues:

> . . . Today by appointment I lunched with him and he confessed that he is doing his best to get married again—that he hates women with the deepest kind of sex-hatred but cannot get on without them. "I need someone's arm to go to sleep upon at night" was the way he put it and one felt it in his nice but pathetically vague apartment. His troubles have made him in some ways more of a person but I am afraid he and I have nothing more to say to each other. We went through the ordeal of seeing each other but too much has happened to both of us—of a different nature. . . . I do not think I see myself blindly when I stick to my systematic thoroughness and decide that I have outgrown him. I have overcome my youthful admiration of the bizarre.

Moving on to Vienna, Agnes had an almost tearful reunion with Dr. Julius Tandler, professor of anatomy and a Socialist leader—one of a group with whom she had spent a month climbing mountains in the Austrian Tyrol in 1909. "We were both terribly touché," she wrote to Eugene of this meeting, "that was inevitable and my old feeling for him reestablished itself immediately. He was a bit uncontrolled at first. Tears came into his eyes and I could feel that he had to struggle to find his relationship toward me." Something funny broke the ice, and they were soon on a friendly basis. The letter goes on: "At lunch which I agreed to eat in the restaurant downstairs he joined me again and our old relationship, only much finer and franker, found itself."

Tandler returned to the hotel later in the day "as pale as death and completely exhausted and . . . utterly dejected." His wife had raised a furor over his meeting with Agnes. In a mood of injured innocence, Agnes called "this hell-hound" on the telephone and asked her to come over. Mrs. Tandler came, "looking fatter and coarser than ever," but full of curiosity about the woman who stirred her husband so profoundly. Agnes accepted a luncheon invitation from Mrs. Tandler and suffered through "hours of her twaddle" only to ease the domestic problem of her unhappy former climbing companion.

Meanwhile the uneasiness in her own home in New York had been sharply accentuated. As soon as Eugene received the letter about her meeting with von Heymel, he sent her a cablegram: ". . . feel surprised hurt, disregard our understanding and my views clearly expressed." On June 15 he followed this with a brief letter:

> I came down this morning hardly able to wait to get the letters that I knew ought to be waiting for me. I was happy to see that you had quite a time in Berlin. I was distinctly annoyed to learn that you had gone to von Heymel's apartment alone. The servants being there have nothing to do with it. It is the sort of thing that a woman cannot do and expect to keep her reputation and especially in going to the apartment of a man like Heymel. Entirely apart from the general proprieties of the case, it is a thing which I have thoroughly discussed with you. . . . I am therefore compelled reluctantly to feel that your action was one showing absolute disregard for my feelings and wishes as well as an entirely unnecessary violation of a very proper and necessary convention.
>
> I am reluctant to write this, but feeling as I do, I believe it is best to tell you.

The next day he wrote again at greater length:

> I have had a most unhappy day.
> The importance of your going alone to von Heymel's apartment must have been great to have justified the cost. . . .
> I am asking myself what I have done to deserve this sort of treatment. I felt so sure after our talks that I could rely upon you. Do you want me to feel, after we reach what I take to be a definite understanding about anything, that I must still feel uncertain as to what course you will pursue[?].

Agnes replied to Eugene's cable: "Sorry Heymel business misunderstood Understanding not forgotten Trust me." On June 18 she wrote that she had been to Versailles with Marius De Zayas, with whom she had

worked at "291." Being "terribly upset" by Eugene's reaction to the
Heymel tea, she related the incident to De Zayas. The letter continues:

> What was my astonishment when De Z said, "Your husband
> is quite right. You are not only careless in your actions but in your
> talk as well," and then proceeded to lay me flat about my loose
> language. From this he went calmly to other points of criticism
> which were equally true and equally unexpected. I was furious, of
> course, felt the whole thing personally as I always do feel criticism.
> Versailles was completely ruined for me because I could not stop
> thinking about myself, and last night as I lay in bed I had only one
> feeling, "How did I ever get anybody to marry me, anyway—most
> of all you."
>
> I have a big picture of Florence in my room, which I swiped from
> Ruth, that comforts me a lot. At least my babies are sweet, aren't
> they, honey?

Her mood of self-pity was short-lived, however. She began to shake
it off even before finishing her letter. "Do not let this letter depress you,"
she concluded. "I am having a wonderful time and realize that temporary
tiredness is affecting me."

To Agnes's plea for understanding of her side of the Heymel incident
Eugene bluntly replied: "What is that side?" In his view the details of
the incident were of minor importance. ". . . what is of importance," he
wrote, "is this—that I must be able to have confidence in you—that is of
the utmost importance to you and to me." With a major difference between them thus out in the open, he reminded her that "this is by no
means the first and only occasion that has given me reason to feel that my
ideas and wishes are not of the moment to you what I might have hoped
for." He wanted her always to have liberty of action but was loath to
have it appear that her liberty might have been abused.

Agnes also took advantage of the occasion to put in a bill of complaints.
". . . the fault is not entirely mine," she wrote. "We have had no leisure.
We have often scarcely seen each other. We have lived in the marketplace instead of building up a shrine of our own. And I will tell you
something I have never dared confess even to myself—I think our town-
house reflects it. We have no room where one feels that you and I actually
live—proof positive that in town we do no living together." The letter
continues:

> I have been thinking hard since I left you and I feel easier because
> part of the answer at least I have found. When I left you I wanted

to have another child because I thought it would keep me occupied, help me feel that I was at least some use in the world—but I want one now not as a soporific but for a very vital reason which I shall tell you about when I come home. Do not let us dodge any more but face each other frankly and our life will develop. I could feel your uneasiness about me in your last letter. I do not blame you. Only a blind man could have failed to be uneasy about the woman who left you but I do not think you will be uneasy about the woman who returns.

Meanwhile, however, there were more art galleries to see, dresses to buy, and friends to visit. She spent "the whole P.M." in the Louvre with Raymond Koechlin, president of the Amis du Louvre, and felt that the galleries acquired a magical charm in the evening after the doors closed and "we had the place all to ourselves." She took Bernard Berenson for a drive in the Bois, despite "a kind of hatred for him," and went to Fontainebleau to see the aged and ailing sculptor Rodin, who had bombarded her with telegrams begging her to come.

When Agnes visited the Steichens at Voulangis in July, she was both "happy and miserable." With nothing to do but rest, she began to worry about Eugene, "the kids, the new cook, the strawberries that probably were not being preserved and a hundred other things." She wrote Eugene a morale-boosting letter, with this conclusion:

> Please go ahead in your tranquil, undisturbed way, Euge. I know you no other way. Be happy and know that I will work for you always—in any and every way.
> Love my babies for me and think kindly if you can of your harum scarum (seemingly so anyway)
>
> Agnes.

Eugene was not entirely mollified by this assurance of cooperation. His reply on July 6 said that he was not troubled by any lack of self-confidence:

> I have never worked better than I have recently. This in spite of the fact that much of the time I have had my mind very much distressed by thoughts connected with yourself. You say, "Be happy and know that I shall work for you always in any and every way." This is a sweet expression—and I am sure you would do so—if you happened to think of it. Thinking after all is what counts.

Despite his needling, Eugene seemed to gain new stature in Agnes's eyes as a result of her trip. Many of the old male friends she had met in

Europe seemed somehow disappointing. She was also bitter about the "human leeches" who were using "faked admiration" as a means of selling books and Italian prints to Eugene's sister Florence. Only slightly less loathsome was Maurice Rothschild, who had sauntered up to the box occupied by Florence and Agnes at a choral and said, pointing a finger at the latter: "*Présentez moi à ca.*" After this experience she wrote to Eugene:

> I just wish I could look at your strong, manly face for a moment to get rid of this horrid feeling. Thank God for you, honey.

Agnes sailed for home July 31 on the *Rotterdam,* one of the last boats to leave Europe before World War I broke out. Incidentally, the home of photographer Edward J. Steichen, where Agnes had recently been a guest, was soon menaced by the sweep of the holocaust. Bewildered by the lack of information on what was happening, Steichen wrote Meyer an emotional letter asking what he should do. "Suggest immediate orderly retreat" was the cryptic cabled reply. Steichen and his family retreated all the way to the Meyer farm at Mount Kisco and spent the remainder of the summer there.

Agnes's return voyage clinched her resolution to take her marriage more seriously. It was not the outbreak of war while she was on the high seas that proved to be the turning point but a terrible nightmare. She dreamed that a beautiful sunrise which she was watching with her father gradually faded until nothing was left but his face, which transfixed her "with an expression of sadistic triumph." Although he did not speak, she read his taunts in his face: "I've got you. You are just another me. And you are doomed to go the way I did."[7] Agnes awoke with a sense of "agony, guilt and self-contempt" because she felt that, in escaping from her home responsibilities, she was imitating the instability of her father, which had caused his family, and especially herself, such bitter humiliation. This sudden flash of awareness led to "a process of regeneration" from which there was no escape for the rest of her life. She acknowledged "relapses from grace," as in any conversion, but the European trip brought to an end her deliberate revolt against the role of mother and homemaker.

In the years that followed both partners tried conscientiously to pull together. Their mutual interests were strong despite the personality clashes. Agnes would say to him: "You are the only man I could have married, but you're impossible to live with." He would say to her: "You've often irritated me but never bored me."[8] And so the strange romance rocked

[7] Agnes E. Meyer, *Out of These Roots,* p. 106.
[8] Sidney Hyman's manuscript, "Life of Eugene Meyer," Part II, p. 329.

along over many hills and hollows. Some of the rough patches were smoothed by Eugene's practice of centering on the humorous side of his wife's foibles and by her ability to laugh at his witticisms even when they were directed at herself. In later years she often repeated his quip when she told him that she was writing her autobiography. "What a pity," he said, "you have already used the proper title for an earlier book." That title was *Journey Through Chaos*.

New interests further tightened the family ties. In June 1915, their only son, Eugene III, was born, giving Agnes "a ridiculous sense of achievement." The father was ecstatic. "Eugene III is a husky one," he wrote to his friend Sir Charles Hercules Read of the British Museum, "and it looks to me as though he will give me as bad a time as I gave my dad. He raises Cain when he does not get what he wants, and he does not always want what his wise and experienced father thinks best. I expect his first words to be, 'I can judge for myself.' "

With their family thus enlarged, the Meyers began discussing a new and permanent home. The only home they had owned was the commodious house at Seventieth Street and Park Avenue, where their daughter Elizabeth had been born. Although they had spent several weeks in London buying three van loads of old English furniture for the place, and Steichen had painted murals for the spiral staircase, Meyer had sold the house during his Wall Street debacle (even before the murals were in place) and the family had moved to the St. Regis Hotel for a couple of years. Then they rented a new apartment, occupying the entire twelfth floor, with 100 feet of frontage on Fifth Avenue and 125 feet on Sixty-third Street, with three additional rooms on the floor below. (Meyer later bought this apartment house as an investment, and he would have the judgment and fortune to sell it for cash a few months before the great crash in 1929.)

Thoughts about a permanent home were centered on Mount Kisco. The Meyers soon gave up the idea of expanding their farmhouse because it was 150 years old and five miles from the nearest fire station. But the hill on Seven Springs Farm, the highest point in Westchester County, with a sheer cliff rising out of Lake Byram, was an ideal spot for a mansion that would afford comfort and enjoyment to a large family and a host of friends. The first step toward realization of this dream came when Meyer called on Charles Freer, the Detroit industrialist and art collector, in his New York apartment in October 1915 and found him studying sketches and blueprints for the gallery he intended to build in Washington to house his art collection, both to be gifts to the government. In response to Meyer's question, Freer said that the architect who had designed the proposed gallery, Charles A. Platt, did indeed plan country homes. "If your taste in architecture runs in the direction of air, light, uncluttered space, simplicity, and harmony of line," he said, "you couldn't do better in your choice of an architect."

At the moment, however, the interest of the two men was centered in the gallery. Freer said that construction of the gallery would have to be deferred for a while because it would cost $1,250,000 and there was no market for his stock in the Parke, Davis Drug Company. Sensing a gentle hint, Meyer volunteered to buy enough of Freer's shares to get his art gallery under way. Such a stock purchase would also help to draw Parke, Davis into the comprehensive chemical combine that was taking shape in Meyer's mind. After a visit to the company's plant and a discussion with its president, Meyer wrote Freer that he was "now prepared to buy as much Parke, Davis stock as you are willing to sell at any rough and ready price that seems equitable to our *instincts!*" When Freer alerted his partners to what was afoot, however, they were outraged by the idea of taking "Wall Street" into the firm. The discussion waxed hot, and Freer threatened: "If you say another harsh word about Eugene Meyer, I won't sell him the 10,000 shares we have been talking about. I'll give them to him as a gift for the unfailing friendship he has shown me."

Meyer himself backed away from the proposed deal as soon as he learned of the partners' reaction. Remembering the factional fighting that had bedeviled Maxwell Motors, he had no desire to enter a business where he was not wanted. His offer nevertheless spurred the Parke, Davis partners into buying the stock that Freer wanted to sell, thus enabling him to go ahead with his project. Construction of the Freer Gallery of Art, now a branch of the Smithsonian Institution, was not quite completed when Freer died. His will made Eugene and Agnes Meyer and Freer's secretary, Katharine Rhoades, lifetime trustees of the gallery, with control over all additions to its art collection purchased through the endowment fund Freer left. Meyer regarded the gallery as "one of the treasure houses of the world."

While these events were unfolding, the Meyers' monument to country living began to take shape in mid-1916. Both Agnes and Eugene worked with Platt in designing the structure for all-year family enjoyment on a baronial scale. Their ardor was not visibly dampened by an ugly anti-Semitic threat that, if they persisted in the plan to build a permanent home in the area, the family would be snubbed socially. Ironically, this threat arose at a time when Meyer himself was buying more land to insure privacy on his estate. He concluded, however, that it might be cruel "to tell them not to worry about the danger of contamination through my pushiness." Neighbors previously divided by their own animosities had united in a common cause against the Meyers. Eugene suggested in a letter to Freer that he could be regarded as a public benefactor for having thus brought his neighbors together. But the real irony of the silly protest would come into full flower only in the last year of Meyer's life when he bought the 262-acre Byram Lake and its adjoining property at a cost of $256,000 in order to save this bit of scenic heritage from subdivision. The lake was then presented as a gift to the village of Mount Kisco on condition that the property be kept in its natural state. The grateful response of the community to this generosity was a far cry from the prejudices of 1916.

The house that the Meyers built on Seven Springs Farm is an imposing three-story structure of stone quarried on the property, with sandstone trimming and a heavy slate roof. It was located so as to fit into the landscape and to afford maximum advantages in regard to sun, wind, and weather—the Chinese concept of Feng-Shui. From the far side of the lake, it has the appearance of an European castle. Inside, a grand hallway running the length of the building gives access to a huge lounging room, indoor and outdoor dining rooms, a spacious library, study rooms, and kitchen facilities suitable for a royal household. On the second floor are bedrooms and sleeping porches for all members of the family and numerous guests. The special features include an indoor swimming pool, a huge playroom, a bowling alley, and an organ that pipes music anywhere in the building. The outside invites relaxation with a formal garden, lily ponds, an orangerie, tennis courts, stables, and trails leading to several hundred acres of woods and open fields.

Remembering their friend who had suggested the architect and encouraged them to go ahead with their venture, the Meyers named one of the most spacious chambers on an upper floor overlooking the lake "the Freer Room," hoping that Freer would occupy it whenever he wished. Meyer's friendship for Freer continued despite Agnes's tendency to go overboard in her admiration of him as a kindred spirit in her world of art. On one occasion when she had gone to spend ten days with Freer and Katharine Rhoades at Great Barrington she addressed a letter to "Dear Old Euge" containing this confession: "Freer and I get so sweetly intimate even before K that I sometimes have a desire to have him all to myself."

She seemed to assume that this would involve no strain on the family ties at home, but when she returned, restored in poise and vigor, she found Eugene "off color" and chafing at the bit.[9] Freer never occupied the room dedicated to him, as he was only a few months away from death

[9] Agnes E. Meyer's diary, November 8, 1917, p. 3.

when the Mount Kisco home was finished. Instead, this gemlike gallery of Chinese and Japanese masterpieces was to become a retreat for Mrs. Meyer when she wrote her book on Chinese art and other works. The invitation to Freer is significant chiefly because it suggests that Meyer had made some adjustment in his thinking in the interests of domestic peace. Tolerance for Agnes's romanticism involving various artistic, literary, and political figures was part of the price he had to pay. In later years he would say to an intimate: "There is always a stranger in my house." Yet in the drama involving himself, Agnes, their children, and their friends, he continued to occupy the center of the stage.

12 /

Adventure in Chemicals

WORLD WAR I OPENED A NEW ERA FOR MILLIONS OF PEOPLE. For Meyer, it meant first some shifts in the nature of his business and then a totally new career. For both changes he was well prepared because of his unusual capacity to foresee approaching events.

Ever since his postgraduate studies in Germany in 1896, Meyer had been concerned about developments in that country. Admiral Alfred von Tirpitz was feverishly expanding the German navy, backed by the new aristocracy of commerce and industry, while the old Junker aristocracy, with its power base in agriculture, maintained a formidable army aimed at Russia and France. Believing that Germany could not long carry this double arms burden and that the Junkers would never allow the new industrial interests to predominate, Meyer feared that events were sweeping Germany toward a military adventure. Heavy shipments of gold to Germany in the spring of 1914 confirmed his conclusion that Germany was mobilizing all her resources for war. Long before the "guns of August" began to boom, his affairs were in order for an unprecedented upheaval.

Meyer's personal worries when the storm broke were centered in the safety of his wife, his sister Florence and her husband, his French kinsmen, and intimates such as the Lyman Kendalls and Edward Steichens who were caught in Europe. In these matters there was little he could do except cable his advice and wait for each situation to work itself out. But he could and did address himself to the panic that gripped the New York Stock Exchange. By July 30 the stock markets had been closed in Montreal, Madrid, Vienna, Brussels, Berlin, Rome, Paris, and St. Petersburg, and only the London and New York exchanges remained open. Meyer clearly saw that both these markets would also have to suspend operations to avert economic catastrophe, despite their traditions of always remaining open.

European investors owned American stocks valued at about $15 billion.

Under pressure from wartime panic or from governments that wanted financial assets brought home, many were trying to liquidate their holdings. Americans too rushed in to dump their stocks out of fear or pressure from their European creditors, for the American economy as a whole was then in debt to Europe. The combined impact of these forces, with few buyers to absorb the sudden outpouring of securities, threatened to inundate the stock market and spread chaos through the national economy. A complete suspension of trading would, of course, impose hardships on some people, but it was the lesser of two evils.

Throughout the morning hours of July 30, Meyer tried to communicate his fears to H. G. S. Noble, president of the New York Stock Exchange, but he was inaccessible. In the afternoon Meyer brought together a few of New York's principal bankers, including Benjamin Strong and Charles Sabin, and asked them to join an effort to close the Exchange. The bankers seemed to agree that such action should be taken, but they were fearful of inviting suspicions of weakness in regard to their own banks. The meeting convinced Meyer that the governors of the Stock Exchange should themselves take the initiative. Back in his office, he resumed his telephone campaign, but the only governor he could reach was Ernest Groesbeck, who was working toward the same end. The two men combined their efforts, each concentrating on one-half of the board of governors.

While this was going on, Meyer's father, then seventy-two, dropped into his son's office eager to talk about the war and its consequences for his beloved France. Eugene was still blasting away at the telephone and in no mood for interruption. The conversation that ensued suggests that father and son were still frequently on different wavelengths:

"What are you trying to do?"

"I'm trying to close the New York Stock Exchange."

"You?"

"Yes, me. And with no success so far. I find that few of the key people on Wall Street have grasped the seriousness of the emergency, and those who do are afraid to say aloud that the Exchange should be closed."

"Why don't you mind your own business? You won't be thanked for your pains. People will suspect that you are getting mixed up in public business because you are in serious trouble personally."

"I don't care what people think. The public business is my business, and your business, and everybody's business. There's no use trying to save yourself if the people who have the power and responsibility to avert a general disaster don't act promptly in the only way that is left."

At that point the father sought more congenial company, and the son resumed his seemingly futile telephoning. At about 10 p.m. Charles Boynton dropped in to report that a meeting of New York brokers at the Metropolitan Club had decided that the Exchange should remain open. "Listen!" Meyer barked. "I haven't time to hash this thing out with you in full, but you can do something for me. Go back to the Metropolitan Club, grab any brokers who are still there, and tell them in my name that if the Exchange opens at ten o'clock tomorrow morning, and if the Comptroller of the Currency enforces the law, every Wall Street bank and practically every brokerage house will be busted a half hour later." Boynton said he would convey the message.

At 11 p.m. Meyer finally made connections with Noble and pleaded for a meeting of the board of governors in time to prevent the opening of the Exchange the next morning. Overwhelmed by problems in his own brokerage firm, Noble refused. But Meyer had the bit in his teeth. "I'm not suggesting," he cried, "that you should close the Exchange on your own. Your duty is to call a meeting of the governors where we can consider as a body what should be done. If you refuse to issue that call, then despite our years of friendship, it will be my business to see that you will be held personally responsible for the disaster that is bound to happen if the Exchange opens tomorrow morning." Dead silence ensued; then came a sigh over the wire and a reluctant whisper: "All right, I'll do as you say." Meyer and Noble then worked together far into the night calling the governors of the Exchange to an emergency meeting at nine thirty the next morning.

As the governors assembled, New York was buzzing with reports that the London stock exchange had closed. Despite a valiant struggle, that great citadel of finance had been smothered by an avalanche of desperate selling converging upon it from all parts of the world. The New York Exchange had the choice of shutting its doors or of making itself and its customers sacrificial lambs in an hour of universal madness. Even so, the meeting was postponed in deference to late arrivals, and the clock on the floor of the Exchange was set back half an hour. With thirty-six of the forty-two governors finally present, Noble began gaveling the meeting to order when he was handed a request from the Clearing House bank presidents to wait until their meeting, then in session, reached a decision. Again the governors waited, and an eerie silence betrayed the tension that was mounting. Thirty-six men with varying interests were about to make a decision that would not only affect millions of investors but would also have profound repercussions on the economic life of the nation.

At 9:45 a.m. by the Stock Exchange clock the governors could wait no longer. As their meeting began, a message from the Clearing House presidents indicated they would like to see the Exchange closed if the governors would take full responsibility for it. A second message from Frank Vanderlip, president of the National City Bank, said in effect that the Exchange should not be closed in any circumstances. By demonstrating its strength in this crisis, Vanderlip said, the New York Stock Exchange could wrest financial leadership of the world from London. "Flag-waving nonsense," Meyer snorted. His disillusionment regarding Vanderlip had begun in the panic of 1907, and now he seemed to have company. Arguments by Meyer and others for closing the Exchange were necessarily brief. There was some opposition, but a motion for closing, offered by Ernest Groesbeck and seconded by Meyer, carried at 9:56 a.m. by a large majority. The cheers that swept through Wall Street were re-echoed through the nation. One of those echoes came from San Francisco, where Sigmund Stern had heard the part Meyer had played in closing the stock market. ". . . it is only a big mind and a big man that accomplishes big things," Stern wrote, "—you are the combination."

The emergency had resulted largely from the massive selling of American securities by European creditors. Meyer foresaw that the situation would be corrected as soon as the wartime demands for American goods exceeded the shrinking imports from Europe, making the United States a creditor instead of a debtor nation. Such a favorable balance of trade was achieved before the end of the year, and the last restraints on the stock exchange were lifted on December 12, 1914.

It was soon evident that the war, despite its terrible sacrifice of life and waste of capital, would bring new prosperity to America. "The prospects of this great war have not yet begun to be realized in this country," Meyer wrote to Charles Freer on August 10, 1914. "But if the carrying trade of the sea is returned to England, France, and Belgium, I look forward to a period of great activity in the manufacturing concerns of this country which can supply the food, clothing and other necessities of Europeans." He also forecast that many securities held in Europe would gravitate to American hands; that many items formerly imported would be manufactured here; that part of Europe's former trade with South America and Asia would be diverted to the United States; and that the great mass of the American people would have no place to spend their increased incomes except at home.

It is characteristic of Meyer that he sought an active role in this expansive transformation. One of the first possibilities that interested him was a new chemical enterprise. The fact that the German dye cartel had supplied 90 percent of the dyes used in this country before the war seemed to offer a great opportunity. Within three months after the war began, American textile manufacturers were screaming for dyes, and no sure supply was in sight. The German government fluctuated between shipping some dyes in neutral vessels and cutting off the supply when it wished to bring pressure upon Washington, and the flow of dyes from Germany would cease altogether in 1915.

Meyer was confronted by the problem in November 1914, when Henri Blum, a manufacturer of raw silk and former dealer in German dyes, called at his office with a tale of woe. If the vanishing German supplies could not be replaced, he said, the textile industry might not be able to survive. The only ray of hope that Blum could point to was a small operation on the second floor of a Brooklyn garage where Dr. William Gerard Beckers was trying to make dyes in pots and pans. Beckers was a German-trained chemist who had been working in the United States as a salesman for a German dye company. Though he seemed to know how to manufacture dyes, he was desperately in need of a laboratory, plant facilities, and capital. Meyer remembered the London basement where he had first seen the mineral flotation process that revolutionized the copper industry. It was arranged that Blum would bring the chemist to Meyer's office. Before the meeting took place, however, Meyer read a news story to the effect that an explosion had wrecked a chemical plant in a Brooklyn garage, blown Dr. Beckers through a window, and killed two of his assistants.

Problems more immediately at hand crowded the dye famine into the background. Otto H. Kahn of Kuhn, Loeb and Company informed Meyer in a secret conference at the Yale Club that he had been selected to act for the American International Finance Corporation in buying control of the International Mercantile Marine, an American company that controlled major British marine interests, including the White Star Line. The Mercantile Marine stock was widely distributed, Kahn said. Secrecy would be absolutely essential if the cost of acquiring the stock was not to be prohibitive. A committee in charge of the proposed acquisition had agreed that Meyer was "the most competent and honorable man" to manage the project and offered a handsome commission.

Remembering the miscarriage of E. H. Harriman's plan to win control of the Northern Pacific, Meyer asked: "Are you going to tell me what to do, or are you going to let me use my own judgment on how best to accomplish the end in view?" Kahn promised him a free hand in deciding when the stock should be purchased, what amounts should be bought, and what price should be paid. Meyer accepted the assignment and reported to Kahn only at his home to assure secrecy. For the same reason he avoided borrowing money on the Mercantile Marine shares he bought. By pulling out of the market a half hour before the Stock Exchange closed each day, so that the closing price would not appear too high compared with that of the previous day, he was able to acquire substantial holdings at relatively low cost.

While this operation was in progress, the sinking of the *Lusitania* by a German submarine, with a heavy loss of American lives, sent a shockwave of fear through Wall Street. Meyer kept buying Mercantile Marine stock at very favorable prices. But a frantic call from Otto Kahn, despite the pledge he had given, halted the purchases. Meyer argued that the selling wave had created a great opportunity to acquire the stock at low prices, but Kahn's committee had put up a stop sign and there was no way of altering it. Ten days later, after the stock market had made a strong recovery because the *Lusitania* incident was not going to take the United States into war, Meyer was asked to resume his Mercantile Marine purchases. When the task was finished, Kahn apologetically acknowledged that the cold feet of the acquisition committee "when the big crash was on" had cost International Finance from $8 to $9 million.

Meyer became involved with Dr. Beckers and the dye problem once more in February 1915. A broker reported that Beckers had recovered from his harrowing experience and was still eager to pit his skills against the growing dye famine. Meyer said he had been waiting four months to meet the man; so the broker brought in both Dr. and Mrs. Beckers late the same day. Mrs. Beckers proved to be "a fine Belgian woman with no frills or nonsense about her," and, despite Meyer's temporary discomfiture in dealing with a husband and wife jointly, she became a highly constructive influence in the new venture.

Beckers' only assets, aside from his technical skill, were an option on some land in East New York and equipment valued at about $25,000. It seemed a long-shot venture, but Meyer's firm and Renskorf, Lyon and Company helped to organize the W. Beckers Aniline and Chemical Works, and each firm paid Beckers $100,000 for stock in the enterprise. Beckers received 60 percent of the total stock, because the business was solely dependent on his skill. Meyer held on to the stock he had underwritten, in accord with his rule never to gamble with other people's money, and also acquired most of the stock in the other broker's hands. The $200,000 was turned over to Beckers on a Friday, and the following Monday he was making dyes in portable quarters. At first the dyes were not very good, but the demand for them was nonetheless fantastic. On one occasion the president of the American Woolen Company drove into Beckers' plant and refused to leave until unfinished liquid dyes had been poured into barrels on a truck he had brought with him.

By the end of a year and a half the new company had a laboratory with two hundred research men, a plant that had cost $2.5 million, and a substantial output. Under Meyer's coaching, all these facilities had been paid for out of earnings, except for the original $200,000 in capital stock. He intended to save the company from the plight he foresaw for many other "industrial war brides" that were living high on wartime profits and would face bankruptcy as soon as the fighting ended.

Even so, the pace was rather breathtaking for Dr. Beckers. At one point he asked Meyer for a confidential talk about a critical situation that had arisen, and showed up at Meyer's office with the look of a scared rabbit.

"My God! Don't tell me there has been another explosion."

"Oh, no. It's the foundations of the plant."

"There has been a cave-in?"

"Not yet. But there is *going* to be a cave-in. I worry so much about it I can't sleep at night."

"Have you had an engineer look your place over?"

"You don't understand. It's the *financial* foundations. I wake up at night and think of all the money we are going to spend this month. . . . Where is it going to come from?"

Meyer's countenance broke into a smile of relief: "So that's your emergency?"

"What are you smiling about? It's very, very serious."

"Not sleeping at night *is* very serious. But I'll tell you what I'll do. I'll fix it up so that you can sleep. Every night when you go to bed I want you to say to yourself: 'Thank God, I've got a million dollars in the bank!'"

"But I haven't got a million dollars in the bank."

"I know you haven't. But if you feel that you want it in order to sleep better, I'll see that you get it."

With Meyer's endorsement, the Equitable Trust Company lent the Beckers $1 million on call. Actually, the money was not needed, but the additional reassurance it gave Beckers enabled him to move forward more rapidly with development of the business. Other companies were emerging in the same general sphere. The Beckers dyes were used for woolen goods. The Schoellkopf Aniline and Chemical Works of Buffalo made cotton dyes, and both were buying the essential aniline oil from the Benzol Products Company. In 1916 these three corporations were merged by an exchange of stock, thus forming the National Aniline and Chemical Company. The marriage was not an entirely happy one. The Schoellkopfs, the largest owners, named the president and dominated the company until Meyer organized a voting trust and ousted them from control. William J. Matheson then became president, but he was ultimately replaced, through a series of maneuvers, by Meyer's associate, Orlando F. Weber.

The company was highly prosperous during the war and immediately thereafter, despite Meyer's pressure for lower prices for its products. It supplied all the blue dyes for the navy. When the economy began to turn sour in 1920, however, Weber came into collision with Meyer. As president of National Aniline, Weber had brought the company through a period of great expansion with an admirable record. At the end of the war its assets amounted to $60 million, of which $16 million was in cash and negotiable Liberty Bonds. On the basis of a large backlog of orders, Weber proposed another big expansion program. Meyer said it was no time to be sinking more money into brick and mortar. To Weber's argument that the contracts were in hand, Meyer replied that government war contracts would be canceled, that private manufacturers would repudiate their contracts, that attempts to enforce such contracts would bankrupt customers and create ill will for National Aniline. Meyer threatened to seek a court injunction if Weber should embark on an expansion program in these circumstances, and Weber bowed to this judgment.

National Aniline was in an excellent position, therefore, when discussion of a larger consolidation began in the summer of 1920. It had been associated in some degree with four older companies: General Chemical, the dominant producer of acids; Solvay Process, whose specialty was alkalis; Semet-Solvay, builder of coke ovens which produced chemical by-products; and the Barrett Company, manufacturer of coal-tar products. The operations of these companies were sufficiently related to make their integration highly desirable, and each already owned substantial stock in National Aniline. Negotiations for absorption of the five into a great new Allied Chemical and Dye Corporation were going forward when Meyer returned to New York at the end of his wartime assignments in Washington.

For years Meyer had dreamed of creating an integrated chemical and dye company that could free American consumers from dependence on the German dye trust. So he was most eager to see the proposed combination come into being. After months of jockeying, however, the negotiations for a five-company merger seemed to be getting nowhere. Leaving no stone unturned, Meyer made an appointment to sound out the Du Ponts on the possibility of a union with National Aniline. On the very day that the meeting was to take place, Dr. William H. Nichols, board chairman of the General Chemical Company, who also acted for the Barrett and Solvay companies, asked Dr. Beckers for the right to conduct a full inspection of the National Aniline plants. When this renewal of interest in a five-company merger was conveyed to Meyer, he sent word to Dr. Nichols that he had an appointment with Irénée Du Pont, that he still regarded the proposed five-way merger as preferable, but the time had come for a "yes or no" decision.

The four older companies then worked out a plan to bring National Aniline into the proposed combine on their terms. With the aid of Nathan L. Miller, soon to be governor of New York, they set up a formula for exchanging stock in the companies that was highly favorable to themselves. This was offered to National Aniline on a take-it-or-leave-it basis. Meyer put accountants and lawyers to work on his side to produce a rival formula that would be, in his words, "fair and reasonable." Nichols seemed to assume that National Aniline was only a "war baby" marked for extinction, while Meyer hammered on the fact that National Aniline "had all the money" ($16 million in cash and government bonds) while the other four companies "had all the debts," amounting in the aggregate to $17 million. With four older companies pitted against him, he was fighting from weakness but felt the "rightness" of his position gave him added strength.

As the negotiations became increasingly rough, Meyer induced Weber to keep out of them, although he was president of National Aniline, because he would be the logical choice for president of the new company if he did not become entangled in the animosities accompanying its birth. The wrangling continued through the remainder of the summer. In the process, stories about the proposed merger appeared in the press, including the values at which the stocks would be exchanged, which led to a ten-point drop in National Aniline stock in the market.

Hope for agreement seemed very slender indeed when the negotiators met shortly before Labor Day, 1920. Dr. Nichols remained at his vacation retreat in the Adirondacks and merely telephoned a message that was repeated by his son: "The proposed combination is like a marriage. If you love a girl, you marry her. You don't marry her if you don't love her. Apparently, Mr. Meyer, you and the interests you represent don't love us enough."

"Oh, but we do," Meyer replied, extending the metaphor. "Moreover, it has been generally assumed that you love us too, because your side has been publicizing the terms of our marriage contract. In effect, our marriage has already been announced. If we were forced to drop out now, it would appear that something very wicked had been discovered about us which you had not previously known. The public would have reason to assume that *you* jilted *us*. I couldn't stand for that."

"What are you going to do about it?" young Nichols inquired.

Meyer suggested that the best thing to do would be to arbitrate the differences between the two sides, but the idea was rejected. Meyer then openly accused the other side of planting false stories in the press, of trying to dictate an arbitrary settlement, and of scheming to deprive National

Aniline stockholders of their rights. He concluded his frontal assault by declaring: "I am going to form a stockholders committee, financed by an assessment on stockholdings, to take legal proceedings against your high-handed methods."

"Who will be on the committee?" he was asked.

"Oh, I don't think we will need many members," he replied. "A committee of one person will do, and I'll be that person. I'll give you twenty-four hours to make up your mind whether you will take our terms or agree to arbitrate. If you refuse to do either, I'm going to announce publicly that I'm a committee of one for protection."[1]

The next day the Nichols contingent asked for more time, and Meyer granted another twenty-four hours. Just before the period expired he was asked to call at Dr. Nichols's New York office. Meyer responded willingly and found Dr. Nichols alone, while his associates in the proposed merger waited in an adjacent office. After pleasantries were exchanged, the conversation, as Meyer remembered it, went like this:

Nichols: You are the toughest horse-trader I ever saw.

Meyer: You flatter me unduly. When it comes to horse-trading, I have to take my hat off to you. There is only one flaw in it. You just want to dictate to the other side what the trade is. You don't want to discuss it.

Nichols: What do you want?

Meyer: A fair deal.

Nichols: Let's split the difference between the price you want and the price we have offered.

Meyer: Let's not. I think our price is low, not high.

At the end of half an hour of gloves-off scrapping, Meyer volunteered a small concession: "I won't split the difference and admit that your position is as just as ours. But I'll give you a little off my asking price to save your face, so that you can go in there and tell your friends what you accomplished. It will be damn little, but it will be something at least."

After five minutes of consultation with his associates in the next room, Dr. Nichols accepted Meyer's terms, and the way was cleared for organization of the great Allied Chemical and Dye Corporation on January 1, 1921. It may have been a shotgun wedding, with the bride herself wielding the shotgun, but the union proved to be a happy one. For Meyer, the outcome marked not only the successful conclusion of a long and hard-fought battle of wits; he felt the exhilaration of right triumphing over might. As Allied began to make its influence felt in the chemical world, moreover,

[1] Dean Albertson's interviews with Eugene Meyer, p. 177; Sidney Hyman's manuscript, "Life of Eugene Meyer," Part V, p. 120.

there was much satisfaction in having participated in the creation of a great new industry. Mere money-making had become commonplace, but employment of the creative instinct carried lasting rewards. Anyone could go into a big thing and make money out of it, he used to say, but creative work with small things of great potential was "more interesting, more imaginative, more fun."

Meyer moved promptly to heal the wounds of the prenuptial fighting by giving a luncheon at Mount Kisco in honor of Dr. and Mrs. Nichols. In the course of much amiable talk Mrs. Nichols told Meyer that she had long been interested in reading character traits from hands and asked if she could examine his. Having studied them, she remarked: "Why Mr. Meyer, your hands are not those of a businessman. They are the hands of an artist."

"Mrs. Nichols," he replied, with a good-natured smile, "that is something I've been trying to impress on your husband for some time now."

When the terms of the merger became known, National Aniline stock regained the ten points it had previously lost under the impact of misleading rumors, and the stock of the other companies in the merger lost accordingly. The new Allied board, with Dr. Nichols as chairman, elected Weber president without any pressure or even recommendation from Meyer. The Nichols faction may have felt that, since National Aniline would have to be recognized somehow, it would be less troublesome to have Weber president than Meyer on the board. In any event, Meyer did not become a member of the Allied Chemical's board until 1950 after he had retired from virtually all other activities.

Weber proved to be a strong, industrious, but highly controversial president. Allied was to become, under his management, as *Fortune* magazine would say nineteen years later, *"the* U. S. chemical company, born to establish a new age . . ."* Fortune* went on to say: "Allied Chemical & Dye is generally considered to be one of the soundest integrations of our time . . . a combination that is to all intents and purposes impregnable."[2] One of its greatest achievements was the construction of the synthetic nitrogen plant at Hopewell, Virginia, which enormously enhanced the productivity of American agriculture. When it appeared that synthetic nitrogen from Hopewell would displace much of the natural product from Chile, Meyer passed the word along to the Guggenheims, who had been pouring large sums into the powerful Chilean nitrate monopoly, but there was no indication that his friendly gesture was given serious consideration. The London *Economist* hailed the shift from natural to synthetic nitrates as "one of the outstanding scientific and industrial achievements of the present age."

[2] *Fortune* magazine, 20:44–51, October 1939, p. 45.

As the years passed, Weber's excessive ego and dictatorial tendencies were accentuated, and his passion for secrecy aroused opposition. Some of his critics felt that he missed many opportunities by not projecting Allied Chemical into new scientific fields. Under his management the company never incurred any debt and held so much of its assets in cash and securities that Wall Street regarded it as "a bank, with a chemical company on the side." At one point a vigorous fight to oust Weber developed, and Meyer, though he was not then a member of the board, bought enough additional Allied stock to thwart it. In order to do this he had to violate one of his own basic investment rules—never to sell Fisher Body stock—for the stock he sold was General Motors, which had been exchanged for Fisher Body when the two companies were joined. It would be a mistake to assume, however, that Weber's conservatism and coolness toward change in a rapidly evolving industry reflected Meyer's views. Weber in his heyday was not taking advice from anyone. When Meyer at last went on the Allied board at the age of seventy-five, long after Weber had retired, he would spearhead a drive for revitalization of the company through more basic research, new and bolder programs, and the employment of younger executives. Sensitivity to changing conditions was a hallmark of Meyer's career in both business and government.

Allied proved to be fabulously profitable. In the decade from 1920 to 1930 the company earned nearly $212 million and paid $134 million in dividends. It was one of the few big corporations that sailed through the great depression without missing a dividend. Meyer's stock in the company was worth about $43 million in 1931. His rich dividends from Allied Chemical would enable him in later years to cover the heavy losses he was to suffer in rehabilitating the *Washington Post*.

13 /

Time of Transition

THE YEAR 1915 BROUGHT MEYER TO THE PERIOD WHEN, IF he followed his "Map of Life," he was to give up business for public service. At the age of forty, he was president of Mount Sinai Hospital; he had made generous contributions to various social service institutions and tried without success to interest his Wall Street friends in building mental health clinics; he had set up at Yale a fund for training young men for public service. But no opportunity for a shift of his own in that direction was in sight.

Meyer himself was ready for the change. His investment banking operations, largely in copper mining, automobiles, and oil, had built up a personal fortune estimated from $40 million to $60 million, before he set aside substantial sums in the form of trusts for Agnes and the children. There was no point in continuing to accumulate wealth. Despite the fears of J. P. Morgan that "that fellow Meyer" would "end up having all the money on Wall Street," money was not an obsession in his life. Money was, to be sure, a useful tool, an absolute essential in banking, but not a *raison d'être*. Meyer's intimates were well aware of the fact that he yearned to employ his talents for the benefit of his country, and this aspiration was notably sharpened by the turmoil of the war years.

Taking stock of himself, Meyer acknowledged that he lacked the skills and temperament usually associated with elective office. His best hope lay in appointment to a government post, but here too the door seemed closed to him, for a Democratic administration was in power in Washington, and he was known to be a heavy contributor to Republican campaigns in addition to being a Wall Street banker. The outlook for any presidential call to service appeared to be dismal.

Meyer confessed his ambition for a public career and his discouragement to Frank H. Hitchcock, who had been Taft's Postmaster General and campaign manager. It was easy for the two to agree that the Republican Party should be returned to power. Both felt that a Republican administration could cope more successfully with the problems arising out of the war in Europe than President Wilson was doing. The outcome of their discussions was an agreement that they would work together for a Republican victory in 1916.

The first essential was to find a candidate with broad popular appeal who could reunite the regular Republicans and Bull Moose Progressives after their disastrous split in 1912. Hitchcock, a shrewd politician, was in a good position to sound out national sentiment as to candidates. Meyer was in a good position to finance the operation. Ostensibly, Hitchcock went into the Meyer firm for help in rehabilitating some mining property; actually, his chief activity was the renewal of his political contacts. When his soundings indicated that Justice Charles Evans Hughes of the Supreme Court was the outstanding choice for the Republican presidential nomination and that he was acceptable to the Progressives, Hitchcock went to work, with Meyer's backing, to line up delegates for Hughes. Having been a successful and moderately progressive governor of New York and having remained completely aloof from the hot Taft–Roosevelt contest, Hughes was widely regarded as the only Republican who could reconcile and reunite the divided factions.

But the justice himself was trying to avoid entanglement in politics; he repudiated the work of Hitchcock and all others in his behalf; when he was nominated by the Republican National Convention in disregard of his wishes, he ignored Hitchcock so as to avoid suspicion that the former party chairman had been acting under cover for him all the time. The political managers he chose proved to be second-rate, and Hughes himself found it difficult to shift in a few brief months from the rarefied judicial atmosphere of the Supreme Court to the hurly-burly of national politics. Hughes's loss to Wilson, by an electoral vote of 254 to 277, left Meyer's hope for a career in public service still in limbo.

Disappointed, Meyer nevertheless moved toward liquidation of his business. Several forces seemed to be pushing in this direction. While vacationing with his wife at White Sulphur Springs early in October, 1916, he had read a dispatch from Berlin quoting the German propagandist Bernhard Dornberg as having said that God would never forgive the rulers of the German people if they were to leave unused any arm he had endowed them with to protect their homeland. As Meyer read it, this was a warning, from a man close to the Kaiser, that the German U-boats would soon be unleashed to resume their assault on American shipping in the Atlantic. Germany had suspended its unrestricted submarine warfare during the American presidential campaign to lend credence to the Democratic campaign slogan—"He Kept Us Out of War"—in the hope of returning

Wilson to power, but that temporary restraint was breaking down. The Dornberg speech was enough to alert Meyer to the approach of war.

On October 4 he wrote to his staff in New York: "I fear new and more acute tensions between Germany and America. Such a development, if it comes, would find the public and the market quite unprepared. I therefore advise that you follow a *very* conservative investment policy for the present." On his return to New York, Meyer refused new business proposals; he asked clients to liquidate their accounts in a reasonable time and to transfer investment portfolios to other firms; he sought to wind up unfinished underwriting projects. In the event of war, he decided, he would volunteer for military duty. When he applied for military training at the "business men's camp" at Plattsburg, however, he was rejected because of his color-blindness. A suggestion that he seek a commission as a "desk soldier" got no response. With the military as well as civilian office seemingly closed to him, he thought he might be most useful in the promotion of new industries that would be essential in wartime.

The country was grossly unprepared for either defense or war. It had no real plans for organizing and equipping a substantial fighting force or for mobilization of the country's industrial resources. When the President and Congress finally created a Council of National Defense, composed of the Secretaries of War, Navy, Interior, Agriculture, and Labor in October 1916, that agency had no place to work and did not hold a regular meeting until December 6. Meyer heard about the council's troubles through Bernard Baruch, a member of its Advisory Commission, and sent Orlando Weber to Washington to secure and organize the necessary office facilities. Even when appropriations for staffing and running the Advisory Commission were forthcoming, they proved to be woefully short and were supplemented by Baruch, and later Meyer, out of their own pockets.

Meyer's evolving interest in defense industry led him to take a close look at aviation. It would be a great industry of the future; the war was giving it feverish impetus. Noting that airplane bodies and motors were usually manufactured in separate plants, Meyer conceived the idea of marrying a motor builder to a body builder. His proposition was accepted by the Curtiss Company, which operated a fuselage plant in Buffalo, but his search for a company to supply motors was less successful.

Early in 1916 William B. Thompson and Charles Hayden had invited Meyer to become an investor in the Wright-Martin Company, which they had organized along with Thomas L. Chadbourne, Charles Payne Whitney, Harry Payne Whitney, William E. Corey, Percy Rockefeller, and others. All were men of general business ability, but none of them knew anything about building airplanes. Meyer had made a token investment to avoid offending his friends, but he had not kept the stock. Some months later, this venture again came under his scrutiny because Lieutenant Gillet of the French Purchasing Mission asked Meyer as a personal favor if he could find out what was happening in the Wright-Martin plant. The company had contracted with France to deliver ten Hispana-Suiza motors a day by September 1, and in November there was no indication as to when the first delivery would be made. The company agreed to open its plant and books to inspection, and, at Meyer's request, Orlando Weber then spent a day in the plant and a day with the company's books. His report was that the French would never get their airplane motors and that Wright-Martin would be bankrupt in three or four months unless drastic changes were made.

Meyer and Weber carried this gloomy forecast to Chadbourne, the leading spirit of the venture, and urged him to bring in a competent engineer and production man, to reduce the labor force by half, and to raise a substantial amount of new capital. It was Meyer's thought, unexpressed at the time, that if these changes were made he would seek a merger of Wright-Martin with the Curtiss Company. Chadbourne procrastinated, however, even after Meyer and Weber had presented their arguments to the board of directors. Reorganization of the company and its merger with Curtiss were not to be achieved until after Meyer had taken up his new career in Washington.

Another facet of the shift Meyer was trying to make proved to be extremely irksome. Up to this time he had made only one public speech—an address on "The Impact of Science on Finance" before the American Association for the Advancement of Science in 1909. After that experience he had rejected many invitations to address public gatherings because of the pen paralysis that afflicted him when he attempted to write out what he wanted to say. In most settings Meyer was highly articulate. His conversation was spontaneous and often marked by wit and wisdom. In the give-and-take of business operations, he was a powerful antagonist; in court, an effective witness. His letters had an easy flow of thought and humor. But he felt that every point in a speech should be made with precision and accuracy as well as eloquence, and the struggle for just the right combination threw him into a tizzy.

Meyer nevertheless broke his own no-speaking rule in December 1916, once more appearing before the AAAS, this time at Columbia University, because he felt that he had an urgent message, and if he was going to enter public life he would have to endure the pangs of speech-making. Choosing as his subject "Some After-War Economic Problems," he used the occasion to declare his disenchantment with the laissez-faire doctrine he had heard at Yale from William Graham Sumner. Wall Street panics, combinations in restraint of trade, and war had reduced to rubble the Sumner thesis that governments need not concern themselves with economic problems because God had provided self-enforcing "laws of political economy." The war had changed the entire face of Europe, and it was changing America too. The U.S. economy was racing toward maturity, and it was foolish to suppose that peace would mean a reversion to the economic relationships of the prewar era.

Meyer's speech called for many reforms in the economy, including "a rapprochement of capital and labor through profit-sharing and scientific management" and restraints on "undue speculation" and depression. "The government can aid in this regard," he said, "by the rigorous curbing of swindlers who annually defraud gullible investors of millions and shake confidence in legitimate financial undertakings." Yet his main thrust was toward improvement in government. In the critical transition from the economics of war to the economics of peace, the United States government would probably be the only stable force equal to the emergency. "The vast machinery of government," he said, "needs a magnified personality—many eyes to see and many hands to do." Even then he saw that the government would need to provide emergency credit for international trade after the war to prevent disaster for American exporters and to make possible the orderly rehabilitation of Europe.

Meyer was walking down Fifth Avenue on Sunday afternoon, December 17, 1916, in a foul mood despite the approach of Christmas that was everywhere apparent. He had just resigned from Maxwell Motors after seven years of turmoil. Efforts to prepare his forthcoming speech had produced only acute agitation. The newspapers were reeking with gloom, rumors, repercussions from the spreading war. Coming down the sidewalk, however, was the smiling countenance of Bernard Baruch.

The two men were friends but not intimates at this time. Since both were out strolling, they fell into step and chatted about the defense program, Wall Street, and many other things. Baruch was brimming over with optimism. As an illustration of his faith that the business boom and the bull market in Wall Street would continue, he volunteered that he had 50,000 shares of United States Steel that he intended to hold for still higher prices. Meyer contended that "it is a very dangerous market." Any major shift in the international situation, whether a widening of the war or a move toward a negotiated peace, he said, could send stocks tumbling. As the two men came abreast of Baruch's home on Fifty-third Street, he invited Meyer to his private preserve on the top floor where the discussion continued, ranging broadly over economic conditions, international affairs, and personal interests. They seemed to be poles apart in their estimate of the immediate economic outlook.

The following day, however, large transactions in United States Steel caused a flurry in the market, and the *Wall Street Journal* disclosed that Baruch was unloading his Steel shares because he "didn't like the looks of things." A rash of speculation by European statesmen about the possibility of peace kept the market churning. On the Thursday following the Baruch-Meyer discussion the press carried the text of a note which President Wilson had secretly sent to the belligerents on the previous Monday, asking that they disclose their peace terms. In explaining Wilson's note to the press, Secretary of State Robert Lansing said that the encroachment on American rights had become "increasingly critical" and that "we are drawing nearer the verge of war ourselves." Panic gripped Wall Street and threw prices into the sharpest tailspin since the Spanish-American War.

In the aftermath of the selling wave, rumors spread that the Wilson note had been "leaked" to favored insiders in advance of the public release, and suspicion pointed to Baruch because he had acknowledged bearish operations three days before the note was published. The fabulously wealthy Baruch was a heavy contributor to Democratic campaigns and a key man in the President's emerging defense operations. The press claimed that Baruch had made a fortune from the market crash with the help of inside tips. Some stories hinted that the information on which Baruch had acted came from Joseph P. Tumulty, the President's secretary. Representative William R. Wood, Republican of Indiana, demanded a congressional investigation.

Baruch was in South Carolina where he customarily spent the Christmas season hunting ducks and wild turkeys on his private preserve at Hobcaw Barony. Under the pounding of the press he suffered a little panic of his own. One visitor reported him close to tears. In his autobiography he acknowledged that "my career in public life nearly ended."[1] Obviously if the incident caused Wilson or the country to lose trust in the new defense chief, he would have to resign. Baruch wired Meyer in New York for details, but Meyer could only telegraph news accounts.

The congressional investigation began on January 5, 1917, with Representative Wood reheating the vapor he had managed to collect. Thomas Lawson, the notorious Wall Street speculator turned muckraker, spewed out a volcano of charges, only casually tossing in the name of Baruch. Meanwhile the victim of this strange Saturnalia returned to New York,

[1] Bernard M. Baruch, *Baruch: The Public Years* (New York: Holt, Rinehart and Winston; 1960), p. 26.

131

with the press at his heels. Thinking that Baruch would be in need of moral support and that most of his friends would be avoiding him, Meyer called him and asked: "Do you want to see me?" Baruch asked him to come over that afternoon.

When the two met, Baruch began to assert his innocence, and Meyer cut him short: "My guess is that since you were so optimistic about the stock market during the talk we had that Sunday afternoon, December 17, it was what I said that strongly influenced you to move from the bull to the bear side when the market opened the next day."

"That's exactly what happened!" Baruch exclaimed.

"Then you have nothing to worry about," Meyer observed.

"Oh, but I do," Baruch insisted. "You see, besides selling the 50,000 shares of U. S. Steel common I was holding as an investment, I sold about 45,000 shares of steel and other stocks I didn't have but meant to buy later on a falling market."

That gave Baruch a more serious problem than Meyer had visualized. "What are you going to say," he asked, "when the investigating committee asks what your business is?" Baruch replied that he had discussed that very problem with his lawyer, Thomas L. Chadbourne, who advised that he describe himself as "a capitalist and an investor."

"Well," Meyer answered, "you sold 45,000 shares that you didn't have. What has that to do with being a capitalist and investor? They'll make you admit that your statement is not accurate—that it's false, or something of that kind."

"What do you think I should say?" the penitent speculator asked.

"I think you should tell them the truth. Tell them you're a speculator. Selling short is a speculator's business."

Baruch went to the telephone and rediscussed the matter with Chadbourne. Both readily accepted Meyer's advice. The Baruch-Meyer exchange, as the latter remembered it, then continued:

"Are you going to have a lawyer?"

"Yes."

"Who are you going to take?"

"Senator Spooner."

John C. Spooner had been a Senator from Wisconsin and chairman of the Republican National Committee, and although he was then practicing law he was still influential in the Republican circles that were trying to make political capital at Baruch's expense.

"I think that's bad."

"Why?"

"If you are guilty of a misdeed, then you would naturally hire a man who had influence. But if you're innocent, you don't need influence. You just need the facts."

"Who would you have?"

"Just by coincidence, I would have picked Spooner's partner, Joseph P. Cotton. I don't think you need a lawyer at all, but you do. So I think you ought to take a man merely to hold your hand and be there in case a legal question comes up that you don't know how to answer."[2]

When this advice was also accepted and Cotton agreed to serve, Baruch reflected aloud on the ephemeral nature of most friendships and asked Meyer if he too would stand by through the ordeal. Meyer did so, taking a seat at the back of the hearing room, after offering one final bit of advice. "If you handle this right," he said, "giving the committee all the facts and figures in a forthright manner, without any dodging or truculence, you can turn this liability into a great personal asset."

Baruch faced the committee "frightened half to death." He confessed that he was a speculator in a voice so low that the chairman asked the stenographer to repeat the answer. His candor produced a flurry of excitement in the committee room and in the country. Although the hearing disclosed from his books and records that his operations had produced a profit of $476,168.47, there was not a shred of evidence that he had any prior knowledge of the President's note. After his initial fright, Baruch regained his poise and came out of the hearing a nationally known figure. The press found an aura of prophecy and statesmanship about his performance. He had also learned a valuable lesson: "If you have nothing to hide, you have nothing to fear . . . because the big dog of truth always catches up with the little cur of lies."[3] Another lesson that he did not acknowledge publicly was that, in time of trouble, his friend Eugene Meyer could be a tower of strength.

The part Meyer played in this episode led to another walk on Fifth Avenue in March 1917. Germany had resumed her savage attacks upon Atlantic shipping. The United States was teetering on the edge of war. As head of the Committee on Raw Materials in the new defense setup, Baruch faced the necessity of securing 45 million pounds of copper for the army and navy in a runaway market. England, France, Belgium, and Italy were trying to buy more copper than all the mines could produce. Prices were soaring—from around twelve to fourteen cents before the war to thirty-eight cents in early 1917. Baruch was well aware that whatever price he might pay for this first major order would fix a pattern for pricing other raw materials and thus vitally affect the government's rela-

[2] Dean Albertson's interviews with Eugene Meyer, pp. 191–2.
[3] *Baruch: The Public Years*, p. 32.

133

tions to industry during the emergency. Again he sought advice from his resourceful friend.

It happened that Meyer was well prepared to deal with the problem. In 1915 he had joined with Baruch and the Guggenheims in floating all the common stock and two-thirds of a $15-million first-mortgage bond issue for Chile Copper. Additional financing had become necessary a year later, and all the parties had agreed to a new $35-million bond issue, but Elihu Root, counsel for the bankers involved, had haggled so long over inconsequential details that the public offering of the issue had come on the very day that the U-boats were unleashed, and not one of the bonds had been sold. Meyer and the other underwriters were stuck with $35 million worth of bonds, which declined to 76; Chile Copper stock fell from 38 to 7¾. Believing this a blind reaction, because war would certainly stimulate the demands for copper, Meyer had bought an additional 50,000 shares of Chile Copper stock.

Despite his enormous involvement in the copper industry, Meyer felt that copper prices should somehow be rolled back to discourage the excesses of wartime inflation. The nation would soon be drafting young men to fight in Europe, and some would lose their lives. It should be clear from the beginning, he said, that the war would not be fought for capitalistic profit. If the leading copper producers could be induced to supply the demands of wartime without inflation or profiteering, they would set a precedent that other industries would follow, or be forced to follow.

But how could a fair and reasonable price be determined? As was his custom, Meyer began playing around with figures. When Baruch asked what formula could be used to strike a psychological blow against profiteering, Meyer had a ready answer: "I think you ought to take the prices for about ten years, which would include eight years of low prices and two years of high prices, and just average them."

"What would the result be?" Baruch asked.

"I figured that out, just by accident, some time last week," Meyer responded. "It would be seventeen and three-quarters cents, down from thirty-eight."

"My God," the raw materials chairman blurted, "I never expected to get copper at a price like that."

"Well," said copper baron Meyer, "it isn't economic, but I think it is important psychologically." The big producers could afford to provide copper at that figure, he added, and if the costs of production should continue to rise, adjustments could be made for later purchases.

"How can I get at it?" Baruch then asked.

"The biggest seller of copper is the American Smelting and Refining

Company," Meyer replied. "The head of it is Daniel Guggenheim. He lives at the St. Regis down the street. He and his wife always receive their friends Sunday afternoon at this time and they serve tea. If we go there, I think we can talk to him."

Guggenheim listened thoughtfully as the two visitors outlined what they had in mind. Meyer, a director of Utah Copper in addition to his large interests elsewhere, spoke from the viewpoint of the industry, outlining what he thought it should do "for the common good." Guggenheim was sympathetic, although he said he would have to consult his brothers and the other major copper interests. If his visitors would pick him up the following morning, he would try to have an answer for them. The next morning as he got into the car he said that four large producers would provide 45 million pounds of copper for the army and navy at Meyer's price of 17¾ cents, and a few days later the agreement was ratified by a formal letter.

News of the coup was electrifying. The fact that large producers were meeting the government's initial needs for copper at less than half the prevailing price profoundly influenced national thinking. "It sounded," in the words of Grosvenor B. Clarkson, director of the Council of National Defense, "the industrial keynote of the war—the note of service and of repudiation of profiteering." Overnight Baruch became a national hero, although there was a good deal of grousing from the steel industry, which resented the precedent, and from smaller copper interests not included in the deal. Only Baruch, Guggenheim, and a few of their intimates knew that the inspiration for this magnificent gesture in the public interest had come, not from the government, but from a copper magnate with a conscience.

With these two incidents recommending him, it is astonishing that Meyer was not immediately welcomed into the organization that Baruch was building to harness industry to the war effort. But Baruch had his own problems, and he may have been reluctant to take into his official family a friend (especially a well-known Republican) whose sharp tongue could be a source of friction. The initiative in finding a war-related job would still have to come from Meyer himself.

14 /

Dollar-a-Year Man

FOR A TIME IT APPEARED THAT MEYER MIGHT BE DRAWN INTO the fund-raising efforts of Herbert Hoover's Commission for the Relief of Belgium. In response to Hoover's request, Meyer pledged his cooperation and suggested that President Wilson create a national committee of prominent leaders to support the Belgian relief effort. With the United States about to become an active belligerent, however, Belgian relief was pushed into the background.

On March 31, 1917, Meyer wrote to Justice Louis D. Brandeis expressing a desire "to give my time and work to the service of the country" and asking for help in finding an opening. Brandeis invited his friend to Washington and wrote a number of letters to government executives in Meyer's behalf. Secretary William Gibbs McAdoo replied that "Mr. Meyer's patriotic desire to serve his country" was "most gratifying," but it was obvious that the offer had merely been pigeonholed. Meyer then wrote directly to President Wilson, volunteering his own services and those of his staff, but by this time the President had asked Congress for a declaration of war, and the White House was inundated by similar offers. A direct appeal to Baruch got nowhere, although Baruch would later claim that he brought Meyer to Washington.

Excluded from office, Meyer began submitting his advice by mail. "It must be made apparent," he wrote to Brandeis for McAdoo's eye, "that in managing the war, no class interest is being served . . ." Certain interests "should be educated to the fact that a marked increase in taxes is not a personal attack on them." Another letter to Brandeis, aimed at McAdoo, protested against exemption of a prospective $2-billion war bond issue from all federal income taxes. The proposed exemption, he wrote, would "lighten the rich man's burden" and provide coupon-cutters with a haven in which to retire while taxes were high. While these letters bore no direct fruit, they may well have created a favorable impression of Meyer's trend of thinking.

At last Justice Brandeis found an opening on the Advisory Commission's Committee on Finished Goods. Meyer received the news joyfully, asked no questions, and promptly took the train for Washington in a mood to interpose his own flesh between the enemy and his country. What he was offered, however, when he walked into the office of Julius Rosenwald, president of Sears, Roebuck and Company and head of the Committee on Finished Goods, was a one-dollar-a-year post as an adviser to the army in the purchase of shoes and cotton duck, about which he knew nothing.

The comedown was unavoidably painful. In New York, Meyer had attained a towering stature in the financial community, with a broad command over men and resources. In Washington he was dropped to the status of a miniature cog in a huge and unwieldy bureaucracy. Nevertheless he accepted the assignment because he had asked for any useful war-related job and because Justice Brandeis had gone to some trouble to find even this opening. At least it brought him into the Washington scene; with his foot in the door, he assumed he could eventually make some kind of satisfactory place for himself.

On the very day of his arrival Meyer smelled potential trouble. One of his fellow advisers on shoe contracts was Stanley King, vice-president of the McIlvain Shoe Company, who was later to be president of Amherst College. The chairman of the industry committee for shoes was the president of the McIlvain concern, so officers of the same company were sitting at opposite sides of the bargaining table. Both were men of integrity and public spirit; yet the seeming conflict of interest worried Meyer, and he communicated his misgivings to Rosenwald.

"There is not a breath of collusion and not a cent of profiteering in the shoe contracts that are being negotiated," Rosenwald retorted.

"*You* know that, and I know that," Meyer replied, "but appearances say something else. Appearances make you personally vulnerable to attack."

Meyer consulted Justice Brandeis, who took a similar view, but Rosenwald was not interested in legal niceties. "I don't care what the legal advice is," he declared. "We've got to win a war. These shoes are good, the prices are wonderful, and we get deliveries." Some months later, however, the conflict of interest in the Committee on Finished Goods did come to public notice when that committee denied a favor sought by Senator Kenneth McKellar, a notorious spoilsman. Rosenwald was so embarrassed by the furor that President Wilson found another job for him. The war effort thus lost a highly competent executive because he had been insensitive to an impropriety even when it had been brought pointedly to his attention.

Near the end of April 1917, Meyer received, to his great surprise, a letter from the White House. President Wilson wrote that the American commission he was sending to Russia to establish contacts with the new Kerensky regime should be "really representative of what we are and what we are thinking" and that he wanted Meyer to serve on the commission, "for I believe that your cooperation will be of the highest value." The commission was to board a government vessel at San Francisco for Vladivostok and travel to Moscow by way of Siberia "where the most dramatic effects of the recent revolution have been witnessed."

A wave of wishful thinking was sweeping the United States in regard to Russia. The giant that stood with one foot in Europe and the other in Asia had overthrown its czar and set up a new government. Would it not now become a great democracy? Wilson's gesture was a reflection of this ideological interest and of the hope that Russia could be kept in the war to prevent Germany from massing her strength on the western front.

Meyer's reaction was a mixture of excitement and incredulity. He realized he had no special qualifications for such a mission, although his wedding trip through Siberia had given him some acquaintance with the country. But he was eager to be helpful in any capacity and intrigued by the prospect of exploring new horizons. Though somewhat conscience-stricken by the thought of leaving his pregnant wife, he immediately telegraphed his acceptance to Wilson. A formal letter followed expressing his "deep sensibility" of Wilson's confidence and his hope that he would have the benefit of the President's "personal views concerning the policy and aims of the Commission."

Determined to prepare himself for the undertaking, the new commissioner wrote to Secretary McAdoo, Felix Frankfurter in the War Department, Professor Samuel M. Harper of the University of Chicago, and others. His enthusiasm was notably cooled when the membership of the commission was announced in the press and he learned for the first time that Elihu Root was to be chairman. Meyer was prejudiced against Root because of the latter's bumbling in the Chile Copper bond dispute, and he felt that Root's age and conservative image would put him at a serious disadvantage in dealing with the Russian revolutionists. Why, he asked himself—a betrayal of his own unawareness of the realities in Washington—had not Theodore Roosevelt been made chairman? Nevertheless, he swallowed his antagonism toward Root, suggesting only that a doctor be assigned to the commission because of the chairman's advanced years.

Meyer also offered to pay for the services of two doctors who could acquaint the Russians with the new vaccine against typhus. As chairman of Mount Sinai Hospital's Pathology Laboratory Committee, he had been instrumental in sending teams of experts to deal with typhus epidemics in Mexico and Serbia and felt that the same technique could be employed to great advantage against the epidemic that was then ravaging Russia, if the Wilson administration and the Russians gave their approval.

While Meyer was working almost night and day to prepare for the trip, he received a telegram asking him to report to the State Department. The logical inference was that the great adventure was about to begin. When Meyer was ushered into Secretary Robert Lansing's office the following morning, however, that official unceremoniously dumped him without so much as a word to soften the fall. "We have some cables," he said, "that make us think that you'd better not go on the Russian mission."

"But it's been announced in the papers that I'm going," the deflated rejectee replied. "What shall I say if I'm questioned by reporters?"

"Tell them that the report was false," Lansing casually volunteered.

"But that isn't true," Meyer protested.

"You can say that," the Secretary insisted, as if deliberate falsification were an everyday practice.

Meyer made his exit feeling as if he had been tossed into a slimy sea. Not only had an attractive assignment, freely offered out of a clear sky and accepted in good faith, been snatched from him without any rational explanation; the Secretary of State had also ordered him to cover his embarrassment by a lie. To a man of Meyer's strict principles, the incident was shocking and disillusioning. Later on, he heard intimations that the objection to his presence on the commission had come from Ambassador David R. Francis in Moscow and it may have reflected anti-Semitism in the Kerensky regime; but no official explanation was ever given.

With this humiliating brush-off on top of his miscasting as a shoe-contract adviser, a less persistent man than Meyer might well have shaken the dust of Washington from his feet. Instead, he asked for release from Rosenwald's office and walked down one floor in the Munsey Building on E Street where Baruch's Raw Materials Committee had its offices. Baruch had not asked him to come and did not invite him to stay; when Meyer stayed anyway, he was not assigned to any particular task. But he began to make himself useful by answering the telephone, organizing papers that he found lying around in miscellaneous fashion, and talking to people, especially the French visitors who could not speak English. There was no organization, no files, no furniture—nothing except Baruch's persuasive personality. The great speculator had had little experience in running an office. His Raw Materials Committee was so much a one-man show that vital committee papers were often stashed away in his pockets or in miscellaneous spots in his hotel suite. As Meyer began to set up an organization and a filing system, he sent a corporal to Baruch's living quarters every day to go through his clothes and return to the committee papers that belonged to it.

Baruch was soon glad to have the help Meyer was giving. With housekeeping details taken care of, Baruch could concentrate more fully on major decisions and the personal contacts that were so essential in a system operating by persuasion rather than law. Meyer was also a fertile source of suggestions, as Baruch had good reason to know. As a working relationship between the two emerged out of this curious beginning, Meyer was permitted to build up a nonferrous metals unit of the committee and acquired the title of "adviser," which meant he was director of the unit. This gave him the heavy responsibility of mobilizing supplies of copper, lead, zinc, antimony, aluminum, nickel, silver, and (later) cement for the war effort.

Meyer exercised great care to avoid conflicts of interest of the type that had caused trouble for Rosenwald. He helped to build up Baruch's organization with able and hard-working executives. Some of the men thus summoned for wartime assignments could not afford to work for one dollar a year, and in several such cases Meyer paid them a salary out of his own pocket. Statisticians and engineers from his office in New York worked on the nonferrous metals unit without compensation from the government. On some occasions Meyer represented Baruch at meetings of the General Munitions Board and was troubled by its impotence in allocating supplies between the rival domestic agencies and between America and its allies. The government had no effective means of establishing wartime priorities or of preventing prices from soaring skyward.

Meyer was sitting in for Baruch on May 29, 1917, when an army ordnance officer asked for approval of an exorbitant price for 15,000 tons of shell steel. The officer had an option on the steel at four and three quarters cents a pound, a figure substantially above the cost tentatively estimated by the Ordnance Department. The option would expire at three o'clock that afternoon, the officer said, and no other shell steel was available for spot delivery. Meyer replied, after on-the-spot calculations of his own, that a fair price would be three cents a pound or a little less, but he could not guarantee that the steel could be immediately obtained at that price from another supplier.

At this point the officer hotly declared that steel was necessary to win the war; he was not interested in the price but only in getting the steel. Did Meyer, he asked, want to live with the burden of losing the war on his conscience? Meyer replied that he would bow to no one in his devotion to winning the war, but that was no reason for letting the government be gouged. If the officer would return later in the day, he said, an answer would be forthcoming. Having had in his own business a policy of showing to the door anyone who argued for acceptance of an option that was about to expire, Meyer was especially irritated by the officer's naïve assumption that the government had to yield to outrageous demands before three o'clock that afternoon in order to win the war.

A call to the steel industry's representative in dealings with the Raw Materials Committee brought the information that the man who had offered the option on the shell steel, a Mr. Fitzpatrick, was in Washington. Meyer soon had Fitzpatrick and the ordnance officer together in his office. It developed that Fitzpatrick was only an agent of a New York jobbing concern. Meyer demanded that the agent put him in touch with the head of the concern, who happened to be a brother of James A. Farrell, president of the United States Steel Corporation. Fitzpatrick replied that this would be impossible as Farrell, the jobber, had left his office for the Memorial Day holiday. Exasperated by this run-around, Meyer ordered Fitzpatrick to pick up the telephone and tell whoever was in charge at the Farrell concern that he (Meyer) had extended the option for two days and that the 15,000 tons of shell steel could not be disposed of until the government had made its decision.

There was no legal ground for such an order from the Raw Materials Committee, but Meyer knew that his response to this emergency would have the support of public opinion. The option was extended; the government acquired the 15,000 tons of shell steel for $2 million less than the ordnance officer wanted to pay, and when the War Industries Board finally got around to setting up a general schedule of steel prices, the figure for shell steel conformed to the fair price Meyer had suggested. The experience led him to conclude: "If you know what you're doing—if you're right and you're not afraid—you can get things done by the force of circumstance as well as by legislation."

With the deficiencies of the country's industrial mobilization for war thus sharply dramatized, Meyer spent Memorial Day writing a memorandum to Baruch and the Advisory Committee. "Confusion is spreading rapidly," he wrote, "because of the informal way supplies are purchased and allocated, and the situation becomes worse with each day that passes." The army was "buying in the market without regard to price." The navy was holding up vital orders because no price policy had been worked out. The needs of the Allies were not being met because there was no central purchasing agency. Some companies were taking advantage of the confusion to cancel contracts for civilian supplies, with the expectation of charging higher prices later. Meyer pleaded for "all possible haste" in creating a centralized purchasing agency along with an effective priorities committee that could "regulate the whole industrial situation," if necessary.

As the weeks passed, Meyer and others continued to bombard Baruch with arguments for better wartime controls. Baruch, in turn, bombarded the Wilson administration. Yet changes were slow in coming. Baruch himself acknowledged that "we floundered during the first year of the war while shortages developed, production lagged, prices rose, and many profiteered."[1]

Washington was agog with discussion of how the war should be conducted on the home front. One interesting focal point of this endless debate was the so-called House of Truth where Walter Meyer lived along with Felix Frankfurter and Walter Lippmann (both on active duty in the War Department), Lord Eustace Percy, and various others. According to his own account, Eugene Meyer was "condescendingly" invited to some of the "highbrow" debates at the House of Truth—"as a sort of Philistine observer and recipient of their superior thinking." Nevertheless, he became an active participant and was stimulated by the intense intellectual fencing. For the first time in his life he felt that he was living in every fiber of his being.

The intellect that impressed him most in this circle was not the brilliant Harvard professor of law, who was already on a high path that would take him to the Supreme Court, or the lucid journalist, Lippmann. Rather, it was a little man with tousled hair and unpressed trousers who seemed almost oblivious while the lightning of cerebration was flashing but who invariably put an end to the debate by a complete, comprehensive, and convincing summary that made further discussion pointless. Gerald C. Henderson, a young man still in his twenties, had graduated from the Harvard Law School with the highest marks in its history. Henderson was the source of many ideas that Meyer passed on to Baruch and Baruch to Wilson. Meyer came to feel such a strong affinity with this young man that he would later seek him out as an associate, and Henderson would become one of only two men who were really close to Meyer in mind and spirit after the death of his brother Edgar.

Meyer's thinking about the war stemmed from his conviction that the United States should make its influence felt with the utmost speed. American forces should be put into the field at the earliest feasible hour. Allied war plants in Europe should be expanded, with American financial

---

[1] Bernard M. Baruch: *Baruch: The Public Years* (New York: Holt, Rinehart and Winston; 1960), p. 54.

aid, so as to supply the American forces. Nonessential production in the United States should be cut back sharply to permit a rapid build-up of military supplies. Meyer had no patience with the argument for mere holding operations in Europe until the United States could expand its manufacturing capacity to win the war, possibly in 1919 or 1920, without much sacrifice of civilian goods.

As Baruch's representative on the General Munitions Board, Meyer fought the War Department order to suspend all truck production until a standard "Liberty" engine could be perfected for mass output. It would be two or three years, he said, drawing on his experience in the automobile field, before a new motor could become an assembly-line reality, free from "bugs." At last permission was obtained to continue production of existing truck models the British and French wanted. The great outlays of the military for a standard "Liberty" engine proved to be of negligible usefulness.

A visit from Colonel Henri Requin of France served to pinpoint one cause of the muddling in Washington. Requin's job was to provide liaison between Marshal Foch and the American general staff. "But I can get nowhere with the general staff," he complained to Meyer in despair. "The old men have all the power, but do not understand. The young men understand but have no power." Meyer put him in touch with Frankfurter and Lippmann in the War Department, fully cognizant of the fact that the useful line of communication thus established was no answer to the general dilemma. "Unless the needs of the Allies are viewed as a single whole—with each Ally producing and getting the things that can best serve the common cause most quickly—" Meyer wrote to Baruch on July 10, "there is a real danger that the Allied Forces in the field may collapse while America is still arming."

Some of the reforms that Meyer and others had been calling for were achieved on August 1, 1917, when the General Munitions Board was superseded by the War Industries Board, plus a priorities committee and the Allied Purchasing Commission. Yet even the new board was advisory only. Its first chairman, Frank A. Scott, broke under the strain of trying to bring order out of chaos without any authority, and his successor, Daniel Willard, resigned and went back to running the Baltimore and Ohio Railroad because he saw no hope of obtaining the power necessary to do the job. For some weeks the board was then left without a chairman.

Meyer shared the belief that the board should have direct authority to provide the sinews of war and civilian necessities. Yet he kept on insisting that the board could make better use of the power it did have. It could use what Meyer called "involuntary voluntary methods" by appealing to public opinion. He needled Baruch to take responsibility for broad policies, feeling certain that public backing would be forthcoming.

Meyer kept aloof from a new controversy over the price of copper, but when the copper industry finally agreed on a compromise price of twenty-three and a half cents a pound in September 1917, and President Wilson approved it, Judge Robert S. Lovett convinced the WIB that Meyer was the logical man to organize the copper industry on the basis of the agreement. A controversy ensued because McAdoo was reluctant to release Meyer from a war-savings job he had undertaken. Meyer induced McAdoo to let him assume a temporarily inactive status because he felt that the WIB had first call upon his services. Although the war was spawning fantastic sobriquets for many men—"king" of this, "czar" of that, and "chief" of the other—Meyer never thought of himself as czar of the copper industry. He remained an "adviser" to the WIB, but that did not crimp his resourcefulness in resolving the problems that arose within his bailiwick.

At first the navy refused to cooperate with Meyer's advisory unit in the buying of cement. Seventeen different governmental agencies had been purchasing cement separately without regard for wartime priorities or the shortage of transportation. Meyer learned of a naval purchase of 2,000 barrels of cement in Los Angeles for use at Mare Island in San Francisco Bay. It would have to be transported 500 miles by rail, although the cement could have been obtained on the water within 30 miles through the industry advisory committee. Meyer was ready to complain in public, but first he went to the navy with his specific case of wasted transportation and obtained its "voluntary" compliance.

The Department of Justice responded to Meyer's bid for cooperation by saying that he was countenancing an outrageous price. Cement had sold for sixty-five cents a bag two years before and had risen to $1.30. A spokesman for the department said that Justice was about to indict the whole industry for profiteering and monopoly. Meyer insisted that, in this case, the higher price was justified by increased costs. There was argument on this point, but it came to an abrupt end when Meyer said that he had $100 in his pocket and he would bet that sum that no cement company would make any money during the quarter at the fixed price. The department withheld its prosecution.

One of his coups proved to be clearly illegal. In New York the editor of a trade journal suggested that he attend a junk dealers' convention at the Astor Hotel. As he was directly responsible for enforcement of the War Industries Board's fixed price for copper, and he knew that junk dealers were reclaiming immense amounts of secondary copper and selling it for whatever the traffic would bear, Meyer saw the convention as a golden

Jacob Meyer, Eugene's great-grand-
father.

The wedding picture of Eugene and
Harriet Newmark Meyer.

The Meyer home in Los Angeles in the early 1880's. Harriet Meyer is on the stoop with several of her children.

The Meyer family in San Francisco in the early 1890's. Left to right: Walter, Elise, Arline, Eugene Meyer, Sr., Rosalie, Ruth, Florence, Eugene, Jr., Harriet, and Edgar.

Eugene Meyer, Sr.

Harriet Newmark Meyer.

Rosalie Meyer, Eugene's eldest sister.

Eugene Meyer, Jr., as a young man.

Eugene Meyer, Sr.

Agnes Ernst at Barnard in 1907.

Meyer in the pre-motor age in front of the old farmhouse on his Mount Kisco estate, Seven Springs Farm.

Eugene and Agnes Meyer being guided down a mountain trail on their honeymoon.

(Opposite) At the liquidation of the War Finance Corporation. Left to right: Andrew W. Mellon, R. R. Burklin, Eugene Meyer, George R. Coosey, Chester Morrill, Floyd Harrison.

Meyer and his four eldest children in the garden at Seven Springs Farm: Elizabeth (left), Florence (top), Katharine, and Bill.

opportunity. He went and, being asked to speak, told the junk dealers they would have to supply copper for wartime use at the price fixed for the industry as a whole or the government would take them over. Distributing proposed pledges of cooperation with the government, he asked the junk dealers to sign. About 4,500 junk dealers, including many who had not attended the convention, ultimately did so.

Back in Washington Meyer reported his achievement to the advisory commission and got a frown from Judge Lovett. "You had no legal authority to do that," Lovett said. The law authorizing the government to commandeer essential war supplies applied only to primary producers. Lovett brought in several law books and convinced Meyer that he had acted illegally. But the pledges of cooperation based on an unwarranted threat continued to stand because the junk dealers would not meet again for another year.

When the next case of excessive pricing on the part of a secondary copper dealer arose, Meyer had to devise a new means of dealing with it. He induced the committee to offer a small amount of copper for less than the twenty-eight cents that an offending firm in Cleveland was charging. By a succession of such operations the uncooperative junk dealers were forced into line, and that was the end of the black market in copper.

Transportation of copper and lead became a critical problem, especially during the hard winter of 1917–18. The delivery of ore from Mexico and New Mexico encountered serious delays. Meyer assigned an engineer from his New York office, Herbert G. Moulton, to study the train movements and then made a deal with Edward Chambers, director of traffic for the Railroad Administration. Instead of shipping miscellaneous cars of ore every day, entire trainloads were scheduled for the refineries at Garden City, Long Island, Perth Amboy, New Jersey, and Baltimore once a week or several times a week. As the special trains did not have to stop en route to have other freight cars cut out, their running time was reduced by half —the equivalent of doubling the number of ore cars. The Railroad Administration then began working on solid trainloads of lumber and other commodities.

Late in 1917 André Tardieu, who was in Washington to speed French purchases, told Meyer that France would "have to get out of the war" if she did not obtain the 500 tons of American aluminum she had been promised. After an investigation, Meyer informed Tardieu that unusually cold weather had frozen the water on which the only producer of the metal, the Aluminum Company of America, relied for electric power. A few days later the Frenchman's histrionic threat came sharply to mind when Meyer walked into a New York drugstore and bought some shaving soap manufactured by the well-known French firm of Roget & Gallet. The soap was wrapped in aluminum foil of French origin. Meyer hastened to fill out an application form of the type used by war agencies for supply requests. It read something like this:

Agency making application:	French Purchasing Mission
Place:	Washington, D.C.
Item requested:	500 tons of aluminum
Disposition:	Application approved
Source of supply:	Roget & Gallet, Paris, France
Price:	Any price the French government wants to fix.

He sent the completed form to Tardieu with the aluminum foil pinned to it. Whether or not the French took the hint, there was no more talk of France pulling out of the war for want of American aluminum.

An alleged crisis over antimony developed because the United States had only small deposits and relied chiefly on China for its supply. Several ordnance officers told Meyer they needed 3,000 tons of antimony for the hardening of lead used in shrapnel. The mere rumor that the army was in the market for such a large supply sent the price from fourteen to twenty cents a pound in two weeks, which would have meant a windfall of nearly $400,000 for the suppliers. Actually, however, the 3,000 tons represented a long-range estimate of requirements. The army's immediate need simmered down to 100 tons.

Armed with this information, Meyer used a form of Chinese torture on the suppliers of the metal. First he wrote the dealers asking the price at which they would sell antimony to the government. All the dealers specified the jacked-up price of twenty cents a pound, except one whose price was a fraction of a cent lower. Meyer rejected the offers on grounds of collusion and pretended indifference for a while. His silence brought an offer from C. K. Li to meet the government's needs at a lower price. Meyer thanked him for his patriotism, but said the government was not in a hurry. After some more suspense, he bid for only 100 tons of antimony and obtained it for less than the previous bids. Then he bought a little more at a still lower price, and continued this drop-by-drop torture until the price was back to the original fourteen cents. By the end of 1917 he had added 3,000 tons of antimony to the government's reserve stocks, while neatly thwarting the would-be gougers.

Lead represented the opposite kind of problem. Delay in the munitions program resulted in a glut of lead; the price dropped to five and a half cents a pound, and lead mines began to close to reduce losses. Eager though he was to keep prices down, Meyer feared that lead would not be available when the munitions program got into full swing. It was more important to maintain production than to reduce prices. He urged the munitions makers in both the United States and Europe to anticipate future requirements for lead and thus maintain a steady demand and output. The temporary surplus was quickly absorbed as the production of munitions increased.

Meyer's resourcefulness as adviser for nonferrous metals reached its apex when the American Smelting and Refining Company complained to him that it would have to close its Baltimore plant, which had been turning out one-fourth of the United States' refined copper, because there was no coal to generate electric power. The shortage of power was also affecting the Bethlehem Steel plant at Sparrows Point and other vital war industries. With the price of coal fixed, the coal companies would not sign delivery contracts unless the purchasers had assurance of cars to haul the coal, and the Railroad Administration denied coal cars until delivery contracts had been signed.

The first step was to discuss the problem with J. Leonard Replogle, director of steel supply for the War Industries Board, who was also fuming over the shortage of coal. "Let's go to the WIB together," Meyer suggested. A joint appointment was made for three o'clock that afternoon. When Meyer arrived at that hour, however, Replogle was coming out of the boardroom. It was obvious from his embarrassment that he had jumped the gun in the hope of getting whatever coal there was for the steel industry.

"I thought we were going in together at three o'clock," Meyer said.

"I just had a talk with them," Replogle apologized.

"And where did you get?" Meyer asked.

"Nowhere," Replogle said.

"I guess I won't bother to go in," Meyer concluded. "I'll have to find some other way."

Personal visits to officials in charge of coal and transportation brought no hope of changing the run-around that was causing stagnation. There was only one thing left to do; Meyer went to the Secretary of War, taking with him two letters, one directing the Fuel Administration to deliver 1,400 tons of coal a day for war-related use in the Baltimore area, and the other directing the Railroad Administration to see that this coal was transported. Secretary Baker signed the letters, which thereupon became orders, and had his aide, Colonel Chester Bolton, deliver them in person to the heads of the fuel and rail agencies. Bolton gave a dramatic fillip to the orders by telling the fuel and rail administrators that if the deliveries were not made, a company of soldiers would take coal out of cars passing through Baltimore en route to New York and New England.

The Baltimore plants got their coal, and Meyer acquired a host of new admirers. The canny spokesman for nonferrous metals said nothing to undercut the idea that he had mysterious powers to get things done. It was a helpful reputation in moving through the Washington wilderness of 1917–18, but he remained in the dark as to how the War Department recorded the incident. Many years later Secretary of Defense Louis Johnson insisted that Meyer had personally ordered troops to take coal from trains going through Baltimore. "It isn't so," Meyer replied, "and it can't be in the record." Johnson said that he had looked up the record, that it showed Meyer did order the troops, and that this civilian encroachment on the military bailiwick caused the generals to agree that the War Industries Board should have greater powers of its own to control wartime production so that civilians would not continue to order troops around. That seemed a gratifying dividend from the incident, but Meyer, tough-minded and resourceful though he was, had not presumed to issue military orders.

Though he found it necessary to discuss many things with his chief, Meyer scrupulously avoided burdening Baruch with his problems. It was his business, Meyer thought, to be as helpful as possible to Baruch without fussing about who would get the credit. From his friendly chats with Elizabeth Bass, chairman of the women's bureau of the Democratic National Committee, Meyer learned that Baruch had passed many of his (Meyer's) ideas along to the President without giving him credit. After chatting with both the President and Meyer, Mrs. Bass would say indignantly: "This fellow Baruch picks your brains." Meyer appears to have harbored some jealousy of Baruch, but publicly he would say: "If I can talk to the President through Baruch, that's all to the good."

For the most part the relations between the two were smooth and cordial. Meyer had no sympathy with Baruch's enemies who were gunning for him or with the rivals who were trying to unhorse him in the hope of succeeding to his job. Yet the two men were very different in temperament, and conflicting views sometimes led to heated exchanges.

"Gene, you're awfully sour," Baruch complained one day. "You're always grumbling about things. Why don't you smile more like I do?"

Meyer replied that Baruch's smile was only "painted on" and did not come from the heart. "You've got a big job here," Meyer continued. "Everybody is telling you you are a wonder and you're blowing up like a balloon. I'm your only friend because I stick a pin in the balloon every once in a while and let out a little of the gas. When things aren't going so well, I'm not going to tell you they are, I'm going to tell you when they're not. If you don't like it, tell me you don't want me around and I'll be glad to find something else to do."

For a moment the two Wall Street titans glared at one another, but they were soon working together smoothly again. When Baruch became nervous and jittery over Wilson's delay in filling the vacant chairmanship of the War Industries Board, Meyer offered both comfort and encouragement. Baruch was given the chairmanship of the WIB on March 4, 1918, and along with it Wilson transferred to him ample power to control American industry—power that Congress had recently delegated to the President. At last the WIB was prepared to cope with the demands of modern war, but the decision had come only a few months before the armistice. It was too late for American production of artillery, aircraft, machine guns, and the like to make any substantial contribution to winning the war. Meyer always felt that much time had been wasted on the industrial front. It was the shipment of American soldiers to Europe at the rate of 200,000 a month, even though they had to rely largely on French and British weapons, that turned the tide of victory toward the Allies.

With the War Industries Board empowered to act, Baruch had somewhat less need for the ingenuity of his Wall Street friend. Meyer felt that it would be better for Baruch and for himself if he turned his energies elsewhere. His organizing ability, his intense dedication to his work, and his capacity to get things done were now widely recognized in Washington. While still in the WIB he had taken on several other wartime assignments. Probably no other dollar-a-year man who came to Washington in those hectic days served on a broader front.

In later years, Meyer would look back upon his year in the War Industries Board as one of his most enjoyable experiences in government. The operation was obviously important to the success of the war, yet it was small enough that he could keep all the reins in his own hands. It was tangible enough so that he could measure the progress made each day and the distance yet to be covered. It was a challenge to his combative instinct and gave him a sense of achievement in a cause bearing directly upon the welfare of mankind.

15 /

Planes for War

LIFE SELDOM RUNS ON A SINGLE TRACK. ITS INTERESTS AND problems ramify in many directions at the same time. That was especially true of the Meyers' first years in Washington; strange new forces pulled them hither and yon.

Agnes had remained in Mount Kisco during the summer of 1917 following the birth of her third daughter, Katharine. When she moved to Washington in October and settled in a spacious rented house on K Street, the children were left in New York where they were to remain for three years, with Margaret Powell, the faithful trained nurse, serving as substitute mother. Agnes was freer than she had been at any time since her marriage to pursue her artistic, social, and intellectual interests.

The most satisfying thing about their new life in Washington was that it permitted her to become, for the first time, a partner in her husband's professional activities. In New York, the Meyers' social ties had not extended very far beyond family and Eugene's Jewish friends and business associates. When guests had come to lunch or dinner, or visited in the country over the weekend, Agnes had often known no more than that they were connected with one of Eugene's ventures, and the business discussions had been reserved for male ears only during the after-dinner cigar-and-brandy hours. In Washington public affairs dominated the discussion, and they were everybody's business. Agnes thus found herself in a congenial setting.

It was not unusual for Agnes to hear from dinner companions that Eugene was the "most brilliant man in Washington." At one of Baruch's parties she met Lord Reading and concluded that he "spreads glory on his race," but this led her to comment: "Bernie and Eugene, I am sure, will do as much for it, if not more, before they get through, and though Eugene is the least of them now I choose him for travelling furthest."[1]

[1] Diaries of Agnes E. Meyer, 1917–18, p. 57.

In any event, Meyer's dedication to his governmental tasks was complete. One day in August 1917, the president of a company in which he had been interested before the war called to ask what price had been set for pig iron as a result of meetings between the Raw Materials Committee and the steel industry representatives. Meyer answered that, to the best of his knowledge, negotiations were still under way and that in any event it would be improper to disclose a decision in advance of its release to the public. His friend was not to be silenced by any such gentle rebuff. What good were friends in government, he asked, if they could not grant such a favor? Had Meyer's head been turned by the Washington heat?

Out of the embarrassment that Meyer suffered from this demand upon friendship came a firm decision. He would dissolve the firm of Eugene Meyer, Jr., and Company to remove all suspicion that he was continuing to serve private interests while in public office. When he first took up war work, he had resigned from the board of governors of the New York Stock Exchange, given up directorships in several companies, and sold all the stocks that might involve him in a conflict of interest. Now it seemed necessary to go further. On August 22 he announced to the press that his investment banking firm would be dissolved within eight days. The occasion brought a chorus of laudatory editorials in the financial press about his Wall Street career. Thereafter his New York office was used only to look after his personal and family interests.

One other factor had contributed to his decision: he had taken a part-time assignment with the Treasury to help finance the war. For months he had been calling for increased taxes and for generous lending by the public. The first Liberty Loan had brought in $2 billion from large investors, but Meyer felt that the rank-and-file should also be asked to save for the war effort—not only to ease the financial problem but also to soak up large sums that were being spent for scarce consumer goods with inflationary consequences. After obtaining details about Britain's saving-stamp program from its director, Robert (later Lord) Kindersley, London head of Lazard Frères, Meyer proposed a similar war-savings program to Secretary of the Treasury McAdoo. The Secretary named Meyer chairman of a committee of Treasury and Federal Reserve officials to review the proposal, and the Meyer plan was approved in both principle and detail. It called for the sale of twenty-five-cent War Savings Stamps which could be affixed to cards and then exchanged (fifteen stamps per card) for a $5 War Savings Certificate that would be payable after five years. Congress passed a bill enacting these provisions and creating the National War Loan Savings Committee to which Meyer was appointed, with Baruch's consent, along with Frederick A. Delano, Mrs. George Bass,

Henry Ford, Charles L. Baine, and Frank A. Vanderlip, who was chairman.

Despite the friction between Vanderlip and Meyer, the committee got off to a smooth start at its first meeting with McAdoo in the chair. Then Vanderlip took off on his own without further contact with either the Treasury or the committee. On a nationwide tour to promote the loan program he left the impression that he had been called to Washington to rescue the country's finances from McAdoo's blundering. McAdoo soon found excuses for not seeing him, and the savings program languished.

Meyer aired his irritation in a letter to Mrs. Bass on August 19, 1918, after a mix-up over the committee's annual meeting. "All in all," he wrote, "I am inclined to think that Mr. Vanderlip ought to know beforehand whether the meeting is to be in New York, or Scarsdale, or Philadelphia— or on the train, as he finally suggested. But I did not think well of having the first annual meeting on the train in a temperature of 115 degrees. Knowing your feelings and mine, I did not think we needed a temperature of 115 to have a warm meeting!" Meyer would always feel that an alert chairman could have brought in many times the sum that the War Savings program raised.

Along with his many other activities, Meyer kept an eye on aircraft production, or rather the absence of it. The contrast between the promise of planes enough to darken the sky and the trickle of actual production was building up to a national scandal. Meyer's old friend Gutzon Borglum, sculptor of the famous Lincoln head, was raising a furor about the delays, and Wilson had made the mistake of giving him a green light for an investigation. Borglum imagined himself a reincarnation of Leonardo da Vinci, but he came up with nothing more than generalities and threw no light on the causes of the failure. Wilson found it necessary to dismiss the raving sculptor, an action that turned his full fury on the White House.

Meanwhile Secretary of War Baker was trying to reinvigorate the Aircraft Production Board and asked Meyer to take a place on it. Meyer declined. About the only bright spot in the aircraft production picture, he told Baker, was the Fisher Body plant making fuselages for war planes and delivering them on schedule. As a very large stockholder in Fisher Body, he could not properly be a member of the board making contracts with that company, and continued production of Fisher Body fuselages, he said, was far more important to the war effort than his presence on the board. "Besides," he added, "you want me to go there and investigate. I don't want to be a member of the board and investigate my colleagues. That wouldn't make sense unless you want the kind of bitter clashes that have paralyzed the Shipping Board."

In late January 1918, Meyer was asked to assemble detailed information about the aircraft program as Baker's "personal representative." He asked for and received a letter that would get him into the aircraft factories and was given the privilege of attending meetings of the Aircraft Production Board. For the second time Baruch consented to detachment of his nonferrous metals adviser from the War Industries Board, although Meyer kept his desk there and was consulted on various problems. When Borglum learned that Meyer was investigating the failures of the aircraft program, with an office in the War Department not far from his own, he bitterly assailed his old friend as the source of Wilson's hostile letters, but the accusation was of a piece with the sculptor's other wild charges.

Within minutes after Meyer walked into his new office, Under Secretary of War Benedict Crowell turned over to him a sheaf of papers and a request from Secretary Baker for advice as to what should be done. The papers showed that the Army Signal Corps had signed a contract with the Engel Aircraft Company, of which H. D. Baker, brother of the Secretary of War, was president and general manager, for $5,924,077 worth of aircraft spare parts. No one in the new company had any experience in building airplanes, and its cash on hand amounted to only a little more than $1,000. It was a promotional venture by H. D. Baker and his friends, who were proceeding to raise capital on the basis of the Signal Corps contract.

Meyer returned the file to Crowell within an hour with a recommendation that the contract be canceled. If the organization that the company was beginning to build was to have any wartime value to the country, he said, H. D. Baker should withdraw from any connection with it in order to avoid potentially great embarrassment to the Secretary of War and the Wilson administration. Crowell asked if Meyer would say as much to H. D. Baker personally, and the two men were soon in conference. Baker argued but finally agreed to do whatever appeared to be necessary.

Secretary Baker then asked Meyer to meet with him late in the evening. It developed that H. D. Baker had asked the Secretary if he would be embarrassed by organization of the Engel Company to build flying boats, and the Secretary had answered that he would not be. But the Signal Corps contract after the war had broken out was a different matter. The worried Secretary had canceled the contract pending an investigation. When Meyer walked into the Secretary's office, Baker acknowledged that the award of a contract to his brother's firm had been a serious mistake and that his brother should withdraw from the company. "Perhaps," he added, "I should resign as Secretary of War."

"Nonsense!" Meyer replied. "The record makes it plain that you knew nothing whatever about the contract when it was entered into between

General Squier[2] and your brother's company. There is not the remotest reason for you to resign. The need is to clean up the whole situation in Cleveland with the utmost speed and thoroughness."

"Will you go to Cleveland and clean it up?" Baker asked.

Meyer answered that he could leave on Sunday night, that he would need a letter giving him authority to do whatever might be called for and another letter to Baker's most reliable friend in Cleveland. Baker dictated the letters immediately, and said he would pay the expenses of the trip. "No," Meyer said, "you can't do that. I'm not doing this for you personally. It's part of my wartime service. All I want is your complete support."

In Cleveland, Meyer explained Baker's predicament to the latter's best friend, banker F. H. Goff, and attorney S. H. Tolles. The two brought the directors of the Engel Aircraft Company together the next morning, and Meyer told them that H. D. Baker's resignation was essential in the national interest; his cash outlays should be returned to him with interest but without profit. Baker submitted his resignation immediately; the board accepted it and promised to send Meyer, by special delivery to Washington, copies of official documents showing the action taken. The documents were placed in Secretary Baker's hands and sent to Capitol Hill on the very day that a Republican Congressman demanded an investigation of the aircraft contract awarded to the Secretary's brother. A Democratic Congresssman arose and read the documents into the record; the great exposé that had been intended turned out to be nothing more than a puff of smoke. Secretary Baker later acknowledged that the greatest personal service rendered to him during his years in Washington came from Eugene Meyer.

The incident gave Meyer a new élan. Agnes recorded in her diary that he "feels the return of power, feels as if some of his chains were falling off, and this tones him up wonderfully. I marvel once again at his great vitality and wonder where it will carry him."

Turning his attention to the larger problem of acquiring military planes, Meyer listened while the Aircraft Production Board decided to build a large plant in northern Italy to manufacture Caproni bombers for the Allies. The Caproni was one of the best heavy bombers then in use, and, with the American aircraft industry in turmoil, there was logic in stepping up its production in Europe. Nevertheless, Meyer was troubled. As soon as the meeting was over, he called on Captain Roger Welles of Naval Intelligence, a friend since their meeting in Shanghai in 1910. How, he asked Welles, did shipping losses from German submarine action in

[2] Major General George Owen Squier, in charge of the army air service.

the Mediterranean compare with losses off the coasts of France and Britain? Welles brought out a graph showing that losses on the approaches to Italy were three times the losses off Britain and France. Armed with that information, Meyer went to the office of General Squier, head of the Army Signal Corps, and said that the resolution just passed by the Aircraft Board would result only in strewing the bottom of the Mediterranean with materials intended for the Caproni plant. Squier called Howard Coffin, civilian chairman of the board, and asked that it be reconvened at the earliest possible moment. The board reversed itself and began studying the feasibility of building the Caproni plant in western France.

This experience confirmed Meyer's suspicion that much of the fumbling in the aircraft program was in the board itself. Composed of three army and three navy officers, along with the civilian chairman, it had no real power or independent sources of information. There was no master schedule for distribution of the few planes that were being produced. The board seemed to be little more than a cushion between the industry and the military. As Meyer prepared for an inspection trip to aircraft plants, Coffin urged him to take along representatives of the Aero Club, a new aircraft industry pressure group. Meyer retorted that the Aero Club had no right to exercise governmental authority. Coffin then suggested that Meyer take along two manufacturers of airplane parts, to which the latter replied: "I am going on the inspection trip as a representative of the Secretary of War without bandwagon attachments." Actually, however, the Signal Corps sent with him two officers designated as "guides" who seemed chiefly interested in watching everything he did.

At the Curtiss plant in Buffalo, Meyer found that production had been seriously disrupted by a short-notice switch from the Spad airplane to the Bristol Fighter. Constant changes ordered by government engineers had delayed the output of DeHaviland 4's by the Dayton-Wright Company. Similar problems plagued other segments of the infant industry. Meyer's written report to the Secretary of War laid much stress on the desirability of keeping experimental engineering apart from production. Too often they were mixed up together, with the result that production could never break clear of disruptive changes in the product.

Meyer's chief recommendations were given orally to Secretary Baker in confidence. He had found the Signal Corps to be hopelessly unequal to its task. Despite General Squier's special talents, he had neither the training nor temperament to oversee the production of aircraft. Nor could any other military officer be expected to risk his future standing in the military hierarchy by issuing the drastic orders that the situation called for. As for the Aircraft Production Board, it could not solve anything as long as it was merely an advisory body at the mercy of military procurement officers. Meyer's conclusion: "You've got to have an Assistant Secretary of War for Air who will devote himself exclusively to the problems related to aircraft—production, supply maintenance, and the training and assignment of personnel."

Baker scarcely had time to hear Meyer's report before leaving on February 26 for a tour of the battlefronts in France. During the seven weeks of his absence the drift continued—a great disappointment to Meyer. Yet he was relieved that Baker had gone to the war zones to see for himself what was needed for an allied victory. Meyer had once suggested to Baruch that preparations for war be suspended for three or four weeks so that all the principal people in Congress and the executive branch could visit the front-line trenches. The time thus lost would be inconsequential, he insisted, in comparison to the stimulus that would come from firsthand acquaintance with the horrors of the battlefield.

So it was in the case of Baker. He returned with new steel in his will. American troops began to move overseas at the rate of 200,000 a month to cope with the massive German offensive concentrated against the western front because the new Communist regime in Russia had pulled that country out of the war. On the domestic front, Baker accepted Meyer's advice to the extent of creating a new Aircraft Division in the War Department to be headed by John D. Ryan. Ryan consulted Meyer and was warned that he would be in trouble if he did not insist on authority commensurate with the job to be done. At the time he did not heed that counsel, but after he had accepted the appointment and found himself helpless in dealing with the officers in uniform who had botched the aircraft program from the beginning, he went back to Baker and obtained a new grant of power along with the title of Assistant Secretary of War for Air. These reforms came, however, in the last months of the war. Meanwhile the furor over the absence of American fighting planes at the front continued, and Wilson appointed Charles Evans Hughes to make a public investigation. Many of his conclusions dovetailed with Meyer's previous findings from within the War Department. Meyer had been released from his assignment, with profuse thanks from Secretary Baker, as soon as Ryan took over.

16 /

The War Finance Corporation

WHILE THE AIRCRAFT INVESTIGATION WAS STILL GOING ON, Secretary of the Treasury McAdoo told Meyer that Wilson was thinking of him as a director of a proposed War Finance Corporation. Legislation to authorize the new agency was being sent to Congress. McAdoo was sounding out the prospective directors as to whether they would "play ball" with the administration. Meyer replied that he made a policy of working with any organization he was a part of, up to the point of disagreement on vital issues. At that point he would not quarrel publicly with his colleagues but would resign if the official opposing him did not.

Absorbed by his work in the War Department, Meyer paid no attention to the War Finance Corporation bill as it moved through Congress and was signed by the President on April 5, 1918. A few weeks later, Paul Warburg, vice-governor of the Federal Reserve Board, offered Meyer congratulations as they met at the Metropolitan Club.

"About what?" Meyer asked.

"You mean you don't know that your name has been sent to the Senate for confirmation as a director of the War Finance Corporation?"

"This is the first I've heard of it," Meyer honestly confessed.

The new assignment was nonetheless welcome. He had nearly finished his investigation of the aircraft muddle, and the unit of the War Industries Board he had built was successfully carrying on without him. The new venture in helping to finance essential war industries was at once a challenge and an opportunity for employment of his special talents. There was some delay in his confirmation by the Senate because Senator William M. Calder of New York had not been consulted, but the enthusiasm of Henry Evans, Bill Thompson, and others put an end to the dilatory tactics. Agnes was much amused by the fact that Baruch's glowing letter about Eugene, which was read on the floor of the Senate, had been written by Eugene himself, but the ghost-writer explained his triumph over modesty by saying that he "could not entrust anything so important to Bernie." Actually it was Baruch's testimony before the Senate committee considering the nomination that resorted to superlatives. So extravagant was his praise that the chairman asked if the nominee were dead. "Why?" Baruch sputtered. The chairman replied that no one ever used language so laudatory about a man still in the land of the living.

Even before the War Finance Corporation got into motion, Meyer was drawn into another operation. Summoned to McAdoo's home one Sunday night, he listened to the Secretary's hope of floating the Third Liberty Loan without any increase in the 4 percent interest rate that the Second Liberty Loan had carried. But the financial community was demanding a higher rate, and this essential wartime venture could not be permitted to fail. "I want you to go to New York tonight in a purely unofficial role," McAdoo said, "and sound out the bankers you know as to their willingness to adhere to the 4 percent rate."

Meyer's mission coincided with a furious German attack which threatened to break through the British lines. All the bankers he consulted, except one, thought the Third Liberty Loan would have to be floated at 5 percent interest or higher. When Meyer reported this gloomy outlook to McAdoo, the Secretary asked pointedly: "What would you do if you were in my place?"

Meyer replied that, with the New York bankers in control of the only nationwide mechanism that could handle the loan, some concession to their judgment would have to be made; he suggested a compromise of 4¼ percent interest, and the rate was ultimately fixed at that point. The bankers did cooperate, and the bonds sold despite the low wartime rate because the fighting spirit of the people had been aroused. The incident was significant to Eugene Meyer chiefly because it led to another assignment that proved to be long, arduous, and troublesome.

At the very first meeting of the WFC, McAdoo noted that Congress had made the corporation the agent of the Treasury in managing a fund (5 percent of most existing government issues) for stabilization of the market for United States bonds. That function had previously been performed for the Treasury by J. P. Morgan and Company, and Congress disliked the arrangement. "The management of the corporation's bond-purchase fund is a one-man job," said McAdoo, "and I want Mr. Meyer to take it on, since he has had experience in the bond market."

"I want no part of that job," Meyer protested as soon as he could break into McAdoo's presentation.

"Why not?" the Secretary asked.

"In time of war," Meyer answered, "the bond market will do many unforeseen things. Anyone who takes this job is going to be attacked no matter how honestly or competently he does it."

"Boys are being killed in the trenches, aren't they?" McAdoo observed icily. "Civilians will also have to take risks."

Meyer surrendered completely at that point, regretting that he had not seen the issue more clearly at the beginning. But not everyone was similarly motivated. When he asked the New York Federal Reserve Bank, by law the fiscal agent of the WFC, to handle the bond orders and deliveries, he was flatly turned down. For want of a better arrangement, he had the transactions handled in his own New York office on the basis of orders relayed from Washington. James W. Hoban had remained with Meyer after his investment banking firm had been dissolved, and he took on this governmental work without extra compensation. Nor did Meyer receive anything for the use of his offices and employees or for the insurance he provided against theft or destruction of the bonds. The volume of work soon overwhelmed Hoban, however, and Meyer arranged to transmit the orders through Hoban to New York banks for processing. But no one bank was used on successive days so that the volume of the operation remained confidential.

The policy Meyer followed was to prevent government bonds from dropping more than one quarter of a point on any day, even if purchases on that day had to be heavy. At intervals the bonds purchased were turned over to the Treasury at the average cost to the WFC, as the operation was not designed to produce a profit or to inflict losses on the corporation. During the last six months of the war, the WFC spent $377,992,205 for bonds to support the market and sold most of them to the Treasury. Since these bonds were purchased for about $80 million less than the par value at which they were originally issued, the Treasury in effect gained that much from the transactions.

Meyer's stabilization operations came to an abrupt end in the spring of 1920. Assistant Secretary of the Treasury Russell C. Leffingwell complained that too much money was going into the purchase of bonds; he was weary of raising funds by the sale of ninety-day Treasury bills at 6 percent interest. Meyer argued that the purchase of Liberty Bonds at about $87 was in the public interest regardless of the cost of short-term money. When Leffingwell persisted, Meyer replied: "If you know how to stabilize this market without money, I think you'd better do it, because I don't know how to do it without money." In addition to his other duties, Meyer had been riding herd on the bond market for two years, with only two weeks of partial vacation, and was tired of it.

"We'll talk it over next week," Leffingwell said.

"No, we won't," Meyer answered. "I'm not going to be in possession of any secrets. I'm going to quit. I want you to put out a release that, as of Monday, the Treasury will handle the sinking-fund purchases."

Meyer refused to budge from that position. Leffingwell announced the shift in responsibility for the stabilization program, and the price of government bonds dropped five points.

The attack that Meyer had feared came only after the war was over. Charles B. Brewer, a sensation-hunter hired by Attorney General Harry M. Daugherty, pretended to uncover a "ring" that had made illicit fortunes through the issuance of duplicate bonds. In his investigation of bonds with duplicate numbers he learned the well-known fact that the WFC's bond transactions had been conducted through Meyer's New York office. Brewer's innuendo made it appear that Meyer had been selling bonds to the government in his private capacity and approving the operation as director of the WFC. The House of Representatives set up a five-man committee to sift these charges, along with Brewer's allegations against the Treasury, and Brewer was made its chief investigator. The committee was given complete access to the War Finance Corporation's books and records, but nothing happened until ten days before the 1924 election. Then Representative Louis T. McFadden, chairman of the investigating committee, telephoned Meyer at ten thirty on a Saturday morning that the committee was in session. Would he care to attend? The last-minute warning was obviously intended to catch him off guard and leave him in the predicament of a helpless witness to his own immolation. Meyer always felt that this trap set for him was related to his evasive reply when McFadden had once sought his support for appointment as governor of the Federal Reserve Board.

As it happened, however, Meyer was not surprised by McFadden's call. Congressman James G. Strong had passed a friendly warning to Meyer. In turn, Meyer alerted Gerald Henderson, who had been general counsel of the WFC at the time in question, and took the midnight train from New York to Washington. When he and Henderson arrived at the committee room, it was obvious from the number of newsmen present that the press had been led to expect a major scandal.

Backed by Under Secretary Gerrard B. Winston, Meyer insisted on the right to answer each of Brewer's charges as it was voiced. As he broke in to do this, Chairman McFadden reprimanded him: "You are interrupting the witness." "And with good reason," Meyer retorted. "The time to nail a lie is when it is spoken—not when it gets so long a headstart that the truth can never catch up with it."[1]

[1] Sidney Hyman's manuscript, "Life of Eugene Meyer," Part VI, p. 265.

In reply to Brewer's charge that he had obtained commissions for selling bonds to the Treasury, Meyer showed that he had received nothing whatever—not even for the use of his New York office, which involved expenses of about $70,000. The small commissions the WFC paid went to the cooperating banks. To the charge that the WFC had sold bonds to the government for more than the market price, Meyer replied that the bonds bought to stabilize the market were turned over to the Treasury, at intervals of about three weeks, at the average price the WFC had paid, and with a falling market this average price would necessarily be above the last market quotation.

By the noon recess the promised exposé had simmered down to a pathetic fiasco. Rigged to discredit Meyer's handling of the WFC's bond operations, it succeeded only in spreading on the record the facts about his skillful and selfless service to the country. After an independent audit of the brokers' slips covering government bond purchases and sales through Meyer's office, Mellon sent McFadden a report noting the "undisputed testimony," that Meyer had not profited from the operation but on the contrary had given "the space and service of his New York office to the government free of charge." Former Secretary McAdoo also sent Meyer a reassuring note, and the *New York Sun* dismissed the hullabaloo as a "tempest in a thimble."

Meyer was one of five directors of the War Finance Corporation. The others were McAdoo, Clifford M. Leonard, Angus W. McLean, and William P. G. Harding, governor of the Federal Reserve Board. As managing director, Harding informed Meyer that, since his Federal Reserve duties would prevent him from attending some meetings of the WFC, he would look to Meyer, as an experienced and responsible banker, to save it from any foolish decisions. Meyer would need to be especially wary, Harding said, in regard to McLean, whom he described as a country boob with no knowledge of finance, although he was a banker, lawyer, and coming governor of North Carolina. Working both sides of the street, Harding also asked McLean to be on guard against any of Meyer's shenanigans that might tighten the grip of Wall Street on the South.

The mutual suspicion thus aroused was a severe handicap at first. McLean would wait to see how Meyer voted on every issue and then vote against him. Meyer accused McLean of drawing a sharp line between good and bad loans, which usually turned out to be the Mason-Dixon Line. The friction ended, however, when the third full-time director, Leonard, a Midwesterner, became aware of the suspicions that Harding had implanted in both of his colleagues and disclosed the facts to them. The three met in a "harmony" session, which marked the beginning of a long and mutually fruitful friendship between Meyer and McLean.

The War Finance Corporation began its operations in May 1918 with an authorized capital of $500 million supplied by the Treasury and the power to borrow up to $3 billion by issuing bonds against the securities it held. Its major task was to help finance essential industries, including banks and railroads, that were threatened by wartime dislocations. Many utilities had been caught in a squeeze between rising costs and stationary rates or lagging adjustments. Banks that had invested in utility securities were also imperiled. Many other banks were under strain from the government's heavy borrowings and the outflow of savings deposits into Liberty Loan bonds.

The first big case to come before the agency was the plea of the Brooklyn Rapid Transit Company for $60 million to pay bank notes soon to be due. The BRT had extended its lines into Brooklyn before there was enough population to make the venture self-supporting. McAdoo thought the problem could properly be left to the bankers who had originally advanced credit to the BRT, but Meyer said that the WFC had a responsibility to preserve confidence in the whole economy; he urged the directors to offer one-third of the sum needed if the bankers would advance the other two-thirds. That advice was rejected. When the WFC directors met with the transit officials and interested bankers, however, Harding asked Meyer to be spokesman for the corporation in turning down the bid for help because he was a New Yorker.

Meyer was especially loath to be the bearer of such tidings; a flat no from him would seem to involve a renewal of his feud with the Brady family, carried over from Maxwell Motor days, because the Bradys were major owners in the BRT and the Central Trust Company, the bank most heavily involved. Nevertheless, Meyer reported the WFC's decision without disclosing his own view. President John Wallace of Central Trust responded by telling Henry Poor, lawyer for the BRT, to go back to his office and draw up the receivership papers.

Harding turned pale. "As governor of the Federal Reserve Board," he said, "I don't know whether I want the Brooklyn Rapid Transit Company to go into receivership at this time. I don't think it would be very helpful to the war effort." On his initiative, the WFC directors reconvened, while the bankers and transit officials waited outside, and agreed to the Meyer formula of supplying one third of the needed $60 million. When the two groups met again, Harding himself, now that there was something to offer, chose to be spokesman for the WFC. The bankers accepted the offer. When everything was settled, Wallace whispered to Meyer: "You boys aren't very good poker players"—implying that the receivership threat was only a ploy. Meyer held to the view that the WFC should make itself useful without resorting to poker.

The BRT loan fixed a pattern for the use of private credit as far as it could be obtained. Meyer demonstrated great resourcefulness in devising new means of enlisting private credit in the war effort. When the Baltimore and Ohio Railroad sought a WFC loan to pay off $10 million in notes, he induced the company to offer the notes for renewal or public sale by agreeing that the WFC would take any portion not disposed of. For this service the WFC collected an underwriter's fee, and, since all the notes were sold, no public funds were used. The Bethlehem Steel Company asked the WFC to underwrite $20 million of a $50-million bond issue to be handled by a syndicate. Meyer agreed to take $20 million of the bonds not otherwise sold if the WFC were paid the same commission of 1.75 percent that was going to the other syndicate underwriters for their portion. Since all the bonds were sold, the WFC had a windfall of $350,000, which helped to offset losses in some other quarters.

Senator James W. Wadsworth of New York interested Meyer in the plight of small canners and farmers in the Genesee Valley. For want of credit, the canneries could not finance the farmers and the farmers could not grow the larger crops needed in the war effort. With the help of Frank Peters, Meyer visited the area and persuaded the canners to set up co-operative warehouses where crops could be stored under bonding safe-guards. Warehouse receipts could then be used as valid security for loans. After Meyer went to Buffalo and induced the bankers to cooperate in the arrangement, ample credit was forthcoming without any use of WFC funds.

Despite the headaches, Meyer found his métier in this war work. Agnes recorded in her diary that he was "happier and stronger than I have ever known him to be." The WFC had been created as a rescue mission for essential war-disrupted industries, and Meyer had shaped it into a powerful instrument of public policy. It was a new role for government in the United States. In the six months of its wartime operations, it made loans amounting to more than $71 million, in addition to its enormous bond stabilization program, and made a net profit of $2.75 million.

A shift in the Cabinet brought Meyer new responsibilities. McAdoo decided to give his whole time to the Railroad Administration, and Representative Carter Glass became Secretary of the Treasury in 1918. Though he was the father of the Federal Reserve Act, Glass himself said he knew nothing about the Treasury job. He thought it was "funny" when Mrs.

Meyer referred to him in conversation as Eugene's boss. Eugene's knowledge and experience, he said, "made him feel like a fool."[2] But the two men got on well together, and Glass relied heavily on Meyer for his initiation into the Treasury.

On December 17, 1918, Meyer went home with a small boy's grin on his face. "Look at me," he said to Agnes by way of challenging her to guess what had happened. "You are going to the peace conference," she ventured, as that was the great event everyone was talking about. Yes, the State Department had asked him to go to Versailles as economic adviser, with John Foster Dulles as his assistant. When Glass heard about this, however, he asked Meyer to delay his trip until he (Glass) had had "time to turn around" in his new office. Two weeks later, he asked Meyer to bow out of the assignment. "Everybody is going to Paris, and I can't find people," Glass complained. "Somebody has got to be around here."

It was a favorable moment for Meyer to strike a bargain, and he made the most of it. For months he had been worrying about economic chaos when the fighting stopped. Now it was an imminent reality. American government loans to the Allies had been cut off as the war ended. Those countries had no gold or liquid investments, and they were desperately in need of food, shelter, and equipment to repair the ravages of war. Over-expanded American agriculture and industry also needed European markets to ease their adjustment to peacetime. Meyer said that confusion and despair on both sides of the Atlantic could be greatly relieved by providing "revolving credit" up to a billion and a half which could be used for loans to American exporters and American banks financing exports.

"I don't know anything about it," Glass responded, "but I'll take your say-so, and I'll stand back of the legislation. You draw [up] the bill."

Meyer helped to nurse the authorizing legislation through Congress. His success in this effort, in March 1919, seemed to mean that the War Finance Corporation would be a vital factor in the transition from war to peace. He had tried to persuade Baruch that the War Industries Board should also continue its operations temporarily as a means of coping with dislocations, but Baruch had hastily disbanded the WIB so that he could go to Paris.

Meanwhile two other problems were dropped into Meyer's lap. In December 1918, he was asked to devise some means of financing the railroads, which were under government control, because Congress had adjourned without passing any appropriation for that purpose in the hope of forcing Wilson to call an extra session. Senators Henry Cabot Lodge and Frank B. Brandegee and other Republican leaders were eager to have

[2] Agnes E. Meyer's diary, p. 137.

Congress on the job so they could continue to haze Wilson. The President was determined to avoid that embarrassment of his peace negotiations if possible.

The problem was presented to Meyer by John Skelton Williams, Comptroller of the Currency and director of finance for the Railroad Administration. Wilson had left, Williams said, with instructions to turn the railroads back to their private owners if no way could be found to finance them without an extra session. But this would require $500 million to replenish the depleted railroad treasuries, and that sum might be more difficult to find than the funds needed to continue government operation. What could the WFC do about it?

"Give me a little time to think it over," Meyer responded. "I can't give you an answer right off the bat."

His first move was to seek legal advice, but the WFC lawyers had resigned after the armistice. Several calls to lawyers proved unfruitful until he reached his brother-in-law, Alfred A. Cook, counsel for *The New York Times* and an eminent corporation lawyer. Cook came to Washington and worked out a plan for paying the railroads with interest-bearing promissory notes without any due date because no one could tell when Congress would make the necessary appropriation. The notes could then be used as collateral for loans. The WFC had about $375 million it could lend to the railroads; so the major problem centered on obtaining another $425 million from the banks or other sources.

Meyer told Leffingwell that it would be impossible to get the cooperation of the New York bankers as long as Williams, a notorious Wall Street baiter said to be the only man living who could "strut sitting down," remained director of finance for the Railroad Administration. Williams resigned. With some difficulty, Meyer then induced the leading bankers of New York, Chicago, Philadelphia, and other cities to meet in Washington for discussion of the problem. When they were all assembled, he deliberately kept them waiting for half an hour—the only time in his life he resorted to this stratagem—to emphasize the fact that they could do nothing until he, representing the government, was present.

The bankers joined in a uniform plea that the WFC lend all its available funds to the railroads, after which the banks would help, but without any commitment from individual banks or groups. Jackson E. Reynolds, president of the New York First National Bank, summed up the argument with an eloquent plea that they follow the example of Marshal Ferdinand Foch who had come in at just the right moment and won the war for the Allies. Meyer intervened at this point, saying that he had been a careful student of Foch's operations, that Foch had refused to take command of the Allied armies until American troops began to pour into France and he knew that he had sufficient reserves to sustain his attack. "What you want us to do," Meyer added, "is to go ahead without any reserves of a definite character. When you show us the reserves such as Marshal Foch had, we'll go ahead as fast as Foch ever went.". His demand for positive commitments from the bankers was finally accepted.

Though Cook and his secretary had spent a month in Washington working on the problem, he refused to accept either compensation or reimbursement for his expenses. Let it be a contribution to the public interest, he said. Pleased by this response and the good work Cook had done, Meyer asked Secretary Glass to write Cook a thank-you letter. Cook hung the letter on his office wall until he was summoned, years later, before a Senate committee investigating Meyer's fitness to be governor of the Federal Reserve Board. Reckless politicians were charging that Meyer had put his brother-in-law on the WFC payroll. Cook's presentation of the letter left them in the ridiculous position of advertising his patriotism.

In those confused days between war and peace there was also crisis in the copper industry. With the signing of the armistice, the government canceled its copper contracts, despite the fact that it had been taking the entire supply. The price plummeted from twenty-six to eleven cents a pound and wages followed, under the terms of the labor contract. Trouble was brewing, especially among the immigrant workers in the Southwest. Meyer was asked to devise a solution because of his previous standing in the industry. His first step was to ask the employers to raise wages and give preference to married men and returning veterans. Having won some concessions from the companies, he joined with the Labor Department in calling a "peace" conference in Washington.

At one point he felt that his efforts were being undermined by Felix Frankfurter and the Labor Mediation Board. A telegram to his friend Frankfurter said bluntly: ". . . your action was based on opportunism and not on principle, and I consider that, having taken the stand you have, you have been negligent in discharging your responsibility. . . ."[3] Frankfurter stoutly defended his conduct.

When the management-labor conference met, Meyer pleaded for patience and cooperation to get the industry into operation on a peacetime basis. Development of new demands for copper, he said, depended largely on the construction industry, and construction was dependent on finance, which required confidence on the part of investors. If there is a lot of rioting, he said, there won't be any confidence, or investment, or demand

---

[3] Eugene Meyer to Felix Frankfurter, January 16, 1919.

for copper. One tough unionist from Arizona responded: "To hell with all this Mark Hanna full-dinner-pail stuff!" Frankfurter told Meyer that he had ruined the meeting.

In the later sessions, however, Meyer's disclosure of the companies' concessions produced a better feeling. He invited the principal contenders to lunch at his home, and Mrs. Meyer described the clash between "Jim" Lord of the American Federation of Labor and "Con" Kelly, president of Anaconda Copper, as "one of the most interesting scenes I have ever witnessed."[4] Following that session Meyer arranged a meeting with three members of the Cabinet, which produced an appeal to the President to clear the way for copper shipments to Germany and an agreement to speed orders for copper wire for telegraph lines. Before the conference ended, the companies had agreed to resume operations at 50 percent of capacity and to keep wages up in disregard of the lower contract scale. The conference voted hearty thanks to Meyer and others involved; the threatened explosion in the Southwest was averted. Mrs. Meyer recorded in her diary: "Dear old Euge felt once more the elation of good work well accomplished." Meyer and Frankfurter patched up their differences, and the latter wrote a thank-you note for the rebuke he had received:

> I am very grateful for the candor which made you say what you said. I concede the validity of your principle—meet and not dodge an issue, and when I say concede I mean that I see I did the unwise thing. But what is more important is that you should show the real friendship of saying an unpleasant truth to me.

Meyer's first step under the modified War Finance Act was to stimulate the organization of export financing corporations by the big banks. Europe was begging for American help. Baruch and Herbert Hoover were in Paris delving into postwar economic problems, and Meyer kept them informed of what he was doing. As transformation of the WFC progressed, Baruch asked Meyer to come to Europe and explain its operations. He sailed on June 1, 1919, and was soon caught in a whirl of luncheons, conferences, and reports from the peace commission. He met with the Supreme Economic Council and with many European officials seeking help for their countries.

Hoover gave a luncheon for Meyer with a group of English, French, and American officials seated at a round table. When all but the Americans had left, the newcomer was asked for his impression.

"I think the shape of the table here is wrong," he said. "You ought to have a long, narrow table with all the Americans on this side and all

---

[4] Agnes E. Meyer's diary, p. 116.

the foreigners on the other side. That's the economics of it. You sit around and let them tell us what to do. Why don't you take the lead and tell them what they should do and what we can do for them if they cooperate along lines that are practical?"

Another Meyer reaction was played up in *Figaro*. When a reporter for that newspaper asked for his comment on the Parisian scene, he answered: "Paris reminds me of San Francisco at the time of the earthquake and fire. Why? The people of San Francisco were all excited and worried about whether the city would ever be rebuilt; a conference to decide the future course was called; the bigwigs talked on and on about what should be done; at last E. H. Harriman arose and said: 'Stop talking and get to work!' The French people could do no better," Meyer concluded, "than follow Harriman's advice to San Francisco."

The United States Treasury representatives in Paris, Norman Davis and Thomas Lamont, were cool toward Meyer's mission, possibly foreshadowing a break that was soon to come. In a detailed report of his trip Meyer wrote: "Vance McCormick, Baruch and everybody else except the fellows from my own department are all right and want to help in every way."

With his sense of urgency heightened by a tour of the battlefields, Meyer went to London and outlined a plan under which the leading industries of Britain would join in issuing guaranteed five-year notes up to $600 million to finance imports needed for postwar recovery. Robert Brand of Lazard Brothers, Sir Richard Vassar-Smith of Lloyds' Bank, Frederick C. Goodenough of Barclays Bank, and others gave support to the idea. But some London financiers were still harboring prewar illusions. Sir Walter Leaf, chairman of the London County and Westminster Bank, became impatient with Meyer's argument that the pound would go down if Britain did not cushion the shock from the termination of American war loans.

"My dear fellow," Leaf remonstrated, "I've been hearing very much about how the pound was going down, but it hasn't, has it?"

"Not yet," Meyer said, "but it will."

With the pound demoralized, the New Yorker continued, food prices would rise and Britain would be in trouble. But the only response he could get from the irrepressible Englishman was: "We'll be lending *you* money very shortly." After one more try to alert the British to the new economic forces the war had set into motion—this time in a conference with Chancellor of the Exchequer Austin Chamberlain—Meyer sailed for home.

America was in a frenzy of inflation. Wartime savings and new installment credit were creating extraordinary demands, while supplies were scarce. In the resulting scramble, prices, wages, and profits mounted, and there was a boom in Wall Street. Meyer watched these gyrations with deepening concern. His countrymen were rushing into a fool's paradise. The worried financier embodied his fears in a letter to Senator Medill McCormick, even though he recognized that his warning would expose him to charges of having contributed to the collapse when it came. McCormick was calling for a report from the Treasury and the Federal Reserve Board as to what they were doing to keep down the cost of living. Up to that time nothing had been done.

Taking alarm from a rising public revolt against the high cost of living, the Wilson administration at last resorted to drastic action. The President had shifted his Secretary of Agriculture, David F. Houston, to the Treasury after Carter Glass had been elected to the Senate. A former university president from the South with limited experience in finance and with strong laissez-faire leanings, Houston set the country on a sharply deflationary course. Wilson's illness and subsequent incapacity left the new Secretary of the Treasury with almost a free hand. Federal Reserve discount rates were raised, and the economy, which had been enormously stimulated for war, was suddenly thrown into reverse, with little regard for the consequences.

Meyer too was working feverishly for adjustments to a peacetime economy, but he pleaded for gradualism and elasticity in making the necessary changes. "I hate to go downhill without brakes," he wrote to Gerard Swope. "I would also think it very poor policy to lock the wheels. The thing to do is to fight for the middle course." In line with that policy the War Finance Corporation, in the spring of 1920, approved loans totaling $150 million to aid the exportation of cotton, tobacco, copper, coal, and fabricated steel. But it was soon apparent that it was spinning its wheels, for the funds had to be obtained from a public offering of WFC bonds, and this offering required approval of the Secretary of the Treasury.

When Meyer sought a go-ahead signal for the bond issue, Houston indicated that he was thinking rather of terminating all the WFC's activities. Houston contended that, since the government was withdrawing from all its wartime involvement with private enterprise, an exception could not be made for the WFC. Exports had attained an unprecedented volume in 1919, he said, and were not in need of governmental aid. His chief interest seemed to be a scaling down of the high cost of living because of the presidential election in 1920.

Meyer replied that the amendment authorizing the WFC to make export loans had been passed and signed by the President after the armistice to meet a postwar emergency; that the emergency was still very real because no peace treaty had been signed and trade relations were chaotic. Some American products such as copper and cotton could not be contributing to inflation, he said, because they were not being absorbed by the domestic market; the great demand for them was in Europe. Private credit was not available in adequate volume for trade of this kind because of fluctuating exchange rates and unsettled political conditions. It was an ironic contest in which the spokesman for an internationalist Democratic administration held fast to laissez faire and an isolationist economic policy while a Republican—a former investment banker and student of William Graham Sumner—argued for continued governmental aid to international commerce.

As the struggle continued, Meyer appealed to Baruch and Under Secretary of State Frank L. Polk for support, but there was nothing they could do while the White House was a virtual vacuum. Then he tried to interest Houston in a conference to survey the domestic and foreign economic situations. That failing, he asked the Secretary to consult the congressional committee which had sponsored the legislation. By this time Meyer felt that the signs of an impending crash were unmistakable and urged that the WFC retain at least a semiactive status so that it could be revived if needed, but Houston replied that there was no danger of a crash.

Bowing to the Secretary's demands, the WFC finally "suspended" its export-lending operation in May 1920. Since Houston had the support of two other Democratic directors, there was nothing Meyer could do about it. He did succeed, however, in getting into the suspension resolution language which made it plain that the directors acted at Houston's request, and not on their own initiative. The Secretary tried to soften the blow by asking Meyer to become Assistant Secretary of the Treasury. Though personal relations between the two men were still amicable, Meyer declined because of his sharp dissent from the Houston policies. On May 17, he sent a letter of resignation to the President. It was neither bitter nor quarrelsome. Conscious of political differences, Meyer was loath to have anyone suppose that his leaving was a partisan gesture. In a letter to his fellow director, F. W. M. Cutcheon, however, he expressed grave fear that "we have been engulfed in a general wave moving in the direction of a narrow and selfish provincialism."

The White House accepted Meyer's resignation, effective May 31, with warm praise for his "effective leadership" of the WFC and his singular dedication to the public service in many assignments over a period of three crowded years. Once more he was free to give time to his family and private pursuits, but not for long. The nature of his leaving made a stormy sequel inevitable.

17 /

Lifeline for the Farmer

THERE WAS NO SADNESS IN THE MOOD OF THE MEYERS AS THEY returned to private life. "The Washington experience with its bigness and its novelty," Agnes wrote in her diary, "ends in a deep, grateful happiness." Both felt that, despite Eugene's wish for a longer public career, he had taken the right course. Agnes was passionate on the subject: "He must become dissociated from this rotten administration before it goes utterly to pieces." Both knew, moreover, that Washington was a place of continuous farewells. They went for a "last ride" along shady Rock Creek "to commemorate the joyous spring hours that we have had in that most lovely of parks." After several farewell parties and an afternoon at the circus with Alice Longworth, they turned their interests toward home, the children, and the farm—a prospect that Agnes characterized as "golden."

Yet private life was not the same as it had been before. Meyer had no strong yearning to return to investment banking. His basic interests continued to be oriented toward national affairs. The new image he had created in Washington was reflected in an invitation to be the principal speaker at the twenty-fifth reunion of Yale's Class of '95 and a request to aid the cause of Herbert Hoover in his pursuit of the Republican presidential nomination in 1920.

For a brief period Meyer toyed with the idea of buying the Missouri and Pacific Railroad because he thought he might have "some fun" running it. From Adolph Ochs came an invitation to join The New York Times organization and to acquire an interest in its preferred stock. For a moment this seemed very enticing indeed, but Meyer lost interest quickly when Ochs said, in response to a question, that he was thinking of Meyer in the business end of the paper.

William L. Ward, the enlightened boss of Westchester County, and Nathan L. Miller, soon to be governor of New York, took Meyer to the Republican National Convention in Chicago, where Miller was to nominate Hoover. All three were in agreement that Hoover would make a better president than Leonard Wood, Hiram Johnson, or Frank O. Lowden, who seemed to be the leading candidates. Meyer had no enthusiasm for Hoover, whom he regarded as a publicity-seeker, but he continued to work for him until the convention decided on Warren G. Harding. Though he "wasn't very happy" with this choice, Meyer felt that it was imperative for the country to turn away from the moribund Wilson administration.

During the campaign, the economic collapse that Meyer had warned against finally hit with a vengeance. The price of cotton collapsed from forty cents to fifteen, and was on the way to eight. Many other commodity prices slid below the cost of production. Business was sluggish, banks were jittery, and the great battle over the League of Nations plunged the country into confusion and bitterness. If Harding and his running-mate, Governor Calvin Coolidge, were nothing to cheer about, Meyer saw even less hope in the Democratic ticket—James M. Cox and Franklin D. Roosevelt. Cox he knew only slightly, and as for Franklin and Eleanor Roosevelt, he wondered why Agnes continued inviting them to dinner, "because I thought they were very dull people."[1]

Meyer was drawn into the campaign despite his original intention not to fight publicly with Houston. Under attack in the distressed farm belt, Houston struck back in a letter that was published in the *Financial Chronicle* on October 9. Acknowledging the spread of economic blight, he came close to saying that it was an inevitable consequence of war and nothing could be done about it. Meyer was fuming over this benighted view when he received a telegram from a friend of his War Industries Board days, George R. James of Memphis. Could not the desperate plight of agriculture be relieved, James asked, by reviving the export powers of the WFC? Meyer replied in a 3,000-word telegram that reviewed the history of the controversy and offered his help in moving the Treasury off dead center.

James organized a group of bankers, businessmen, and journalists in Memphis and arranged a meeting with Meyer in New York. About the same time the American Bankers Association was convening in Washington, and the Memphis group sought a place on the program for Meyer. Houston threatened to cancel his scheduled address if Meyer were allowed to speak. The Secretary was under mounting attacks from hostile farm groups calling for his impeachment and a march on Washington. A group of bankers organized a rival session at the Raleigh Hotel where Meyer answered Houston, declaring that the collapse of farm prices in America

---

[1] Dean Albertson's interviews with Eugene Meyer, p. 310.

and the hunger in Europe demanded rational use of governmental power to relieve both situations.

The bankers at the Raleigh passed a resolution directly appealing to Wilson for restoration of the WFC's export operations and asked Meyer to speak for the group at a Senate committee hearing in New York on the country's worsening economic problems. Meyer was thus deeply involved in a national debate on the use of governmental power to meet the emergency, a debate that ended with the election of Harding by an overwhelming vote. Houston probably contributed much to that outcome, even though the chief issue was United States adherence to the League of Nations.

After the election there was considerable talk of Meyer being named Secretary of the Treasury "because of his wide knowledge of the country's commercial activities."[2] But Harding's choice of Charles Evans Hughes for Secretary of State seemed to foreclose any possibility of awarding the second place in the Cabinet to another New Yorker. The Memphis *Commercial Appeal* and many of Meyer's friends then said that he would make "an ideal Secretary of Commerce," but that place went to Hoover. Meyer was asked to be Hoover's assistant secretary, but he declined in the belief that the War Finance Corporation would be revived and that he would be asked to head it once more.

Shortly after the election, the Senate Committee on Reconstruction and Production, with Senator Calder as chairman, began a tour of the country to investigate economic conditions. Meyer's campaign for restoration of the WFC won him an invitation to accompany the committee and sound out national sentiment on that issue. Meetings were held in Cleveland, Chicago, Des Moines, Omaha, Denver, Kansas City, St. Louis, Memphis, and New Orleans. Meyer bore down with special emphasis on the plight of 35 million people who drew their livelihood from cotton, insisting that their impaired purchasing power was a drag on the entire economy. After the Des Moines meeting and a luncheon attended by Henry C. Wallace, soon to be Secretary of Agriculture in the Harding Cabinet, the entire Calder committee embraced the Meyer thesis and made revival of the WFC its chief mission. The idea won hearty support, and resolutions endorsing it began to converge on the Treasury, but they made no impression on Houston. By this time Meyer had lost both patience with, and respect for, the Secretary. "Houston," he wrote to Leffingwell, "is one of those who would rather be wrong than change his mind. . . . I can forgive anything but this irresponsibility." Neverthe-

[2] New York *Evening Post*, December 31, 1920.

less, he called on Houston at the suggestion of a friend to report his findings in the West and South, only to find the Secretary's immovability further stiffened by bitterness.

Meyer went from Houston's office to Capitol Hill, where the House and Senate Committees on Agriculture were to hold joint hearings on means of relieving the farmer. Though he had intended only to listen, he was asked to be the first witness. Once more he described the consequences of postwar stagnation and pleaded for revival of the WFC. Senator Wadsworth recounted what Meyer had done for New York's Genesee Valley in wartime and asked if the solution in that case could be applied "at the level of the agricultural producer." Meyer replied: "The first step in doing a thing is to want to do it, and then you can find a way."

The following day Secretary Houston told the joint committee: "I know of no solution for the problem presented by falling prices." Senator George Norris asked Meyer if he cared to cross-examine Houston and William Harding of the Federal Reserve Board. Noting that everyone was tired and that most of the newspapermen had left, Meyer asked only a few questions and volunteered to return the following week. The committee so agreed.

En route to Mount Kisco for the weekend, Meyer lay awake in his Pullman berth mulling over the Houston testimony. If the issue were dramatized in human terms, he concluded, Congress might pass a resolution for revival of the WFC. The following day he drafted a statement that was presented to the joint committee on Monday. Imitating Wilson's "Fourteen Points," Meyer riddled the Houston testimony in "Thirteen Points of Error." His indignation reached still greater intensity in a letter to Franklin K. Lane, then treasurer of the European Relief Council. Sending a contribution of $2,000 in the name of "four happy, well-fed children," Meyer concluded:

> We accept the idea that in war life and property must be freely sacrificed to maintain a great principle. History records no precedent, however, for the wholesale sacrifices imposed upon the civilized world by the Secretary's present policies for the purpose of maintaining the petty platitudes of the outworn political economy which he professes.
>
> The cheeks of the children of Europe are gaunt with hunger, but the cotton seed that would furnish them with the needed fats is rotting in the fields of Mississippi; they walk in tatters, and the cotton fields are white with cotton it does not pay to pick. . . .
>
> The corn and wheat of our great granary states lie in the bins because the farmer cannot sell, in the present demoralized market,

without making himself a bankrupt, yet we are told by the head of finances in this country that "nothing can be done."

I should feel like a slacker for the rest of my life if I failed to lift my voice in protest against such an absurd and disgraceful admission.

"Man alive," Lane replied, "you talk as if you were in earnest and un-afraid—which is a glorious treat." There was some criticism of Meyer for personalizing the issue, and in later years he acknowledged that he had been overwrought at the time, but his indignation produced results. On December 13 both houses of Congress overwhelmingly passed a resolution directing the Secretary of the Treasury to revive the export loan activities of the WFC. One observer gave Meyer sole credit for the outcome, and congratulations flowed in from many sources.

But the fight was not over. Wilson was still inaccessible, and Houston could be expected to insist on a veto. Meyer went to see all the members of the Cabinet he knew and urged them to oppose a veto, which would probably be overridden if it came. All of them said that Wilson, a stickler for protocol, would follow Houston's advice. Not only did he do so; he also asked Houston to write the veto message and apparently sent it to Congress without change.[3] The reading of the message in the Senate interrupted a speech by Senator Pat Harrison, Democratic wheelhorse from Mississippi, who had just declared: "I pray to God that President Wilson does not veto the resolution." On the same day the Senate overrode the veto by a vote of 55 to 5, and the House followed suit a day later by 250 to 66.

Even this striking victory was not the end of the road. The New York *Financial America* attributed to bankers the conclusion that revival of the WFC was "unsound, unethical and uneconomic." Meyer was shocked by this reaction. The bankers could cripple the revived agency by refusing to cooperate with it, or their hostility could turn President-elect Harding against it. Meyer wrote to Harding soliciting his support of the congressional action but received a noncommittal reply.

A story in the *Wall Street Journal* of January 6, 1921, deriding the WFC so nettled Meyer that he went straight to the Ritz Tower apartment of his friend, publisher Clarence W. Barron. Barron was in bed under steaming blankets, a routine practice because of his excessive weight, but this did not inhibit a friendly battle of wits. In the course of their exchange of insults Barron said that Meyer was about to be "torn apart" by the

[3] David F. Houston, *Eight Years with Wilson's Cabinet*, Vol. II (New York: Doubleday; 1926), p. 110.

Chamber of Commerce of the State of New York which was meeting at noon. Had he not seen the report of the special committee appointed by the Chamber which blasted the WFC out of the water? Meyer had to confess that, although he was a member of the Chamber, he knew nothing of the report and had never attended a Chamber meeting, because he had never known it to do anything worthwhile in the public interest.

Rushing back to his office, Meyer found a copy of the report, signed by Thomas W. Lamont of the Morgan Company, Herbert K. Twitchell of the Chemical National Bank, James S. Alexander of the National Bank of Commerce, and Paul M. Warburg, former vice-governor of the Federal Reserve Board. The leading tycoons of Wall Street had denounced the WFC and urged the country not to "return to the apron strings of government." The argument seemed especially menacing because it was so close to the back-to-normalcy doctrine that Harding had been ardently preaching. Meyer decided that a frontal assault on the report was in order and induced W. Averell Harriman to join him in that venture.

As the two men stepped into the elevator at the Chamber of Commerce Building on Liberty Street, they met Warburg.

"I see, Mr. Warburg," Meyer began, "that you signed a report objecting to my recommendations about the War Finance Corporation."

"That's true," Warburg acknowledged.

"But I have a letter from you," Meyer continued, "strongly endorsing my position when I first started to stir up interest in reviving the corporation. How can you now support and sign a report to an opposite purpose?"

"Did I write you a letter?" the embarrassed banker asked.

"You did and I can show it to you," Meyer replied.

"Well," Warburg lamely admitted, "I didn't like the way you treated my friend, Secretary Houston. That's the reason."[4]

There was little time to reflect on this petty explanation of a report dealing with a vital national issue. The Chamber meeting began, and Lamont was soon asked to present his report. While acknowledging that Congress had already decided the issue by overriding the President's veto, Lamont asked the Chamber to receive and file the report because it contained a statement of basic principle. As the motion was seconded, Meyer was on his feet expressing fear that the filing of a report that had been widely distributed to the press would be construed to mean that the bankers of New York were unwilling to cooperate with an economic recovery measure that had been overwhelmingly passed by Congress. For

---

[4] Sidney Hyman's manuscript, "Life of Eugene Meyer," Part V, pp. 173–4.

this reason, he declared, "I move that the report be laid upon the table." Harriman seconded.

Having no familiarity with Roberts' Rules of Order, Meyer was quite unprepared for the action that followed. Warburg, flushed and excited, started to reply, but the chairman, Darwin P. Kingsley, cut him off with a ruling that a motion to "lay on the table" was not debatable. Meyer's motion then carried by a vote of 66 to 57; the report went into the ashcan. Meyer kept his surprise to himself, but he had learned for the first time the meaning of the potent phrase that had accidentally slipped off his tongue in a moment of excitement.

The press reported the meeting in terms of personal conflict, which the *Wall Street Journal* reduced to "MEYER DOWNS LAMONT." But it was no time for gloating. Meyer was mulling over means of shielding the WFC from any personal enmity that the incident might have aroused when Lamont called to say that he had had nothing to do with the writing of the report. Then Warburg called to say that, although he had written the report, others had changed it, and he was not responsible for its final form. The report had probably inspired much of the hostile New York comment on revival of the WFC, but the damage had been overcome by a fortuitous interment.

Harding lost no time in reappointing Meyer to the War Finance Corporation board. The Senate confirmed the nomination on March 14, 1921, and Meyer was again elected managing director, succeeding Angus W. McLean. The family settled in what Agnes called "a big, old-fashioned barn at 2201 Conn. Ave." The children were happy "in their semi-country life," she recorded in her diary, "and we are glad to be living together again." Washington's cosmopolitan atmosphere was particularly welcome "after the dullness of New York." We get a glimpse of the family at home in this period from Agnes's account of Eugene's "very nice" birthday party on October 31, 1921:

> The children recited pieces in French and German and gave him presents which they had made or bought for him out of their own money. I wrote him a letter which might have been entitled "To any man who is on the road to fame." In the evening we had a violin concert and Bill who had also been begging for a fiddle was promised that he should have one.

The first task at the WFC was to rebuild the organization, which had been reduced to caretaker status. The post of chief assistant to the managing director went to an able young administrator, Floyd R. Harrison, who had been assistant to Secretary of Agriculture Edwin T. Meredith. The Secretary had mentioned Harrison as a capable young man who was seeking a place in business. Meyer had gone to Capitol Hill to hear Harrison testify on the agriculture appropriation bill and had learned from Congressman James F. Byrnes that Harrison made a better presentation before the Appropriations Committee than any other department's spokesman. With that recommendation, Meyer had offered Harrison a place in his New York office on the theory that it is better to hire a good man when you find one than to hunt for one after a specific need has arisen. Before Harrison reported for duty, Meyer was back in the WFC and persuaded Harrison that he would get better training for business there than in New York.

Search for a general counsel turned Meyer's thoughts back to the House of Truth where he had met Gerard C. Henderson. He was located in New York where he was beginning to develop a private practice, and Meyer persuaded him to spend four months with the WFC, organizing its legal department. Actually Henderson remained more than three years as general counsel and was consulting counsel for another year. Henderson's untimely death from sinus thrombosis while mountain climbing, soon after he returned to private practice with former Governor Miller, would be a severe blow to his devoted friend at the WFC.

Additional legislation was necessary to equip the WFC for its new role, and it brought Meyer into his first collision with Hoover. The new Secretary of Commerce sought a number of changes in the bill without clearing them with either the WFC board or the White House. Meyer went to the President and asked whether he or Hoover was to guide the legislation. Harding said it was Meyer's responsibility, and, at the latter's request, promised to ask the chairman of the Banking and Currency Committee to ignore the Hoover proposals. Lobbying by the Hoover men nevertheless continued until the chairman denounced that interference. The incident served to alert Meyer to Hoover's penchant for meddling in affairs outside his jurisdiction.

Passing with little difficulty on Capitol Hill, Meyer's bill was signed by the President on August 24 and became known as the Agricultural Credits Act of 1921. Its chief purpose was "to provide relief for producers of and dealers in agricultural products." Although the name of the War Finance Corporation remained the same, it was transformed into a rescue mission for the nation's distressed farmers.

Meyer, Harrison, and Henderson spent September in the Middle West and Pacific Coast states explaining the new law to bankers and agricultural groups, establishing local agents, and surveying the credit needs of the farm belt. They frequently encountered skepticism. Was not the WFC just another political gesture? Meyer argued tirelessly that it was not. Dramatic proof of his words came at Salt Lake City where the sugar-beet industry was in dire straits. The inability of sugar factories to pay farmers for their beets had spread distress beyond the farm to merchants, laborers, banks—the entire economy. The WFC could not make loans to sugar factories, but it did lend $11,458,000 to a Sugar Beet Finance Corporation set up with the help of local banks. The sap of life began to flow once more within the industry, and every cent of the loan was eventually repaid. The *Deseret News* of Salt Lake City characterized the operation as "a splendid piece of financial work in which all concerned have cause for the utmost satisfaction."

Meyer insisted that the WFC must not become just a bail-out operation. Its loans had to be made on good security. Its function was to provide credit so as to allow farmers time to work out their problems and thus arrest the hemorrhage of distressed selling and mortgage foreclosures that were spreading chaos and demoralization.

On Meyer's return to Washington, spokesmen for the newly organized congressional farm bloc came in and asked some sharp questions as to what he had done. His response was that a new banking system that must operate all over the country cannot be put into operation overnight—that machinery had to be set up, forms prepared, procedures worked out; he had felt the need for personal acquaintance with the problems the WFC had to deal with. As the delegation prepared to leave, Meyer took over the questioning. "Now I want to talk to you," he said. "We want to cooperate with you, but we also want you to cooperate with us." The WFC would be working day and night, he continued, to speed aid to the agricultural areas. "If you have any complaints, don't get up on the floor of the House or Senate and attack this operation, because it is the white hope of the situation. Just appoint a committee to come down and tell me that I'm not making good. I will be very glad to resign and you can then have someone else appointed who can do the job." That candor helped to cement the good standing Meyer already had among both Republicans and Democrats on Capitol Hill.

Meyer made a similar appeal to a gathering of farm journal executives. The legislation, he insisted, was right. With vigorous action by the WFC and cooperation by all the agricultural interests, the job could be done. The farm journals gave him consistent support, except for *Wallace's Farmer* of which Henry A. Wallace, later President Franklin D. Roosevelt's Secretary of Agriculture and Vice-President, was then associate editor.

With his left hand, Meyer was fighting off the McNary-Haugen bill which was making substantial progress in Congress. That highly controversial measure was designed to subsidize wheat exports. Meyer concluded that Britain, our chief customer for wheat, would never permit the dumping of American wheat at less than market prices at the expense of Canadian and Australian growers. The McNary-Haugen bill, he insisted, was not only economically unsound; it was merely a publicity stunt cooked up by George N. Peek, president of the Moline Plow Company, and General Hugh Johnson, then president of the Moline Implement Company. The dynamic spokesman for the WFC was troubled because Harding's Secretary of Agriculture, Henry C. Wallace, was flirting with the McNary-Haugen idea. As the fight warmed up, Peek went to see Meyer and threatened that the farm organizations would withdraw their support from the WFC if he continued to fight McNary-Haugen, but Meyer replied that he would not be intimidated.

Meanwhile Harding's political debts to the "Ohio gang" became a problem. Trying to operate the WFC without partisanship, Meyer recommended that Angus McLean, a North Carolina Democrat, be reappointed a director when his term expired in 1922, but Harding insisted on naming one of his own camp followers, Fred Starek, a journalist-politician who seemed to be more interested in poker, dining, and wining than in the work of the WFC. Harrison often had to spend two hours a day getting Starek to sign official papers, and the board was sometimes embarrassed by Starek's failure to pay his debts.

But Starek was only a minor figure on the bandwagon of licentious living and corruption that was allowed to roll through Washington during the Harding administration. Like the Hugheses, the Mellons, the Hoovers, and other serious-minded people in governmental circles, the Meyers saw little of this seamy side of the Harding regime. They were not among the "ins." All official Washington, the Meyers included, went to the lavish parties given by Harding's friends, Edward B. (Ned) and Evelyn Walsh McLean, owners of the *Washington Post*, but these sybaritic affairs brought no intimacy with either the McLeans or the corruptionists who were pushing Harding toward a tragic end. One eminent Democrat, Mrs. George Bass, condensed her estimate of the Washington scene into this salutation in a letter addressed to Meyer: "The Most High and Puissant Over-Lord of the Far-Flung . . . Cattle Lands; Only Workable Brain among the Feeble-Minded Supporters of an Amiable and Spineless Administration."

Meyer worked hard to keep politics out of the WFC. Congressmen were not allowed to plead a case before the board, although they could communicate with individual members. When Senator Ralph H. Cameron of Arizona insisted on a hearing and came to a board meeting without an invitation, he was ultimately admitted but received an embarrassing reception.

"Now, Senator," Meyer began, "tell us what's wrong with your loan application."

The Senator sputtered and said nothing was wrong.

"Oh," Meyer replied, "I thought there must have been something wrong with it, because you felt it needed your personal presence to get it approved."

The disconcerted Senator left without making the argument he had apparently intended to present.

As the emergency in agriculture was eased, the WFC modified its policy from assistance in the financing of immediate exports to assistance in financing deferred exports. The change was made possible by the emergence of the co-ops. Aaron Sapiro had organized the Staple Cotton Cooperative Association, which obtained the first WFC loan under the new policy, and the pattern was widely followed. By the summer of 1923, the WFC had advanced $172 million to these co-ops in addition to the $182 million it had lent to rural banks. Meyer was building for the future. The grower associations were able to store crops at reasonable costs, thus promoting orderly marketing and more stable prices. Aid to the rural banks not only put credit at the disposal of many farmers who could not otherwise have been reached; it also helped to strengthen ties between rural banks and farmers for the period when the WFC would cease to operate. The policy was not to build a self-perpetuating empire but to facilitate the normal flow of credit to agriculture.

Extending credit to the depressed livestock industry proved to be a special problem. Livestock breeders need loans over much longer periods than other farmers and most businessmen, and the banking system was not well adapted to this kind of credit. Under the pressure of forced liquidations, the price of steers had dropped from $120 to $20 and the price of sheep from $20 to $3. Meyer addressed himself to the problem at a meeting of the American National Livestock Association in Denver in the summer of 1922, urging the industry to seek special legislation to overcome its handicap. In turn, he was asked to prepare a bill for that purpose in consultation with a livestock committee.

Following the Denver meeting, Meyer rejoined his wife and daughters Florence and Elizabeth who had been enjoying a "glorious camping trip" through Rito de los Frijoles Canyon in New Mexico. At Santa Fe, he received a telegram from Rosalie indicating that their mother had been ill but was feeling better. Two days later there were letters from Rosalie and his mother. The dutiful son sent his mother a telegram and then took his family to a Spanish-Indian fiesta. While there he was handed a telegram with alarming news. He obtained tickets for New York on the first train out of Santa Fe, but en route to the station from the lodge where the family had been staying a messenger delivered to him another wire saying his mother was dead. Harriet Newmark Meyer's tired heart, weakened by diabetes and nearly forty years of invalidism, had finally given way at the age of seventy-one.

At Newton, Kansas, the following evening Meyer learned from another telegram that, because of his father's distress, services for his mother and cremation of the body would take place on Friday morning before he could reach home. On Saturday, he joined the family circle at Port Chester where the chief concern now was to comfort his grieving father. The elder Meyers had celebrated their golden wedding in 1917 and Eugene Senior's eightieth birthday a few months before Harriet's passing. Despite his preoccupation with government business, Eugene had visited his parents frequently, and after his mother's death he remained a steadying anchor for his lonely father until his death on January 18, 1925.

Back at the WFC, Meyer concentrated attention on the livestock bill, which ran into competition from a measure prepared by the Joint Committee on Agriculture to deal with the same problem. The Meyer bill called for a system of federally incorporated, privately capitalized agricultural credit corporations that would be subject to examination by the Comptroller of the Currency. The joint committee proposed a system of intermediate credit banks to be capitalized by the government and financed by tax-exempt borrowings. In the struggle that ensued, Harding twice pledged his support to the Meyer version, but the President later suggested that Congress resolve its dilemma by passing both bills, and that course was followed. In practice, little was done under the Meyer system, which could not compete with the tax-exempt financing of the intermediate credit banks.

The Meyer family had advance notice of the Harding tragedy that was to plunge the nation into mourning in the summer of 1923. After the President had been stricken in San Francisco, following his return from Alaska, the Meyer family doctor, who had recently observed Harding at a political meeting, called Mrs. Meyer in Mount Kisco and said, contrary to the current bulletins about the President's condition, that he had suffered a stroke and would never return to Washington alive. The warning was prophetic. Vice-President Calvin Coolidge suddenly inherited the nation's problems, including a crop failure in North Dakota and adjacent states. The new President was scarcely sworn in when he was confronted by a clamor for an extra session of Congress.

Meyer felt that the politicians and grain interests were trying to dump their problem on the White House steps without adequately trying to help themselves. Before leaving for Atlanta on WFC business, he went to the White House and warned C. Bascom Slemp, the President's secretary, against what he believed to be a scheme to embarrass the new President. Slemp kept asking: "What can be done?"

Meyer replied: "Send a committee out there to investigate and tell them to take plenty of time so that you won't have to call an extra session of Congress."

Meyer said pointedly that he did not want to be on such a committee, but as he was catching the train out of Atlanta two days later he was handed a telegram asking him to be at the White House the following morning at eleven o'clock. Coolidge would accept no excuses; he wanted Meyer to head the investigating committee. "It's your idea," he said. "You know what ought to be done." When Meyer acquiesced, Coolidge asked him to take Frank Mondell, who had succeeded Dwight F. Davis on the WFC board, and a representative of the Agriculture Department. Meetings were held in many western cities. By the time the trip was over it was too late to call an extra session of Congress, and Meyer had convinced a large number of wheat growers that cooperative marketing was the best approach to their problem.

The authority of the War Finance Corporation to make loans for the benefit of farmers and livestock growers was extended three times and finally expired at the end of 1924. Meyer himself took the initiative in putting the agency into liquidation, moving adroitly one Saturday afternoon in early January 1925, after Congress had adjourned for the day. By this means he prevented the two members of the board who were trying to protect their $12,000-a-year jobs from running to Congress to stop the liquidation. Before Congress could intervene the following Monday the board had retired its capital stock (except for $1 million) and Meyer had handed the Treasury a check for $499 million. It was ultimately sent to the National Archives in the belief that it was the largest check ever drawn in the history of the world. What remained for the WFC was the collection of about $60 million in loans still outstanding. It had lent $700 million—$300 million for war purposes, $100 million to finance postwar exports, $300 million to aid farmers—without loss and with enough return to pay interest on the bonds it had issued and the funds obtained from the Treasury.

The achievement was widely acclaimed. David Lawrence, then president of the Consolidated Press Association, said the WFC had completed "one of the most amazing financial operations in the history of the U.S. government." A headline proclaimed: "WAR FINANCE BODY ENDS WORK IN BLAZE OF GLORY." William Hard, Washington correspondent and magazine writer, visualized the $700 million of public money that had been put into business and had come back—"every cent of it—and more" as a medal being pinned on Eugene Meyer. While many were saying he had saved American agriculture from disaster, Meyer himself was content to observe: "The war is over at last."

18 /

The Board Smells Sweet Again

As early as the summer of 1925, Meyer had become concerned about the operation of the intermediate credit banks. One major purpose of those banks was to provide "breeder loans" to livestock men, and that phase of their operation was being neglected, throwing a heavy burden on the WFC. Meyer urged Secretary Mellon, and through him the President, to fill a vacancy on the Federal Farm Loan Board, which supervised the intermediate credit banks, with a man who understood livestock finance. The place went to Albert C. Williams, who had demonstrated his capacity in the WFC. Williams soon told Meyer of negligence, sloth, nepotism, and outright violations of law within the Farm Loan Board. The inadequacies of the board were a serious blight on agriculture because it supervised the entire farm loan system.

Fearing a scandal that would hurt the Coolidge administration no less than the farmer, Meyer arranged for Williams to report his findings directly to Mellon, who was ex officio chairman of the Farm Loan Board. Mellon then named Assistant Secretary Charles E. Dewey to represent him at meetings of the board, and Dewey uncovered shady operations in the "Huston group" of joint stock land banks. The board ordered examination of the Huston banks, and the Department of Justice launched an investigation.

The corrective measures were attacked as a scheme to intimidate the farm loan system and extend Treasury control over it. The problem of the reformers was further complicated by the fact that inadequate records had been kept and even those on hand were in a state of disorder. With nearly eighty banks in the farm loan system, its five examiners could make only superficial examinations, and there appeared to be virtually no check on the farm loan associations through which the federal land banks made their loans. Months passed, therefore, with little progress in cleaning up the mess.

In June 1926, Mellon asked Meyer if he would accept a vacancy on the

Farm Loan Board and launch a thorough overhauling. Meyer replied that Williams was the only member of the board on whom he would be able to rely in such an undertaking. To do the kind of job that ought to be done, Meyer said, he would need at least another member favorable to his views, with reliance on Mellon as ex officio chairman to break three-to-three tie votes in case of necessity. Mellon thereupon challenged the competence of Farm Loan Commissioner Robert A. Cooper in a letter to Coolidge on June 16—a delicate matter because he was known to be a personal friend of Coolidge's. The President compromised by shifting Williams into the top position while leaving Cooper a member of the board. Williams and Dewey then came up with some improved forms for the system, and Mellon again sought Meyer's advice.

"These forms clear up many contradictions and sources of confusion," Meyer concluded. "But your trouble isn't printed forms. Your trouble is people."

"I can't do anything more about it," Mellon sighed.

In January 1927, Guy Huston and five others were indicted by a federal grand jury in St. Paul on charges growing out of their operation of the Southern Minnesota Joint Stock Land Bank. Several receiverships in this banking system were to follow, thus intensifying pressures for a house-cleaning, but Mellon's sponsorship of a bill to bring all farm loan bank examinations under supervision of the Treasury gave the exploiters an opportunity to scream that the Treasury, often interpreted to mean Wall Street, was trying to take over the farmer's credit system.

Shortly after Congress adjourned in March, Mellon asked Meyer if he would accept the farm loan commissionership with two like-minded men on the board. Meyer replied that conditions in the farm loan system had disintegrated a good deal since he had made his first offer. With Mellon in no position to break tie votes in the board, since he was about to leave for Europe, Meyer said he would need two new members besides himself and Williams. Smiling wryly, Mellon yielded to the new terms and left on his trip.

Rumors as to what was afoot leaked to the press and caused a hot national debate. The Atlanta *Constitution*, the Kansas *Union Farmer*, and many other journals welcomed the idea that Meyer would head the farm loan system, because of his wide experience and the good work done by the WFC. But columnist O. M. Kile reported that farm leaders were indignant over the proposal; the St. Paul *Pioneer Press* said that such an appointment for Meyer would be a "political blunder" that would be costly to the President; the *National Farm News* expressed fear that the proposed shake-up would "destroy" the Farm Loan Board as an effective agency of farm credit. Charles Michelson of the New York *World* interpreted it as a move to "take the minds of farmers off the McNary-Haugen bill" and forecast a fight against Meyer's confirmation by the Senate.

While that fight was warming up, the Kansas City Joint Stock Land Bank went into receivership with $50 million in bonds outstanding. The collapse came just after the bank had been given a clean bill of health by examiners of the farm loan system that Meyer's critics had been praising. The White House took advantage of the occasion to announce recess appointments for Meyer as farm loan commissioner and two of his trusted associates at the WFC, Floyd R. Harrison and George R. Cooksey, as members of the Farm Loan Board. Cooper, Edward E. Jones, and Elmer Landes had resigned. Williams had shifted from the top position to membership on the board, and two old-line members, John H. Guill and Lewis H. Pettijohn, retained their posts. Meyer was clearly in command.

Despite the evidence of disintegration within the farm loan system, the Meyer appointment brought a good deal of grumbling. There was widespread repetition of the superficial assumption that "Wall Street" was invading the sacred precincts of farm finance. William Hard tried to clear up this misconception in one of his columns. "President Coolidge," he wrote, "has simply taken the most experienced financier in Washington to clean up a complicated and perilous financial situation. That is all; and it has nothing in the wide, wide world to do with 'Wall Street.'" Yet gunning for Meyer continued through the summer and fall. Some who recognized his eminent qualifications seemed nevertheless irritated because agricultural finance was to be directed by a Jew, a millionaire, and a non-farmer.

The task that Meyer took over proved to be monumental. As head of the Farm Loan Board, he supervised a conglomerate consisting of twelve intermediate credit banks, fifty-two joint stock land banks, twelve federal land banks, and 4,670 National Farm Loan Associations, with assets in excess of $2 billion. Although it was supposed to be a going concern, many units within the system had to be rebuilt while day-to-day operations continued.

The files that the new board inherited were virtually useless. Minutes of the board containing its policies and rules for the previous decade were an unbound heap of paper without an index. The bylaws of some of the banks and associations were missing. As the board had no general counsel, the land banks had differed widely in what they approved as collateral for farm loan bond issues. In some cases delinquent mortgages had been accepted as security, and in one instance extensive losses had resulted from loans improperly granted on cut-over timberland. Another notorious case involved the sale of 114 farms that had come into the possession of a joint stock land bank to a single bank speculator at 50 percent of what the bank had lent on them. Some of the lending units in the system had never been examined; accounting methods were often chaotic; interest charges on mortgages were sometimes higher than the law allowed. The Louisiana Federal Land Bank had passed out thirty-year loans of $100 to anyone requesting the same on the ground that this was "the first Yankee money to be on hand in Louisiana since reconstruction days."

One of Meyer's first moves was to name Chester Morrill secretary and general counsel to the board. Morrill brought order into the board's files and organized a legal staff that redrafted the board's rules and regulations. The examining and appraising divisions of the Farm Loan Bureau were reorganized and their work coordinated; a uniform accounting system was installed in all the operating units; bank examinations were stepped up in accord with the law and irregularities were systematically dealt with instead of being concealed; a statistical division was created to give the board an accurate reading on what the system was doing.

Emergencies nevertheless continued. The Milwaukee Joint Stock Land Bank went into receivership on July 1, 1927. The joint stock land banks in Cincinnati and St. Paul were also in trouble, and the intermediate credit bank in South Carolina had sustained losses of some $1.3 million. Fear spread that disclosure of these conditions would undercut investor confidence and bring about a collapse of the system. Meyer came under pressure, even before the first of these misfortunes was known to the public, to stem the receding tide of confidence by reassuring statements. On the political front he was importuned by Senator Joseph T. Robinson of Arkansas and on the financial front by George W. Norris, governor of the Philadelphia Federal Reserve Bank. Knowing that mere words could not wipe out the consequences of bad banking, Meyer replied to Robinson: "I wish I could feel justified in saying that there will be no loss to the bondholders. I am really not in a position, however, to make such an unqualified statement, for I do not know at this time what the final outcome will be." To Norris he pledged only that each cancerous situation would be cleared up as promptly as possible.

More troublesome interference with the clean-up operations came from higher sources. The farm loan commissioner whom Coolidge had recently ousted, Robert A. Cooper, asked Meyer to approve an arrangement under which he (Cooper) would appear before the new board as counsel for a group of joint stock land banks. Cooper added that the President saw no objection to the arrangement and would soon speak to Meyer about it.

Then came a letter from Coolidge to Meyer saying that he had told Cooper "I felt sure you would be pleased to assist him in any way you could." Meyer took the problem before the board and found that it was no more disposed to tolerate such a conflict of interest than he was. Aside from the implication that certain banks wished to employ Cooper because of his inside information, the law forbade any former officer of the government to act as counsel or agent of any private interest having business with the branch of the government where he had served for two years after his departure.

When the board rejected Cooper's scheme, he complained to the President, and Meyer was asked to call at the White House. Coolidge was playing the political game, but he took no offense when Meyer reminded him that he himself had found it necessary to fire Cooper and that morale in the organization would be shattered if the President should direct the board to accept this kind of unethical, if not illegal, arrangement. Before the interview ended, Coolidge said he would back the decision of the board and invited Meyer to call on him at the "summer White House" near Rapid City, South Dakota, if he should find himself in the vicinity. Meanwhile, the President suggested, Meyer could carry any problem that might arise to Senator Curtis of Kansas.

The President's departure did not dispose of the Cooper business. Slemp called from the White House and wanted to know what had been done about Cooper. Meyer answered that he thought he had an understanding with the President that the board could not do what Cooper wanted. Nevertheless, Meyer took the issue to the board again, obtained a reaffirmation of its previous decision, and wrote the President about it. Then he reviewed the entire farm loan problem with Curtis and incidentally brought in the Cooper request. Curtis agreed with the position of the board and volunteered to telegraph his view to Coolidge. Meyer suggested instead a long letter to the President. "And take your time about it," he added, "since I'm not going to give way on this point even if it means my resignation as commissioner."

When Meyer did call at Coolidge's vacation spot later in the summer, he was asked to stay for lunch and a private chat with the President. As the other guests departed, the atmosphere was heavy with silence, as if each was loath to say what was on his mind.

"That was quite a letter you got Charlie Curtis to write me," the President finally said.

"I didn't see the letter," Meyer truthfully replied, "but I hope it satisfactorily explained why the Farm Loan Board could not give its consent to what Cooper wanted to do."

Coolidge managed a quizzical smile. He may have been amused by the fact that the only trouble at the Farm Loan Board that Curtis had found it necessary to write him about was the trouble he himself had caused. In any event, it was evident that this board would not bow to a presidential wish that was too indefensible to be made a command. The subject was never mentioned again.

Meyer continued on good terms with Coolidge and, despite the foregoing incident, considered him "the most underestimated of all the Presidents." Indicative of their easy relationship was Meyer's response when Coolidge casually invited the Meyers to come to dinner after they had stopped their car on Pennsylvania Avenue to greet him as he was out for a stroll. "Oh, I'm terribly sorry," Meyer replied, "but we have a long-standing engagement for dinner with our children tonight." As soon as they were out of the President's hearing, Agnes chided Eugene: "You can't refuse an invitation from the President." "But I just did," he replied.

The dismissal of several incompetents from the Farm Loan Board raised a storm on Capitol Hill. Senator Kenneth McKellar declared that he would not for a moment stand for such "political persecution." At his request, Senator W. Cabell Bruce took advantage of his friendship with the Meyer family to protest against the dismissal of good Democrats and to accuse Meyer of being a "patronage hound" in the services of Senator Reed Smoot, an influential Republican. In response, Meyer offered proof that a protégé of Smoot's had been dismissed along with the McKellarite.

Another fracas followed the Farm Loan Board's refusal to appoint a political ally of Senator Duncan U. Fletcher's as president of the federal land bank in Columbia, South Carolina. The board felt that the man's previous service as superintendent of Florida prisons had not necessarily qualified him to run a bank. Fletcher retaliated by launching a furious campaign to deny confirmation to Meyer, Harrison, and Cooksey, whom he denounced as "men from Wall Street, none of whom has the slightest knowledge of agricultural needs."

Senator Smith W. Brookhart also complained that Wall Street had captured the farmer's credit system, but the myth of Wall Street gouging the farmer took a rude jolt when the Farm Loan Board called the heads of the land banks to Washington to discuss their projected $30-million bond issue in September 1927. Some of the presidents felt that the 4.5 percent interest paid on previous issues of this sort (the funds were used for farm mortgages) would have to be raised. Meyer insisted that the 4.5 rate was already too high for tax-exempt bonds and that the interest should be reduced to 4 percent, which would be the lowest in the history of the farm loan system. After much discussion, Meyer was authorized to test his contention that the market would absorb the bonds at the lower rate.

Calling a meeting of the chief dealers in federal land bank issues, Meyer argued not only for the lower interest rate but also for a clear statement in the descriptive circulars that these so-called instrumentalities of the United States were secured by mortgage holdings of the banks and not by the federal treasury. There was stiff opposition on both points, but the bankers ultimately yielded, and the $30-million bond issue at 4 percent was bought by investors within an hour on October 24. Other bond issues followed at 4 percent, with the result of substantially lowering the interest farmers paid on their mortgages. It was a mark of confidence in the rehabilitation of the farm loan system that was still far from being completed.

The fight against confirmation of the new board members came to a head in a meeting of the Senate Banking and Currency Committee on January 12, 1928, eight months after the recess appointments had been made. Senators Fletcher and Brookhart blocked a move to report out the nominations without further delay, and Meyer was summoned for questioning the same day. Fearful that a candid disclosure of all the weaknesses and mismanagement he had found might undermine the confidence that was beginning to congeal around the system once more, Meyer frequently asked that his testimony be off the record. What went into the record was largely intracommittee wrangling and rambling questions by Fletcher and Brookhart designed to embarrass Meyer. At one point Senator Glass complained that not a single question had been asked "relevant to the proposition of the fitness of these members." Harrison and Cooksey had not even been asked to appear. There was one light moment in the dreary session, however, when Meyer, in response to a question as to what he knew about "practical farming," admitted that he did not support himself on his farm in Westchester County. "The ground is so rocky," he said, with gross exaggeration, "that the only way one could plant it would be to ascend in an airplane and shoot the seed into the soil with a rifle."

The opposition having produced nothing of substance, the three nominations were confirmed by an overwhelming majority. Meyer's demonstrated capacity to hammer down interest rates on farm mortgages had given a ridiculous twist to the campaign to save the farmer from the toils of "Wall Street." In this instance the recess appointments, which had given the new board a chance to demonstrate what it could do before the Senate voted, proved to be a shrewd maneuver.

There remained to the Farm Loan Board the drudgery of extending and institutionalizing its reforms. Since the board was not a bank and did not exercise dictatorial powers over the numerous lending agencies in the system, it often had to operate through subtle influence and indirect power. Direct emergency steps were necessary where banks faced receivership, but in most cases the influence of the new board on the system came through education of existing personnel in sound principles of agricultural credit.

Meyer's faculty for inspiring loyalty and devotion on the part of his employees was affirmed by the Farm Loan Board's chief examiner. That official was called into Meyer's office and asked about his financial situation because he was shabbily dressed. When the examiner confessed that he had accumulated debts of $750 in his struggle to support his wife and seven children on a modest salary, Meyer raised his pay and wrote him a personal check for $1,000 to be repaid without interest whenever the employee felt able to do so. That kindness—typical of Meyer's action in many similar cases—was still remembered three decades later.[1]

At the end of two years as Farm Loan Commissioner, Meyer asked to be relieved as of May 10, 1929, because the clean-up operation was well advanced and he did not like the agricultural policy of the new Hoover administration. Hoover accepted the resignation with thanks to Meyer for having strengthened the system and restored confidence. William Hard, writing in the Washington *Star*, gave Meyer credit for having completed a "gigantic and terrific" purifying process without making any noise about it. The Federal Farm Loan Board, he wrote, "smells very sweet again." Many farm journals expressed their gratitude, in contrast to their grumbling when Meyer was appointed: ". . . a fine talent for generalship . . . an almost irreparable loss . . . public confidence is now at high tide." A few Meyer-baiters in Congress were still vocal, but they were a small minority. The former Wall Street banker had so thoroughly identified himself with the interests of the farmer that he had been frequently mentioned for Secretary of Agriculture in Hoover's Cabinet-picking days and later for director of Hoover's farm board. But the President was thinking of Meyer in a very different capacity.

[1] V. R. McHale to Eugene Meyer, December 28, 1954.

19 /

In the Toils of Depression

By 1929 THE MEYERS HAD BECOME AN INTEGRAL PART OF THE Washington scene. Eugene was known as a man of ideas, a brilliant conversationalist, and a generous benefactor. Agnes was one of the city's most popular hostesses; she had buttressed her standing in cultural circles by publishing a book on Chinese art[1] dealing chiefly with paintings in her own collection; her friendships in the literary world had been greatly extended. A society editor found it "good news indeed" that the city was not to lose the Meyers—"one of the most stimulating and interesting families ever associated with the official group."

The standing of the Meyers in the social world came sharply into the limelight because the most notorious feud of the Hoover administration broke out at one of their lavish parties. They had invited 150 guests to dinner and several hundred more to dance later in the evening. Their home and garden in Crescent Place were beautifully decorated for the occasion, with eerie illumination, crystal fountains playing, and the trees "blooming" with great clusters of colored balloons. Most of Washington's *grand monde* was present, except the highest-ranking invited guests. Agnes had carefully arranged four tables, with herself at one, Eugene at another, Vice-President Charles Curtis at a third, and his official hostess (Mrs. Dollie Gann) at a fourth, so as to blur the question of highest official rank. But Speaker Nicholas Longworth felt slighted, and his wife, Alice Roosevelt Longworth, sent regrets, which produced a furor that also kept the Vice-President and his hostess at home. For months after the event the social caldron bubbled with the rival claims of the two families to precedence.

The parade of the great through the Meyer homes in Washington and at Mount Kisco was not merely social ritual. When H. G. Wells was

[1] *Chinese Painting as Reflected in the Thought and Art of Li Lung-mien* (New York: Duffield; 1924).

a dinner guest, the conversation was largely about the British monetary system, with the host dominating the discussion. On other occasions, as when the guest was the French ambassador and poet, Paul Claudel, Agnes claimed her hours of glory. Whether the guest of honor was a justice of the Supreme Court, an eminent professor, a foreign statesman, diplomat, businessman, government official, or journalist, the conversation was likely to range over a broad field. Debate was often intense, and it was not unusual for Eugene and Agnes to be on different sides. After a weekend at Mount Kisco, Claudel said that he "felt like a cat that had been thrown into an electric fan."

Mrs. Meyer was deeply involved in many activities outside the home. She was chairman of Westchester County's pioneer Recreation Commission which, largely through her efforts, dedicated its $1-million recreation center in White Plains in 1930 with a music festival presented by twenty-one choral groups. She became widely known as an authority on recreation, and the New York *Evening Post* gave her credit for making White Plains "the music center of the metropolitan area and even of the Empire State." Eugene often taunted her at the dinner table by telling the children, with mock solemnity: "You must understand, my dears, that Mother is teaching little children to play." The youngsters would then shout in unison: "How about a little recreation at home?"[2] But there was evidence of appreciation for her work in the community. In later years John Lord O'Brian, eminent Washington lawyer, would describe her as "a great lady whose whole mature life has been devoted to expanding the horizons of the human spirit."

At home Agnes was firmly in control of the housekeeping. Eugene once complained that he felt like a boarder in his own house, but the complex pattern of living they had established made it necessary for Agnes repeatedly to achieve engineering miracles to keep the family functioning in high gear. Her task was greatly complicated by the frequent moves from Mount Kisco to New York (or Washington) and back again. When the children were small these ordeals involved transportation in the family limousine full of children, nurses, dogs, birds, goldfish, milk bottles, diaper pail, and so forth. If the road were muddy, the limousine would invariably get stuck, and the entire ménage would have to be unloaded while the chauffeur put rocks and planks under the wheels to get it started again. After one of these trying moves to New York, Agnes entertained twenty-four guests at a formal dinner the same evening. It seemed a triumph over almost insuperable obstacles, but when a beautiful salmon was served

[2] Agnes E. Meyer, *Out of These Roots, The Autobiography of an American Woman* (Boston: Little Brown; 1953), p. 165.

as the first course, Eugene, at the other end of the table, complained: "Ag, you know how I hate salmon."

Seven Springs Farm was a beehive of well-organized activities. Meyer held the children to strict rules, requiring their presence at the breakfast table on time, after having made their beds. Breakfast was a time for reporting to Father how each child was doing in school or in other activities. Mrs. Meyer seldom came down to breakfast. After seeing Father off to the office, the children had lessons from 9 A.M. until noon—chiefly arithmetic and French taught by Mlle Otth, a Swiss governess. Later Mlle Meyer, who had been brought from France to make French a second tongue in the family, drilled the children in language, history, and literature. On weekends the routine was riding and swimming in the morning, tennis and more swimming in the afternoon, and resting in the garden before dinner. Meyer played tennis with the children and guests. Agnes proved to be a whiz at baseball.

In its heyday the Meyer farm was almost a little village. Charles Ruthven was overall foreman; John Commons ran the farm; Al Phillips was in charge of the chauffeurs and automobiles. Members of the staff and their families—often a total of twenty-four persons—lived on the farm, and all the children played together in democratic fashion. To most observers, life on the high bluff above Lake Byram was the acme of luxury, but when the Meyers returned from their annual visit to the E. H. Harriman mansion, Eugene was wont to say that it made his house "look like a shanty."

Summer on the farm was usually broken up by an extended pack trip, cruise, or European excursion to get the children "out of the groove of conventional living." When Florence was eleven and Elizabeth nine, Agnes took them on a "hair-raising" pack trip through the Jemez Mountains of New Mexico. Two years later Bill (Eugene III) and Mlle Meyer joined the trio in a "perilous expedition" through the Kern and Kings River Valley of California. The family rule was that no child under nine could go on these trips. Kay joined the group in 1926 for a jaunt in the Canadian Rockies. Meyer was sometimes lured into fishing with his family, but he found excuses to avoid the more strenuous expeditions.

In alternate years there were cruises. On one of these the family used Felix Warburg's "marvelous schooner," the *Carol*. Two years later when they cruised up the coast of Maine on the *Kalmia*, a 110-foot motorboat, Eugene found amusement in notifying friends along the way what time he would dock in their harbor. As the captain maneuvered the *Kalmia* toward Edward G. Lowry's dock, Eugene, watch in hand, shouted to his waiting host above the clanking of the anchor that he was within thirty-five seconds of being on time. The excursions in Europe included visits with relatives and artist friends of the family as well as sightseeing. Agnes carefully supervised the viewing of art galleries, telling the children not to look until she gave the word, so as to minimize bewilderment from too many visual impressions.

The mainspring of the Meyers' intense activity was competition. It started with the rivalry between Eugene and Agnes themselves. Symbolic of this relationship was their endless domino game, later changed to gin rummy. At Mount Kisco two big chairs and a card table in front of the fireplace bore evidence of the intermittent contest. At Crescent Place the game was played in the library between the fireplace and the window, but it was also resumed on trains, in hotels, or any other suitable place. The score was kept on a lifetime basis, and sometimes one player would be thousands of points ahead of the other. The children were often fascinated kibitzers, and Elizabeth once described the game as "not a time-passing gimmick" but "a joyous confrontation looked forward to by all, and often embarked upon after mobs of guests had departed, and we all settled down for fun by ourselves."

Agnes relished her victories and often had long winning streaks. When chance ran against her and Eugene forged ahead with deceptive chatter and magician-like manipulation of the cards, she would exclaim, "Isn't he wicked?" as if noticing his ploys for the first time. That seemed to be part of his reward for winning. The game highlighted their contrasting personalities and sharply differing techniques but also evidenced their continuing disposition to function as partners in the game of life.

Forgetting his own irritation when his father had expected him to be first in everything, Meyer drilled a competitive spirit into his children. Whether it was tennis, grades in school, or conversation, they were expected to win or excel. As a means of helping the children think for themselves, they were encouraged to participate freely in the debates that swirled through the home whether or not guests were present. When necessary to maintain a semblance of order, Meyer would intervene and give each child a chance to express his or her views. As the children grew older, his challenges and sallies would often be greeted by boos and hilarious laughter. On one occasion he put a sign on the breakfast table: "Even fathers can sometimes be right." Yet neither parent took time to teach the children the routine mechanics of living, and Father's goading in the direction of success was often undercut by Mother's penchant for criticism and belittlement of what they did.

Everyone closely associated with Meyer was a victim of his incurable teasing, which took many forms. Desperate for money, Elizabeth once wired from college: "Allowance or bust!" The reply from her father was simply: "Bust." Lowry wrote that he was about to undergo an operation for appendicitis. "I always had a feeling," Meyer replied, "that something in you ought to come out; that it wasn't doing you or anyone else any good. At last the doctors have agreed with my diagnosis."

Katharine consulted her father about a stock she owned: should she sell it or keep it now that a profit was in sight? "You've got to start making decisions of this sort for yourself," he said, but he accommodatingly reviewed the pertinent facts about the stock. "I guess I'll keep it," Kay then concluded. "Many people lose money," her father replied, "by being too greedy." "Well, then," she said on the basis of that hint, "I guess I'll sell it." "Others have lost a lot of money," he teased, "by being greedy too soon."

The Alaska Juneau gold mine became a source of exasperation as well as mirth. As a Christmas present Meyer offered his children a choice between $100 and 100 shares of Alaska Juneau, and they all took the stock. From time to time he told them that the mine had been flooded by seawater or visited by some other catastrophe. One night when Herbert Hoover, then Secretary of Commerce, was a guest in the home Meyer said that the price of Alaska Juneau had risen by five points. The children cheered. But then he confessed that he had previously sold their shares. This brought screams and shrieks from Bill and his sisters. Hoover was flabbergasted. The clamor continued until Meyer reimbursed the children for their loss, but Alaska Juneau never emerged from the category of a costly family joke.

In theory the Meyer children were wealthy because of the trusts their father had set up for them soon after their births. Actually, however, they knew nothing of the trusts when they were young and could draw no income from them until age twenty-one and no capital until age thirty. In grammar school they had allowances for minor incidentals and in college "clothes allowances" intended to cover travel and minor items as well. Despite their opulent surroundings, the children were taught to abhor waste. There was a frenzy in the family about turning off lights when not in use.

Meyer wrote to his friend Fred H. Bixby on October 15, 1929:

> We spent the first part of the summer abroad, because my wife wanted to have her bust done by a sculptor in Paris. Then we spent a few weeks on the farm, where I tried to renew my youthful days with the result that I cut my head open on the springboard in the swimming pool and crashed a couple of ribs on the tennis court. After that—here comes the worst—I bought a small ranch in Wyoming, near Jackson Hole, and am going to run a few cattle. . . .

Florence is at college in Bryn Mawr; Elizabeth is starting in at Vassar and having a great swirl there; and Bill is still with us before starting at Taft next year.

Purchase of the Red Rock Ranch on Crystal Creek stemmed from a conversation with Ruth Hanna McCormick. Meyer complained to her one day about Agnes's dangerous pack trips. What he wanted, he said, was a ranch where he could ride into the mountains but return at night to a hot bath and a decent meal. "I know just the place for you," she said, describing a former dude ranch near her own in the Tetons. "Buy it for me," Eugene said. Within a week he owned, sight unseen, a 600-acre cattle ranch.

The bust referred to in his letter is a classical likeness made by Charles Despiau, a pupil of Rodin. Agnes thought the "reality" of the bust was "somewhat appalling" and tried to conceal the fact that she had posed for Despiau from her modernistic sculptor friend Constantin Brancuşi, because of the intense hostility between the two schools; but a friend inadvertently let the secret out, and Brancuşi looked at her as if she had "driven a dagger into his heart." As they parted, he threatened: "I'll show you what a portrait of you is really like." The result was a black marble abstraction which he called "La Reine Pas Dédaigneuse," but which the children scornfully dubbed "Agnes's Knee."

The Meyers often visited Brancuşi in Paris, and he was a guest in their household on many occasions. The children watched with fascination while he worked in the garden at Mount Kisco, shaping a massive block of oak into a base for the white marble "Bird in Flight" that Meyer had purchased. As the work progressed he joked and talked profoundly of the relation between nature and art. The bond of friendship he established with the younger generation became evident when Elizabeth visited an exhibition of his work at the Brummer Gallery. A couple unknown to her was moving from piece to piece with smirking comments about each. Standing before the black marble "La Reine," the man said to his companion: "Now what in hell do you suppose *that* is?" Unable to contain her indignation any longer, Elizabeth wheeled around to face them and haughtily interjected: "That, sir, is my *mother!*"

Brancuşi was present at a gay luncheon party in the Meyer home on Connecticut Avenue which ended with a series of performances by various guests. Someone demanded that Meyer perform, but how? What could a banker or government official do in that artistic atmosphere? *"Mais c'est le patron!"* Brancuşi shouted. *"Il va jeter de l'argent à la foule."* Responding to the challenge, Meyer hopped onto the sofa, reached into his pockets, and threw bills and coins in every direction, while the guests, along with the children, screamed and gathered up the booty.

Agnes's infatuation with the arts, her zest for life, and her romantic fixations contributed much to what she called "the perpetual ferment" that enlivened the family atmosphere. She was "haunted by beauty of every kind" and by enchanting male companionship. At dinner parties she unashamedly stood by the door as the men returned after their smoking interval and picked off the most alluring male. "To have a brain and to be a woman is very often to be at war with one's self," she wrote in her diary, "but oh, the exquisite compensation when the whole machinery functions together—when in short the rare man happens along who is big enough to integrate our whole being." In her early days in Washington she enjoyed "sweet rides" with Herbert White, and after death removed the first object of her art-oriented adoration, Charles Freer, she spent sentimental interludes with Shrinvasi Sastri, a sensitive Indian diplomat. Her diary recording one of his many visits tells us that they "journeyed through leagues of emotion together." When Sastri called to say goodbye, their "few hurried moments of conversation" were interrupted by her daughter Florence, who came into the room and said: "Daddy wants you to know that he is home"—at which "both laughed appreciatively."

In 1929 it was Ambassador Claudel who was putting her soul on the rack and stretching it "to the limit of its capacities." Their first meeting at a dinner party had produced a profusion of sparks, but a "passionate friendship" soon developed as the ambassador-poet launched an intense campaign to convert his new friend to Catholicism. For several months Agnes was "torn to pieces" by the "problem of body and soul"[3] that Claudel kept foremost in her consciousness. Though she clung steadfastly to her Protestantism and her pragmatic belief in social work, both of which were obnoxious to Claudel, their friendship surmounted all differences, and Agnes described it as "one of the real inspirations of my life." Claudel spent weeks at Mount Kisco, and when Agnes last went to see him in his château near the Swiss border, ten years after he had left Washington, both wept for joy.[4]

While this extramarital romanticism contributed to the lightning that flashed and the thunder that reverberated through the Meyers' household, it did not destroy the dependency of each upon the other. There were still numerous amenities in their life together. On one of their many European

[3] Agnes E. Meyer's diary, p. 390.
[4] *Out of These Roots*, p. 181.

jaunts, Agnes recorded in Paris: "Eugene enjoying himself thoroughly in England, Florence ecstatic about Constantinople and everybody well and happy at home. What a healthy, exuberant, joyous lot we are."

For Eugene, however, relaxation came at rare intervals. The months following his resignation from the Farm Loan Board were one of the few periods in his lifetime when he could loaf, and for a while he resented efforts to get him into harness again. Brandeis put heavy pressure on him to head a delegation that would study economic and industrial possibilities in Palestine for a year and then raise $25 million in the United States to finance the program. Meyer replied that his twelve years of government service had earned him the right to a vacation and time with his wife and children. The argument waxed hot but did not erode the friendship of the two men. Meyer later told Norman Hapgood he was so fond of Brandeis that he enjoyed "being roasted by him better than I enjoy being patted on the back by some others."

But the flow of events toward the precipice of 1929 left no possibility that Meyer could remain on the sidelines. As early as May 29, 1928, he wrote to Edward G. Lowry: "This country has gone a little crazy on speculation. . . ." From that period on, he warned many friends of the approaching danger, and some of them, including Louis S. Cates, president of the Utah Copper Company, gave him full credit for saving them from ruin. Meyer's apprehension grew as stock prices spurted to dizzy heights in the spring and summer of 1929, and the Federal Reserve Board did virtually nothing to curb the gusher.

It was the "new era" in which many businessmen convinced themselves that economic principles of the past were outmoded, and speculators bought and sold wildly. Meyer got a heavy dose of the "new thinking" when he went on a yachting party with a group of big industrialists who drank seemingly endless toasts to prosperity, to the dawning of the "new era," and to the great captains of industry who were bringing it about. After this had gone on for some time with mounting enthusiasm as the cocktails flowed freely, Meyer commented to Walter Huston, the actor, that no mention had been made of the role that would be played in the new era by the arts or by government. When he could stand the self-glorification no longer, Meyer arose, glass in hand and a mischievous grin on his face. "I offer a toast," he said, "to the captains of industry of Babylonia, Egypt, Greece, Rome, and I'll throw in Venice. Let's drink to these captains of bygone days. They were all great men in their time, but not one of them is mentioned in history and today no one knows who the hell they were." The industrialists resisted their temptation to throw the Cassandra overboard, but his attempt to cool their fever apparently made no impression whatever.

Meyer, of course, was not the only one bemoaning the gyrations of Wall Street. Hoover and some of his followers were also worried by the excesses to which speculation had been carried. Shortly after his election, Hoover indicated that he wanted Meyer on the Federal Reserve Board. "As governor?" Meyer asked. "No," the President-elect replied, "but I have in mind a still more important assignment for you as head of an economic council to help the President coordinate all the economic policies of the government." The council was to include the Secretaries of the Treasury, Agriculture, Commerce, and Labor and the heads of certain independent regulatory agencies. So bizarre was the concept of a Cabinet-level council headed by a member of the Federal Reserve Board that Meyer dismissed it as a frivolous concoction designed to pay a campaign debt. The debt itself was real enough, for Meyer had helped to swing the New York delegation behind Hoover at the Republican National Convention and had contributed $25,000 to the GOP campaign, as usual. But he refused to be drawn into an organizational mish-mash that would probably be either mischievous or impotent.

After Hoover's inauguration, he again consulted Meyer: what could be done about the "crazy and dangerous" stock market? Meyer agreed with that characterization of the market, but he had no ready panacea. If the President should warn the country that the market was too high, he said, the President would then be expected to say when it was too low and when it was just right. The last thing the President ought to do was to imitate a stockbroker counseling his clients. The Treasury and Federal Reserve could, however, Meyer suggested, launch a campaign to encourage the buying of bonds. While stock prices were skyrocketing, bond prices were sagging. A vigorous effort to center interest in bonds would divert funds from speculation into business expansion.

Hoover did not disclose his reaction to the idea, but on March 14, 1929, Secretary Mellon issued a brief statement which he refused to discuss or amplify in any way: "The present situation in the financial markets offers an opportunity for the prudent investor to buy bonds. Bonds are low in price compared to stocks." The next time Meyer encountered Mellon, the latter complained icily that the President had forced him to make the statement about buying bonds. Meyer kept a stony face, not knowing whether Mellon's anger was directed at him or at the President. Many years later he learned from Hoover that Mellon did know the source of the suggestion. Meyer was much amused, therefore, when a friend credited Mellon with having saved him from bankruptcy by advising the purchase of bonds. "You owe me a drink," Meyer said by way of introducing his tale of the short-circuited bond-buying campaign. It went no further than Mellon's stark and stingy statement.

It is strange that the country's foremost expert on agricultural finance was not consulted about Hoover's Federal Farm Board, except as to some of the appointments to it. Meyer was asked to head a committee to meet the 1929 cotton crisis but declined on the ground that the job could be done better by the established agricultural agencies. Hoover then tried in vain to interest him in heading a St. Lawrence Seaway commission and in taking a ceremonial trip to Haiti. Meyer consistently refused to take an incompatible assignment merely to have a job.

With plenty of time to watch the booming economy, Meyer was shocked by what he saw. Samuel Insull and many others seemed to be demonstrating that fantastic risks offered a new road to great wealth. The Lehman Brothers were organizing a $100-million holding investment company, with stock that would sell at a 30 percent premium when issued. This kind of financing, he said, "is the supreme expression of lunacy. It is the straw that will break the camel's back." The wild and sometimes fraudulent inflation of real estate values, he said, could prove even more calamitous than the antics of Wall Street. Mass psychology had produced a kind of temporary insanity.

As for his own interests, Meyer was well prepared for the coming storm. During his years in government he had continued to make money in the stock market, operating through his New York office. In 1929 his wealth was centered in the Allied Chemical Company, which was well stocked with cash and short-term government securities and had no debts. Weber did not follow Meyer's advice to sell some of the company's investments when it would have been profitable to do so. Nevertheless, Allied could sail through a long period of rough weather. Feeling secure in his personal affairs and incapable of changing the course of events, Meyer sought relaxation on his Jackson Hole ranch and was there when the great stock market crash came in October 1929.

After the big shake-out through the fall and early winter, Meyer's customary optimism began to reassert itself. On December 17, he advised his friend Angus McLean that "good securities are cheap and worth buying" and that he looked for an improvement in business. Two days later, in a letter to Dwight F. Davis, he acknowledged that the outlook was uncertain but expressed the view that "whatever the conditions are we may view them with greater confidence than when we were up in a balloon with a question mark as to what kind of landing was going to be made." Unfortunately, the landing which had been made at that time was on a very uncertain slope, and the perilous slide into depression was to continue for another two years, with Meyer in the midst of the fight for economic survival.

In the early struggle, the President enlisted Meyer to convey messages to key people in financial and industrial circles, including a suggestion that big companies buy up their own stock. Hoover was struggling mightily, though often ineffectively, to prevent the "recession," as he called it, from becoming a depression. With one of the items in his program, the Smoot-Hawley tariff passed at an extra session of Congress in June 1930, Meyer had no connection, but he did not regard it as a major cause of the global dislocations that followed. History would have been much the same, he would often say in later years, without enactment of that American tariff. The fact remains that it was another disturbing element in a world economic situation that was already bordering on chaos.

Nearly a year after the stock market crash, Hoover phoned Meyer and said that Governor Roy Young of the Federal Reserve Board was resigning to become governor of the federal reserve bank in Boston. "I'm going to appoint you a member of the board and then governor," Hoover said. "I won't take no for an answer." Without giving Meyer a chance to reply, the President hung up. His commanding manner was quite unnecessary, for Meyer wanted this job and felt he could handle it properly. The recess appointment was announced on September 5, 1930.

The general reaction was favorable. The Federal Reserve Board had been under sharp criticism for its failure to cope with the speculative blitz of 1927-29. A survey by *Time* indicated that the bankers and financiers of New York were confident that Meyer would exercise more forceful and aggressive leadership. The St. Paul *Pioneer Press* thought the Meyer appointment would mean "more banking and less politics in the Federal Reserve Board." *World's Work* said no more distinguished appointment had been made in the Hoover administration. There was some complaint in the labor press that "Wall Street" had captured the federal reserve system, and Senator Brookhart called Meyer a Judas Iscariot to the cooperative movement, but this superficial ranting was all but lost in the general approval. Mark Sullivan likened Meyer to "one of those old Dutch burgomasters in a Holbein painting" who could take the problems of a whole community on his broad shoulders and carry "a world of troubles like a gravely smiling Titan." William Hard credited Meyer with a remarkable combination of amiability, pugnacity, reliable judgment, and special audacity. Baruch told *The New York Times* that "if the President had taken a thousand good men and rolled them into one" he would not have a better man for the job than Eugene Meyer.

When Congress met, it appeared that the nomination would be confirmed with little ruckus. The Senate Banking and Currency Committee made a favorable report on December 10, but Congressman McFadden of the House Banking and Currency Committee launched a campaign of opposition, and the Senate recommitted the nomination because Brookhart complained that he had had no opportunity to question the nominee.

McFadden invented a conspiracy, alleging that Young and Edmund Platt had been ousted from the Federal Reserve Board, with the connivance of Alfred Cook (Meyer's brother-in-law), in order to make a place for Meyer. Cook was erroneously linked with J. P. Morgan to make it appear that a cabal of international bankers was trying to subvert the federal reserve system for ulterior purposes. The whole fabrication fell apart at the hearing, however, when Cook testified that he had never represented Morgan and that he had known nothing of Meyer's appointment until he read it in the newspapers; Young testified that Meyer had nothing whatever to do with his retirement; he had simply left a $12,000 job for one paying $30,000; Platt, too, had simply taken a more lucrative job. The two resignations were not connected, and Meyer had no advance knowledge of either of them. No doubt Hoover welcomed Platt's decision, as he was a New Yorker and the law forbade the appointment of two members from a single state, but there was no evidence that anyone had urged Platt to leave.

With these charges utterly deflated, Brookhart and McFadden fell back on less specific complaints. Meyer could not escape from his Wall Street background. His "training and associations" made it inevitable that he would manage the great fountains of American credit for the advantage of international bankers—for Europe and not America. By innuendo, Brookhart made it appear that Meyer had enriched himself while in the government service, that he was a wrecker, an enemy of the farmer, and a chronic office-seeker. The hearing droned on and on. As Frank Kent explained it, Brookhart at last had a real, live "money devil" in a position where he could be exploited for the Progressive cause, and he made the most of it. The hearing became "a ridiculous exhibition of a Senator at his worst." Kent concluded: "For sheer futility and inanity he [Brookhart] nearly established a world record. . . ."

Through most of the ordeal Meyer was a cool and accommodating witness. He explained in great detail the policies he had followed in the War Finance Corporation and the Farm Loan Board. He patiently countered innuendo with facts, whether the subject was the cotton crisis of

1926 or his handling of the government's bond-stabilization program during the war. But he came into direct collision with Brookhart when the latter asked how the nominee would cope with speculative orgies in the future. After a little sparring, Meyer said flatly:

> There are certain lines of questioning that I will not reply to, and they have to do with how I will conduct myself in office if I am confirmed.
>
> I have been here in public office for the best part of the last thirteen years. The Senate of the United States, for the most part, knows my record and knows me. It is a question of confidence in a man for a place. You can not do much more than express either confidence or lack of confidence. I will not declare myself on questions of policy to be decided in the future by the board, of which I am a member temporarily, and will be a member if confirmed. I want that to be very definite and clear.[5]

Chairman Robert D. Carey, Senator Robert F. Wagner, and other members of the committee backed Meyer in this stand, and it won wide popular support. The New York *World* said it was "a wholesome example of courage and further demonstrates his fitness for the position." Yet the grilling continued for ten days. At one point Meyer opened his mouth to ask Brookhart: "When did you stop beating your wife?" But he restrained the impulse and continued to respond patiently. When the controversy was shifted to the Senate floor, after a second favorable committee report, Meyer's supporters let the abuse run without reply in order to save time. Confirmation finally came on February 25, 1931, by a vote of 72 to 11.

Meyer's performance in the hearings led a friend to suggest to Agnes that the presidency could well be the next step for him, but the suggestion got an adverse response. "E and I will never bite" on such a feeler, Agnes wrote in her diary. "I am profoundly thankful that E is a Jew for this will effectively protect him from the lure of that fata Morgana."

At last the energetic Californian, still vigorous at fifty-five, was the key figure in the nation's monetary and credit systems. It was the position he had dreamed of in his moments of greatest ambition to serve his country well. Yet, as he responded to the flood of congratulations, he was keenly aware of the problems that beset him. By some twist of fate, the great prize he had worked for with such herculean efforts had come to him at a time when the outlook was clouded by a series of critical emergencies.

[5] "Nomination of Eugene Meyer to be a Member of the Federal Reserve Board," hearings before a Subcommittee of the Committee on Banking and Currency, United States Senate, Seventy-first Congress, third session, 1931, p. 130.

One immediate problem was the feuds within the board. Dr. Adolph C. Miller, an intelligent and cultivated but also overbearing and unreliable member of the board since its beginning, was at war with George R. James, a merchant from Memphis. Charles S. Hamlin of Boston, who had been the first governor of the board, was a mild-mannered old gentleman, but he kept an extensive diary (which he later willed to the Library of Congress) that was full of carping remarks about his associates. Meyer thought he was on very good terms with Hamlin, but the latter assailed him in his diary as a cold and domineering governor who worked too closely with the President. Division within the board was accentuated by the practice of having one member assume major responsibility for a particular region. The staff served members of the board individually but not the board as a collective body. Meyer soon put an end to this splinterization by having the staff report to the board and by having the board act as a body on federal reserve business.

The task of unifying policy was further complicated by conflicts between the New York and Chicago federal reserve banks. Headed by a weak president, the Chicago board was dominated by the city's private bankers. In New York the governor of the federal reserve bank, George L. Harrison, a strong and able man, often tried to run the whole system. Meyer's objective was to establish central control in Washington, where it belonged, while helping each regional reserve bank to function smoothly in its own sphere. To strengthen his own hand he brought into the system two of his reliable aides in the WFC and the Farm Loan Board, Floyd R. Harrison and Chester Morrill. As soon as the new leadership at the Fed was in the saddle, Washington rather than New York emerged as the financial capital of the United States.

There was much interest in the course that Meyer would take to reform the banking system. In some circles he was considered a monomaniac on banking reform. In 1923 he had told a joint congressional committee that all eligible nonmember banks, nearly 10,000 of them, should be in the federal reserve system and had criticized the federal reserve authorities of that day for their failure to recruit the country banks. The dual system encouraged both state and federal supervisors to shrink from maintaining proper standards—a self-defeating competition in weakness. The rescue efforts of the WFC in 1921–22 had clearly demonstrated the need of country banks for access to a "central reservoir of credit."

In the first days of the Hoover administration Meyer had discussed banking reform with the President. Hoover was interested, as his autobiography makes plain. But many small banks had been hostile to reforms in the heyday of the boom, and Hoover knew from his experience in

California that banking reform could be a hot political issue. Nothing effective was done, and by the time Meyer became head of the federal reserve system the opportunity for any major accomplishment in this sphere had passed. Wholesale failures had undermined public confidence in the banks and the bankers' trust in one another. Even some large eastern banks were in peril. Reform had to give way to emergency rescue operations.

The worsening abscess of reparations and debts from World War I came in for prompt attention. Reparations had been scaled down by the Dawes plan and then the Young plan, but the payments were still beyond Germany's capacity to pay, given the unwillingness of the victorious powers to accept goods. Britain and France insisted they could pay their war debts to the United States only from reparations. The United States was no more willing to accept goods in payment than they were. In lieu of facing realities, Americans had been lending Germany money, which she paid as reparations and the Allies paid the United States on their war debts. Meyer insisted that the arrangement was impractical, deceptive, and disruptive both economically and politically.

Soon after his appointment, he met with Owen D. Young, George Harrison of the New York Federal Reserve Bank, and Assistant Secretary of State Joseph P. Cotton. They agreed that reparations and war debts should be drastically cut. Meyer was deeply concerned about the mounting tensions in Europe because of the vulnerability of the United States to potential demands by European creditors. Foreign deposits in U. S. banks and liquid investments—mostly trade obligations—amounted to about $2.5 billion, and America's total stock of gold was about $4.5 billion. A run by foreign creditors, Meyer said, would drain away the greater part of that gold.

As governor of the central banking system, Meyer was keenly aware of his responsibility to protect it against all hazards. America was the keystone in the arch of the world economy. If any other country went down, it would be a tragedy. But if foreign creditors should demand their gold and the United States should be unable to deliver it without calamity, the whole world would be in chaos. Foreign withdrawals would stimulate domestic withdrawals, and American banks were already failing at an alarming rate. Such was the nightmare that the governor of the federal reserve system had to live with.

After the conference with Young, Harrison, and Cotton, Meyer went to the White House with a plea that reparations and war debts be scaled down from 40 to 70 percent as a relatively painless contribution to world stability. The official view was that reparations and war debts were entirely separate, but Meyer insisted that they were obviously interrelated and urged the President to call an international conference to slash both at the same time. It was not a question of justice or legality, he argued, but of facing up to the fact that Germany could not pay, or would not, and the Allies had no intention of forcing her to do so. "Germany will default and repudiate," Meyer said, "and this will mean the economic collapse of everything in Germany and east of Germany. Then France and England will follow, and we will go in on top of the heap."

"Why shouldn't Britain or France make the proposal?" the President parried.

"No government in Britain or France which now proposed to curtail or eliminate German reparations could remain in power," Meyer responded. "You are the head of a state which doesn't change its government on a temporarily unpopular issue. Being right, the measure will succeed, a calamity will be avoided, and in the end the people will understand the measure and support the man who proposed it."

Hoover said both Congress and the people would object. Meyer disagreed. He thought the people were tired of the phony arguments that had been made for a decade and that they would respond to an honest, courageous presentation of the facts. Frank recognition that the debts could not be collected, he added, would be a political asset and source of strength. Hoover indicated his impatience with the whole argument by saying that there was "a lot of propaganda" in the air about the war debts, and the conference ended with Meyer protesting that he was neither an agent of nor a victim of propaganda—that he was speaking from strong convictions in line with his duty to the President.

Still smarting from his rebuff, Meyer crossed the street to the Treasury, where the Federal Reserve Board was then housed, and reported to his colleagues. "In my opinion," he said, "this is the last opportunity to save Germany from disaster." But he feared that, when the disaster came and the President had to face worldwide repercussions, with a possible shattering of his own political future, he would seek to involve the federal reserve in a futile rescue effort. Indicating his own determination to resist any such maneuver, if it came too late to be effective, Meyer asked his colleagues if they would stand by that policy, and there was no dissent. The breach between Hoover and Meyer had reached formidable proportions.

The depression continued to run its devastating course, with repercussions from each collapse spreading weakness to other parts of the world economy. In December 1930, 344 banks closed, making a new record of 1,300 suspensions for the year. The rise of the Nazis in Germany accentuated both political and economic uncertainties, causing a further withdrawal of short-term credits and capital. In May 1931, the Kreditanstalt in

Vienna failed, and a month later Germany declared the end of reparations. Gold and currency were being hoarded in many lands. At last on June 30 the President proposed a moratorium on reparations and war debts some nine months after he had rejected Meyer's proposal.

There were rumors that Ogden Mills and Meyer had converted Hoover to the moratorium "at the pistol's point." It may have been figuratively true of Mills, but Meyer was not even consulted at the time. Presumably Hoover could not face an open acknowledgment that Meyer had been right in the first place. In his autobiography he makes no mention of his discussion of debts and reparations with Meyer and presents the moratorium as if it originated solely in his own mind. It is this characteristic of Hoover's version of history that caused Meyer to remark in later years that the Hoover autobiography should have been entitled "Alone in Washington." But the friction between the two men was not due solely to Hoover's shortcomings. Meyer's bluntness and lack of diplomacy were galling thorns to the President's vanity.

Welcome though the moratorium was, it came too late. Germany was fighting to keep afloat economically. Even before the moratorium was ratified, the Reichsbank sought and obtained credit amounting to $100 million from the Bank of International Settlements, the Bank of England, the Bank of France, and the New York Federal Reserve Bank, and before this was taken up, Berlin was asking for five times that amount to ease the spreading panic. Harrison in New York conveyed this appeal to Meyer and received no encouragement. There is considerable difference, Meyer said, between temporary assistance and a huge long-term credit. The Federal Reserve Board in Washington and the bank in New York as well as the Bank of England and the Bank of France seemed to be fully in accord in the matter.

With the crisis in this posture, Meyer flew to New York on Friday afternoon, July 10. It was his custom to spend weekends at Mount Kisco when possible, partly to get away from the heat of Washington and partly to enable him to talk with people in New York. On Saturday he remained at the farm but spent much of the day on the telephone. Discussion of the German crisis was intense, in the press and elsewhere, and even though the German bid for massive credits had apparently failed, there seemed to be an assumption that the Federal Reserve Board would somehow be asked to rush to the rescue. Meyer called board members Miller and Hamlin, who were away from Washington, and asked them to be on hand for a board meeting on Monday. The governor himself made plans to return on Sunday afternoon.

Before his departure, Meyer was handed a copy of a "strictly confidential" statement of the German situation. Though it purported to be an unofficial communication, it was actually a warning from the German government that "a complete collapse of the country appears unavoidable" unless credit assistance were "immediately forthcoming." There was a special request for a reassuring statement by the federal reserve bank on the "fundamental soundness" of the German economy. Copies of the appeal had also gone to Hoover's camp on the Rapidan and to the New York Federal Reserve Bank. But the President was reported in the press to be giving his weekend to relaxation and conferences with Vice-President Curtis. "It is well known," said Acting Secretary of State William Castle, who was also at the Rapidan, "that in any case the Executive has no authority over the Federal Reserve Board and does not attempt to influence it."

Sometime on Sunday, Meyer changed his mind about entraining to Washington. Instead, he would take a plane from Newark after stopping in Englewood for a talk with Thomas W. Lamont, a well-known authority on international finance. As the two men greeted one another, Lamont casually remarked that he supposed Meyer was on his way to the meeting at the reserve bank. Two Morgan partners would be there, he said—Russell Leffingwell and Parker Gilbert. Meyer "pricked up his ears" without letting Lamont know that this was the first he had heard of such a meeting. As soon as he could leave without arousing suspicions, he rushed—not to Newark or Washington—but to the federal reserve bank in New York. If there was to be a meeting involving the destiny of the central banking system, he was determined to be there.

It was strange, Meyer mused as his chauffeur whizzed through the traffic, that no one had told him of the meeting. He had talked to Harrison only a few hours previously. Arriving at the bank, he found the meeting well under way. In addition to Leffingwell and Gilbert, those present included Harrison, Owen Young, Deputy Governor W. Randolph Burgess, Albert Wiggin of the Chase National Bank, and Acting Secretary of the Treasury Ogden Mills—a formidable constellation of banking talent. Mills was talking by private wire to the President at the Rapidan.

While that conversation ran on, Young gave Meyer a fill-in: since Germany's Darmstadter and National Bank would not open the following morning, the President wanted to issue a statement expressing interest and sympathy. Meyer looked over the proposed text and exploded: "You can't do this. It's a commitment."

Young insisted that the statement was not a contract to do anything in particular. "It's worse than a contract," Meyer replied. "It's a moral commitment of American resources to help the Germans. Tomorrow the

German newspapers will say that the resources of the American government and American banks are back of Germany and her financial institutions. You leave it to the Germans to fill in the terms. They will say what it means, and you will have either to follow through or repudiate their interpretation and make the news worse than ever."

Moreover, he continued, the proposed statement involved a question of major policy to which the group present should not, and could not, commit the federal reserve system and the government. Only the Federal Reserve Board could legally take such action, but the presence of many high officials at the current meeting would seem to make the statement official. As Meyer paused for breath, Mills could be heard to say: "I agree with you, Mr. President. We ought to issue this statement. But Gene is here and he says we shouldn't. Perhaps you better speak to Gene."

Meyer took over the telephone and listened to the President's arguments that the statement would be helpful in a crisis. In reply, Meyer repeated all that he had said to the group and insisted that no such statement should be issued. The argument went back and forth with neither protagonist yielding an inch, until Hoover's irritation reached a breaking point. "Oh hell!" he exclaimed and hung up.

Though he continued to fume over this attempt to initiate a momentous financial policy behind his back, Meyer decided not to magnify the crisis by resigning. Nor did he seek a showdown with Hoover or Harrison. The President could have called Mills or Harrison in New York to suggest the preparation of a statement such as the Germans wanted. With Mellon in Europe, Mills was acting ex-officio chairman of the Federal Reserve Board. The officials in New York, and presumably the President, knew of Meyer's intention to return to Washington on Sunday. It would have been possible to submit the proposed statement to him there before issuing it. Yet the arrangement of a meeting on so vital an issue without a word to the governor of the board, who was nearby in Mount Kisco, still seemed to be a devious end run to circumvent his known opposition. When that venture failed, Hoover seemed relieved that Meyer did not resign, for, as the governor remarked, there was no archangel in the wings to take his place.

Mills did issue a statement in his own name, but it was wholly noncommittal and emphasized the independence of the federal reserve system. The President, in a conciliatory mood, called Meyer while he was reporting the events of the weekend to the board in Washington and said that he hoped the reserve authorities would do all they could to relieve the situation. The board decided that it could go in no deeper than participation in the $100-million credit to the Reichsbank previously arranged, but that was not the end of the matter. On the following Saturday and Sunday, July 18 and 19, the Meyers and several other couples were guests at the Rapidan. Hoover was still toying with the idea of providing more short-term credits to Germany. Mrs. Meyer recorded in her diary that the President "behaved like a tired child and a little like a spoiled one." On Monday and Tuesday there were almost continuous conferences at the White House attended by Meyer, Mills, William R. Castle Jr., Senator Dwight W. Morrow, and Charles G. Dawes, then ambassador to Britain. The situation in Germany had worsened. Banks were failing, and creditors outside Germany were withdrawing short-term credits, which threatened to destroy Germany's foreign trade and cause further demoralization.

Hoover was greatly alarmed, as he later disclosed in his *Memoirs*, by the volume of German indebtedness to American banks, but he grossly exaggerated it on the basis of a report from the Comptroller of the Currency. He accepted the comptroller's figure uncritically, even though it was more than three times the estimate he had previously obtained from the Federal Reserve Board, which later studies showed to be more accurate. Incidentally, his *Memoirs* tell nothing about his controversy with Meyer and even fail to mention Meyer as one of those with whom he conferred on July 20–21, though the others are named. As Hoover tells the story, he stepped into the breach with a standstill agreement under which banks everywhere would continue to hold their German and Central European short-term obligations. But as Meyer remembered it, the President and the State Department fought doggedly for direct credit to Germany, and reluctantly fell back upon the standstill idea, which was a reflection of federal reserve policy. At Hoover's request, Mellon and Stimson then induced the Seven Power Conference to accept that principle on an international scale. It was an extension of the solution applied to reparations by the moratorium—a complete but belated triumph for Meyer and his colleagues.

The collisions with Hoover in this and various other instances led Meyer to some generalizations about the man. Able and hard-working though he was, he had the great weakness of being unable "to admit even to himself that there were limits to what he understood and could do. He was the Great Engineer, from whom all really important ideas must emanate. So if something had nevertheless to be done, on the advice of others, things began working in his mind which made it seem that after all the course adopted was first thought of by him. In this process, the reasoning and the facts involved in the matter might become badly confused; and this explains, I think, why Mr. Hoover's account of the German crisis of 1931 is so ragged and superficial, at the same time that it is so dogmatic."[6]

Meyer was keenly aware of the possibility that his frustration of Hoover's wishes might contribute to charges that he had worsened a worldwide economic trauma. In later years he would acknowledge that the same line of reasoning could lay at his door the rise of Hitlerism out of Germany's desperation and World War II, resulting from Hitler's aggressions. But he continued to feel, even in his old age, that he had taken the right course. No American gesture at that late hour could have changed the forces sweeping over Europe. Weakened by the depression, America could not prop up failing banks everywhere. In the hour of crisis the international banker who had been accused of being overly sensitive to pressures from abroad clung tenaciously to his primary duty of keeping the United States solvent.

The perilous signs on the domestic horizon which had buttressed Meyer's caution were soon plainly evident. Production was down, unemployment was mounting, commodity prices were sagging, and fifty-cent wheat spelled ruin for farmers. American banks were closing at a rate that would take the total to more than 1,700 in the last six months of 1931. And in September of that year Britain abandoned the gold standard.

Meyer was forewarned of the British action when he visited the federal reserve bank in New York on September 19. The announcement was to be made the following day. "The British are hauling down the flag of commercial empire," he said, "and trade everywhere will be impaired." Since about nine-tenths of the world's commerce was carried on in terms of the pound sterling, the suspension of gold payments in London was an even more severe blow than the stock market crash of 1929.

As the shock waves spread out from London, sharp demands were also made on gold held in American banks. In the first year of Meyer's governorship he had repeatedly favored reductions in the federal reserve rediscount rates, partly to encourage withdrawals of foreign balances in New York, and about $700 million in gold had been exported. But orderly withdrawals were one thing, and panicky shipments of gold as fast as vessels could be found to carry it were quite another. After Britain went off gold, the federal reserve system raised rates to slow down the hemorrhage.

Yet Meyer vetoed what otherwise might have been a hasty step in that direction. On the day when the demand for gold reached its peak he was sitting in Harrison's office at the New York Federal Reserve Bank. An official walked in and said that Chase National had just sent in 60 million

[6] Sidney Hyman's manuscript, "Life of Eugene Meyer," Part VII, p. 115. This part of the manuscript was written with the help of Bray Hammond.

of "acceptances" to sell. Since the gold that the banks had to ship to their depositors overseas came out of their reserves, they had to replenish these reserves by selling their most liquid assets or borrowing from the Fed. The distressed official asked Harrison if they should not raise the acceptance rate—the rate of discount at which the federal reserve bank was making the purchases. Without even giving Harrison a chance to reply, Meyer shouted, "No!"

"Raise the rates in the midst of the rush," he said, "and you'll show you're jittery, and then the market will get jittery. We mustn't turn this crisis into a panic. The federal reserve banks were created to serve the public. The thing to do is to stand there and take everything the banks want to sell. Let the world know there is one place of strength and power. But after closing time, the rate can be raised effective tomorrow without causing any excitement." This advice was followed. It is a good illustration of what Meyer meant when he insisted that central banking is an art. Though it seems to call for mechanical reactions, the questions of when and how to act can be answered only through experience and judgment of a high order.

A week later Meyer again intervened in the rate-making process even though the law gives the initiative to the federal reserve banks, leaving to the board only power to approve or disapprove discount rates. Fully conscious of this limitation, Meyer called Harrison after the October 1 meeting of the New York Federal Reserve Bank's directors and asked what had been done about the discount rate. The directors had done nothing, fearing that any increase in rates in the face of heavy gold withdrawals might be interpreted as a sign of weakness. Meyer disagreed. The normal and natural thing to do, he said, was to raise the discount rate to discourage withdrawals. Such action would be counted a sign of common sense and strength. New York should not follow the British example of not raising the discount rate when the pound was under pressure, he said, because the British were acting from weakness and the American system could act with much greater strength behind it. The New York Federal Reserve Bank responded by boosting its rate 1 percent in each of the two following weeks—a drastic total jump from 1½ to 3½ percent—with the board's approval.

The hemorrhage that had drained $700 million in gold from the United States in September and October subsided. November saw a net increase in American gold holdings, and fairly normal in-and-out movements continued for several months thereafter. When the crisis was over, Charles Rist, the eminent French economist, confided in Meyer that Paris had interpreted New York's sharp boosts in the discount rate as a sign of strength. "And that," Meyer replied, "was the way I expected our action to be interpreted."

Whatever else may be said about this critical period in financial history, the United States played its central banking role with a high degree of finesse and seasoned judgment, and the dominant figure in formulating and carrying out that policy was Eugene Meyer.

20 /

The Reconstruction Finance

Corporation

BRITAIN'S DEPARTURE FROM THE GOLD STANDARD SENT OUT shock waves far beyond the depositories of monetary metal. Confidence was shaken all over the world. In such a climate marginal banks had little chance for survival, and 522 such institutions in the United States with $471 million in deposits suspended operations in the first month that Britain was off gold.

For some time Meyer had believed that revival of the War Finance Corporation was in order, and the new wave of bank failures clinched the argument. Other bankers and some legislators were thinking along the same line. Meyer urged Hoover to declare a financial-economic emergency of world proportions and to call a special session of Congress for enactment of a bipartisan program, including revival of the WFC. But Hoover, remembering the trouble that had come from his special session to revise the tariff, would not risk another burn from the same stove.

The President was pursuing a different line. Even before the British went off gold he had summoned the Federal Advisory Council, the Federal Reserve Board, and Treasury officials to discuss plans for the creation of a National Credit Corporation which could make loans to banks on assets that the federal reserve banks could not accept. The bankers were very cool toward the idea. Eleven days after the collapse in London, the administration brought the reluctant leaders of the banking, insurance, and loan agencies together with federal officials in a secret meeting at the home of Secretary Mellon. The bankers were said to have agreed en route to Washington that they would not put up money for any venture they believed to be impractical. Hoover's plea for a $500-million corporation to help banks with frozen assets received a glum reception. Meyer urged acceptance of a National Credit Corporation because action was needed immediately and Congress was not in session. If the arrangement should prove inadequate, he said, he would use all the strength he could summon to revise the War Finance Corporation. The bankers agreed to go along with that understanding.

Hoover then summoned key members of Congress from their homes to a White House conference on October 6 and told them what was afoot. He said he would ask Congress to broaden the discount powers of the federal reserve banks so that they could be more helpful to banks in need of funds and that, if necessary, he would recommend the creation of a governmental finance corporation similar to the old WFC. Within a few months the National Credit Corporation had lent $155 million to 575 banks, but its efforts were puny in the face of the plague that had fallen upon banking. As soon as the new credit agency was set up, Meyer told the President that it was not big enough or strong enough to do what was needed. If we take the assets of the strong banks and freeze them in slow loans to weak banks, he said, we will make things worse, not better. The strong banks should be kept strong. Only governmental action can fill the vacuum, he added, and it ought to be taken soon.

Since neither the White House nor the Treasury initiated any move in that direction, Meyer asked Chester Morrill, secretary of the Federal Reserve Board, to review pertinent legislation of the past and to write a bill for a new lending agency with broad powers to stem the tide of depression. Board Counsel Walter Wyatt and Floyd R. Harrison also worked on the bill. As first drawn, it made no provision for Meyer in the proposed Reconstruction Finance Corporation, but the Democratic leader of the Senate, Joseph T. Robinson, indicated that his party would support the bill if Meyer wrote it and ran the agency. Hoover agreed to this. The bill was then modified to include the governor of the Federal Reserve Board as an ex-officio member of the RFC board of directors.

The finished draft went to Capitol Hill—not to the White House. Hearings began before a Senate Banking and Currency Subcommittee on December 18, with Meyer the first witness. He described the bill as a major effort "to bring the resources of the nation, through the Government, into action on a scale and in a manner that will be adequate to accomplish an important and desirable result." Though the proposed Reconstruction Finance Corporation could lend up to $2 billion to banks, trust companies, building and loan associations, insurance companies, and other financial institutions, Meyer felt that its greatest contribution would lie in "the removal of fear."[1] The RFC would not be a cure-all for the depression, which was really worldwide, but it could function as "a movable fortress" against critical situations in any part of the country.

The extent to which it was "Meyer's bill" became evident at the hearing. When Mills testified as Undersecretary of the Treasury, he asked Meyer to sit beside him because of his unfamiliarity with the details of the bill. But as the questioning warmed up, Meyer had to leave to take a telephone call from the President. Mills sought to cover his embarrassment by telling the committee: "Governor Meyer is not here at this time. I think he is more familiar with the exact language."[2] His anger flared openly when the two men were alone together, and it was not substantially assuaged by Meyer's explanation of his absence.

Congress modified the Meyer bill in some particulars. The authors were especially disappointed by the elimination of the section designed to revive commodity prices. Meyer wanted a subsidiary to the RFC that could function much as the Commodity Credit Corporation did after the advent of the New Deal. He always felt that this section of the RFC bill was deleted solely because the Democrats in Congress could not swallow a Republican bill in its entirety. Senator Glass told Meyer that he was asking for more power than any man ought to have, but the latter replied that he had no interest in power for its own sake; power was important only as it advanced the country toward recovery.

However reluctant Hoover may have been at first, he accepted the RFC bill as a part of his program and signed it as soon as it reached his his desk on January 22, 1932. His chief interest at that time seemed to lie in preventing Meyer from dominating the new credit agency. Because of the agreement with Senator Robinson and the text of the act, Meyer could not be eliminated, but the President let it be known that he wanted former Vice-President Dawes to be chairman of the board, with Meyer in second place as president. That led to another sharp clash with the redoubtable governor.

It was not merely a contest for high position. Meyer lacked confidence in Dawes's ability and was loath to see the RFC fail to achieve its potential. The family view was reflected in Mrs. Meyer's diary: "I know that D and E will never agree. D is too much of a bluff, too disorganized in his thinking and too sketchy a personality. He is sure to enrage E before long and then the feathers will fly because D will resent E's treatment of him." Within a

[1] "Creation of a Reconstruction Finance Corporation," hearings before a Subcommittee of the Committee on Banking and Currency, United States Senate, Seventy-second Congress, first session, p. 15.

[2] *Ibid.*, p. 45.

few days, Meyer convinced the President that the roles should be reversed—that he should be chairman, since the act itself made the governor of the federal reserve an ex-officio member of the RFC board, and Dawes should be president. That compromise was accepted. The Secretary of the Treasury and Farm Loan Commissioner Paul Bestor were also ex-officio members of the board. The other directors named by the President were Harvey C. Couch of Arkansas (Robinson's choice), Jesse Jones of Texas (Speaker John N. Garner's choice), and Wilson McCarthy of Utah.

Even before the bill was passed, Meyer began setting up an organization in a dingy brick building at Nineteenth Street and Pennsylvania Avenue. For several days he was almost constantly on the telephone talking with bankers, community leaders, federal reserve officials, and others in many different cities. Most of them consented to join the new agency or to give the help requested. The human dynamo who now spoke for a hopeful new rescue mission refused to take no for an answer. In an incredibly short time he had RFC units functioning in the chief financial centers. Under the law the RFC had to insist on a reasonable prospect for repayment of the money it lent. Yet funds were flowing into banks in distress ten days after the act was signed, and loans ranging from $10,000 to $10 million were soon being made at the rate of one hundred a day.

The White House complained that the RFC was "all Meyer and not enough Dawes." That was precisely what Hoover had tried to guard against. Meyer feared that Hoover, Dawes, and Mills would try to use the RFC for political purposes, and was determined to keep it strictly non-partisan. As the fight to control the RFC's $2 billion warmed up, Agnes recorded in her diary: "I know the whole Wash. crowd consider Eugene unbearably dictatorial but I doubt whether a really great intellect ever got anywhere with soft words. What they cannot get away from is that he knows his stuff as nobody else does."[3]

One of the RFC's first problems was a run on itself—a run for jobs. Victims of the depression and patronage-seeking politicians besieged the new agency with the persistence of hungry wolves. The task of expanding the staff was delegated largely to Floyd Harrison and Chester Morrill; yet the burden that fell directly upon Meyer was enormous. Agnes was so worried about his health that she secretly made an appointment with the President to tell him that Eugene would break down physically unless the President protected him against "senatorial greed" and "White House pounding on political appointments." Hoover, looking "old and worn," surprised her by saying: "Eugene Meyer is the most valuable man I've got.

---

[3] Agnes E. Meyer's diary, p. 504.

My chief occupation is to keep Eugene well. The only real detriment to his health is his constant smoking of big black cigars which he calls 'light.' "[4] It was this interview that caused Agnes to liken Hoover to a chameleon "with all the fascination of that creature."

After the new lending agency was well established, Meyer usually spent his mornings at the Federal Reserve and afternoons at the RFC; evenings and nights were divided between the two. Speed was often paramount. One morning Edward O. Howard of Salt Lake City called Meyer out of a board meeting and said that his bank needed two or three million dollars to avert a run upon its scheduled opening at 10 a.m. It was already past ten o'clock in Washington. Returning to the board while Howard kept the telephone line open, Meyer convinced his colleagues that the loan should be granted on the spot. This was possible, he said, because Howard was a thoroughly honest, able, and reliable banker who would be as careful with RFC funds as with his own. It was agreed that the federal reserve bank in San Francisco should advance the necessary funds through its Salt Lake City branch and that Howard could send the RFC a list of his collateral later.

But extraordinary speed in exceptional cases did not mean disregard for security. The RFC was not a pork barrel or a lottery. On one occasion a group of Tennessee bankers went before the board with an emotional appeal for help without submitting any data on the condition of their bank. General Dawes, in a flag-waving speech, seemed to assure the applicants that the board would "go the limit" for them when they came back with the facts. Fearing that this might be regarded as an unsound commitment, Meyer tried to refocus the issue by saying: "Gentlemen, don't forget to bring your collateral with you."

Within three months, the RFC had lent $500 million, most of it to banks in rural areas and small cities. At the same time the federal reserve system was pumping more credit into the economy. Currency began to come out of hoarding and bank failures nearly stopped. Signs of returning confidence began to appear, but the storm was not over. Before the end of April, Meyer was very worried again about the general outlook. More banks began to totter. In some instances the mere fact that they asked for an RFC loan aroused depositors' fears and thus encouraged withdrawals. Meyer concluded that the RFC could greatly enhance its usefulness if it were permitted to buy preferred stock in banks, thus strengthening their capital structure, instead of merely lending them money. Jesse Jones sounded out Garner about this idea and reported that the Speaker

---

[4] *Ibid.*, p. 506.

would not cooperate, although the Roosevelt administration later did obtain such authority for the RFC.

On May 1 the failure of a Boston bank brought another tense White House session. Something more had to be done to arrest the downward momentum, and Hoover and Meyer were once more at loggerheads as to what it should be. Mrs. Meyer's diary gives a close-up view:

> This week Hoover's impetuous way of acting on the spur of the moment—rashness after timid delay—has again caused a grave uneasiness. Instead of thinking out unemployment relief slowly and carefully, the Pres. let Jo Robinson get ahead of him by proposing a $2,000,000,000 bond issue for necessary and productive public works. The very next day Hoover announced his own plan of increasing the RFC funds $1,500,000,000 and empowering them to lend to the states. He also wanted the RFC to lend to private individuals to which Eugene is emphatically opposed. The bond market broke from two to three points at the publication of so many more gov. bonds to be thrown on the market and H. had to amend his statement to quiet the alarms. He is incapable of visualizing, as E so accurately can, the effect of his sudden announcements on the business world and the market. When the effect is bad and E has told him it would be, it only serves to increase his irritation with E. Today Garner has put out a biting and not inaccurate interview that the Pres's many and changeable statements confuse and alarm the public.[5]

Even such routine matters as publicity for the RFC brought Hoover and Meyer into collision. Hoover managed to get Henry Allen installed in the RFC to tout its achievements for political purposes, but Meyer arranged that the board would pass upon all publicity. Hoover's tendency to leap into print while his plans were in the formative stage was anathema to Meyer, whose practice was to keep quiet until he could speak from a tangible background of action. Allen left the RFC in a state of frustration.

Early in June 1932, the Meyers were again at the Rapidan along with the Daweses, the Hurleys, and others. The chief worry at that moment was the encampment in Washington of veterans who were demanding payment of a bonus for their service in World War I. Secretary of War Patrick Hurley urged military dispersal of the veterans as a lesson to the country in law and order. Meyer argued for some means of advance payments on the bonus that the veterans would ultimately receive because many of them and their families were destitute. The argument continued

[5] *Ibid.*, pp. 531–2.

far into the night, the majority standing firm against any weakness in the face of intimidation. As the Meyers went to bed in a "hot and stuffy cabin . . . disgruntled by the uncomfortable surroundings and atmosphere," Eugene summed up his impressions: "Hoover is convinced he will be re-elected only if he shows a strong hand. Instead, it'll kill him."

The next morning at breakfast, when the President commanded Agnes to sit next to him, she tried to smooth the feathers that Eugene so often ruffled. When Eugene appears to be "too set on his own opinion," she told the President, "it is usually because of important principles which are involved." But there was no indication that the President appreciated her intervention.

Shortly after this visit to the Rapidan, Agnes rushed to the White House to save the President from what she regarded as a political blunder. Eugene was organizing banking and industrial committees in all the federal reserve districts to help the economy get into motion again. Owen Young was chairman of the first committee set up in New York. The Federal Reserve Board was extending the pattern to other parts of the country, but the President wanted the committees transferred to the RFC so that he could claim credit for them. Agnes naïvely supposed she could make the President see that his attempt to "grab the committees" would cause Democratic resignations, thus hurting rather than helping his campaign.

Hoover responded in "loud, angry tones," insisting that the idea of the committees was his, that Owen Young was using the New York committee to further his presidential ambition, and that the RFC staff was composed mostly of Democrats. At one point he seemed to hint that Meyer was aiding Young against him. "Eugene thinks I am nothing but a politician," he protested, "but there has got to be leadership in this situation. I am President for better or worse, and I have got to do the leading."[6] This experience convinced Agnes that "Eugene is trying to save the country and the President is trying to save Hoover."

The President's troubles in dealing with a stubborn and unyielding chairman of the RFC had not been substantially relieved by the presence of Dawes in the organization. Dawes was indeed a source of irritation to Meyer, but he remained only a figurehead. The relations between the two men never reached a breaking point but often came near it. Meyer was increasingly annoyed by Dawes's habit of banging on the table to emphasize his points. One day when the banging attained unusual proportions

[6] *Ibid.*, p. 554.

for no apparent reason, Meyer cried: "Stop it, General, you're among friends."

The friction between the two men would have been ample cause for Dawes's resignation in June 1932, but the more immediate reason was the precarious condition of the Central Republic Bank in Chicago to which he had given much of his life. According to Hoover's *Memoirs*, Dawes had not owned any interest in the bank since 1924, but he was honorary chairman of its board. On Saturday, June 25, the Central Republic became the focal point of several runs in Chicago. Dawes warned Melvin A. Traylor of the First National that the Central Republic would not open on Monday unless help was forthcoming. Traylor called Hoover at his Rapidan camp and said that every bank in Chicago would have to close its doors unless the RFC stepped in and saved the Central Republic.

Meyer received a similarly alarming report from the RFC's Chicago office shortly after noon on Sunday. A telephone call to Dawes confirmed the latter's intention to close his bank the next morning unless mammoth loans were forthcoming. Meyer was irritated that so little warning had been given. "You ought to think about the country as well as yourself," he told Dawes. Governor Harrison and W. Randolph Burgess had previously been invited to lunch with Meyer at Mount Kisco on Sunday to discuss the Chicago situation. As soon as they could escape from the almost constantly ringing telephone, all three left for the federal reserve bank in New York. Mills, Lamont, and Parker Gilbert had also been asked to come, and that group spent the evening until 1 A.M. chewing over the Chicago predicament.

Meanwhile similar sessions were being held in Chicago and Washington and all kept in touch with one another, and with Hoover at the Rapidan, by telephone. RFC directors Jones and McCarthy were in Chicago attending the Democratic National Convention. After surveying the bleak outlook from that vantage point, Jones reported that he and McCarthy would take the responsibility for an RFC loan of $90 million to the Dawes bank.[7] The New York group was thinking in terms of a smaller loan, but it was obvious that the bank had to be kept open if a financial collapse in the Chicago area were to be avoided. The loan would be secured by collateral of $118 million book value. Meyer was concerned about the nature of some of this collateral, but there was no time for quibbling. The condition he did insist upon was that the loan be used to keep the bank open and not to liquidate it. The RFC directors who were not in at-

---

[7] Jesse H. Jones, *Fifty Billion Dollars* (New York: Macmillan; 1951), p. 78.

tendance at any of the Sunday night meetings were kept informed by telephone, and the board met at 9 a.m. Monday morning to ratify a Dawes loan of $90 million, with the understanding that the Chicago banks would supply another $5 million.

Everyone connected with the loan seemed to be keenly aware that it would be embarrassing to the Republicans. A huge RFC loan to the former RFC president who had been Vice-President of the nation was irresistible political ammunition. Yet Meyer made no apology for it. In the circumstances, the loan was a national necessity. "If the RFC was to be blamed for anything," he said, "it was for its failure to make more such loans. Its purpose was not investment but the curbing of disaster."

In fact the Dawes loan had been recommended by two Democratic directors of the RFC. As the political campaign warmed up, Congress passed a bill forbidding loans to any institution if one of its directors had been an RFC director within a year. The bill also opened the door to public disclosure of the names of borrowers and the amounts borrowed. The result of the latter provision was gravely to impair the usefulness of the agency because banks under pressure were fearful of starting runs on themselves by asking for an RFC loan.

There was a brief respite from the gloom of depression when the Meyers and their daughters Florence, Elizabeth, and Katharine went to Yale in June 1932 to see Eugene obtain an honorary doctorate. In a highly complimentary speech, Professor Phelps declared that the problems Meyer had to meet every day "would crush a lesser man." Yet the ceremony left the Meyer family unsatisfied. Somehow the atmosphere at Yale seemed stilted and divorced from the real world, and the honor had been so long delayed that it had little meaning.

By midsummer a feeble ray of hope began to filter through the dismal reports on the state of the economy. The RFC had sharply reduced the number of bank failures. Its loans to more than 5,000 financial institutions approached the $1.3 billion mark, and it had helped to liquidate or reorganize several hundred other banks—an amazing record. But there was no secure foundation for the new feeling of confidence that Meyer had labored so hard to create. Politics was the order of the day. The country had lost faith in Hoover's ability to pull the economy out of its funk. Many of his supporters were disillusioned, yet hopelessly committed to him. On the other side, some Democratic leaders seemed to be acting on the principle that continuation of the depression was the surest road for their return to power. Meyer himself was torn between his dissatisfaction with Hoover and distrust of Roosevelt, then the Democratic nominee for President.

Another tussle with Hoover developed when the President indicated that he wanted Harvey Couch to succeed Dawes. Unimpressed by Couch's performance on the board, Meyer interpreted this as a means of opening the RFC to congressional patronage (Couch was Senator Robinson's protégé) and ultimate Democratic control. Sentiment was mounting on Capitol Hill to make the RFC a sort of general relief agency. The trend of events brought home to Meyer how utterly exhausted he was. At fifty-six he had been working from 8 a.m. until the small hours of the next morning six days a week, with an overflow of homework and telephone calls on Sunday. Neuritis made it painful for him to walk; his weariness was so acute that he absentmindedly collided with a wall in his bedroom. As he mulled over his problem, he also concluded that he should resign on grounds of principle. His two jobs gave him more power than any one man should have. At the beginning he had felt it necessary for him to set up the RFC because of his background of experience, but it would be wrong to keep the job indefinitely.

Returning to Washington from Mount Kisco in early July, he conveyed his wishes to Secretary Mills and sought an appointment with the President for the same purpose. Forewarned by Mills, Hoover twice refused to give Meyer an appointment and ignored a letter that Meyer then wrote suggesting that all the ex-officio members of the RFC board, including himself, be replaced by people who could give full time to the work. While waiting for an answer, Meyer was called to a series of White House conferences on the relief bill before Congress, the last of which broke up in a row with Speaker Garner. Meyer emerged from this three-hour session so exhausted that his wife was summoned.

In cold fury, Agnes called Ogden Mills and told him bluntly that unless Eugene were removed at once from the RFC it would have no chairman and the Federal Reserve Board would have no governor, "as Eugene would not last a month."[8] Mills conveyed the message to Hoover later in the day, with the result that Owen Young was asked to become RFC chairman, but Young declined. The next day Meyer came home at 1 p.m. in a state of such exhaustion that Agnes rushed to Mills's office to plead for immediate legislation to get him off the board whether or not a successor had been found. Meyer was then summoned to the White House, and the President asked Congress to separate the two offices because of the "danger of a physical breakdown among the ex-officio members in their endeavor to carry dual duties." Congress responded in the Emergency Relief and Construction Act of 1932, which became effective

---

[8] Agnes E. Meyer's diary, p. 572.

July 21, and Meyer was succeeded by Atlee Pomerene, former Democratic Senator from Ohio.

The shift brought to light some criticism of Meyer for having held two such exacting and powerful positions, but this was tempered by wide appreciation of the work he had done. Felix Frankfurter telegraphed Mrs. Meyer that "Gene . . . has been the only brave and effective leader in Administration in dealing with depression." Lewis B. Williams wrote Meyer that "the importance and brilliance of your contribution to recovery" overshadowed the efforts of everyone else in the struggle. Agnes's proud comment was that, although the many terrible disasters that Eugene had prevented through the RFC would probably never be entirely known, the work he had done was that of "a Titan and a hero."

The RFC had not, of course, saved the country or ended the depression. Some of the ragged holes in the economic fabric had been too enormous for any kind of emergency patchwork. By its nature the RFC necessarily left many critical human problems untouched. Yet it supplied reserve strength that could not have been obtained in any other way. No doubt the RFC, like the WFC, both essentially Meyer creations, will stand as a historic precedent for governmental aid when the economic weather becomes too stormy for private banks and other essential institutions to survive on their own resources.

21 /

The Banking Holiday

BEFORE THE FINAL BOUT WITH THE DEPRESSION, THERE WAS A brief respite for the Meyers. Taking Bis (Elizabeth), Kay, and Ruth, they went on a ten-day yachting cruise on the *Idler*. Florence was in Salzburg, and Bill remained at home, free to come and go as he pleased, which, according to his mother, he "loved above all else." The boat was comfortable and the weather superb. Agnes and Eugene had their first rest in months. Her diary reports that "the children were charming, Kay especially beautiful and Ruth more independent every day."

At the age of ten Ruth demonstrated her independence by informing her father that she had been looking over the stock market and felt it was a good time to invest her money. "How much do you have?" Meyer asked. "My nickel bank is full and I have five dollars," she replied. "Mr. Woolley's stock is selling for five dollars, and I'd like to buy a share." Even the Old Maestro seemed a bit shaken when it developed that she hit the absolute bottom of the depressed market and her share proved to be worth $28 a few years later.

Bill's independence took a very different form. Asking his mother to sit down for a talk, he awkwardly handed her a piece of paper. "Don't be afraid," he said. "This isn't a marriage license." Rather, it was a pilot's license. The following day Bill went zooming over Seven Springs Farm in his "lovely silver plane" as the family sat on the terrace watching an eclipse.

Meyer's absorption in the national trauma was the most pressing reality the family had to live with. Even while he was setting up the RFC, he was deeply involved in revising the country's banking laws. For years the Federal Reserve Board had been asking for broader lending powers, but Senator Glass had stood in the way as a sort of Horatius at the central banking bridge. Glass had immense prestige in Congress, and, despite the close friendship that had grown out of their work together in the Treasury, he and Meyer were now looking in different directions.

The Senator from Virginia was engaged in a broad study of the national banking system with the aid of H. Parker Willis as technician for his committee. Willis was a professor of banking at Columbia whose rigid theoretical views collided with Meyer's more pragmatic concepts. Together, Glass and Willis seemed to regard themselves as the architects of the federal reserve system, and they were highly critical of the way in which it was being run. The reforms they were sponsoring were chiefly designed to curb inflation, despite the fact, as Meyer saw it, that "the country was almost dead from deflation."

While the contest over basic federal reserve policy was going on, a further worsening of economic conditions forced emergency action. Bank suspensions were mounting, foreign gold withdrawals had seriously depleted bank reserves, and currency was being hoarded in increasing volume. The result was a terrible tightness in the money market that frustrated recovery. "Free gold" held by the reserve banks had been reduced to about $500 million—less than one-half the short-term balances held by foreign banks in this country. The law required the reserve banks to hold, not only a 40 percent gold reserve against their federal reserve notes, but also collateral to the full value of their notes. Since the banks did not have enough "eligible paper" to use as collateral, they had to lock up $930 million in gold for this purpose, with the effect of causing a monetary famine. It was imperative to provide a different kind of collateral behind federal reserve notes, and Meyer proposed the temporary use of government bonds for this purpose.

The first problem was to convert Senator Glass to this relief from monetary strangulation. Glass had recently laid aside his basic reform bill for one emergency measure—the RFC. Realizing that only a tour de force would induce him to sidetrack his pet project a second time, Meyer tried to "scare the hell" out of the Senator and everyone else concerned. George Harrison, Randolph Burgess, and Russell Leffingwell also took a hand in the attempted conversion.

Meanwhile Meyer was once more at loggerheads with Hoover. For some time the President had been working for a broadening of the eligibility requirements of the Federal Reserve Act. At a White House conference in October 1931, he had obtained agreement from congressional leaders, along with Mellon, Mills, Harrison, and Meyer, on this objective. When Meyer sought means of meeting the new crisis, the President held doggedly to the October formula, which was not directly responsive to the most urgent requirement.

The two men attempted to iron out their differences at a conference in December. The President then wrote Meyer, asking him to review the

October agreement and not to "retreat from that position." Meyer was furious. He had no thought whatever of retreating from the agreement or of opposing broader powers for the board over eligibility. Indeed, he had been urging this reform for ten years. What he was trying to make the President see was that this particular reform was not as urgent at that moment as the authority to use government bonds in place of gold as collateral behind federal reserve notes. The President, he said, "wanted to talk about the necessity of fireproof construction when what we needed was water, quick, to put out the fire."

The controversy was finally resolved at a White House breakfast on February 9. The guests included Senators Glass, Robert J. Bulkley, Frederic C. Walcott, and John G. Townsend, Jr., in addition to Mills, Dawes, and Meyer. Before it broke up, Glass had promised the President that he would introduce an emergency bill, despite his continued dislike for it. His concession helped to bring leaders of the House into a receptive frame of mind at a second White House conference the same day. The compromise finally worked out partly satisfied Glass and Hoover and fully satisfied Meyer. It was divided into three parts: (1) Section 10 (a), for which Glass was largely responsible, allowing the federal reserve banks to make advances to groups of banks on sound assets not previously eligible; (2) Section 10 (b), reflecting Hoover's special concern, which permitted the discount of noneligible assets "in exceptional and exigent circumstances" and at higher rates; and (3) Section 3, Meyer's contribution, permitting the use of government bonds as collateral behind federal reserve notes.

Meyer assumed the chief burden of explaining the bill to the House Committee on Banking and Currency. The squeeze in the money market, as he explained it, resulted from the hoarding of about $1.25 billion in currency, amounting to nearly half the total of federal reserve notes outstanding. Ordinarily the reserve banks would back up their currency by the statutory 40 percent gold reserve and 60 percent commercial paper. But the depression had almost dried up the supply of commercial paper, so the reserve banks had had to substitute gold for it, with the result that $2.9 billion of federal reserve notes were backed by $2 billion of gold. Passage of the bill, Meyer said, would allow the reserve banks to free a large part of this gold by putting United States securities in its place.

The compromise bill passed the House by a vote of 250 to 15 under the most drastic procedure known to Congress, and the Senate followed suit soon after Glass finished explaining at length why he was advocating a bill that he disliked. Senator Blaine complained that Congress had been told bear stories with the lights turned low. Meyer acknowledged that a "technique of terror" had been used because of the gravity of the emergency. The advocates of the bill had been scrupulously careful, however, to avoid alarming the public.

As soon as the bill became law on February 27, the reserve banks began buying large quantities of government bonds—more than $1 billion worth in the next five months. Credit was eased, interest rates declined, some currency came out of hoarding, gold began to return from abroad, and there was a notable gain in industrial production and employment. The psychological impact came not only from more plentiful credit but also from the fact that the complex and impractical conditions imposed by the original Federal Reserve Act on central banking operations had been lifted. At last the system could make effective use of its assets no matter what their category, origin, or denomination. In this sense the Glass-Steagall Act, though a temporary emergency measure, proved to be a vital turning point in federal reserve legislation. Its more important provisions were made permanent, and rigid theoretical limitations gave way to greater reliance on judgment and choice of action in the light of realities.

About the same time the federal reserve system was confronted by a mischievous demand that it should thenceforth maintain stable commodity prices. This sweeping antidepression measure, sponsored by Representative T. Alan Goldsborough, proved to be popular in Congress and elsewhere. Its purpose was to authorize and direct the Federal Reserve Board to restore the wholesale commodity price index to the 1926 level and keep it there. While pointing out that the board was already exerting its powers to stimulate business and raise commodity prices, Meyer opposed the bill with all the force at his command. The very idea of maintaining a static economic condition in a dynamic world was repulsive and beyond the powers of a governmental agency in a free country. Despite the warnings, the House passed the bill, 289 to 40. In the Senate, however, Glass succeeded in displacing the fanciful Goldsborough scheme with a harmless authorization for an increase in national bank note circulation, which satisfied the congressional yearning for a gesture against depressions.

On a different front, Glass himself was causing the harassed federal reserve governor more trouble than Goldsborough. He was continuing to push his long-range banking reform bill which Meyer considered both drastic and reactionary. A copy of the bill, drafted largely by Glass and Willis, went to the board on March 17, 1932. Since Meyer was devoting long days to federal reserve and RFC business, he undertook a study of the Glass bill at night sessions in his home, with the aid of Chester Morrill, Walter Wyatt, Floyd Harrison, Winfield Riefler, and Dr. E. A. Goldenweiser. The meaning of every word and paragraph was analyzed in great detail. Many of these sessions continued until 4 a.m. and contributed much to the later breakdown of Meyer's health. At the end of eleven days this group had drafted a report on the bill, which won unanimous support from the board.

When Meyer testified on the bill before the Senate Banking and Currency Committee on March 28, he and Glass were in full agreement on one aspect of the problem. Both considered the country's dual banking system a curse. But the bill left this problem entirely untouched, because the Senator had not been able to find any constitutional means of requiring unification. Meyer was confident that Congress did have authority to unify the nation's banks and volunteered to supply the committee with a legal memorandum to point the way; Walter Wyatt prepared such a memorandum, but nothing came of it.

Many of Meyer's objections to the Glass bill involved loose drafting and technicalities, but basic principles were also at stake. In order to discourage use of the central banking system for speculative purposes, Glass was trying to force the reserve banks to confine their member banks to short-term, self-liquidating transactions. Meyer also feared that the provision aimed at the abusive use of banking affiliates might do more harm than good and that the bill would produce further deflation at a time when the board was trying desperately to move in the opposite direction. Its excessive rigidity threatened to substitute crippling restraints for administrative judgment and moral courage in the Federal Reserve Board. Finally, Meyer tried, without success, to win support for a system of bank reserves, worked out by Winfield Riefler, based on the velocity of deposit turnover. The effect of Meyer's report was to leave the Glass-Willis bill a shambles, but Glass accepted help from Morrill and Wyatt in recasting the bill in the light of the board's criticism. It would ultimately become law, but not until after the country had been convulsed by still another crisis.

With the RFC in operation, the Glass-Steagall Act on the books, and fundamental banking reforms in process, the outlook for recovery substantially improved. Thanks to the Federal Reserve Board, credit was plentiful and interest rates low. For a time production increased, and conditions abroad were more stable. But the economic gains were repeatedly undermined by political confusion as the country muddled through its quadrennial presidential election campaign.

After Franklin D. Roosevelt's decisive victory in November, hopes for a new start were blighted by a perilous interregnum of four months. The "ins" could only mark time, and, with hostility and distrust between the two parties at high tide, no basis for cooperative action could be found. There were persistent rumors that Roosevelt would devalue the dollar, and his silence on all matters of policy contributed to increasing drains upon the banks. Nearly a billion dollars in currency went into hoarding in February 1933. So the period became, not one of recovery or of heroic action, but one of confusion, futility, and partisan brawling. For Meyer and his colleagues, it would always remain an unhappy memory. Deeply involved in an on-going operation, they could only continue playing their respective roles to the best of their ability and judgment, and that course would arouse further enmity on the part of the President they were trying to help.

The first of the statewide bank holidays was proclaimed by the governor of Nevada in November 1932. Others followed, and when Michigan closed her banks on February 14, 1933, the alarm reached epidemic proportions. Hoover wrote a letter on February 22 reminding the Federal Reserve Board of its "great responsibility in the control and management of the currency," and asking advice as to whether the situation had "reached a public danger" and whether new authority should be sought. It had the ring of a trivial note for the record. Instead of bluntly acknowledging that nothing could be done as long as the stalemate between the President and the President-elect continued, the board replied sotto voce without making any recommendations. The President would later pounce on the board's statement in this letter, that it was weighing every proposal with great care so as to avoid any action that "would be likely to bring even greater disturbances," as evidence that it was minimizing the danger.

On February 27, Meyer met with Mills and William H. Woodin, who had been designated as Roosevelt's Secretary of the Treasury. New trouble had broken out in the District of Columbia, and Mills was worried that banks might not be able to absorb the Treasury's refunding issue due about the middle of March. Meyer did not see how the Fed could engage in open-market operations to support the bond issue, as Mills requested, at a time when it was stiffening rates to discourage the exodus of gold. Such an attempt to help the Treasury, he told Mills, might hurt it instead and would raise questions about the independence of the federal reserve system.

The President wrote to the board again on February 28. Did the board "consider it desirable: (a) to establish some form of federal guarantee of banking deposits; or (b) to establish clearing-house systems in the affected areas; or (c) to allow the situation to drift along under the sporadic state and community solutions now in progress." Again the discussion of fire insurance in the face of a raging conflagration! The guarantee program he was talking about would have insured bank deposits up to 50 percent at a time when no one knew what that would involve. But the board could have replied constructively without swallowing Hoover's specific idea. Instead, it lamely reported that it was "not at this time prepared to recommend any form of federal guarantee of banking deposits." Though the board could not safely move toward a guarantee of deposits when the banking system was collapsing, Meyer and his colleagues were open to criticism for this negative response. The Federal Deposit Insurance Corporation established by the New Deal, with a guarantee of deposits up to $5,000, demonstrated that depositors could be protected without subsidizing bad banking.

The idea of issuing clearing-house certificates or script had been pressed on the President by a personal adviser, Henry M. Robinson, a Los Angeles banker, and it became the subject of a meeting in Meyer's office the night the letter was received. Even Robinson seemed to have little faith in it. Meyer and George Harrison regarded it as an exercise in utter futility. Clearinghouse certificates had served a purpose in the panic of 1907 when currency was not obtainable, but in 1933, with the federal reserve system and the RFC in operation, any bank with assets could obtain currency. The debate on an almost forgotten relic of the past proved to be only a waste of time.

It was painfully obvious that the third alternative the President had posed before the board—that of doing nothing—was petty scapegoating. If the board did not accept his useless last-minute suggestions, it would bear the onus of the approaching disaster. That aspect of the letter was infuriating, but Meyer and his colleagues let it pass.

On March 1 the big banks in New York, which served as depositories for other banks in the United States and abroad, were overwhelmed by demands for funds. Meyer spent the day trying to get the federal reserve bank in Chicago to relieve the resulting stringency and then rushed to New York in the evening, with Mills and Woodin, to survey the emergency there. Bank holidays or legislative restrictions on the withdrawal of deposits were in effect in ten states, and six more states would join the group the following day. Fear gripped the whole country. The economic structure painfully built over two centuries appeared to be in danger of toppling.

The need for a national banking holiday was no longer open to question. Yet there was still hesitation because no clear-cut authority for the President to act could be found, the hope of getting an immediate response from Congress seemed nil, and Roosevelt steadfastly refused to join Hoover in any action. Hoover's approach to the President-elect had been inept and self-serving. In effect, he attempted to use the crisis as a bludgeon to commit F.D.R. to Hoover's own rejected policies, and the President-elect used this as an excuse for doing nothing whatever in cooperation with Hoover. So the drift toward disaster continued.

On the afternoon of March 2 Dr. Miller went to the White House with a plea reflecting the views of all the appointive members of the board that the President proclaim a national banking holiday. Miller took the initiative because he was a personal friend of both Hoover's and Roosevelt's. By this time Hoover's enmity toward Meyer was painfully evident. The President gave Miller a letter to be laid before the board at its meeting scheduled for that evening, "thinking that the board's support might yet secure Roosevelt's approval of this plan."[1] The letter said that the President would "be glad to have the advice of the board" on the use of his emergency powers "for the purpose of limiting the use of coin and currency to necessary purposes," along with a proposed proclamation, if the board felt the powers should be used, "as it would seem to me that it should be issued by me before banking hours to-morrow morning."

Once more the President and the board were operating on different wavelengths. Hoover was talking about curbing withdrawals of currency and gold. Meyer and his colleagues thought only the more drastic remedy of temporarily closing all banks would suffice. Even before the crisis became acute, the board had had its counsel prepare an executive order declaring a national bank holiday, to be used in case of necessity. It drew upon the President's powers under the 1917 Trading with the Enemy Act —an admittedly dubious source. After consulting counsel for the Treasury and the board, Attorney General William D. Mitchell had told Hoover there was sufficient "color of authority" in the old wartime statute to warrant issuance of the proposed proclamation if he thought the emergency was serious enough, but Mitchell had refused to advise such action unless Roosevelt would give it his blessing. Meyer felt there was too much fussing about acquiescence of the President-elect, since it could not enhance the validity of the proposed order, but he thought there should be agreement, if possible, to call Congress promptly to ratify the action.

At about 11 p.m. on March 2, Mills reported the board's plea for a national banking holiday to Roosevelt, who had arrived earlier in the evening at the Mayflower Hotel. About midnight Dr. Miller tried in vain to bring the two sides together. According to Raymond Moley, F.D.R. was confronted by both Hoover's idea of a proclamation to stop gold and currency hoarding and the holiday proposed by the Treasury and Federal

[1] *The Memoirs of Herbert Hoover, The Great Depression* 1929–1941 (New York: Macmillan; 1952), p. 212.

Reserve Board.[2] Although he appears to have concluded that a banking holiday would be necessary, F.D.R. refused to join Hoover in action of any kind.

The day before the inauguration (March 3) the crisis worsened. The board approved advances in the discount rates by New York and Chicago and authorized two of its members to approve increases by other reserve banks up to 4½ percent. Banking holidays were ordered in seven additional states. By afternoon withdrawals from the reserve banks were threatening to reduce their reserves below the legal minimum. Universal closings had become imperative.

In the late afternoon Meyer left a meeting of the board to report the mounting disaster to the President. While he was waiting to be ushered into the inner office, Theodore Joslin, a presidential secretary, introduced his young son to "Governor Meyer."

"What state are you governor of?" the boy asked.

"The state of bankruptcy," the weary governor replied.

Meyer concluded from his interview with the President that he was at last ready to proclaim a banking holiday, but only with Roosevelt's concurrence. Hoover insists in his *Memoirs*, however, that he "refused to declare a holiday but constantly proposed, up to the last minute of my Presidency (eleven p.m. of March 3rd), to put into effect the executive order controlling withdrawals and exchanges if Mr. Roosevelt would approve."[3] In any event, no action was taken. Hoover discussed the threat of calamity hanging over the country when F.D.R. made his courtesy call at the White House, but without altering the deadlock.

At 9:15 p.m. Meyer assembled his colleagues for a third time that day, summoning Hamlin from a concert. All hope that Congress might intervene with emergency action had passed. Once more the board reviewed the reports from the country and once more unanimously concluded that the holiday proclamation should be issued. Secretary Mills agreed. Meyer called the President and said that the board felt that immediate action had become imperative. Hoover seemed more reluctant than he had been a few hours earlier. Miller again tried to impress Roosevelt with the gravity of the crisis.

From the New York and Chicago federal reserve banks came alarming messages that a holiday was necessary to save their remaining gold and currency. Meyer tried to reach Mills again and learned that he had gone to the White House. A call there was taken by the President, and Meyer tried once more to convince him that a holiday was essential, with

[2] Raymond Moley, *After Seven Years* (New York: Harper; 1939), p. 144.
[3] *The Great Depression 1929–1941*, p. 213.

or without Roosevelt. Mills came back to the board's conference room, and Meyer also sent for James, who was sick. There was no compunction about calling a sick man because everyone in the toils of this nightmare was sick by this time.

Having failed to convince the President by oral argument, the board decided to put itself on record. There was some controversy over how the President's letter should be answered, but this was only because Mills sought to shield the President from the inevitable repercussions that would follow disclosure of his stubborn resistance to the essential banking holiday. At Mills's request, a reference to the "conversations" between board members and the President was eliminated from the letter. In its final form, it cited the latest perils, noted the calls for a holiday by the federal reserve banks in New York and Chicago, and concluded with this urgent plea: "The Federal Reserve Board feels that it can not too strongly urge that the situation has reached a point where immediate action is necessary to prevent a banking collapse." The letter was accompanied by a proposed executive order proclaiming a national banking holiday from Saturday, March 4, to Tuesday, March 7, both dates inclusive.

Meyer sent his secretary, Frank Fahy, to the White House with the letter and proclamation. The President had gone to bed, and no one was willing to disturb him, until Lawrence Richey was called and gave his consent. Hoover's wrath boiled over. Awakened in his weariness, near the point of prostration, he was confronted by another prod from a board whose advice he had repeatedly rejected. The only excuse for that encroachment upon his rest was the peril that hung over the entire nation— a peril that only the President could arrest. The weary board itself continued in session until 4 a.m., trying to get the states in which banks were still open to declare holidays the next morning if the President should not. Word came shortly after 3 a.m. that state holidays would be in effect in the two most critical centers—New York and Chicago.

One of Hoover's last official acts on March 4 was to write Governor Meyer a sizzling reply. His complaint was that the board had urged issuance of the banking holiday proclamation despite the facts that: (a) Roosevelt did not want it; (b) the Attorney General was dubious about the authority to act without F.D.R.; and (c) the governors of New York and Illinois were ready to act if bankers in those states thought it necessary. "In view of the above," the letter concluded, "I am at a loss to understand why such a communication should have been sent to me in the last few hours of this Administration, which I believe the Board must now admit was neither justified nor necessary."

When he wrote his *Memoirs* many years later, Hoover was still bristling over this fight with the Federal Reserve Board. "The majority of the Board," he wrote, "again declined to have any part in the proposed recommendations to Roosevelt or the Congress. I concluded it was indeed a weak reed for a nation to lean on in time of trouble."[4] In attempting to sustain that charge, he quoted his own letter inviting the board to propose a proclamation and completely ignored the board's reply in which it submitted a different kind of proclamation. He made no reference to Meyer's oral pleas for a banking holiday. The record conclusively shows that, instead of being "a weak reed," the board was working day and night for action much stronger than Hoover would take. It was neither confused nor divided. Its recommendation was well considered and presented with vigor and tenacity. Of course, the board could not issue an executive order of its own to close the banks. Short of that, it went as far as it could to avert national disaster. In effect it forced a banking holiday on its own responsibility by closing the federal reserve banks. The continued drift toward a banking collapse was a result of the deadlock between Hoover and Roosevelt and of Hoover's timidity in the face of that political stalemate. Shortly after the inauguration, F.D.R. issued the board's proclamation in slightly modified form.

Incidentally, Hoover's assumption in his irate letter that F.D.R. "did not wish such a proclamation issued" was clearly erroneous. So was his assumption that the board knew Illinois and New York would declare banking holidays. The assurance came only after the board's letter had been written. In his fatigue, Hoover lashed out recklessly. What really distressed him was the firmness and vigor of the board's efforts to push him farther than he was willing to go.

The final strain on the Hoover-Meyer relationship was the President's wish to lead a general exodus when Roosevelt came in. To this end he urged not only Meyer but also Chief Justice Hughes and other high officials to resign as of March 4, 1933. Both Meyer and Hughes refused for the same basic reason. The offices they held were not political. In Meyer's case, he had served only two and a half years of a ten-year term. No governor of the Federal Reserve Board had ever resigned with a change of administrations, and Meyer refused to degrade the office by making it a political football. When F.D.R. specifically asked the governor to carry on, the latter had no thought of trying to work with the New Deal for any length of time, but his going would not be a mere partisan gesture.

Fearing that his intervention might not be welcome, Meyer did not inject himself into the planning for reopening the banks. The inexperienced

---

[4] *Ibid.*, p. 212.

Woodin left that task largely to Mills and Arthur A. Ballantine, former Under Secretary of the Treasury. Woodin did ask Meyer to manage the operation after it had been worked out, but Meyer declined on the ground that he did not have sufficient staff and that he would be suspected of favoring the national banks. Mrs. Meyer feared that her husband was "failing physically" during this aftermath of the banking crisis, and his secretary described him as "dazed," but he felt much better after getting a few nights' sleep.

Meyer was once more aroused when the Senate, in passing Glass's banking bill, attached an amendment by Senator Robinson to permit all state banks to borrow from the federal reserve system without meeting the qualifications or accepting the obligations of membership. With Glass and Miller, the governor rushed to the White House to tell the President that this would give state banks an irrational advantage over national banks, but F.D.R. brushed off the objections with a generalization that it would be "just a matter of administration." The implications were alarming. Apparently the President felt free to shape banking policy without so much as consulting the board or its governor. Nevertheless, the board sent a strong protest against the Robinson amendment to Capitol Hill, along with a proposed substitute. On March 16 Agnes recorded in her diary:

> Eugene is nearly killing himself over the bill to admit state banks to the Fed. Res. System because he has no support anywhere. The Pres. goes ahead without consulting him, the board is of no support whatsoever, and Woodin flutters between the W. H. and the Treas. like a butterfly with a broken wing. Tonight E. managed to insert in the legislation that st. banks must pay for membership in the Fed. Res. Sys. just as national banks do. That will keep out the busted banks.

A satisfactory compromise was worked out, but the incident was portentous. Even more troublesome was F.D.R.'s experimentation with the dollar. Meyer concluded that since he was not in a position to help determine "what the Roosevelt dollar should be like" it would not be advisable to appear to be in such a position. There is no evidence that he winced under the onslaught unloosed against him at this time by Senator Huey Long, but it certainly highlighted the hazards of public life at a strategic moment. Long was thundering that, despite the Democratic victory, which was supposed to have swept away the predatory classes, this awful Wall Street banker was still at the helm. F.D.R. was then trying to appease the fiery Louisiana kingfish, seemingly unaware that the irrepressible rantings would soon be shifted from Wall Street to the White House.

Only the timing of the governor's exit remained open to question. He was determined not to leave in a huff. With the fight over the banking bill ended, he asked for an interview with F.D.R. and was invited to a "tray luncheon" with the President and Mrs. Roosevelt on March 24, 1933. While the President did the lunching, Meyer sat around waiting for a chance to tell him that he wanted to quit. A follow-up letter written the same day tendered his resignation and requested the President to accept it "as soon as you can conveniently arrange to do so." Roosevelt asked that the governor remain until a successor could be chosen.

The day was significant in the Meyer family for another reason. That night Ignace Jan Paderewski, the great Polish pianist and statesman, played in the Westchester County Music Festival, and went to the Meyers' apartment in New York afterward for supper, with the result that Agnes fell in love again. While "studying the tablecloth," wondering how much of Walter Damrosch's chatter Paderewski could stand, she chanced to raise her eyes and found the great man looking at her. His gaze sank into hers so powerfully that she looked down again, but only for an instant. When their eyes met a second time, Agnes, in her own words, "let him have my soul entire." Slowly his head nodded in recognition, and, unable to endure it, Agnes raised her glass to his, proposing a toast in German. Explaining the incident in her diary, Agnes recorded:

> I do not care that he is one of the greatest living statesmen. I do not care that he is the world's greatest living artist. I am captured and held by the greatness of his soul and its indescribable beauty. Is it of any significance that on the 24th a great meteor fell from the heavens? What a day! A great star falls from the heavens. Eugene resigns from the political firmament and I fall in love with Paderewski.

In Washington the weeks of marking time were disconcerting. Congress was jumping at F.D.R.'s bidding and a new feeling of public confidence was everywhere apparent. In the Meyer household, however, it seemed that the New Deal was saving millions with one hand and spending billions with the other "in a rash, dashing, blind sort of way." Agnes was also depressed by the departure of the Claudels at the conclusion of the ambassador's tour of duty. "All that was fine and decent in Washington is disappearing, even among the foreigners." The only consolation was the Meyers' acquisition of the entire Claudel wine cellar, which Agnes welcomed in those prohibition days "with Robinson Crusoe's emotions when he landed his supplies from the boat on his raft."

Eugene's worst fears about the new administration were confirmed when F.D.R. issued his gold embargo proclamation on April 20. Impatience for release was further accentuated by a suggestion from Bill Ward that Meyer take over the job of running Westchester County. One day during the long waiting period the governor was accosted by a new guard at the door of the Treasury Building as he returned from lunch. "Do you work here?" the guard asked. "I don't know," the governor replied genially. "Have you heard anything?"

At last Meyer wrote the President that he would leave on May 6, if convenient, but Woodin pleaded for a few more days. On May 8 the following letter came from the White House:

My dear Governor Meyer:

In accordance with your request, I hereby accept your resignation as Governor and member of the Federal Reserve Board, effective at the close of business May tenth. Thank you very much indeed for complying with my request to remain until that date. I know this has been an inconvenience to you.

I am glad to assure you of my high appreciation of the fine service you have rendered the Government and the country, and to send you my best wishes for your future welfare and happiness.

Very sincerely yours,
Franklin D. Roosevelt

At last the ordeal was over. Meyer had been working for the government for sixteen years, often day and night, for a dollar a year or a relatively small salary. Hostile politicians had scrutinized his record without finding anything whatever that reflected on his integrity. No one could explain his extraordinary devotion and boundless energy except on the basis of sincere public service. There was never any indication that he might seek elective office. Meyer had simply proved to be an exemplary warhorse in the service of his country.

As governor of the Federal Reserve Board he had suffered many cruel disappointments. His two-and-a-half-year tenure included the worst crises the board would have to face in its first half century, but he had met them with courage, insight, and resourcefulness, often charting new courses because of the absence of any experience with a depression of such magnitude. Many of the measures that helped to stem the tide of disaster had an indelible Meyer stamp. An amusing cartoon of the period showed

Meyer as a magician pulling rabbits out of his hat—the National Credit Corporation, the RFC, the Glass-Steagall Act, the open-market policy, and the Commodities Finance Corporation. There were other contributions to stability—liquidation of the war debts and the Glass Banking Act—for which he shared credit, and many lonely struggles for solvency and sanity that remained unknown to the public. With more experience behind it, the board might well have done better, but its performance in the face of unprecedented depression was a highly creditable one.

"It was at all times evident," said *The New York Times*, "that a firm and experienced hand was on the tiller." "Governor Meyer did more than any one man, with the single exception of the President," said the New York *Herald Tribune*, "to turn the tide of the depression." There were many others in similar vein: ". . . perhaps the most sincere 'career man' in the Capital"; ". . . one of the most useful public servants . . . in many years"; ". . . the government's handyman when there was work to be done with money." Several decades after Meyer had left the board some experts in the sphere of central banking would continue to regard him, despite his relatively brief tenure, as the best governor the system ever had.

In Meyer's own mind, however, the experience remained an unhappy one. Despite his love for reminiscence, he was reluctant to talk about his days and nights at the Fed. In this highest official post that ever came to him, his cherished dream of giving the country a sound, manageable, and unified banking system had been thwarted. He had only the comfort that he had striven mightily, with shrewdness and boundless energy, against the greatest economic debacle that ever afflicted the nation.

22 /

Plunge into Journalism

THE GREATEST MISCALCULATION EUGENE MEYER EVER MADE about himself was his assumption, as a young man, that he would want to retire at age sixty. When he left the Federal Reserve Board at fifty-seven he was indeed exhausted, and Agnes spoke of him as being at "death's door." But two weeks of sleep and rest restored his spunk. Walking down the front-hall stairs at Mount Kisco with a hand on the bannister, he detected dust and snorted accusingly at Agnes: "This house is not properly run."

"You'd better go buy the *Washington Post*," she snapped.

It was not a suggestion out of the blue. On several occasions Meyer had toyed with the idea of a journalistic career. Publishing a good daily paper could be another form of public service. Back in 1920 he had rejected Adolph Och's suggestion that he join *The New York Times*, because it was related to the business end of the paper. But if he bought a newspaper of his own, he could choose for himself the role he would play. In 1925 he had made a bid for the Washington *Herald*. William Randolph Hearst was then publishing both the morning *Herald* and the afternoon *Times*. Meyer had asked Arthur Brisbane, the Hearst columnist, to arrange a meeting for him with the publisher when the latter came to New York. The result was an invitation to lunch with Mr. and Mrs. Hearst in their Ritz-Carlton apartment. Meyer's offer to buy the *Herald* had elicited Hearst's customary reply: "I always buy newspapers, never sell them." But Hearst could not resist fishing a little in the troubled waters of his Washington publishing venture. "What," he had asked, "makes you think it would be a good idea to sell one of my Washington newspapers?"

"You are reported to be losing about a million and a half dollars a year," Meyer had replied. "This is not likely to change because these papers conform to the policies of the Hearst chain of twenty-four papers. Your type of paper is set for you by the proletariat of New York, Chicago, and San Francisco, but it doesn't have much market in Washington, which does not have an industrial working class. I can understand why you want one outlet in Washington to influence legislation, but you don't need two papers for that purpose—especially two that are fighting one another and costing you a lot of money."

Meyer had half-expected Hearst to be incensed by this candid talk from one who had had no experience whatever in the journalistic field. But the luncheon had ended on friendly terms. Hearst merely ignored Meyer's offer. When the publisher found it necessary a few years later to cut his losses in Washington, he turned to a friend of the Meyer family, Eleanor (Cissy) Patterson, who first became executive editor of the *Herald* and then acquired a lease on both the *Herald* and the *Times* after she bailed Hearst out of a payroll crisis.

Meyer's interest shifted to the *Washington Post*, a once lively and influential paper which had hit the skids because its playboy owner, Edward B. McLean, was milking it to satisfy his passion for horses, jewels, and women. Adolph Ochs had volunteered the advice, at Meyer's request, that a newspaper ought to be worth $5 million if its gross amounted to half that sum. But Meyer had no idea what the *Post*'s gross was and feared any attempt to find out would tip his hand. In any event, he had reasoned he could buy a newspaper at a phony price by selling stocks at a phony price. In May 1929, he offered the trustee in control, the American Security and Trust Company, $5 million for the *Post*, feeling that such an offer could not be resisted. Apparently McLean and the trustee bank were willing to sell, but Evelyn Walsh McLean, wife of the publisher and owner of the famous Hope diamond, insisted on keeping the paper as a buttress to her social prestige and a power base for her sons.

After his retirement from government service in May 1933, Meyer told his colleagues that he intended to go back to Westchester County and grow apples for the Washington applesauce market. His jest was only a camouflage for the serious ideas that were taking shape in his mind. From Wall Street came suggestions that he could become the dominant voice of American business in the recovery period and boost his fortune into billions. But there was no lure in merely amassing wealth for its own sake.

One venture to which the retiring governor gave more than passing thought was the management of Westchester County. Bill Ward, the enlightened county boss, had picked Meyer as his successor, and the latter had agreed to try his hand at the job, under Ward's guidance. But then the Meyers read in the press that the *Washington Post* would be sold at auction on June 1, 1933. Under the blight of depression, the *Post* had slipped deeply into debt; the trustee had finally ousted the incompetent publisher, who was confined to a psychiatric hospital, and the International Paper Company had forced the drifting journal into receivership in an effort to collect unpaid paper bills.

In his later years Meyer liked to relate his renewed interest in the *Post* to a telephone call from Cissy Patterson late one afternoon at Mount Kisco. The colorful and erratic editor of the *Herald* asked if she could dine with the Meyers that evening. "Yes, come on up," Meyer responded. "We have a few friends coming, but there is no reason why you shouldn't join us." The reason for her unusual request was soon evident. She asked her host point-blank: "Are you intending to buy the *Washington Post?*" As Meyer remembered it in later life, he really did not intend to buy the *Post* at that time, and it did not even occur to him that Cissy was sounding him out because of her own and Hearst's interest in it.[1] But Agnes's diary makes clear that Eugene had been thinking seriously of buying the *Post* even before his resignation from the Federal Reserve Board became effective. "If he succeeds," she wrote, "it will be a sensation and we shall have a reputation for Machiavellian behavior"—because they had prepared all their friends for their departure from Washington. She dismissed concern about the enormous expenses that would be involved: ". . . what after all is money for if not to be used. . . . It is a great opportunity for E. to be a dominant influence in this formative period of the new America . . . a great chance to be creative."[2]

Of course, the decision to buy the *Post* could not have been final at the time of Mrs. Patterson's visit, since it was to be sold at auction. But it is evident from the record that the old yearning for an amplified voice in public affairs was in ferment before her call. Meyer was too cagy to tip his hand to a competitor, and he still had a tentative commitment to Westchester County. He went to see Ward with the demeanor of one seeking release from a promise. "Do you think it is more important for me to buy the *Post*," he asked, "or to take the job you want to hand me in the county?" Ward looked pained. The burden he had hoped to unload was once more on his back. "I think you ought to buy the *Post*," he said, "if you can get it."

Since he had offered $5 million for the paper a few years earlier, Meyer concluded that any open bid of his at a public auction would be an invitation to price-boosting. Hearst would be a formidable competitor despite his financial troubles. Mrs. McLean was reported to be trying to pawn the Hope diamond to save the paper for her sons. After conferring with Alfred Cook in New York, Meyer returned quietly to Washington and, in the

---

[1] Dean Albertson's interview with Eugene Meyer, April 6, 1953.
[2] Agnes E. Meyer's diary, p. 655.

interest of secrecy, hired a young lawyer he had never seen before, George E. Hamilton, Jr., who happened to be an intimate friend of Samuel Kauffmann, assistant business manager of the Washington *Star*. Hamilton discreetly surveyed the assets of the *Post* and concluded that the ramshackle plant and run-down equipment were worth no more than $100,000. But the Associated Press franchise which the paper held and its historic prestige were assets of considerable value. The night before the sale Meyer gave Hamilton precise instructions on what to bid and when. About $1.7 million was placed at his disposal, and he was told not to bid more than $2 million.

The sale took place after dark on the steps of the old Post building on E Street, near its intersection of Pennsylvania Avenue. Evelyn McLean, resplendent with her Hope diamond, was the most conspicuous figure in the tense crowd of hopeful bidders, curious townsfolk, and worried employees. At first the lawyers for the McLeans, Hearst, and several other bidders sparred cautiously. Hamilton threw the proceedings into turmoil by jumping the previous bid by $50,000, as if to suggest that any further offers would be futile. Mrs. McLean dropped out at $600,000. Hearst's lawyer chased Hamilton up to $800,000. In accordance with his instructions, Hamilton at that point was topping each bid by going to the next multiple of $25,000. Cissy Patterson begged the auctioneer to delay knocking down the property to Hamilton while she telephoned Hearst for authority to go higher. Confusion mounted as the hammer was stayed. Three times the auctioneer came up to the point of declaring the property sold and then shied away from it, until Hamilton threatened to withdraw his top bid. Then the paper was knocked down to an unknown buyer for $825,000.

Hamilton was besieged by reporters seeking the identity of the purchaser. Hamilton's friends at the *Star* were especially mystified because he had jokingly told Kauffmann when they were playing golf together some weeks before that he was going to buy the *Post*. At that time he hadn't the remotest idea that he might be asked to buy it for someone else. To avoid being followed when he left the sale, he walked to Sixteenth Street, took a cab to the Meridian Hill Hotel, walked through the building and out the back door, where he crossed the street to the Meyer residence. Meyer and Floyd Harrison listened with much satisfaction to his report on the sale. The two men had been hiding in the Crescent Place home, which had been closed for the summer, taking care that no lights would show on the outside. Nevertheless, an automobile came up to the door. Hearing it, they waited in silence, but no one rang the doorbell. Harrison opened the door and saw that it was an *Evening Star* truck. "What do you want?" he asked.

"Is Mr. Meyer in?" a voice inquired.

"No," Harrison fibbed, "what makes you think he is in?"

"Well, we didn't know. We were sent to find out if he was here."

Meyer then called the airport, changed his plane reservation to the name of his secretary, and traveled to Mount Kisco incognito in an attempt to sustain the pretense that he had been there while the sale was taking place. The *Star* also sent a reporter to Mount Kisco, but he returned with the butler's assurance that Meyer had been injured by falling out of a tree while pruning it and could not be disturbed. Meanwhile rumors spread —one to the effect that Meyer had bought the paper at the request of a Republican faction which sought to harass the Roosevelt administration from the White House doorstep. Another said that the new *Post* would boom Ogden Mills for the Republican presidential nomination in 1936 so that Meyer could become Secretary of the Treasury.

The mystery persisted because the sale was not immediately confirmed by the court. Through his attorney, Meyer consented to a ten-day delay to avoid any suspicion of railroading. At the end of that period Attorney Charles Evans Hughes, Jr. sought to reopen the bidding so that Mrs. Mc-Lean could retrieve the paper. But the receiver, Benjamin S. Minor, reported that the highest bidder was ready to pay the entire price in cash, and the court ruled that the sale on June 1 had been both legal and conclusive. Meyer then disclosed his sole ownership of the paper and said that it would be published by a new Washington Post Company, with himself as president, Mrs. Meyer as vice-president, and Harrison as secretary-treasurer.

The new ownership was announced on the front page of the *Post* on June 13 in these words:

> It will be my aim and purpose steadily to improve *The Post* and to make it an even better paper than it has been in the past. It will be conducted as an independent paper devoted to the best interests of the people of Washington and vicinity, and hopes to have their interest and support.
>
> I think I should, in this connection, make it clear that in purchasing *The Post*, I acted entirely on my own behalf, without suggestion from or discussion with any person, group or organization.

The intent, of course, was to refute the rumors that the paper would become a Republican organ. When Meyer said the *Post* would be independent he meant independent with no "ifs" or "howevers," as readers would soon come to understand. Inexperienced though he was in the sphere of journalism, he knew that if the paper were to become an influential voice in the nation's capital, which was increasingly becoming a world capital, it would have to speak with its own voice. It would have to specialize in facts and seek wisdom from all sources—not grovel along a party line. Meyer was well aware of Lord Northcliffe's observation that "Of all the American newspapers I would prefer to own the *Washington Post*, because it reaches the breakfast tables of the members of Congress." But it would have to reach them with accurate news and editorials that would command both readership and respect.

The response to the announcement was generally favorable. Even Mrs. McLean expressed relief "that the *Post* has come into fine and honorable hands," although she was talking about starting another morning paper in Washington for her sons. The *Evening Star* said it was pleased that the *Post* would "be now under the direction of so broad-minded, capable and public-spirited a man." Adolph Ochs saw "unlimited potentialities" for the new *Post*. The *Louisville Times* rejoiced in the fact that "the *Washington Post* has gone into the strong hands of Eugene Meyer." Others said that the news about the *Post* was "too good to be true."

Beneath the congratulations and the great confidence in Meyer as an individual, however, there were many forebodings. How could an inexperienced publisher transform a failing newspaper into a great national organ under the intense competition then prevailing in Washington? Five dailies were fighting for advertising and circulation. The *Daily News*, Scripps-Howard's afternoon tabloid, was then a lively exponent of the New Deal. The *Star* dominated the journalistic scene with its bulging ads, extensive local news, and bland editorial policy. Though the Hearst papers, the *Herald* and *Times*, seemed out of place in Washington with their vitriol and their benighted views on foreign policy, Cissy Patterson had given the *Herald* a ranting and unpredictable quality that made it a formidable competitor in the morning field. It was an unhealthy climate for a paper on the skids. Even before the depression Oswald Garrison Villard had expressed doubt "whether it would ever be possible to have in Washington a really national newspaper."

The most pessimistic of Meyer's friends was Gardner Cowles, publisher of the Des Moines *Register and Tribune*. Though he had been well aware of Meyer's ability ever since the latter had arrested the agricultural slump in Iowa after World War I, Cowles bluntly told his friend that all the cards were stacked against him—he could not win. The landscape was cluttered with the wrecks of newspapers taken over by wealthy men who wanted to try their hand in journalism. While acknowledging the formidable odds against him, Meyer responded to Cowles's warning with unwavering cheerfulness: "The capital of this great nation deserves a good paper. I believe in the American people. They can be relied upon to do the right thing when they know the facts. I am going to give them the unbiased truth. *When an idea is right nothing can stop it.*"

In this mood Meyer began, at the age of fifty-seven, what was to be in many respects the greatest adventure of his life.

23 /

Every Mistake in the Book

THE NEW ERA FOR THE *Washington Post* OPENED WITH A furious fight over comics. In his first hours on the job the new publisher learned from A. D. Marks, business manager, that several syndicated features and the most popular comics published by the *Post*—"Andy Gump," "Dick Tracy," "Gasoline Alley," and "Winnie Winkle"—were in jeopardy. The *Post* held rights to these features and comics under a five-year contract with the New York *News*–Chicago *Tribune* syndicate, but Cissy Patterson was trying to snatch them for the *Herald*. Marks had written the syndicate during the receivership to reaffirm the *Post's* hold on the comics but could get no reply.

"Are comics important?" the financier-public-servant-turned-publisher asked. Marks eyed his new boss in amazement. Could any aspiring journalist be *that* dumb? "Yes," he replied earnestly, "they are extremely important, and we can't get a letter from Chicago."

They tried, without success, to telephone the head of the syndicate in New York. Meyer then sent a telegram asserting the *Post's* right to continue using the comics. No answer came. Warming to his task, he had Alfred Cook serve legal papers on the syndicate. The next morning the *Post* received a letter saying that the receivership had broken the contract and that the comics were being transferred to the *Herald*.

Meyer's answer was a suit in New York to compel specific performance under the contract. In Washington he obtained a temporary restraining order forbidding the *Herald* to publish the four comics. At this point Mrs. Patterson phoned to let her old friend know her personal feelings in the matter. Her brother, Joseph Patterson of the New York *News*, regarded himself as the godfather to these cartoon characters and since Colonel McCormick of the *Tribune* was her cousin and she herself was a major stockholder in the *News-Tribune* syndicate, she looked upon these comics as a family affair. Meyer replied that he owned the cartoon rights in Washington openly and fairly and had no intention of giving them up. After all, business was business.

"You know, of course, Eugene," she said, "this means a fight."[1]

Meyer was well aware of the fact that it meant a fight—a fight that he could not afford to lose. He was challenging the two biggest kingfish in the sea of journalism, Hearst and McCormick, at the outset of his new career, and defeat on such an issue would be extremely costly in terms of prestige no less than in newspaper circulation. But it was a fair settlement that he sought, not a public hullabaloo or a showdown in the courts. He wrote to Hearst saying that, although the case was in the hands of his lawyers, he would rather deal with it in a friendly way. Apparently neither Hearst nor McCormick was eager to fight on such a slippery battlefield. At one point Hearst wired his editor: "Never mind the *Tribune* features." But Cissy had the bit in her teeth. She concluded that, in any event, she had nothing to lose. If by any chance her raid should succeed in the courts, she would acquire valuable circulation-building features; meanwhile the furor itself would help to keep the *Herald* in the public eye.

When a judge dissolved the restraining order forbidding use of the comics in the *Herald*, that paper began printing the comics on July 16, although they continued to appear in the *Post*. Making good Cissy's threat to fight, the *Herald* proclaimed that it would be the exclusive outlet for the comics and invited *Post* readers to shift their allegiance. Parades, movies, and other forms of promotion trumpeted this invitation. In New York, however, Judge Peter Schmuck ruled that the *Post* was the legal owner of the comic rights, and before the year was out that decision had been upheld by the New York Court of Appeals. The appellate court in Washington ultimately got around to the same view, but even then Cissy petitioned for a stay of the mandate and a rehearing. When this failed, she went to the Supreme Court of the United States, which refused to hear the case, some felt because it could not endure the indignity of Andy Gump parading through its sacred precincts. The final mandate forbidding publication of the comics in the *Herald* was issued on April 10, 1935, more than two years after the fight had begun.

Even then Cissy pleaded for one more use of the pirated comics. The color-page features for the following Sunday had already been printed, she said. Meyer talked it over with his lawyers, and they urged him to "be nice" about it. He gave his consent on condition that the *Herald* print a front-page box indicating that the comics were appearing by the courtesy of Eugene Meyer, who, in the future, would have the sole right to publish

[1] Alice Albright Hoge, *Cissy Patterson* (New York: Random House; 1966), p. 128.

them in Washington. Cissy exploded with indignation. She had previously been incensed by Gene Elderman's huge cartoon showing the comic characters parading back to the pages of the *Post* by order of the Supreme Court.

For a fleeting moment, however, appearances were otherwise. Mrs. Patterson sent her old friends a present, seeming to acknowledge that they had won the case fairly. It was beautifully wrapped and decorated with flowers. "How nice of Cissy," Agnes exclaimed as Eugene proceeded to open the gift. "I wonder what it is?" With the fancy trimmings peeled away, they gazed in astonishment at a piece of raw meat.

"A pound of flesh!" Agnes moaned.

Indeed, Cissy had left nothing to the imagination. She had scribbled on a card: "Take your pound of flesh!" For once, the tough fighter with thick cartilage in his nose was deeply wounded. A friend who formerly signed her notes "Affectionately yours," accused him of being a Shylock because he had resisted her raid on his newspaper and the courts had ruled in his favor.

The Meyers had first met Eleanor Patterson in 1917 when she was the glamorous Countess Gizycka. Both had been charmed by her red hair, sharp wit, and free-wheeling demeanor. At that time Agnes had characterized her new friend as "extremely feline" and had noted in her diary that she would see to it that she "did not get scratched." But there was no protection against Mrs. Patterson's fury when her emotions were aroused. Shaken though he was by her insult (his generosity was the antithesis of Shylock's merciless exactions), Meyer did not allow the incident to canker his soul or to cut off all communications with his former friend. On one occasion they happened to sit together at a Soroptimist Club luncheon at the Willard Hotel and joined in singing, with arms about each other's shoulders: "The more we get together, get together, get together, the happier we'll be." But Cissy's persistent badgering prevented their rivalry from attaining an amiable basis. While the fight over the comics was still going on, the *Herald* tried to pirate the name of the *Post*'s special column for government employees, "The Federal Diary." Again Meyer won in the courts. The poison-peddling at the *Herald* became so offensive at one point that Meyer called his nemesis on the telephone and said: "Cissy, if you don't stop telling lies about me, I'm going to tell the truth about you."

Yet the needling from H Street was a minor problem in the resuscitation of the *Washington Post*. *Fortune* once said that all Meyer got for his $825,000 "was an Associated Press membership, a run-down building and plant, and a name chiefly distinguished by the fact that John Philip Sousa had written a march in its honor." In the days of its prestige, carried over from the energetic management of John R. McLean, the *Post* had attained a circulation of 75,000. Under the management of McLean's playboy son "Ned," the circulation had slid to 51,534 in the receivership period, and about one-third of this was padding on the books for the sake of media records. Advertising had shrunk to a pittance, and rates had dropped to six cents a line for the big department stores in a desperate effort to keep some ads in the paper. The worn-out presses were matched by other defective equipment. The old building on E Street was a rat-infested shell that was wholly inadequate to the needs of a modern newspaper. The *Post* had lost most of its ablest writers because of the severe pay cuts imposed by the McLean regime during the depression. It was indeed a bleak picture that the new publisher surveyed. For the first few days he even had difficulty getting his name spelled correctly in the paper.

Meyer soon found, moreover, that his statement of intentions had been read with a great deal of skepticism. Would not the independent label he had attached to the paper turn out to be only a cover for a Republican organ? And if it did not, could a journal with such limited facilities be anything more than a rich man's toy? Many of the able people he tried to hire took a wait-and-see attitude. It required a tour de force on his part to line up the kind of persons he wanted in this new venture.

His problem was one of building a newspaper while at the same time keeping his readers informed in a period of fantastic and almost revolutionary changes. On the date that Meyer assumed the role of publisher, Congress passed the National Recovery Act. The New Deal was winding up its first fabulous one hundred days. Washington had become a sort of journalistic paradise. Roosevelt was experimenting with devaluation of the dollar in an effort to raise the general price level. A gigantic $3.3-billion public-works program was being launched, and the Tennessee Valley Authority was ushering in a new era of public power. The NRA was imposing codes on the country's leading industries. Farmers were being subjected to compulsory crop reduction. Prohibition was coming to an end, and F.D.R. recognized the Soviet Union for the first time since the Communists had taken control following World War I. Meanwhile a great drought had extended its grip over twenty-seven states. The year 1933 thus became possibly the most exciting in our peacetime history. To follow and understand these swift-moving events was a challenge to the most seasoned veterans of the press. For a newspaper undergoing a rescue operation it seemed to demand miracles.

Though his interest was centered in the editorial page, Meyer concluded that his reorganization should start with the news and business departments. He eliminated the 10 percent wage cut that the receiver had ordered, and began a search for outstanding writers and executives. Because of his own inexperience in the field, he sought a general manager, and, in his haste, took the first seemingly acceptable candidate who applied for the job, Eugene MacLean. A large, easygoing man, MacLean claimed credit for having lifted the Scripps paper in San Francisco from fifth to second place in circulation. Meyer's consultation with two friends in the business and an investigation of MacLean by Milton H. Esberg seemed to buttress the conclusion that he was the right man.

Meyer himself, however, took the initiative in recruiting a staff, offering some salaries that were far out of line with the pay scale then in effect. One of his first moves was to cable Elliott Thurston, then in London, because he had admired Thurston's reporting for the old New York *World*. Thurston signed a contract and became one of the *Post*'s leading correspondents. Other early additions to the news staff were Franklyn T. Waltman, a rising star on the Baltimore *Sun*, and William Harlan Hale, who stayed only a few months. Ralph E. Renaud, also formerly of the *World*, became managing editor, and Felix F. Bruner, city editor. Ralph W. Robey wrote a column largely on New Deal economics. Carlisle Bargeron was induced to shift his whimsical column from the *Herald* to the *Post*. On New Year's Day, 1934, Raymond Clapper of the United Press Bureau in Washington joined the *Post* staff and began a new phase of his career that was to lead to fame and tragedy. Clapper developed a close working relationship with Meyer that soon blossomed into friendship. As they discussed news coverage one day, Clapper emphasized the thousands of interesting aspects of the news that do not fit in news stories. Meyer responded: "Why don't you write them into a column?" That was the origin of Clapper's column which proved to be so popular that he was lured away by the United Features Syndicate and was writing for 180 newspapers when he was killed in a collision of war planes in the Pacific in 1944.

In his relations with his staff, as in his previous business associations and government service, Meyer was sometimes brutally frank. With a glance or a word, he could transfix an errant copy boy or make a careless reporter quiver. But the Clappers saw him as a human figure with a rare capacity for compassion. Invited to bring their two children to lunch at the Meyer home in Crescent Place, Ray and Olive coached the youngsters in proper behavior in such dignified surroundings. Everything went well at the big table until Peter, age six, was served a gleaming red lobster. Never having seen one before, the child found it impossible to restrain a flow of tears. Meyer was the first to notice it. Getting up from his chair and kneeling beside the boy, he put an arm around him and said: "Pete, I don't like these red monsters either. You and I are going to have roast beef." His kindness cemented an emotional bond between the two families.

Moving with great caution, Meyer imposed a virtual ban on the expression of any editorial opinion by the *Post* until he could effect a reorganization of the staff. Editorial conferences were held in his office—MacLean's authority did not extend to the editorial page. Floyd Harrison, who had long been Meyer's faithful alter ego in and out of government, became a sort of editorial hatchet-man to eliminate everything that might conceivably offend his chief or even express a positive view on any subject. It was a painful interregnum which plunged the staff into a frantic effort to fill the editorial page without saying anything.

Ira Bennett, the editor, was an able and fluent writer, though conservative and isolationist in his views. He had been worn out, in the years before the Meyer regime, trying to save the *Post* from Ned McLean's idiosyncrasies and Hearst's scheming to absorb it. The other members of the editorial staff were Captain Paul Hudson and myself.

Meyer told Elliott Thurston that he hoped to hire a great editor and a great cartoonist. His aim was to develop an independent paper that would be as powerful and as useful in America as was the *Manchester Guardian* in Britain. His first choice for the editorship was Douglas Southall Freeman, distinguished author and editor of the Richmond *News Leader*, but Freeman was tied too closely to his home town. Charles Ross was also considered, but he was under contract with the St. Louis *Post-Dispatch*. Thurston suggested Charles Merz of the editorial staff of *The New York Times*, and Meyer sent his new correspondent to New York to sound out Merz.[2] It was no use. Already on his way toward top editorial duties on the *Times*, Merz felt no pull toward the uncertain venture in Washington. A few days later Thurston met Felix Morley at the National Press Club and mentioned to Meyer that he might be the kind of vigorous, unlabeled young man he was looking for. Similar advice had previously been given by Frank Kent who had known Morley on the Baltimore *Sun*. At the time Morley, a brother of novelist Christopher Morley, was in charge of public relations for the Brookings Institution, having recently received a doctorate from Brookings for his book on the League of Nations. Inviting Morley to call on him, Meyer outlined his ambitions for the *Post* and asked him if he would like to take charge of the editorial page. "It would be a big job," Morley commented. Sizing up this thirty-nine-year-old former Rhodes scholar with a piercing stare, Meyer replied: "It's always good for a man to take a job bigger than he is."

[2] Elliott Thurston to author, February 27, 1972.

Intrigued by this challenge, Morley accepted the job with the under-standing that he would work in close consultation with Meyer, that he would be "editor in fact as well as name," and that he "would never be expected to write or sponsor an editorial expression with which I might be in thorough disaccord."[3] The publisher reserved the right, however, to make his views prevail in case of a showdown.

Morley took over the editorial staff in November 1933. Meyer had previously hired two new editorial writers: Dr. Anna Youngman, an economist with broad experience in the federal reserve system and the *Journal of Commerce*, and Mark F. Ethridge, formerly of the Macon *Telegraph*, who in later years would become publisher of the Louisville *Courier Journal* and *Times*. "Here's the baby," Ethridge told his new chief as the latter assumed control over the editorial page. "You hold it, and God bless you."

The new editor brought in Reginald Wright Kauffman, who supervised a change-of-pace column, "The Post Impressionist," and wrote light edi-torials. Other early additions to the editorial staff were Karl Schriftgiesser, Bett Hooper, and John M. Clark, who had been church and school editor. When Meyer called Clark into his office and told him he was to be promoted to the editorial staff, the young man fainted, apparently from shock added to a touch of food poisoning. Meyer rushed to his safe and brought out a bottle of brandy reserved for such occasions. Clark became a valuable contributor to the page until he left a few years later to operate a newspaper of his own and was tragically drowned at an early age in a boating accident. Morley also hired Joseph M. Lalley, a gifted and eccentric writer who commuted every day from Baltimore, and Barnet Nover of the Buffalo *Evening News*, who wrote a column as well as editorials on foreign affairs. The only carry-over from the previous editorial staff was myself.

Under Morley's direction, the editorial page began to acquire, as *Fortune* reported, "insight, vigor, and prestige." Editorial conferences were no longer held in Meyer's office, but he kept closely in touch with Morley, and for a few years they got along very well together. Morley encouraged his staffers to use their legs as well as their heads; they should know the city and the officials who made news and policy; they should probe into the background of the problems they wrote about. They should investigate both sides of a controversy, consult experts whenever possible, and then draw independent conclusions. The policy reflected Meyer's own lifelong respect for facts and his concept of the newspaper as a public institution.

As he had done in banking and government service, Meyer gave careful

[3] Morley to Meyer, November 28, 1933.

thought to where he was going. The set of principles he drew up to guide his publishing venture was printed on March 5, 1935, as follows:

> The first mission of a newspaper is to tell the truth as nearly as the truth may be ascertained.
>
> The newspaper shall tell ALL the truth so far as it can learn it, concerning the important affairs of America and the world.
>
> As a disseminator of news, the paper shall observe the decencies that are obligatory upon a private gentleman.
>
> What it prints shall be fit reading for the young as well as for the old.
>
> The newspaper's duty is to its readers and to the public at large, and not to the private interests of its owner.
>
> In the pursuit of truth, the newspaper shall be prepared to make sacrifice of its material fortunes, if such course be necessary for the public good.
>
> The newspaper shall not be the ally of any special interest, but shall be fair and free and wholesome in its outlook on public affairs and public men.

Meyer wanted the paper to attain a sound economic footing, and he was eager to have those who labored for it amply rewarded. But the satisfaction which he sought for himself was of a different sort. "In publishing *The Post*," he wrote to Samuel Crowther, "my only interest is to make a contribution to better knowledge and better thinking. If I could not feel an ability to rise above my personal interests or the interests of any and every faction or class, I would not have the slightest pleasure in being a publisher."

As for editorial policy, he wanted it to be consistent with freedom and the broadest concept of the general welfare. Editorials should be guided by (1) a belief in constitutional government; (2) a belief that civil liberties of all are best defended by protecting the civil liberties of each individual; (3) a belief that an expanding free economy will best satisfy the material needs of the people; (4) a belief that international cooperation is the safest road to peace and stability.

The neophyte publisher soon discovered, however, that it was one thing to lay down principles of integrity and fairness and quite another thing to make them count in day-to-day operations. The Sunday editor, Laura Vitray, needed a picture to illustrate a story about an African safari, and, finding nothing suitable, she had the art department paint an arrow into a picture of a lion so as to make it appear that he was dying in agony. The fakery might have gone unnoticed except for the fact that the *Star* printed the same picture on the same day, merely showing the lion frolicking on his back in the Washington Zoo. Meyer hit the ceiling. Ethridge conveyed the publisher's wrath to the hapless editor, but without any suggestion that heads would roll. Indeed, his rebuke was so suave that Vitray credited him with real executive genius.

Ethridge himself was involved in another incident which Meyer regarded as an infringement of his "fairness" rule. He wrote a sizzling editorial assailing Frank J. Hogan's tactics in defending William P. Mac-Cracken, Jr. against a contempt citation by a Senate committee. In effect, Hogan was accused of indulging in "silly procedure" and "smart practices and trickery." The lawyer demanded a retraction on the grounds that the editorial was "utterly untrue in fact" and that it reflected upon his personal and professional honor. Meyer was in Miami, but he telephoned MacLean, asking that he see Hogan and "do full justice to him and the facts." A second editorial three days later put the controversy in the MacCracken case in a somewhat different light, and Hogan telephoned his appreciation to Meyer for his "high sense of honor and fairness." The case became an important precedent. If an editorial proved to be factually inaccurate, or if a conclusion were based on faulty or inadequate information, the writer was expected to correct it without squirming or quibbling.

When a public official complained about an editorial, Meyer would often ask the writer to visit the official for a full discussion of the points at issue. Such confrontations were not always unpleasant. On one occasion Meyer sent a member of the staff to see Secretary of Agriculture Henry A. Wallace because the latter had complained that the export figures in an editorial criticizing his cotton policy were inaccurate. The writer explained to the Secretary that the figures had come from his own department. Wallace said that could not be so, but when the writer went to the Bureau of Agricultural Economics to recheck the figures he was summoned back to the Secretary's office. Wallace had also done some checking and wanted to apologize. "You were right," he exclaimed, with disarming candor, "and I was cockeyed."

Meyer demanded the appearance as well as the substance of fairness and objectivity. Thurston wrote a column about Justice Brandeis and was flabbergasted to hear the boss say that he hoped people would not get the idea that he was crusading for Jews. To avoid suspicion of racial favoritism or divided loyalty, Meyer refrained from any connection with the Zionist movement. During his Wall Street days, he had given both time and money, at the behest of Brandeis, to the cause of establishing a homeland for persecuted Jews. But he had stayed clear of Zionism while in the government, and this policy carried over into his journalistic career. Though he was alert to any injustice to Jews or other ethnic groups, he was determined to give no ammunition to those who might charge his newspaper with racial bias. For the same basic reason he refused a proffered decoration from the Mexican government and urged *Post* employees to assume a similar attitude toward any decoration or honor from a foreign power.

Assuming that the facts were straight and the reasoning sound, Meyer liked hard-hitting editorials and would back his editors to the limit. Fairness did not mean mushiness or quibbling. The new publisher seemed to relish a fight when the paper stood on grounds of high principle.

One of the first campaigns undertaken by Meyer's *Post* was aimed at amendment of the stringent 1933 act controlling the issuance of securities. Though Meyer was in full sympathy with the chief purpose of the law—to protect investors against fraud and loose practices in the sale of stock—he insisted that this objective could be attained without retarding the recovery that the country so urgently needed. Chairman Sam Rayburn of the House Interstate and Foreign Commerce Committee responded to the *Post*'s editorial pressure by a flat denial that the act was preventing the sale of securities. Meyer immediately wired leading financiers, bankers, industrial and insurance executives and printed their replies in the *Post*. All were in agreement that the act was stifling the issuance of securities, and their unanimity caused the Roosevelt administration and Congress to accept a liberalizing amendment. The *Post* had demonstrated that it could exert a powerful influence on public policy.

In January 1934, the paper launched a very different type of crusade aimed at Washington's hidden slums—the rotting and rat-infested alley dwellings that were contributing heavily to the city's crime, juvenile delinquency, and high death rate. Congress passed a bill authorizing replacement of the alley dwellings by good, low-cost housing, and the President assigned the job to John Ihlder, who had come to the top in a *Post* survey of available experts in that field.

Meyer was keenly interested in everything his paper did. Roaming through the old Post building, he became acquainted with printers, pressmen, and circulation people as well as writers, accountants, and executives. His presence in many places served a double purpose. He wanted to learn the business and at the same time infuse into those who put out the paper a new concept of their role in the community. One reporter credited the new boss with changing his whole thinking about journalism. Working for the *Post* was no longer just a job. Since the paper, in Meyer's words, was "engaged in a public service," the reporter concluded that he too must be "working for the people . . . quite a switch."

No task seemed beneath the dignity of the new publisher. He solicited ads and subscriptions; he investigated complaints that the paper was not delivered; he became a prolific source of news tips as well as editorial suggestions. Returning to the paper after dinner, he often remained far into the night, but he would be back again the next morning at ten o'clock. These working hours were so long and erratic that he stopped using his limousine at night out of consideration for his chauffeur, Al Phillips, and went home by taxicab. By the time the cab reached Crescent Place the driver would be feeling wormlike if he did not subscribe to the *Post.*

The victory of the Washington Senators in the 1933 American League pennant race was a great event for the *Post.* The sports department "played" the crucial games on a huge magnetic board erected in front of the building as each play was telegraphed from the stadium. Meyer liked to carry the play-by-play reports from the wire room to the magnetic board. He was so interested in the crowds watching the game that he would sometimes ask the board operator not to play a home run until he could get down to the street to see the faces of the cheering fans. The following year, however, the Senators fell upon hard times. The aspiring publisher asked sports writer Shirley Povich what had happened to the team, and when he was told that its pitching was weak he talked of lending $50,000 to purchase a first-rate pitcher.

Despite his great interest in editorial policy, Meyer himself seldom wrote editorials. Taking a hint from Mrs. Meyer, Morley asked his boss to write a piece on a change in the Federal Reserve Board's rediscount rate. Meyer asked how long it should be, and Morley suggested about a third of a column. When Morley went to the publisher's office later in the day, he found DeVee Fisher, the secretary, in tears. She had typed ten drafts of the editorial, and it still was not satisfactory. Meyer's desk and the floor around it were strewn with crumpled paper. "I can't possibly put this into a third of a column," the distracted publisher exclaimed. Morley then took the latest version and made a draft of his own which proved to be satisfactory. After this unhappy experience, Meyer passed his editorial ideas to members of the staff orally or dictated rough memoranda.

At first it was a strain for the former governor of the nation's monetary system to mix with reporters, copyreaders, advertising men, and printers. Though he made a conscious effort to understand his new employees, the gulf between them was not immediately bridgeable. On some occasions it seemed to be significantly narrowed, as when Meyer got down on his knees at a farewell party in the Willard Hotel for a departing employee and shot craps with the reporters. Surprised though they were by this unbending, no one seemed surprised when he won, despite his unorthodox method of throwing the dice against the wall. The habit of winning seemed deeply ingrained in his nature.

But some other efforts to narrow the employer-employee gulf clearly misfired. As the deficit in the company's operations became more and more conspicuous and troublesome, someone suggested that Meyer call the staff together and explain the growing pains the paper was experiencing. Meyer thought well of the idea and addressed himself to the theme that sacrifices on the part of everyone would be necessary. He wanted the staff to know, he said, that he was making sacrifices; he didn't take his usual trip to Europe last year, and he hadn't added a single painting to his collection of French Impressionists for two years. Many employees snorted over these "sacrifices" and continued with their plans to organize a unit of the Newspaper Guild.

The sometimes happy, sometimes awkward give-and-take between publisher and employees inspired Ed McSweeney, a financial writer, to fasten a nickname on the boss. Thereafter when reporters laughed at his inexperience behind his back and printers speculated about his fortune, they called him "Butch." Apparently Meyer first learned about the nickname from an article in *Time*. When he dropped into the newsroom one night he questioned Bill Nessly, night news editor, with more amusement than irritation: "Mr. Nessly, do you call me Butch?" Nessly couldn't conceive of anyone taking such liberties with the boss, but in time the name acquired an affectionate ring. One of the men in the city room explained: "I kind of have to hang on to myself because I'm getting to like the old man."

Many employees had special reasons for liking him. He lent money at low interest rates, or no interest at all, to help struggling writers buy homes. One reporter told Meyer about an explosion in the furnace of the new home he had just bought, which would cost him $800 he did not have. Meyer wrote a check for the amount and made it clear that no repayment would be expected.

One of the new men who came to regard the publisher as almost a father was Charles F. Moore, Jr., manager of public relations. At the end of the day Moore was often invited in for an extended period of reminiscence. He would park himself in a large mahogany wastebasket beside Meyer's desk and listen with rapt attention to his stories. One evening as Moore sat in the wastebasket (he insisted that its contours fit his own) he looked so dejected that Meyer asked what the trouble was. Moore replied that his small savings had been depleted since he had come to work for the *Post* and that his "economic anchor was dragging."

"What is your salary?" Meyer asked.

Moore named the figure, and the following week it was almost doubled.

Charlie, as everyone called him, supplied many of the promotional ideas that heightened public awareness of the "new *Post.*" When Mrs. Meyer suggested that the paper sponsor an art show, he worked with her to arrange the display of hundreds of paintings in all the Washington department stores. Local artists participated enthusiastically; many of the paintings on exhibit were sold; and the *Post* won new laurels for community service. At one of the exhibits Moore bought a painting of a Georgetown street. When he attempted to claim it, he was told vaguely that someone else had bought it. Furious, he demanded the name of the person who had taken the picture and learned that it was Mrs. Meyer. That information intensified his boiling, and he went home swearing that he would quit the paper the next morning. As he opened the door to his living room, however, there were the Meyers hanging the picture on his wall, Eugene on a rickety ladder and Agnes giving directions as to just where it should be hung. The promotion manager was almost speechless with mortification.

As the *Post* struggled to find its new role, it was often at odds with the New Deal. Meyer felt that fundamental changes in national policy were being made with little regard for their constitutionality or long-range soundness and that many critics had been silenced for fear that they would be charged with fostering self-interest. His own policy was to avoid carping, yet to speak out candidly when he thought the public interest was endangered. An analysis of the *Post's* editorial columns, he told the American Society of Newspaper Editors, would show that it had supported as many administration measures as it had opposed, and the paper had "never once stooped to criticism for the sake of mere opposition." Its harshest words had been directed at F.D.R.'s "policy of extreme federal regimentation."

"The principal fault I have to find with your friend in the White House," Meyer wrote to Felix Frankfurter on December 24, 1933, "has to do with his fondness for expediency against principle. I am old-fashioned enough in my philosophy to believe that policies based on decent and wise principles will stand up in the long run, and that expediency takes more brains than anybody has, especially in the kind of world in which we live." A few months later Meyer wrote Frankfurter in London that it was time for him to return. "The young men you left behind you," he continued, "have come pretty near wrecking the country, and some of their performances, while high-minded, do not reflect glory on you as the 'practical' man I know you to be."

Thurston was the first correspondent to report that Roosevelt was about to devalue the currency. *Post* editorials assailed the concept, which seemed to be prevalent at the time, that commodity prices could be controlled and prosperity restored by manipulating the gold content of the dollar. Thurston, Ralph Robey, and Anna Youngman wrote voluminous explanations of F.D.R.'s monetary experimentation and its probable consequences. The paper accommodatingly changed its type so that it could get billion dollar figures, so common in New Deal stories, into its headlines. At the same time, however, the paper warned: "If Mr. Roosevelt throws one more digit at us, *The Post* will match the rubber money, dollar for dollar, with rubber type."

Having no sympathy with regimentation, Meyer also resisted the bid of the National Recovery Administration for his cooperation. When he arrived at the office one morning, the NRA's "Blue Eagle" was conspicuously displayed through the building and the elevator. Meyer had the cards thrown out and refused to put the Blue Eagle on the front page of the *Post*, as requested. He compromised, however, by having a small Blue Eagle printed inconspicuously on one of the back pages so as to avoid, he said, any charge of "treason."

As NRA administrator General Hugh Johnson intensified his "crackdown" on uncooperative corporations, the *Post* repeatedly warned that attempts to enforce the codes by criminal prosecutions would lead to intolerable regimentation and chaos. The general threatened: "You ain't seen nothin' yet." To this the *Post* replied on March 9, 1934:

> His words may well be prophetic. But we have seen enough to know that we stand at the crossroads in our national history, and to know further that if a truly "planned economy" is to be substituted for our present system there must be changes of which the country has as yet no real conception.

The Washington scene had been enlivened in 1933 by many colorful figures in addition to the dashing and seemingly reckless new President and General Johnson, the fire-eating head of the NRA. By way of acquainting its readers with the new crew of policymakers, the *Post* serialized an anonymous book entitled *The New Dealers*, without endorsing its conclusions.

Enraged by some references to himself, General Johnson denounced the book and the *Post* in a nationwide radio broadcast. The writer, he said, had "more than a trace of rodent blood" in his veins and his drivel had been printed by "a dying newspaper, recently purchased at auction by an Old Dealer—a cold-blooded reactionary—who was one of the principal guides along the road to the disaster of 1929." The *Post* printed the Johnson blast and along with it a statement by Meyer showing that the "dying newspaper" had increased its circulation 37 percent under its new management and stood third in advertising lineage gains among all the newspapers of the country. Instead of replying in kind, the statement said the *Post* had a high regard for Johnson's ability, energy, and devotion to the public interest and expressed regret that it could not "also admire his self-control or temperance in public utterance." The Associated Press carried the statement, and Meyer considered it the best advertising the *Post* ever had. At that point he ceased to advertise *The New Dealers* in other publications and explained to magazines that solicited such ads that General Johnson had done a better job than they could—that "his circulation is greater than yours and the price is nothing."

The *Post* was indeed making notable strides. Almost from the first day of the Meyer regime the improvement was apparent. News coverage was more extensive and less stodgy. The paper seemed to be gaining a sense of purpose. Senator Arthur H. Vandenberg credited the *Post* with "the most amazing improvement in the past 12 months of any newspaper ever to come to my attention" in a quarter century of journalism.

Yet the improvements were spasmodic and uneven. Meyer was often discouraged. "Do you think I was a fool to buy a newspaper?" he asked Elliott Thurston as they left the building one morning at two o'clock. "I suppose anyone is a fool to buy a newspaper," Thurston responded candidly, "but it is a great adventure." Though he was working day and night to build a great institution, Meyer retained a sense of humor about his operation. He often described himself as a "freshman student in journalism," and a letter to his old friend William Hard invited that veteran newsman to visit the *Post* on his return from Europe so that he could "have a good laugh at me as a newspaper man."

From the inside, the progress seemed minuscule when compared to the distance yet to be covered. A confidential survey of the *Post* by John K. Gowen, Jr., Boston newspaper analyst, gave fairly good marks to the editorial and financial pages, but noted that local news writing was "feeble," art was poor, the society layout was "atrociously mechanical," the whole paper was "typographically monotonous," and its magazine section was a dull "canned product." The new publisher commissioned three separate surveys of his paper, but critical deficiencies proved to be easier found than corrected. Nor were all the troubles in the area of news coverage. Expenses had mounted far out of line with gains in circulation and advertising. Meyer repeatedly complained: "We could not get circulation because we did not have advertising and we could not get advertising because we did not have circulation."

Most discouraging of all was the fact that some of the men whom Meyer depended upon were not meeting his standards. The advertising manager he had brought in from Buffalo, Joseph Melia, proved to be a disappointment. Ralph Renaud, the managing editor, seemed incapable of shaking off a psychological hangover from the failure of the *World*, and after a few months he was replaced by William Haggard. Still more troublesome was the vacuum at the top of Meyer's new organization. General Manager Eugene MacLean, when he was not nursing a hangover, seemed to spend most of his time with his feet on a desk reading magazines. When Meyer discovered him in that posture one night while news was exploding on a dozen fronts, he concluded that drastic action would have to be taken. Ethridge was shifted from the editorial staff to be assistant general manager, but Ethridge left in December 1934 to take a job on the Richmond *Times-Dispatch*.

The departure of a man as talented as Ethridge was in itself a bad omen, and it led to further complications. Meyer agreed with Ethridge that it would be to his advantage to accept the opportunity that had opened to him in Richmond, but asked him not to take any other *Post* men with him. Ethridge replied that he would not indulge in raiding. Once ensconced at the *Times-Dispatch*, however, he asked Leon Dure, an old friend on the *Post* staff, to sound out another promising writer on the *Post*, Sid Olson, about joining the *Times-Dispatch* as city editor. When Meyer heard of it, he responded with a furious telephone call to his former assistant general manager. Ethridge found it impossible to break in to explain that he regarded Olson as a minor employee not covered by the "no-raiding" pledge he had given, but he wrote a letter to that effect (a lame excuse) and accused Meyer of "unnecessarily aggressive and offensive, and even bulldozing" conduct. Dure was fired as notice to the staff that Meyer expected a stricter sense of loyalty.

The incident seemed to portend disintegration within the *Post*'s staff. The scuttlebutt in the newsroom was that the revolving door had developed a hot box from the numerous comings and goings. Thurston left to take an important job with the Federal Reserve Board. Robey also resigned. Bargeron's column had deteriorated, and his contract was not renewed. MacLean was a dead weight the paper could no longer afford to carry. Meyer and his trusted business manager, Charles C. Boysen, drafted a letter terminating MacLean's services, and Boysen was asked to deliver the letter in person. As he entered MacLean's office, the general manager handed him a letter saying that he (Boysen) was fired. "I have something for you, too, Mr. MacLean," Boysen said as he presented his letter with a somewhat more authoritative signature.

The disintegration of Meyer's team came to a climax in November 1935 when Managing Editor Haggard and eleven other editors and desk men threatened to walk out. The newsroom had become a costly, wasteful, and inefficient operation. As many as five different editors had a right to make over pages, and it was not uncommon for them to make up twice as many pages as they used. The paper was being run as if it were a rich man's toy, free from the pressures of sound business management. Lacking confidence in Haggard's ability to straighten out the mess, Meyer had ordered him to clear any further salary increases and promotions with the business manager, apparently without realizing the implications that journalists would see in such a step. Haggard fought the order with strong support from other editors who feared business encroachment on journalistic freedom. The controversy thus assumed serious proportions, and it began to appear that a general walkout on a basic issue might inflict disaster on the still anemic enterprise.

Alarmed by the outlook, Morley conferred with Clapper and Waltman, and the three induced Meyer to come to the office and face the revolt, despite a case of grippe which had been keeping him at home. After a long discussion about changes that would be necessary, Haggard agreed to cooperate, providing his demands were met. One of those demands was a sharp increase in salary for himself.

"And if I don't meet those demands?" Meyer asked.

"About twelve of us will walk out," was the reply.

The harassed publisher let them walk. By this time he was convinced that he had to have a new team anyway. In his first two years he had, as he would often confess, made every mistake in the book. Aside from his blind spots in choosing personnel, he had been insensitive to journalistic traditions and habits of thought common to practitioners of the trade. His decision to deny Haggard control over his news budget was apparently an interim step toward firing him, but Meyer failed to realize that it would add combustible fuel to Haggard's revolt. Other editors, reporters, and desk men who were well aware of Haggard's deficiencies were nevertheless troubled by the specter of business interference with the newsroom. Meyer learned the hard way that there is a vast difference between managing a banking business and orchestrating an assemblage of prima donnas capable of putting out a modern newspaper.

Nor were his mistakes confined to the newsroom. His circulation department was also a dubious operation. On the surface, the *Post*'s rapid gains in circulation were heartening. In the two years since the receivership the number of papers turned out had nearly doubled. Meyer had spent $50,000 in a circulation drive, but most of the new subscribers soon dropped out because the product itself was not very good. His first circulation manager was a hard-driving, tyrannical professional, Harold Fenton, who browbeat underpaid subordinates into miracles of performance for brief periods. The turnover in "Fenton's Flying Circus" matched the shifting subscriptions. Under this system it was necessary to write 100,000 new orders a year to maintain a circulation ranging from 98,000 to 100,000. The cost of this circulation was about 130 percent of the revenue obtained from the sale of papers.

In April 1935, Meyer abolished the *Post*'s so-called honor racks because 60 percent of the papers dispensed by this means were stolen. Cissy Patterson's *Herald* printed an allegedly faked picture of *Washington Posts* dumped in the river and openly accused the *Post* of fraudulently padding its circulation figures—a practice that others said was standard for her own organization. Meyer had some of his most trusted executives ride the paper routes and make delivery surveys without finding any substantial irregularities. Yet it was apparent that a successful newspaper could not be built on the kind of ramshackle foundation his circulation department was providing.

The *Herald*'s accusations were indicative of Cissy Patterson's relentless warfare against her rival. For the most part the *Post* ignored the *Herald*'s needling, but sometimes the temptation to strike back was irresistible. When the *Herald* printed a sensational "eyewitness" account of an execution, giving details of how two felons had died, one of them "cursing the law, himself and God," the *Post* called it a "scoop" and said it was "the most astonishing performance in local newspaper history," for the story had appeared at 6 A.M. and the executions had not actually taken place until 7:50 and 8:06 A.M., long after a "Washington morning newspaper—NOT the *Post*" had the gory details in print and on the street.

Eugene Meyer was no stranger to battling for survival. Most of his contests, however, had been on a different level. He had fought the tycoons of finance and industry and jousted with public officials on major national issues. Now he was immersed in a struggle that often seemed petty, mean, and hopeless. As he faced his family at the breakfast table, qualms about his venture often came to the surface. Maybe Gardner Cowles was right. Perhaps even now, after he had sunk a fortune in the paper, he should sell it and leave to younger men the task of scratching around for subscriptions and advertising and the development of high news and editorial standards.

Yet retreat was a dismal road. Every time that he reviewed his predicament, Meyer concluded that the chagrin of quitting an adventure in public service at the apex of his career would be less tolerable than the hazards ahead. His decision was to correct his own blunders and to drive forward.

24 /

The Neophyte Digs In

THE SECOND PHASE OF THE *Post's* REHABILITATION BEGAN IN 1935 with Meyer in active command. He had learned that the horizontal-type of organization he had known in government and business was not well adapted to journalism. A newspaper is a triangular affair that needs strong men of very different types in charge of news, advertising, and circulation. It had been almost fatal to have misfits in these key spots reporting to a general manager who did not manage. Henceforth he could blame only himself if he did not find the right men and hold them to a high standard of performance.

In line with his lifelong habit of seeking out experts, Meyer cultivated his friendship with Carl W. Ackerman, dean of the Columbia University Graduate School of Journalism. Ackerman was invited to Mount Kisco, and Meyer frequently wrote him for advice. The dean was asked to recommend young men and women of "brains and character." It was also Ackerman who alerted Meyer to the readership surveys that were being made by a new scientific sampling method. This led to fruitful relationships with Harold Anderson of the Publishers Syndicate in Chicago and Dr. George H. Gallup, who had been a professor of journalism at Drake and Northwestern universities. Both Anderson and Gallup were applying to newspapers and magazines a fact-finding process reminiscent of that which Meyer had used in investment banking many years before. Anderson was soon surveying not only the *Post*, but also its competition. Every page of the papers was analyzed to determine reader appeal or lack of it. The findings became an indispensable guide in building the type of newspaper that people wanted to read.

Anderson was then retained as consultant because of his wide acquaintance in newspaper circles—the area in which Meyer's handicap was most evident. The first fruit of this relationship was the recruitment of Donald M. Bernard of the Knoxville *Banner* who had made a specialty of rescuing crippled newspapers. At first Bernard declined an offer from the *Post* but after Floyd Harrison had importuned him to visit with Meyer at his home and Meyer had fully outlined his aspirations for the *Post*, Bernard changed his mind. He had caught a vision of a vital role for himself in journalism's big league.

For some months after his arrival Bernard functioned as a general handyman, trying to firm up a foundation on which the paper could attain more secure growth. The first task was to build a good organization. Several of the departments were realigned, and the head of each was made directly responsible to Meyer. The most important decisions regarding the management and conduct of the paper thus came directly to him. Harrison continued to work with the publisher as a knowledgeable and energetic assistant. Charles C. Boysen remained as business manager, and Bernard became advertising manager.

After the walkout in the news department, the major task was to find a new managing editor. The *Post* could not afford another whirl of the revolving door. Meyer's consultation with Anderson and Bernard resulted in the preparation of three lists of promising editors. The name of Alexander F. "Casey" Jones, city editor of the Minneapolis *Journal*, turned up on all three lists, and Jones took charge of the demoralized news staff in November 1935.

Marquis Childs, writing a few years later in the *Saturday Evening Post*, would describe Casey Jones as a Welshman with a low boiling point and would note that he was one of the chief reasons why the *Washington Post* was "as full of fight as a wildcat." *Fortune* would characterize Jones as "a tall gray veteran of the business"—a "cyclonic, convivial" managing editor who was "incurably romantic about his profession." Everyone agreed that he knew his business—the display of news and features as well as the gathering of information. Though he had grown up in the Middle West, his interests were broad, and his crisp, punchy style attracted a large audience for what he wrote personally.

Jones transformed the news department into a smooth-functioning unit. There was less emphasis on assembling a galaxy of big journalistic names and more on the development of a competent team. Edward T. Folliard, who had returned to the *Post* after an unhappy flirtation with the *Herald*, began to enliven its pages with special stories on many fronts. William Nessly was ably covering the White House. Shirley Povich, who had gotten his start with the old *Post* by reason of the fact that he had been Ned McLean's caddy, continued to make the sports pages sparkle. Jones gave special attention to improving the paper's local news coverage so as to compete more successfully with the *Evening Star* in this field. To attain a solid footing in the community, he said, the paper would have to appeal to Georgia Avenue as well as Capitol Hill.

Relieved of detailed supervision of the news department by a competent managing editor, Meyer devoted himself to building up other segments of the paper. One of his special interests was the Gallup Poll. Before Jones's arrival, Meyer had committed the paper to publication of Gallup's public opinion surveys. By use of a scientific sampling method Gallup had predicted the results of the 1934 congressional elections with only a 1 percent margin of error. He had then asked Meyer's reaction to a periodical poll of public opinion on the momentous issues of the day, and the publisher responded enthusiastically.

Not only did Meyer share Gallup's conviction, borrowed from Talleyrand, that "the only thing wiser than anybody is everybody"; his standard definition of a political leader was: "a man only six months behind public opinion." If Dr. Gallup could accurately determine what the rank-and-file were thinking on the major issues of the day, his surveys would prove immensely interesting and highly useful in a democratic society. Haggard and some other editors violently opposed identification of the *Post* with any such experiment, but Meyer overruled them and published the first poll by the American Institute of Public Opinion in October 1935.

The poll proved to be a success, and after Gallup had repeatedly demonstrated his ability to sample public opinion, with relatively narrow margins of error, the surveys came to be printed in more than 120 daily newspapers in the United States. Meyer remained closely associated with the poll, submitting many questions for suggested surveys and often criticizing the questions asked and some conclusions drawn from the returns.

Meyer wanted to give his paper a special appeal to women. It should contain a feminine-interest section that would stay at home with the wives when the men carried the news and sports pages to the office. The task of creating such a section was turned over to Malvina Lindsay, an unassuming but extraordinarily talented journalist from Kansas City. The women's pages that she edited came to be used as models in many schools of journalism, and their brightest spots were often her own column, "The Gentler Sex," noted for its humor and mild satire. Later she was to write a column —"Of Human Affairs"—for the *Post's* editorial page and syndication by the Women's National News Service.

One of the "musts" that Meyer emphasized was a column that would provide expert psychiatric advice on a wide range of human problems. He found a psychiatrist who was interested and offered him $10,000 a year for part-time guidance of a feminine columnist who would do the actual writing. The psychiatrist rejected the offer, but meanwhile Ethridge had induced Elizabeth Young, a new $25-a-week reporter in the department, to write a column on "This Business of Living" under the name of Mary Haworth.

Though her first columns dealt with imaginary problems, letters soon flowed in and the column attracted wide readership. Miss Haworth avoided answering questions casually or flippantly. Instead, she took the readers' troublesome problems to psychiatrists, lawyers, clergymen, social workers, and others, and translated their advice into nonprofessional language, adding a large measure of her own shrewd judgment. Though she wrote about many problems of love and sex, *Newsweek* credited her with replacing "the traditional saccharin with 'psyche salt.'" Another admirer said her writing was "no more a lovelorn column than Lippmann's is a gossip column." Within a few years she had more readers, both men and women, than any other feature in the paper.

After the column was established, Meyer told Mrs. Young about his efforts to hire a professional psychiatrist and added: "It seems that someone has invented you and I think you'll do." As time went on he came to regard her column as "one of the best things we have done on the *Post*." Half-apologetically he showed Miss Haworth an article entitled "Little Words Have Guts," which embodied one of his favorite journalistic theses. It was a gentle criticism of her sometimes involved style, but her candor and sincerity were always refreshing. She could flatten a fop or singe the ears of the selfish with admirable dispatch. To a pregnant wife who did not want to have her baby she replied with "nausea and dismay." Another wife who was fearful of a friend's advances toward her husband was advised to use her wits, tongue, and elbows "openly and unashamed if necessary, to keep her from muscling in." A mother-in-law who complained about growing antagonism between her two sons' wives was told that she was "perhaps even fueling the antagonism . . . as neurotic relief of sorts from unsuspected jealousy that lurks in your own bosom." Meyer credited his columnist with sincerely searching for truth —a quality he prized above all others. The column was ultimately renamed "Mary Haworth's Mail" and by the mid-1940's was syndicated internationally to an estimated twenty million readers.

Meyer himself was a fertile source of news leads. When Lord Lothian, who was later to become British ambassador to the United States, was a guest at the Meyer home the conversation turned to King Edward VIII's love affair, and Meyer felt that the hints and solid information that he elicited could be pieced together into a sensational scoop. On October 17, 1936, the *Post* broke what was probably the greatest story of the year in these words:

> King Edward VIII of Great Britain plans to marry the glamorous American, Mrs. Ernest (Wally) Simpson. . . . He may not be able to make the erstwhile Baltimore belle his Queen, but he is determined to make her his wife, even if it costs him his throne.

The story, which carried no by-line, was written by Edward Folliard, but Meyer was its source. Although many refused to believe it at the time, events over the next few months brought complete confirmation. The *Post* had the satisfaction of having brought into the open a dramatic situation that would shake the government of Britain to its foundations.

Not all of the Meyer contributions to the paper were of equal moment. In a whimsical mood he sent Karl Schriftgiesser to interview a gargoyle on the facade of the 1935 addition to the old Post building, and when no gargoyle could be found to match the embellishments on the older wing of the building, Schriftgiesser interviewed the blank wall, with amusing consequences.

The *Post* refused to sensationalize. One of the most bizarre and exciting stories of the middle thirties was the kidnapping and murder of Charles A. Lindbergh's infant son. Instead of sending a battery of top reporters to cover the story, as some other papers did, the *Post* relied on the restrained and factual coverage of the Associated Press, which led to a serious blunder. In the struggle to be first in reporting the verdict, AP reporters at the trial had arranged a series of signals to facilitate the race to the telephone, but a mix-up in the signals led to the filing of a story which the *Post* printed under the caption: "Hauptmann Guilty But Escapes Electric Chair." The error (actually Hauptmann had been sentenced to death) was corrected before the paper reached the streets, but the *Herald* reproduced the inaccurate headline and printed a story about the *Post* fooling its readers with a false verdict, as if the error had not been corrected. Meyer ignored the distortion.

The struggle in Washington's journalistic arena continued to be intense. To most of the participants, the big question was not whether five newspapers could thrive in a city of 600,000 people, but which of them would survive. The only one that seemed secure at the time was the *Evening Star*, with its strong hold on advertising from the big department stores, although the tabloid *Daily News*, part of the Scripps-Howard chain, appeared less vulnerable to competition. The *Times* lacked a firm foothold in the community, and both the *Herald* and the *Post* were losing about $1 million a year. Even for William Randolph Hearst and Eugene Meyer this could not continue indefinitely.

After 1935 Meyer trimmed his losses somewhat by converting the Washington Post Company into a partnership between himself and Mrs. Meyer. This enabled them to deduct the losses of the paper from their taxable income, a substantial saving, but it stopped far short of making the *Post* a viable institution. However willing Meyer might be to sustain losses during his lifetime, his creation could not endure without a stronger economic base.

In the third year of his publishing venture, he tried to buy the *Herald*. Meyer's own biographical interviews are silent on this point, but Cissy Patterson told her staff that on August 6, 1936, "the *Herald* was all but signed, sealed and delivered to Mr. Meyer,"[1] who had offered more than $600,000 for it. The negotiations had been going on without her knowledge. When she heard what was afoot, Cissy called Hearst at three o'clock in the morning and wept over the telephone until he relented and let his tempestuous editor have her way. Cissy had once remarked that all she had to offer the *Herald* was "dynamite," but she had forgotten the tears. The result of her deeper involvement in the destiny of the *Herald* was a $1-million loan to Hearst, which led to a lease on the *Herald* and the *Times* and finally to outright purchase of the two papers and their merger into a ten-edition, 'round-the-clock operation, which further intensified competition with the *Post*.

Eugene Meyer was not ready, however, to quit. His old friend and former associate in government, Andrew Mellon, came in one day and asked if Meyer would sell the *Post*, making clear that he would pay whatever the Meyers had lost on the paper plus $1 million. Since 1936 was a presidential election year, it was a reasonable assumption that Mellon's motive was political, but he did not disclose the trend of his thinking. Gratifying though it was to have Mellon, who was worth at least $300 million, offer to bail him out, Meyer responded simply: "Mr. Mellon, I didn't buy it to sell it."

"If you change your mind," Mellon requested, "will you give me the first opportunity?"[2]

"Certainly," Meyer answered.

It was an acid test of the seriousness of the neophyte publisher's intentions. In 1935 he had lost $1,306,036 in operating the *Post*, and the outlook for the year ahead was still forbidding. Yet the psychological compensations were sufficient to stifle any thought of retreat.

It was no secret that Meyer was hoping for an attractive Republican

[1] Alice Albright Hogue, *Cissy Patterson* (New York: Random House; 1966), pp. 162–3.
[2] Meyer's biographical notes dictated to Sidney Hyman, Part VIII, p. 29.

Agnes Ernst Meyer in the 1920's. (Edward Steichen)

Meyer and his daughter Katharine, then five or six, now publisher of the Washington Post.

Seven Springs Farm, the Meyer estate at Mount Kisco, New York.

The Meyers riding together in Rock Creek Park.

The auction on the steps of the old Washington Post *building on June 1, 1933, when the newspaper was sold to an unknown bidder, later revealed to be Eugene Meyer.*

(Left) *Despiau's bust of Agnes Meyer.* (Right) *Brancuṣi's black marble abstraction, supposedly a bust of Agnes Meyer.*

Dining together on Crescent Place in Washington. Left to right: *Katharine, Agnes, Florence, Eugene, Bill, Ruth, and Elizabeth.*

Washington's newspaper publishers at a 1937 Community Chest luncheon. Left to right: *Frank B. Noyes,* Star; *Eugene Meyer,* Post; *Eleanor Patterson,* Times *and* Herald; *Lowell Mellett,* Daily News; *and Earle A. Nash, luncheon chairman.*

Meyer visiting the Post *composing room on the fifth anniversary of his publishing venture.*

Lord Halifax and Meyer *in a London air raid shelter, September 1941.*

A *happy family reunion during World War II.* Left to right, standing: *Bill Meyer, Katharine Graham, son-in-law Philip Graham, Ruth Meyer, son-in-law Pare Lorentz.* Seated: *Mary Bradley Meyer, Florence Homolka, Eugene, Agnes, Elizabeth Lorentz.*

Meyer and his grandson Vincent Homolka, about 1945.

The Famine Emergency Committee meeting at the White House, March 1, 1946. At the head of the table are former President Hoover (seated) and President Truman (standing). On the left side of the table are (from left) Eric Johnston, Anne Lord Strauss, Justin Miller, Emily Dickinson, Sheldon Clark, Herbert H. Lehman, Henry A. Wallace. On the other side (beginning at Truman's left) are Secretary of Agriculture Clinton P. Anderson, William L. Clayton, Eugene Meyer, Chester C. David, George H. Gallup, A. S. Iglehart, and (at the end) John W. Snyder.

alternative to President Roosevelt in 1936. The *Post* had tried to deal objectively with the New Deal, but Roosevelt's monetary experimentation, the regimentation of industry under the NRA, the agricultural policy, and the mounting New Deal deficits cut sharply across the newspaper's concept of sound public policy. Without directly involving the paper, Meyer took a lively interest in the search for a candidate to run against F.D.R.

One politician thought Meyer himself should become a "dark horse" candidate. R. B. Hartman, who had been a lieutenant of Mark Hanna's for many years, wrote Meyer that his "wonderful record" and his "unselfish work . . . for the country" made him "a real possibility." But Meyer replied that he had no such opinion of himself and that "the paper is independent and nonpartisan, and I have no other purpose in mind than to continue my present occupation."

Very early in the sifting-out process it became apparent that Governor Alfred M. Landon of Kansas was the only hopeful candidate as far as the moderate Republicans were concerned. Meyer journeyed to Topeka to "look over" the governor in the fall of 1935 and was "considerably impressed." He stimulated Ray Clapper, Frank Waltman, and others to write articles about the little-known governor. After another visit to Topeka by Mr. and Mrs. Meyer, Agnes wrote an article about him that was widely distributed by the Landon-for-President Committee. Meyer consulted Roy Roberts of the Kansas City *Star* and various others about getting Landon speeches and interviews "on the air." When the candidate's appearances betrayed his meager experience, Meyer took a radio engineer to Topeka to design a microphone that would be specially suitable for Landon's voice and technicians to teach him the art of broadcasting. "Every time I see him," Meyer wrote to an old friend, "I have a higher opinion of his ability and character." But it was obvious that Landon had a long way to go.

While the political contest was warming up, the *Post* received its first major accolade from the journalistic profession—a Pulitzer Prize for Felix Morley. Although the Pulitzer board did not, in the award itself, single out any one of Morley's editorials, members of the board divulged that they had been especially impressed by a piece entitled "A President Leaves His Party." It was typical of the candor, objectivity, and public-interest orientation for which both the staff and the publisher were striving. Meyer was as delighted as the recipient. At last his venture seemed to be paying off in coin that was meaningful, despite the continued monetary losses. Throughout the Roosevelt-Landon campaign the *Post* made a conscientious effort to report the news on both sides fairly and accurately. Its editorials commented freely on speeches and other developments on both sides, without commitment to either. Some of Morley's editorials on Landon's shortcomings brought protests from Mrs. Meyer, but Meyer advised him: "Pay no attention to her." Shortly after the election was over, Meyer acknowledged in a letter to Clapper, who had left the paper in 1935, that "even when people try to be fair and as truthful as possible, you and I know it is not always easy to accomplish." The same letter explains the rationale behind the *Post's* decision not to endorse either candidate:

> After thinking the whole matter over as to our policy I became convinced that we had an unusual opportunity to approach politics somewhat differently from other newspapers. The major part of our constituency does not vote. Therefore, it would appear unnecessary for The Post to undertake to give, or attempt to give, suggestions . . . as to how people should vote . . . This freedom may be taken advantage of to deal with issues separately on their merits, approving and disapproving some on both sides, and preserving in fact as well as nominally the description of "Independent" that we carry on our masthead.

Meyer's hope for a new face in the White House had actually begun to wane soon after Landon's nomination. In August the Gallup Poll had showed a marked gain in Roosevelt's popularity. No one with strong faith in polling by the scientific sampling method could cling to the Landon illusion. There was much discussion of polling when Gallup, Anderson, and Meyer met; all of them felt certain that the *Literary Digest*, which predicted a Landon sweep on the basis of a poll among telephone subscribers and automobile owners, was "going to lay an egg." As it turned out, the *Digest* was buried under the Roosevelt landslide, and about the only comfort Meyer found in the outcome was the reasonably accurate Gallup forecast. On the basis of Gallup's findings, Meyer dictated a letter to Landon a few days before the election expressing regret that he had not made it. Some of Meyer's colleagues persuaded him not to jolt the candidate in that fashion before the votes were cast. But as soon as the election returns showed evidence of a Democratic tide, he called to his secretary, through the din of the city room: "Mr. Fahy, mail that letter."

The *Post* congratulated the President and wished him success. Then, seizing a suggestion from Charles Moore, Meyer sponsored a great welcome for F.D.R. as he returned to Washington. A two-column front-page editorial, slipped into the paper of Thursday, November 5, at the last minute, under the heading, "Let's Give the President a Real Welcome!" was an irresistible call to action:

AT SOME HOUR tomorrow, the President of the United States returns to the community in which he has lived for the past four years and in which he will live for the next four years.

AS CHIEF EXECUTIVE of the country, he is, through his appointments, the chief executive of this city.

THE WASHINGTON POST respectfully suggests that the people of Washington should greet Franklin D. Roosevelt in a manner deserving a man who has won a great victory and is now returning to his home.

WE WOULD like to see his car tomorrow cover the distance between the Capitol and the White House between throngs of citizens lining Pennsylvania Avenue.

WE WOULD like to hear thunderous cheers.

WE WOULD like to see a marching escort of men and bands.

WE WOULD like to see the Avenue appropriately decorated and men and women shouting their greeting from the windows.

WE WOULD like to see government workers and non-government workers allowed sufficient time from their duties to share in the demonstration.

THE TIME is short. But with the cooperation of all and under able leadership, it can be done . . .

The following morning, the day of F.D.R.'s arrival, the *Post's* lead story was about the great demonstration that had been organized for the President's homecoming. Large maps showed the townsfolk the President's route through the city. As the hour of the President's arrival approached, Meyer stood at the window of his office on the third floor of the Post building looking out on Pennsylvania Avenue. For a while the Avenue seemed to be empty. "Well," he said, "I guess that idea wasn't too good." Before the President's car came into view, however, the Avenue was swarmed by an estimated 200,000 persons who gave him a tumultuous welcome. As he passed the Post building, he waved a personal greeting to Meyer.

For Roosevelt, it was the beginning of a new chapter in his fabulous career. The nation appeared to be at his feet. For Meyer too the incident seemed to carry symbolic significance. After three and a half years of struggle, he was on top of his job and the *Post* was beginning to hit its stride. The remaining problems were enormous, but the flounderings of those first three years had given way to more solid growth and a more seasoned brand of journalism. The *Post* was at least in a position to forge ahead with a chance of survival in the furious race that lay before it.

25 /

The Fight over Packing the

Supreme Court

NEAR THE END OF 1936 MEYER LAUNCHED A NEW POLICY THAT was to have momentous consequences. ". . . we are not trying to get mass circulation," he wrote to his friend Samuel E. Blythe, "but quality circulation. . . . I am being very sordid about this. I am not selling the paper to many who haven't got an interest in buying goods." Recognizing the integral relationship between circulation and advertising, he had decided to seek readers who would also be good customers.

The key figure in evolving this policy and in carrying it out was Donald Bernard. Meyer and Bernard often mulled over the *Post*'s dilemma together. Out of these ruminations came detailed studies of the *Post*'s circulation and the buying habits of the people of Washington. The circulation which the paper was paying so much to retain proved to be concentrated in Anacostia and other low-income areas, while most of the purchasing power was located in Takoma Park and the northwest section of the city. Bernard's department made a seven-foot map showing the average income of the residents in each census tract. Researchers then went to Lansburgh's Department Store and studied the sales tickets by census tracts to determine where its business came from. The sales of other department stores were subjected to the same type of analysis. All these surveys showed a common pattern: the bulk of the sales came from those census tracts where the average breadwinner earned more than $45 a week. The *Post* then made a determined effort to build up its circulation in those areas.

Since the content of the paper had an intellectual appeal, in contrast to the sensationalism of the *Herald*, the *Post* found ready acceptance in the families of average or higher income. Soon it was possible to demonstrate to advertisers that a *Washington Post* ad had more than ordinary power because it reached homes with a capacity to buy. Bernard adopted a policy of not selling advertising unless he honestly thought that the buyer would profit from it; advertisements suspected of being phony were rejected despite the difficulty of devising a reliable screening process.

Meyer was enthusiastic about this policy because he wanted the paper to grow on a solid foundation and to qualify under any test of its integrity. High standards were not solely for the news and editorial departments. "The good advertising man or woman," he said, "is one who studies deeply and in detail the business of the merchants whom he seeks to serve, in order that he may talk with them intelligently about their advertising messages, and make his newspaper useful to them, in an advertising sense, in the highest possible degree." The business side of the paper ought to reflect "the ethics, the ideals and the enthusiasm that belong professionally to the good news writer."

Under the impact of this policy and the energy that the new advertising team put into the job, the *Post*'s lineage mounted and the *Evening Star*'s near monopoly on department store advertising began to crumble. Meyer often attended the sessions in which his salesmen presented the story of the *Post*'s transformation and joined in the sales pitch. Even when these forays led into blind alleys, his shrewd business judgment sometimes turned the occasion to his advantage. One friend in a high corporate position flatly rejected his appeal for advertising in the *Post*, but in the course of the discussion Meyer learned so much about that corporation's business that he bought some of its stock and realized a substantial profit which helped to ease the paper's continued losses.

One element in the new policy—home-delivery circulation that would stick—proved to be especially elusive. Having fired his first high-powered professional in this field, Meyer took a more cautious approach. It would be better to have a reliable though inexperienced executive run the circulation department, he decided, than to trust a professional whose methods aroused suspicion. This led to a succession of thirteen circulation managers from 1933 to 1949 and kept that segment of the *Post* organization in turmoil until it finally settled down under the professional management of Harry Gladstein. Circulation remained the weakest part of the paper throughout the Meyer regime.

In the day-to-day operation of the paper Meyer necessarily left most of the decisions to his executives and editors. They were permitted and urged to exercise independent judgment, but they could expect to hear from the publisher if it was not informed and rational judgment. They were under constant pressure, moreover, to avoid favoritism and self-serving conclusions. Alarm signals went up at any suggestion that stories or editorials were being influenced by individual friendships, organized propaganda, or special interests. The broad-gauged freedom of action that he allowed his editors was thus disciplined by a feeling of responsibility to ideals and objectives bigger than themselves.

The pervading sense of public interest in the Meyer organization was reflected in special attention to the worsening plight of the District of Columbia. Washington was a city of gleaming marble monuments, broad avenues, historic buildings, and extensive parks, but its core was corroded by disease, slums, lax education, and chaotic government. The *Post* began a systematic exposé of these conditions in its editorial columns, having assigned one member of the staff to give full time to local problems. Its campaigns for better government in the District brought the paper into frequent collisions with petty tyrants on Capitol Hill, and one of them, Representative Thomas L. Blanton of Texas, sued the *Post* for $600,000, charging malicious libel. Meyer ultimately settled the case for $3,000 in the interest of conserving time and energy.

Beyond the operations of the paper, Meyer assumed an active role in community affairs. In 1936 he sparked a mass meeting which led to the organization of a Criminal Justice Association in Washington to cope with the problems of delinquency and crime. Meyer accepted the chairmanship and made the agency a sort of civic conscience for many years. It was credited with modernizing arrest practices, inspiring the establishment of a juvenile bureau in the Police Department, speeding up trials, and improving bail bond procedures. In the first five years of its operation felonies in the District were reduced 30 percent despite a large increase in population. Meyer also became director of the National Probation Association in Washington and president of the National Committee for Mental Hygiene. For this civic work the Council of Social Agencies gave him its annual award in 1945.

Overshadowing every other issue in 1937 was President Roosevelt's attempt to pack the Supreme Court. The President's bombshell was exploded on February 5. Though it was camouflaged with the trappings of judicial reform, its central purpose was to permit the President to appoint six additional justices to the Supreme Court if the members then over seventy did not resign. Viewing the bill as the most daring and ruthless attack on the Supreme Court in its history, the *Post* joined the fight immediately. Along with the text of the President's message on the front page, it carried a story by Franklyn Waltman and a survey of congressional reaction by Robert C. Albright. Cartoonist Gene Elderman pictured F.D.R. in the role of Samson pushing down the pillars of judicial balance in the edifice of American democracy. The lead editorial assailed the

President for not taking the people into his confidence during the campaign, urged separation of the court-packing and reform aspects of the message, and said that this "dangerous and . . . indefensible . . . plan" would bring about a major alteration in our system of government.

Curious about the reaction within the Supreme Court, Meyer asked Waltman to seek an appointment with Justice Owen J. Roberts. Waltman was too polite to tell the boss that an experienced reporter did not attempt to interview justices of the Supreme Court; he just did nothing about it. The following day Meyer found out that Waltman had disregarded his request and said that if Waltman was reluctant to go he would do it himself. The justices, he said, were well aware of the law of self-preservation, and they would not stand on their ivory-tower tradition when the integrity of the Court was in jeopardy. Waltman went and found Roberts's door open to him. Instead of discussing the problem himself, however, Roberts referred Waltman to Chief Justice Hughes, who gave him an appointment that afternoon at his home. Without quoting the Chief Justice, Waltman then wrote a series of widely read and widely reprinted articles packed with facts about the Supreme Court, the circuit courts of appeals, and the federal district courts. The result was to show that the Supreme Court was not behind in its work, that only a few of the circuit courts were overburdened, and that the delays that did occur had no ascertainable relationship to the ages of the judges.

Meyer also discussed the problem with Hughes, without disclosing the talk even to his close associates. He was careful, however, to avoid any approach to Justice Brandeis. The reports that he interviewed Brandeis on the court-packing venture are in error. As the oldest of the justices whom the President sought to replace, Brandeis was sorely grieved by the indiscriminate assault upon age, but he was also extremely sensitive about being involved in the controversy. Meyer feared that if the *Post* did obtain some inside information from the Court, Brandeis would be suspected as the source because of their long friendship.[1] The only contact between the two men during this period was Brandeis's invitation to "drop by the Cape" during the Court's recess and Meyer's responding letter on July 26 begging the justice not to resign from the Court under any circumstances.

Editorially, the *Post* kept the Court bill under a withering fire. The President's pretense that the Court was behind in its work, that aged justices were contributing to injustices, and that six new members would speed up the work was called "A Case Built on Sand." The actual purpose of the bill was "to secure constitutional interpretations in line with the

---

[1] Eugene Meyer to Alexander F. Jones, October 26, 1954.

President's views." The *Post* accused the President of "wittingly or unwittingly distorting facts to foist this revolutionary choice upon Congress."

Senator Glass declared that Congress would commit suicide if the President so requested. But he had not reckoned with the power of aroused public opinion. With the *Post* and many other newspapers speaking out fearlessly, legislators and other national leaders began to find their voices. The debate was centered on the naked issue of packing the Court. An Elderman cartoon entitled "To Furnish the Supreme Court Practical Assistance," showed six Roosevelts behind the bench whispering advice to the so-called nine old men. The President responded to the mounting avalanche of criticism by accusing the Supreme Court of usurping power and vetoing his program. On the same day the *Post* reminded him that he had been largely responsible for the loosely drawn legislation that the Court had invalidated; in the case of the Guffey Coal bill he had openly advised Congress to let no doubts as to its constitutionality, however reasonable, interfere with its passage.

As several liberal Democrats emerged to lead the fight against the Court bill, the *Post* accused the President of "driving a wedge in his party." Senators Burton K. Wheeler, Edward R. Burke, William H. King, Millard E. Tydings, and others set up an organization to mobilize opposition. The Republicans on Capitol Hill fell discreetly into the background. Party lines were thus obscured and the opposition brought together those who feared that enlargement of the Court to clear the way for the President's proposed "new instruments of power" would undermine the U.S. constitutional system and tip the balance of power dangerously toward the executive side. Remaining with the President were Democrats who felt that some action against the Court was imperative and those whose party ties were dominant.

When the Senate Judiciary Committee began hearings on the issue, the *Post* suggested that the Court would supply the committee with any information that might be requested, and when Chief Justice Hughes's letter to Senator Wheeler was read some days later, an editorial hailed it as a "powerful blow" against the Court proposal. Most of the data and the carefully guarded arguments in the Chief Justice's letter had previously appeared in the *Post*.

Meyer and his editors were greatly relieved when a majority of the Supreme Court began to turn away from some of the ultraconservative decisions of the past. One of the most important of these cases, in which the Court upheld Washington's minimum wage law, had been decided before the Court-packing bill was announced, but the illness of Justice Stone had caused delay in handing down the decision. When the Court upheld the Wagner Labor Relations Act in a resounding opinion by Chief Justice Hughes, support for the Court-packing venture sagged visibly. The *Post* felt that the Court had "conducted itself with dignity and restraint under severe pressure" and that it should "never again be subjected to such an outrageous attack." Nevertheless, the fight continued, with the *Post* clamoring for an emphatic defeat of the bill on the floor of the Senate as a warning against any possible future attempt to make the Court subservient to the White House.

In May the resignation of Justice Willis Van Devanter gave the contest an ironic twist because F.D.R. had long before promised the first vacancy on the high bench to Senate Majority Leader Joseph T. Robinson, who was now spearheading the fight for the Court-packing bill. If the President fulfilled his promise, it would not only undercut his chance of getting the bill enacted but also make ridiculous his campaign for "younger blood" on the Court, for Robinson was a conservative Arkansas politician of sixty-five. So no appointment could be made. Meanwhile the Senate Judiciary Committee blasted the Court bill in a lengthy report which the *Post* hailed as a sort of coup de grace.

In a desperate effort to save the administration from defeat, Robinson tried to rally his forces behind a substitute bill that would permit the President to name one justice a year to supplement the work of any justice over seventy-five. The *Post* continued its opposition because this substitute bill would give any future President a club over any aged justice who might remain on the bench. Under the strain of his hopeless predicament, Robinson died of a heart attack. The fight was so near to being won that a *Post* editorial of July 22 expounded upon its salutary consequences:

> For the most part it has been an inspiring fight. It has brought to many members of Congress a quickened sense of their responsibility. It has broken down the dangerous assumption that Administration measures ought to be accepted with little or no questioning. Moreover, the entire country has been awakened to a new appreciation of constitutional government and to the necessity of safeguarding the institutions through which such government has been achieved.

When seventy Senators voted that same day to recommit the bill, the *Post* restrained its exultation, thinking of the problems ahead. Its editorial, "Victory Calls for Restraint," expressed fear that the revolting Senators might run wild after a great triumph of this sort and called for the restoration of harmonious working relations within the Democratic Party and in the country. The struggle for democratic government and wise public policy was a never-ending process involving the ability of diverse groups to work together.

But F.D.R.'s selection of Senator Hugo L. Black, one of his most valiant lieutenants in the Court-packing venture, as a successor to Justice Van Devanter, raised a new ruckus when the press discovered, after the Senate had voted confirmation, that Black had once been a member of the Ku Klux Klan. The *Post*'s dislike for this turn of events was pointedly expressed in Elderman's cartoon showing a hooded figure on the Supreme Bench—an extreme view that would be discredited by subsequent history. The struggle involving the Supreme Court carried over into the 1938 congressional campaigns when Roosevelt attempted to "purge" from the Democratic Party a number of Senators and Representatives who had fought his Court bill on grounds of principle. Once more the *Post* plunged into the controversy, vigorously defending the legislators who had defied the President to protect the independence of the courts. In most of these contests the voters rebuffed the President, as Congress had done on the central issue.

Roosevelt always contended that, although he lost both these battles, he won the war, for the Supreme Court did not thereafter upset New Deal legislation. Defenders of the Court insisted, with more factual support, that Congress did not thereafter legislate with reckless disregard for constitutional limitations. In any event it was evident that neither the New Deal, the country, nor the *Washington Post* would ever again be quite the same. A tide of public opinion had risen to prevent the President, in the moment of his greatest popularity, from extending his control over the courts and possibly upsetting the constitutional barriers to one-man rule. The country felt new confidence in the democratic process, and the *Post* had won new recognition as a crusading journal.

F.D.R. swallowed enough of his wrath to congratulate Meyer on his paper's sixtieth anniversary in November 1937, and to express the hope that "as the Post goes on from decade to decade it will ever uphold the noblest traditions of American journalism and thereby serve the highest interests of the community and the Nation." In the circumstances it was a generous recognition of the paper's independence. The sixtieth anniversary brought forth many other less restrained comments. The *Post* was widely praised for being "always farsighted and fairminded" and was variously described as an "outstanding civic and cultural asset" and "one of the nation's great journals." Meyer took advantage of the occasion to issue a statement saying: "The *Post* will go on trying to do its duty as an independent publication, seeking to advance itself by advancing the causes of truth in the news, intelligent editorial comment, competent

special treatment of interesting subjects, good features, and good entertainment, and by making itself generally useful in advancing and promoting the welfare of the community."

A survey showed reprints from the *Post* amounted to three times the
total for the other Washington papers combined. Oswald Garrison Villard
noted the appearance of a new star in the journalistic firmament in these
words: "He [Meyer] is afraid of nobody, not of lawsuits, or feuds or battles
with political magnates."

At last the new *Washington Post* appeared to have hit its stride regardless of how uncertain or stormy the future might continue to be.

26 /

The Zigzag Road to War

WHILE THE STRUGGLE OVER GOVERNMENTAL CHANGES AND ECO-
nomic policy continued at home, dark clouds were gathering over Europe.
Italy's blustering dictator, Benito Mussolini, had brought the first great
challenge to the League of Nations by his aggressive assault upon Ethiopia
in 1935. The League fumbled, and the United States naïvely buried its
head in the sand. The isolationist forces which had been in control of
Congress since World War I passed a neutrality bill blindly forbidding the
shipment of arms to aggressor and victim alike. The strongest power in
the world hoped to avoid further entanglement in war by coolly ignoring
the marauders who were beginning to run amok in Europe.

Both Meyer and Morley viewed this isolationist mania with grave misgivings. The *Post's* fight against the Neutrality Act and its renewal in 1937
was one of its major editorial preoccupations. Morley saw neutrality as a
calculated effort to destroy the first notable experiment in collective
security—the League of Nations. Meyer increasingly felt that the United
States had a moral responsibility to stand up against dictators whose con-
quests would ultimately threaten our own freedom and security. In the
hope of averting a new world war, the paper had long advocated revision
of the harsh Treaty of Versailles which had provoked the German people
into support of Hitler. Morley argued that Article 19 of the League Cove-
nant envisaging the revision of treaties should go hand in hand with Article
X outlawing aggression. His editorials also warmly supported the Stimson
doctrine denying recognition of any territorial change brought about by
military conquest. The *Post* was well ahead of the government in its campaign for collective defense against the menace arising in Europe and Asia.

To get a closer view, Meyer went to Europe in 1937, taking Mrs. Meyer
and Morley with him. In London the publisher felt that the British were
not sufficiently alert to the mounting peril. In Paris the quest for information was greatly facilitated by Meyer's sister Elise, wife of Luis de Souza
Dantas, the Brazilian ambassador in Paris, who invited Premier Leon

Blum, Edouard Herriot, and many other politicians and foreign-service officials to meet the visitors at the embassy. Meyer was again depressed by what he learned. In the face of a rising menace in Germany, France had weakened its economy by adopting an eight-hour day; the Nazis were using money to corrupt the press; Pierre Laval was trying to align France with Mussolini against Hitler.

From Paris, Morley went to Berlin and met Meyer again in Prague. Hjalmar Schacht, the Reichsminister who had financed Hitler's rearmament program, had invited Meyer to Berlin, but he kept out of Germany because of Hitler's pogroms, although he did visit with Schacht in Vienna. In Prague there were interviews with Prime Minister Eduard Benes and other political and industrial leaders of Czechoslovakia. Benes was candid in reply to Meyer's questions as to where he stood in the dangerous situation that was developing. "If England and France will fight for Czechoslovakia," he said, "we will fight and Russia will support us. If England and France will not fight, we will have to make terms." Meyer had previously asked French Foreign Minister Yvon Delbos if the French would fight to save Czechoslovakia from a Hitler invasion, and Delbos had responded: "Of course we will. We're bound by treaty to do it." But that was far from being conclusive. France would be swayed by the British attitude, and Meyer found no disposition in London to go to war over the Czech issue.

In Vienna, American Ambassador George Messersmith took Meyer to see Premier Kurt von Schuschnigg while Morley was in Munich. Engelbert Dollfuss had been murdered three years before in the office next door to where they were sitting. Hitler had then sent troops to the Austrian border and Mussolini had responded with a show of strength at the Brenner Pass as if he intended to protect Austria. With a Berlin-Rome Axis now in the making, Meyer pointedly asked Schuschnigg: "Have you lost your Italian friends?" Schuschnigg replied weakly: "I cannot believe that Mussolini would want Hitler in Vienna any more now than he would have three years ago."[1] Schuschnigg's uncertainty as to where Mussolini stood seemed to remove all doubt about the emerging German-Italian Axis which threatened disaster for Europe.

Traveling in Germany, Morley got a view of the evolving crisis that differed substantially from Meyer's. The editor talked with many Germans who were critical of Hitler's saber-rattling, but they all seemed to be united in the determination to break free from the oppressive Treaty of Versailles. An interview with Dr. Karl Haushofer, the geopolitician who had shaped Hitler's foreign policy, confirmed Morley's feeling that there should be a

---

[1] Dean Albertson's interviews with Eugene Meyer, April 6, 1953.

rational means of relieving the pressures on Germany without another war. Yet Hitler was obviously poised for a hammer-blow against Austria, and Czechoslovakia would probably be next.

The divergent attitudes of the editor and the publisher came to the surface in long discussions on the boat as they returned home. Both were fearful that Europe was moving toward war; their differences concerned the proper reaction of the democratic nations in the face of the Nazi menace. Meyer, the internationalist, was ready to move wherever logic and reason might dictate to save Western civilization from fascism. Morley's Quaker background would not allow him to pursue his passion for international cooperation to the point of supporting war.

"Sometimes you argue almost to the point of exasperating me," Meyer said as the debate waxed hot.

"If you wanted a yes-man editor," Morley replied, "you got the wrong person."[2]

Meyer also felt that his editor had not taken full advantage of the trip to examine the crisis. "You could have written at least half of the articles you sent back," he complained, "without leaving your desk." In Morley's view, however, the trip had been "a grueling six weeks" in which he had produced twenty articles and several cables in addition to the traveling and interviewing. He felt that it was Meyer who had missed the center of action by not going to Germany. So the trip became a considerable wedge between them. At the time these differences were not crucial because both were trying to prod the United States into a more active international role in the hope of averting war. But they would become increasingly troublesome as the months passed.

Back in Washington, Meyer invited Sumner Welles to lunch for a discussion of what he had learned in Europe. Welles was Under Secretary of State and a key figure in the making of foreign policy because of Roosevelt's limited confidence in Secretary of State Cordell Hull. In relaying his sense of grave concern to Welles, Meyer concluded: "The dictators are on the march and things are going to break soon, in my opinion. I think you'd better get ready and do something about it in this country."[3]

"I think you ought to see the President," Welles replied.

Two weeks later Meyer was invited to the White House, and he repeated most of what he had said to Welles. Winding up his gloomy forebodings, he expressed fear that Hitler would invade Austria and that Austria would then open the way to Czechoslovakia. "It seems to me," he said bluntly, "that you've got to get busy."

[2] Author's interview with Felix Morley, July 11, 1972.
[3] Albertson interviews, April 6, 1953.

Roosevelt surprised his visitor by asking, in a disarming fashion, what he could do.

"There is one thing you can't do," Meyer replied.

"What do you mean?"

"You can't do nothing."

The State Department had been urging Roosevelt to make a strong speech in the Middle West and had prepared a text for him. The President decided to make the speech as a warning, not only to Hitler and Mussolini, but also to Japan, which had embarked on an aggressive course in China. Stiffening the final text with language supplied by Secretary Ickes, the President denounced the spreading "epidemic of world lawlessness" and called for a "quarantine" of the aggressors. Morley warmly praised the speech in a front-page editorial entitled "America Finds Her Voice." Americans could again "take pride in their country as one which is at last willing to take a stand on principle. . . . the President has made a tangible contribution to peace."

In many other quarters, however, the speech was harshly criticized. Hull later complained that it set back the educational campaign for international cooperation by at least six months. Meyer did not challenge Morley's editorial support of it, but when Ickes confessed that he had supplied the word "quarantine" to the speech, Meyer told him: "Well, you did a disastrous thing, because instead of being constructive the speech was nonsensical in the face of a major menace."[4] It was the vast gap between F.D.R.'s words and actual U.S. policy that troubled Meyer. Weak and disarmed as it was, the United States was not in a position to impose any kind of international quarantine, and the administration was quibbling as to whether it would cooperate with the League of Nations in the mildest kind of restraints on aggressors. In another speech on October 12, Roosevelt made it clear that he would not attempt to "quarantine" Japan, and the Brussels conference that was trying to devise means of coping with aggression in Asia collapsed.

Some months later, when the President got around to asking Congress for funds to build the biggest navy in the nation's history, he had Meyer's full support. Here was a meaningful response to the country's danger. "It is one way," said an editorial of January 29, 1938, "of awakening Congress to what the Administration's naval and military advisers regard as imperative realities."

Meanwhile the intense journalistic competition in Washington became even more acute. Cissy Patterson's combination of the Washington *Times* and the *Herald* into a single 'round-the-clock newspaper reduced the *Post*

[4] *Ibid.*

once more to third place in circulation. In the ensuing struggle the *Post* tried to squeeze some advantage out of the fact that it was the only Washington paper published exclusively for morning readers, but it felt the pressure of Mrs. Patterson's consolidated operation. Meyer often commented in his whimsical moments that "the *Times-Herald* was first in circulation, the *Star* first in advertising, and the *Post* first in operating expenses." At one point he devised a "share the progress" plan intended to give employees two-thirds of any net improvement in the paper's financial operations, but it was abandoned after a year passed with no trimming of the losses.

Nevertheless, enrichment of the *Post*'s content continued. On the fifth anniversary of his management, June 13, 1938, Meyer announced the acquisition of the Herald Tribune Service, which meant the addition of Walter Lippmann, Dorothy Thompson, and Mark Sullivan to the battery of *Post* columnists. Some *Post* editors and other observers felt that Meyer had gone overboard in buying columns. In addition to the new crop, the paper was already publishing columns by Harlan Miller, Barnet Nover, Malvina Lindsay, and Westbrook Pegler. With the addition of three more, one wit quipped that now "all the garbage is available in one package." The preponderance of columns was questionable judgment at a time when the coverage of local news was spotty and the paper had no foreign correspondents of its own. Local news coverage was improved somewhat in 1939 by a new city editor, Frank Dennis, who had worked on the *Daily Oklahoman* and the Boston *Herald*, but recruitment of a staff was still handicapped by low salaries and the persistent belief that the *Post*'s future was still uncertain.

Harlan Miller had come to the *Post* at the suggestion of Gallup, and for a time Meyer pushed syndication of Miller's supposedly salty and down-to-earth output. After the columnist became a regular "ham-and-egg" guest at the White House on Sunday nights, however, Meyer concluded that the salt had lost its savor and let him go. Feeling a need, nevertheless, for some balance in the comment offered to readers, he induced Ernest Lindley to write what he called a "good New Deal column." In the years ahead he was especially pleased when Lindley seemed to get inside information that was available to no one else.

The struggle that Meyer went through to retain the column of Westbrook Pegler was one of the strangest episodes of his career. Pegler's ferocious animadversions, mislabeled "Fair Enough," were syndicated by Scripps-Howard's United Feature Syndicate, but not used by the Scripps-Howard paper in Washington. The *Star* printed the column for a year and dropped it. Meyer bought it, and during the next seven years the column proved highly successful, especially while Pegler was exposing corruption in labor unions. The *Post* promoted it heavily and fought tenaciously to retain the column when the Scripps-Howard *Daily News* tried to preempt it in 1941, despite initial assurances from the syndicate that this would not happen. Meyer complained in a series of letters that the refusal to renew his contract for the Pegler column was "hitting below the belt," violating "fair trade practices in journalism," and creating a scandal. Pegler wanted his column in the *Post* because he regarded it as "one of the best newspapers in the world." But the syndicate persisted in its refusal to renew the contract, and Meyer, regarding that action as a breach of faith, severed all relations with United Press. As the years passed, Pegler's ranting became more venomous, and, ironically enough, was sometimes turned against Eugene Meyer and the *Washington Post*.

Near the end of the prewar period *Time* saluted the *Post* as "the capital's sole big-league newspaper," noting that its news lineage had gone up 68 percent since 1933, its advertising lineage 111 percent, and its circulation 173 percent. "Besides," the article continued, "it has become a journal of national importance, a reading must on Capitol Hill, an institution of high character and independence, a force for good in its bailiwick." The compliment almost bowled over the *Post*'s editors, and they responded with an expression of shock. For eight years they had lived on a Spartan diet. Nothing was good enough. Everything had to be better. Fearing a psychological lapse as a result of *Time*'s glowing compliment, they invited their readers to "let us have it" whenever the paper lacked snap and punch. They wanted "no stretched hat-bands around The Post" because "this newspaper has just started to grow."

Despite the *Post*'s antagonism toward many New Deal measures, President Roosevelt gave the paper an occasional boost. At his January 29, 1937, news conference he responded to questions about the Labor Department's request for subpoena powers in investigating labor disputes: "When I woke up this morning, I read two editorials on the subject. The *Washington Post* has what I call a completely intelligent editorial on it. The *Herald Tribune* has what I call an uneducated editorial on the same subject. So if you will all read those two editorials my position will be clear."

On one occasion the President said he almost fell out of bed because the editor of the *Post* had read his mind so accurately. In April 1939, the President had told a group which assembled at Warm Springs, Georgia, to see him off that he would "be back in the fall, if we don't have a war." Editor Morley commented the next morning: "In using the collective 'we' the President told Hitler and Mussolini, far more impressively than he told Warm Springs, that the tremendous force of the United States must be a factor in their current thinking. . . . He made it plain that a war forced by them would from the outset involve the destinies of a nation which, as they fully realize, is potentially far stronger than Germany and Italy united." President Roosevelt had properly linked the United States, the editorial continued, with the efforts of Britain and France to avert war. F.D.R. was so pleased that he asked the reporters present to read the editorial if they wanted to know the trend of his thinking. Both the American and foreign press services carried the editorial on their wires, and it was widely quoted and reprinted.

Chamberlain's surrender to Hitler's demands at Munich did not immediately crush all hope of "peace in our time." Morley sought to interest his chief, the State Department, and several embassies in the idea of an international conference that might turn Munich to constructive ends. In an editorial entitled "A Turning Point" he pleaded with the powers to use the debacle of Czechoslovakia as a beginning for a new policy of reconciliation and reconstruction that would bury the mistakes of the past on both sides. His appeal to sanity won a good deal of applause, and Meyer rewarded him with a salary increase. But with the 1938 congressional elections approaching, the President was not disposed to assume leadership in any such venture, and it was all too evident that Hitler had the bit in his teeth.

The elections proved to be a setback for the administration and thus hastened the turning of a momentous corner—the subordination of domestic reforms to the worsening international situation. Roosevelt came to realize that his Court-packing bill, the subsequent attempted "purge," and his executive reorganization bill had divided the country at a time when the security of the nation demanded unity. Without abandoning his domestic reforms, he struck a new note in his annual message to Congress on January 4, 1939: "Events abroad have made it increasingly clear to the American people that dangers within are less to be feared than dangers from without."[5] The gist of his appeal was for national unity in pursuing "methods short of war" against the aggressors. The *Post* gave strong support to his "methods short of war," and the result was more frequent harmony between the White House and E Street.

Hard-headed realist though he was, Meyer continued personally to pursue rapprochement even after the pogroms began in Germany. The Meyers went to Europe again in July 1939, and while Agnes visited the

[5] Basil Rauch: *Roosevelt from Munich to Pearl Harbor* (New York: Creative Age; 1950), p. 105.

haunts of Thomas Mann, whose books she was reviewing, Eugene sought out Dr. Schacht, who had been ousted from Hitler's cabinet. Through the help of Mrs. Meyer in Berlin, he located Schacht near Locarno, Switzerland, and spent an afternoon and evening with him exploring the possibilities of substituting a peaceful solution for the arms race that signaled the approach of war. There was much agreement between the two that the economic and social needs of Germany should have been recognized after World War I; that Germany, lacking colonies, was suffering from a shortage of food and raw materials; that statesmen should be able to face these problems without bloodshed. As a result of the discussion, Schacht wrote Meyer a letter suggesting an offer to Germany and an authoritative study. He had already made clear, however, that he no longer had any voice in the government but was an exile just returning from India whence he had gone to escape Hitler's wrath. It was too late for any peaceful solution.

The expected invasion of Poland came on September 1, 1939, after Hitler had concluded his deal with Stalin. It brought into sharper focus the perils confronting weak and defenseless countries everywhere. Chamberlain's hope for "peace in our time" had evaporated; Britain and France sent Hitler an ultimatum. At the *Post* an alert assistant managing editor, Lowell L. Leake, noted at the end of a London dispatch which came in about midnight on Saturday one sentence saying that Chamberlain was to speak on BBC at what would be 5 a.m. in Washington. After checking with Casey Jones at home, Leake slowed down the presses, tipped off the circulation staff, held a stereotype man and an extra newsman. A few minutes after Chamberlain declared war on Germany, Leake was ready with a replate, and the *Post* printed 47,000 extra copies, being one of a few morning papers to have the story.

Once more the *Post* sounded an alarm in a front-page editorial, "Is Neutrality Possible?": "The unbelievable has become reality. Civilization is caught in the current of the maelstrom. The outcome, for much that we take for granted and for everything that we hold most dear, is wholly unpredictable." The *Post* was not deceived by the "phony war" that followed the division of Poland. After Hitler seized the Scandinavian seaboard, its editorials warned that invasion of Holland and Belgium was a virtual certainty. Britain and France would be in the gravest danger. As these events unfolded and disaster for the democratic countries spread, the *Post* repeatedly supported broader American aid for the beleaguered democracies. When the President talked of acquiring a fleet of 50,000 planes, the *Post* said it was more important at that moment to continue sending military aircraft to Britain and France.

As the crisis in Europe worsened, Roosevelt pushed his lend-lease policy through Congress. The *Post* gave it strong support and praised the President for letting Congress debate the issue without any arm-twisting. Nothing the paper had to say, however, was as pertinent as Meyer's personal comment to his niece, Elise S. Haas, and her husband Walter, after the new system got into operation. "No one with any fiscal knowledge would have dreamed up a plan like lend-lease," he said, "and it has worked."

Through the catastrophic summer of 1940 the editorial task was largely one of weeping over tragedies and applauding the magnificent speeches of Prime Minister Churchill. On June 1 the paper accurately saw that the "epic retreat . . . of the British and French troops from Flanders will be remembered as one of the most magnificent operations of the war and perhaps of all military history." When Churchill delivered his heroic pledge to fight to the bitter end, the *Post* commented: ". . . so long as Britain's fighting spirit is not crushed no battle lost can be counted as a final defeat."

Italy's attack on France brought indignation from the *Post* no less cutting than that from the White House. Mussolini's treachery was seen as a bitter illustration of the "stupidity, folly and lack of foresight" of those Americans who had stood for neutrality in an age of aggressive plunder. The enormous American interest in the outcome in Europe was now unmistakable. Yet the *Post* continued to argue that increasing aid to the Allies would not necessarily lead to American participation in the war. With France prostrate and Britain fighting desperately, an editorial commented on June 19:

> The British people must not be misled, however, into assuming from this [American aid] that the United States is likely to enter the war. The resolve of the American people to avoid participation in this struggle is exceedingly strong.

This inconsistency reflected a transition that was taking place within the *Post*. Morley had resigned on March 26 but would not leave the paper until the following August when he was to become president of his alma mater, Haverford College. The editor had convinced himself that a return to Haverford would give him more peace of mind, leisure to do some political writing, and a revival of sentimental and spiritual values. Undoubtedly more persuasive, however, was the widening breach between himself and Meyer in regard to the war. Though Morley had been preaching international cooperation, first in the hope of averting war and then in the hope of ending it, he was unalterably opposed to military involvement of the United States. The brightest prospect that he could visualize was a negotiated peace between Hitler and Britain, which would at least keep communism from spreading over eastern Europe.[6]

Meyer, in contrast, had come to view a clash with Hitler as inevitable. In a letter to Robert H. Brand of London he removed all doubt as to where he personally stood:

> There is considerable difference of opinion as to *when* we shall have to meet the ruthless power of Hitler. There is no substantial difference of opinion, I believe, as to the fact that we shall have to meet it.

Meyer's feelings were shared by Barnet Nover, the editorial writer and columnist whom Morley had brought in from the Buffalo *Evening News*. Nover was clamoring for wider American participation in the struggle. It became more and more difficult to keep the resulting schizophrenia within the organization from being reflected in the editorial output.

Despite their differences, Meyer was reluctant to lose an editor who had brought unquestioned distinction to the editorial page. At first he concluded that Morley was fishing for a raise, because the Haverford position would pay a little more than he was getting at the *Post*; but no offer of an increase was forthcoming. Unable to see any logic in the reasons Morley gave to support his decision, the publisher told him: "You have the most important editorial job in the country, and you are leaving it to become head of a boys school." Behind the verbal fencing, however, each saw that continuation of their relationship would lead to inevitable clashes—clashes that neither was eager to face. Even before the resignation became effective, the mounting disasters in Europe demonstrated the necessity of a new face in the editorial slot. For a time Morley wrote a weekly article for the *Post* from his Haverford sanctuary, but Meyer ended the arrangement because the gulf between those pieces and the *Post*'s reoriented policy was too painfully evident.

The search for a successor was thorough. At one point it appeared that the new editor would be Elmer Davis, then a newscaster for the American Broadcasting Company and later director of the Office of War Information. Having studied all Davis's articles and books, Meyer offered him the job at $20,000 a year, and Davis agreed to take it, even though he was earning twice that amount, because he was bored with broadcasting only five minutes a day. When ABC heard about his decision, however, they made Davis news editor, and he reneged at the *Post*. Meyer then turned to Herbert Elliston, a native of Britain, who had been a foreign corre-

---

[6] Morley's Memoirs (manuscript), p. 349.

spondent in China and was then financial editor and columnist for the *Christian Science Monitor*. Morley had recommended Elliston, whom he had previously tried to hire as an editorial writer. Elliston had not been interested at that time but, with Morley out of the picture, he welcomed the top assignment and would guide the editorial policy of the paper for thirteen years with skill, foresight, and dashes of brilliance. At the outset, however, he was not given the title of editor. Meyer himself became editor and publisher on October 17, 1940, and Elliston was designated associate editor. On the same day Meyer made a speech at White Sulphur Springs calling on the country to prepare itself for the great struggle ahead and for aid to the British "with all the material resources at our command."

It was soon evident that the *Post* had gained new vigor and pungency in the international sphere. In December, the Meyers were saddened by the death of Lord Lothian (Philip Henry Kerr), British ambassador in Washington and a frequent guest at Crescent Place. The paper printed well-informed tributes by Justice Frankfurter, William Mackenzie King, and others, and when it was suggested that Lothian's successor in Washington might be David Lloyd George, Britain's premier in World War I, the *Post* complained that "exhumation of the Welsh wizard" would be "a confession of bankruptcy in statesmanship." Lloyd George was not appointed.

Elliston proved to be a liberal with his feet on the ground. A naturalized citizen, he had great respect for constitutional principles and human rights. A candid internationalist, he was not afraid to face the consequences of joint action with like-minded countries in a world aflame with violence. Though he had no experience in directing an editorial page and his broad tolerance for different viewpoints sometimes left readers guessing just where the *Post* stood, he contributed much to the paper's reputation for insight, independence, and fairness.

For some months the *Post*'s backing of the administration's foreign policies had been complicated because Roosevelt was running for a third term. Long before the nominating conventions, Meyer had expounded his belief that no President should depart from the unbroken two-term tradition that George Washington had initiated. In Roosevelt's case, Meyer was especially fearful that a third-term campaign would revive hostility on domestic issues and thus handicap the President in dealing with the international crisis. On March 4, 1940, the *Post* had printed a story by Ernest Lindley under the headline: "Roosevelt Won't Run—Hull His Candidate." It reflected what F.D.R. was saying to congressional intimates at the time. Meyer had sent out a great number of reprints, fearing nevertheless that the report was too good to be true. After the Democrats renominated Roosevelt, Meyer returned from the convention emphasizing the "dissension and dissatisfaction" in the party and the feeling that the President had "used himself up" during his eight years in the White House, but it was mostly wishful Republican thinking.

One reason for Meyer's feeling about Roosevelt was expressed in a letter to Bernard F. Gimbel: ". . . I like him personally and distrust him as President. He is too ignorant about too many subjects. He is too quick to decide on inadequate considerations and his megalomania has reached proportions which, in my opinion, make him positively dangerous to himself as well as to the country."

The outlook for terminating Roosevelt's presidential career appeared more hopeful in 1940 than it had been in 1936 because the Republicans had nominated a dynamic industrialist, Wendell L. Willkie, who was demonstrating charismatic qualities that Landon had conspicuously lacked. Meyer contributed much to the groundswell that had swung the nomination to Willkie over Senator Robert A. Taft and District Attorney Thomas E. Dewey. In the gallery at the nominating convention in Philadelphia, Meyer and his friend Herman Phleger, San Francisco lawyer, sat next to a state legislator from Pennsylvania who was yelling wildly for Willkie. Meyer asked him why. "Willkie is the only man mentioned," the legislator replied, "who will help me get elected." From this Meyer reasoned that Willkie's name on the ticket would be a great help to many convention delegates who would be running for local office.

The Washington publisher and San Francisco lawyer began a series of visits to state delegations on the convention floor. Everywhere they were asked: "What's going on?" "Who's going to be nominated?" The conspiring duo would reply that it would be "Willkie on the fifth."[7] If an opportunity arose, they would also suggest the great advantage of getting on the bandwagon before it was overloaded. With many enthusiasts clamoring for Willkie, the sentiment behind him became a swell, then a tide, and then a flood on the sixth ballot. Once more the Republican Party seemed to be alive, and the enusing Willkie-Roosevelt contest was an exciting one.

Editorially the *Post* had welcomed Willkie on the political scene as a man who had conducted a "truly electrifying campaign." On his nomination an editorial surmised that many voters would rally to him because his character inspired "confidence and trust." During the campaign the *Post* was favorably impressed by Willkie's declaration that "only the strong can be free, and only the productive can be strong." It praised his candor in saying: "I shall lead you down the road of sacrifice and service to your

[7] Eugene Meyer to Henry L. Corbett, April 25, 1952; author's interview with Herman Phleger, February 24, 1972.

country." An editorial preference for Willkie could be read between the lines, but the *Post* held to its policy of not endorsing any candidate, and it continued to stand with Roosevelt on some issues. As an independent publisher, Meyer refused to contribute to the Republican campaign fund, and he appears to have retained little hope that the Roosevelt landslide of 1936 would be reversed. After the election the *Post* devoted an entire page to greetings addressed to President Roosevelt as he returned to Washington and resumed his practice of reading the paper in bed before breakfast.

In January 1941, Meyer recognized that the United States was in a state of undeclared war, although the government was trying to maintain the fiction that all its measures to aid the Allies were "short of war." It was an agonizing period in which many conscientious citizens winked at presidential war-making because it seemed the only practical means of safeguarding the national security. The country could not bring itself to face realities. Throughout this period the *Post* was more candid than the President in recognizing the inexorable trend of events, yet it too moved from expedient to expedient without ever calling upon Congress to declare war to save Western civilization.

Meyer and his colleagues were far ahead of the administration in arguing for vastly increased defense preparations. Yet even in this area there was some fumbling. Stacy May and Robert R. Nathan of the Bureau of Research and Statistics of the Advisory Commission to the Council on National Defense assembled information about the acute shortages of steel, aluminum, and other metals as measured against the mounting requirements of wartime. Their work came to the attention of Alfred Friendly, an alert reporter who had a special assignment in the sphere of defense production, and he wrote an article that extended to America the too-late-and-too-little saga that had so bedeviled western Europe. Casey Jones took the story to Meyer, and Meyer showed it to William S. Knudsen, director of the Office of Production Management, who was in part responsible for the failure to get industry into high gear. The article came back heavily annotated by complacent experts in the defense organization, and Jones refused to print it. An official report seemed to sustain the Knudsen view, but within a couple of months the government itself launched a big expansion of steel production. Jones apologized to Friendly and acknowledged that he had suppressed one of the most important stories of the year.

By way of redeeming that error, the *Post* launched a series of front-page articles under the caption "Guns for Soldiers." Written by Folliard, Friendly, Robert C. Albright, John G. Morris, and Marshall Andrews, these pieces accused the administration of trying to "pile a 30 or 40 billion dollar defense load" on top of full peacetime production, with chaotic results. More than a year after the defense program had begun, it was lagging perilously.

In June 1941, Hitler cynically tore up his alliance with Stalin, which had lasted only twenty-two months, and invaded Russia. Without any sense of surprise, the *Post* denounced the action and recognized the desirability of giving military aid to the Soviet Union. But it refused to go along with Roosevelt's attempt to whitewash the Soviet system as an inducement to the making of common cause with the Russians. When the President suggested at a news conference that the Soviet constitution provided freedom similar to America's, an editorial concluded that such nonsense was more likely to produce a reaction against aid to the Russians than sentiment favorable to it.

Meyer decided to visit beleaguered Britain in September 1941 for a firsthand glimpse of the war. Along with Robert Sherwood and Gerald Gross, a Federal Communications Commission engineer, he spent twelve hours in a frigid Catalina bomber, after waiting four days for the takeoff in Montreal. Though Meyer was nearing his sixty-sixth birthday, his chief worry was Sherwood, who was not warmly dressed and whose great height prevented him from either lying down or standing up in the space allotted to them. In London, Meyer found himself immediately on the defensive because of the failure of Congress to declare war.

Many doors were opened to Washington's best-known publisher. Brendan Bracken, then Minister of Information and a member of the war cabinet, arranged interviews with nearly all the high officials of Britain. Meyer spent an hour and a half with Lord Ismay, head of the Committee on Coordination of the Services, just before Ismay left for Moscow to see Stalin about joint war plans. Interviews with Anthony Eden, Lord Woolton, Herbert Morrison, Ernest Bevin, American Ambassador John G. Winant, and many British publishers brought new confidence that the British would be able to retain control of the air over Britain and perhaps over the channel.

As the publisher was about to leave London, he was invited to lunch in Downing Street with Prime Minister Churchill, who had been out in the country making speeches. When the other guests left, Churchill asked Meyer to stay, because he had something to say to him alone. "I don't want to fail to impress on you," the great Premier then said, "that anything you can do to hasten your entry into the war, which is coming sooner or later, will be helpful."[8] Britain's material resources were running short.

[8] Albertson interviews, April 10, 1953.

Meyer merely agreed that the United States would be in the war in full force "sooner or later."

One evening as Meyer was leaving the Foreign Office he heard someone call his name. It was Vincent Massey, the Canadian representative in London, whom he had known in Washington. Massey invited Meyer to dinner, and Mrs. Massey gave him a recital of what the women of Britain were doing to win the war. She insisted that he must first see Major General Jean Knox, head of the Auxiliary Territorial Services, and then the WRENS and the air force women, because if he visited Lady Stella Reading's volunteers first she would dissuade him from seeing the others.

Calling on Jean Knox, Meyer found her "extraordinarily interesting and attractive, with a great vision, a clear mind and a great ability to . . . express herself clearly and briefly." She took him to see camps where women were operating and repairing trucks, servicing and operating anti-aircraft guns—doing everything except pulling the trigger. Although he inspected the other women's auxiliary groups, he was so "terribly impressed" by Jean Knox's operation that his wife began to question whether his interest was in the heroic women of Britain or in one heroic woman.

After his return to Washington, by way of Lisbon, Meyer communicated his enthusiasm over what he had seen to Sumner Welles, as he had done in 1937. Once more Welles advised: "I think you ought to see the President." When Meyer was invited to the White House, he repeated to the President and his aide, "Pa" Watson, what Churchill, Bracken, and the others had said. "All this you have doubtless heard from the State Department," Meyer commented, "but there may be one new thing they have not reported on: the wonderfully brilliant performance of 75,000 British women in uniform"—a force that was to be expanded to 250,000 within a year.

Meyer concluded with a plea for American women in the military services. If you take men only, he said, you will draw out of the factories many who ought to remain there. F.D.R. pounded the table and roared with laughter: "Pa, what do you think? Gene wants us to get the women into the services. Won't those old brass hats go crazy?"

Creation of the women's auxiliary corps was not a laughing matter, however, at the *Post*. The paper continued to campaign on this front until legislation was passed and the WACS were organized by Oveta Culp Hobby some months after Pearl Harbor. Meyer's continued interest was evidenced by the devotion of an entire page, during the days of paper shortage, to stories by British women on what they were doing to win the war.

America's confused struggle to stay out of the war while rushing headlong into it finally ended with Japan's deadly blow at Pearl Harbor. Suddenly the nightmare of indecision and conflicting purposes gave way to new energy and resolution. The *Post* struck a resounding note that had been only cautiously suggested before:

> With a blinding flash the true inwardness of the world crisis now stands revealed for the American people. This war was never an "intra-European war." It was intended from the beginning as a world war. And America was marked out as the final object of attack. This newspaper had gone on that assumption since Hitler and the Italians leagued themselves with the Japanese. It would be fantastic folly to think of the Japanese engaging on their cosmic adventure alone. On that assumption—thank heaven!—all our defense plans have been prepared.

The hour having struck, the *Post* assumed that there would be "no rest till victory has been secured. This is our rendezvous with destiny." With the interests of the paper thoroughly merged with those of the nation, it embarked upon a new era that would be more momentous than anything in its past.

27 /

The National Defense

Mediation Board

MEYER HAD NOT WAITED FOR THE ENEMY TO STRIKE. HAVING concluded in January 1941 that the United States was in a state of war no less grim and momentous because it had not been formally declared by Congress, he decided to volunteer his services to the President. For the first time since he left public service in 1933 he asked for an appointment at the White House, reminded Roosevelt of what he had done during World War I, and offered to take any assignment if the President thought he could be useful.

"How old are you?" the President asked.

"Sixty-five," Meyer replied.

"You don't look that old," F.D.R. commented.

"I'm not recommending myself to you," Meyer said, "but I just felt obliged to place myself in the service if anybody wanted me."[1]

About the same time John Lord O'Brian, general counsel in the Office of Production Management, was trying to get Meyer into the central war-time control setup, but OPM Director Knudsen was wary of becoming involved with the press. Meyer began to fear that the President would name him a member of the National Defense Mediation Board. The program for stepped-up defense production and aid to the Allies was plagued by strikes in several key industries, and the White House had not been able to settle them. In the absence of controls reserved for full-scale war, the President had set up a board to bring the weight of aroused public opinion to bear upon the most stubborn labor-management disputes. It was an essential task requiring a high degree of skill and prestige, but Meyer felt

---

[1] Dean Albertson's interviews with Eugene Meyer, April 10, 1953.

that his meager experience in labor negotiations did not qualify him for such an assignment. He asked Sidney Hillman, associate director general of the OPM, to keep him off the mediation board. At a National Press Club luncheon Hillman told Meyer that the President had agreed not to make the appointment, but a few minutes after the publisher returned to his desk the newsroom asked for a photograph.

A search of the *Post* library had disclosed that it had no picture of Meyer, although he had been publisher of the paper for eight years. His likeness had never appeared in his paper. "What is this all about?" he asked. "You've been appointed a member of the mediation board," an editor replied. Roosevelt may have relished the idea of giving a critical publisher a job he would not like, knowing that he could not refuse. Aside from Meyer's unlimited offer to serve, the *Post* had been repeatedly demanding more effective machinery for the settlement of labor disputes in defense industries. Meyer swallowed his distaste for the assignment, and threw his full energy into the work.

The board was to mediate only the major disputes referred to it by the Labor Department. It could investigate issues and practices, take testimony, and make public its findings and recommendations when necessary to the attainment of industrial peace. Dr. Clarence A. Dykstra, president of the University of Wisconsin, was chairman but was soon succeeded by the vice-chairman, William H. Davis, a New York lawyer. The other public member was Dr. Frank P. Graham, president of the University of North Carolina. The employer members were Meyer, Roger D. Lapham of the Hawaiian-American Steamship Company, Cyrus Ching of the United States Rubber Company, and Walter C. Teagle, ex-president of the Standard Oil Company of New Jersey. Philip Murray and Thomas Kennedy represented the CIO and George Meany and George Harrison the AFL. Though he was in fact an employer, Meyer felt he should have been designated a public member because of his long service in government; in practice he would often function as a public member, to the irritation of his fellow employers on the board.

On the day that the board met with Secretary of Labor Frances Perkins, the *Post*, by coincidence, carried an editorial on the strikes that were botching defense production and suggested that she resign. Though crediting Secretary Perkins with many achievements, the editorial concluded that "in the present emergency, the office she holds ought to go to a man who would give positive leadership in the development of a practicable labor policy." Meyer was embarrassed when the Secretary greeted him, but he did not complain about the editorial, and there was never any suggestion that he disagreed with it.

The first dilemma awaiting action by the board was the strike that had kept the Allis-Chalmers plant in Milwaukee idle for three months, thus cutting off production of powder-making machinery and essential destroyer parts for the navy and for Britain. It was the most troublesome of several strikes that were costing the country 120,000 man-days of war work per week. That blight on the defense program had reached a critical point when the mediation board held its first meeting in the Social Security Building on March 25, 1941, but the board merely completed its organization and decided to meet on alternate Thursdays. Meyer reminded his colleagues that the board had been set up to meet a crisis and suggested that it remain in continuous session. His motion was voted down, and the members departed for their usual weekends at home. The press roasted the board for this, and its members were soon back on the job, but it took nearly a week to get the Allis-Chalmers disputants to a hearing.

Meyer concluded early in the proceedings that both sides had behaved badly. The company had been combative and not very candid. The union, headed by Harold Christoffel, suspected of being a Communist, had called the strike on the basis of fraudulent ballot-stuffing operations. Since this was the period of the Hitler-Stalin alliance, it was broadly assumed that Christoffel was trying to disrupt defense production here to aid the Fascist-Communist conquest of Europe. But many workers were involved, and it was a question of seeking a settlement that would be fair to them.

The board worked all day and far into the night without making an appreciable dent in the controversy. Relations between the two sides were in a state of acute hostility. As Meyer mulled over the problem that night, however, he thought he saw a ray of light. Charles E. Albright was the largest stockholder in Allis-Chalmers and a director. Many years previously Albright, then the country's leading writer of insurance, had sold Meyer a million-dollar policy in what he said was "the shortest time that it has ever taken to write any prospect that I have approached." Ordinarily Meyer insisted that he could insure himself cheaper than any company could, but he had taken a term-insurance policy that would pay $1 million in forty-eight hours as a safeguard for his brother Edgar when they were in business together. Now he drew upon his reputation with Albright for decisiveness and good judgment. When the two men met the following morning, Meyer asked, man-to-man, if Allis-Chalmers were trying to get the government to take over its plant.

"Well," Albright responded, "it couldn't be any worse, could it?"

"Yes," Meyer replied. "If Roosevelt takes you over, being a politician, he's not going to strafe Mr. Christoffel and pin medals on you. . . . You've left some things on which he can make quite a fuss. He would magnify your mistakes into crimes and put you on a parity with this union as obstructing the public interest."[2]

Following this conversation, the company was much more conciliatory. The board conveyed to both sides a sense of national urgency they had not felt in Detroit. Chairman Davis kept running from one side to the other with suggestions and requests for approval. The usual response was: "Yes, but I want to add a few words." Then the other side would want to add or change a few more words. At the end of the second day Albright's concessions resulted in a breakthrough on some issues and agreement to arbitrate all future disputes arising under the contract. Seeing an opportunity to enhance the prestige of the board, Meyer drafted a resolution thanking Davis for his unremitting toil and devotion to the principle of conciliation and asked each side to sign it. Christoffel said he would if the employers would. The employers agreed, and Meyer went back to Christoffel.

"Will they agree to it?" the labor leader asked.

"Yes, they will agree," Meyer replied, "if you will just change a word."

That mockery of what both sides had been doing all day brought a roar of laughter, which caused *Post* reporter Alfred Friendly, listening outside the closed door, to rush to the telephone and tell his editor that the long strike was over. With such a manifestation of mirth, he concluded, it was not necessary to wait for the board to report its success. The Gridiron dinner was held the same night, and among those who came to Meyer's table to express amazement that the stubborn dispute had been settled in forty-eight hours was John R. Steelman of the Labor Department, who had been trying for months to end the strike.

When the General Motors case came before the mediation board, Meyer was once more confronted by old friends. One of the company representatives was Lawrence Fisher of the Fisher Body Corporation which Meyer had financed before it was merged with GM. The company's spokesmen seemed to take it for granted that they had a friend in court. Actually, however, Meyer had no sympathy with the company's stalling and its assumption that it could continue producing automobiles in disregard of the worsening world crisis. His trend of thinking was much closer to that of Walter Reuther of the United Automobile Workers, whom he regarded as "a very intelligent young fellow." Reuther was campaigning for the conversion of industry to a wartime basis.

But Meyer resisted Reuther's demand for a wage increase of ten cents an hour on the ground that it was inflationary. Two other big companies

---

[2] *Ibid.*

had granted such increases, and Meyer insisted that if GM should follow suit it would become an unfortunate general pattern in the hour of the nation's peril. Meyer told his new friend candidly that he would oppose an increase of ten cents an hour even if he were the only member of the board to do so. No such information was conveyed to the company.

The negotiations continued for two weeks without noticeable progress. Meyer was troubled by the rudeness and insensitivity of some of the company spokesmen. The director of industrial relations, a former labor leader, was insulting to the union men, and Charles E. Wilson, the General Motors president, who was on crutches because of an accident, demonstrated that the company had not adjusted to the era of collective bargaining. At one point Wilson made a long speech to the effect that the issue in dispute was not a matter of money but of principle. People would not be able to see much naked principle, Meyer replied, when the company's profits, investments, and operations were so enormous. General Motors had just issued a quarterly statement showing the highest profits in its history and book values making it the largest corporation in the world. Wilson replied with obvious irritation that "the book value should not be a source of reproach or a limitation on earnings." Meyer continued his needling and, despite his worries about inflation, the case was settled on the basis of a ten-cents-per-hour wage increase. Wilson was still irritated by this incident when the two men lunched together years later, but Meyer found comfort in the revolution that had then taken place in the company's attitude toward organized labor.

While Meyer was serving on the mediation board, the *Post* kept independently hammering at Congress to grant the board power to effect settlements, where necessary, instead of merely making recommendations that were sometimes flouted. The paper applauded when the President took over the Air Associates plant at Bendix, N. J., to avoid a breakdown in the production of warplane parts, but was troubled by the disparity in the treatment of recalcitrant employers and recalcitrant labor. With the administration resisting emergency strike-control legislation, the *Post* urged Congress to act on its own initiative, but the issue had not been resolved when the attack upon Pearl Harbor came.

The most difficult case that the mediation board had to deal with was John L. Lewis's demand for a closed shop for 43,000 workers in the so-called captive mines operated by steel companies to supply their own fuel. The board felt that it should not impose that policy on the steel companies by government edict and it should not allow a wartime strike for that purpose. Lewis rejected pleas for arbitration of the issue and called a strike in late October 1941. The board reviewed the case and concluded that the powerful United Mine Workers Union did not need either collaboration by the government or a work stoppage in order to organize the "captive" mines. But Lewis continued his defiance; the *Post* accused him of trying to hamstring the nation because he hated the President.

Lewis's intransigence led to disruption of the mediation board. At his request, Murray, Kennedy, and the five CIO alternates resigned in a body. The board never met again. The coal mine dispute was settled by giving in to Lewis's demands. The key figure in that outcome was John R. Steelman, F.D.R.'s chief trouble-shooter in the labor field.

Meyer's irritation over that outcome did not readily lift. Nearly a decade later he wrote to Frank P. Graham:

> The most interesting day in the Defense Mediation Board was the last day when we got 9 to 2 against the closed shop for John Lewis. Roosevelt had indicated that "no man should be compelled to join a union to pursue his vocation." But he arranged with John Lewis to compel a man to join a union to pursue his vocation. The absolute power of John Lewis dates from that wobble on the part of F.D.R., announced the day of Pearl Harbor, you will remember. A lot of trouble has followed that incident.

Under the impact of the war, the President called an industry-labor conference on December 10, 1941, and obtained a no-strike, no-lockout pledge from the participants. A War Labor Board was then created to police the agreement. Though the *Post* applauded these developments, it continued to call for legislation, and Congress ultimately gave the President authority to seize and operate plants in cases where the board was unable to prevent strikes in war-related industries.

On the outside, Meyer hammered away at better utilization of the labor force in wartime. In a speech on Town Meeting of the Air on November 5, 1942, he complained that contracts carried over from the depression were still "spreading the work" at a time when it was vital "not to spread work but to spread men." But he wanted contracts modified in a way that would maintain decent standards of living and prevent employers from increasing their profits in wartime. There was impressive evidence that he had not burned the bridges between himself and the labor camp. In November 1944, when he was trying to catch a plane in Chicago in order to get home for Thanksgiving dinner, he passed the Hotel Stevens and noted that the CIO was holding its annual convention there. When Philip Murray, who was presiding over the meeting, observed his former colleague, he escorted Meyer to the rostrum, introduced him as a very valuable member of the mediation board, gave him a badge indicating that he was an honorary guest of the CIO, and asked him to address the convention.

The tenor of Meyer's remarks was that the unions had now achieved power and no longer had to fight for it as they had done in the previous ten years. Their position was strong and they could obtain good wages and working conditions without indulging in class warfare. Since the delegates were circulating a book entitled *The War Is Only Beginning,* Meyer concluded that his advice did not carry very far, but he was received with courtesy and respect.

Meyer's attitude toward labor was further illustrated by his hiring of Dr. Leo Wolman, economist and researcher in industrial relations, to write on labor problems for the *Post* to offset the extreme views of both employers and union leaders. While welcoming the rise of organized labor, his influence was always on the side of encouraging responsible use of labor's new power.

28 /

A Newspaper Goes to War

DESPITE THE SUDDEN STIFFENING OF THE NATION'S RESOLUTION in the days following Pearl Harbor, there was a lag in the adjustment of many habits and practices to the new realities of world war. The *Washington Post* joined lustily in the task of preparing the country for its ordeal.

From the beginning Meyer and his editors embraced the Churchill-Roosevelt strategy of crushing Hitler first. It was beside the point that Japan had struck the blow that forced us into the war. The overriding fact was that Hitler, Mussolini, and the Japanese warlords had joined forces in a conquest aimed at domination of the world. Since Hitler was the chief inspiration as well as the central force in that alliance, logic as well as sound military judgment demanded that the victims concentrate their striking power against him first.

Necessity similarly dictated embracement of the "Grand Alliance" which united Britain, the United States, and the Soviet Union in a struggle for survival. The *Post* called the alliance "a triumph of common sense." When Russia signed the Atlantic Charter in June 1942, the *Post* noted that the first article of the charter "is a renunciation of aggrandizement, territorial or otherwise." It was hopeful thinking, but the vital consideration was that the ring was beginning to close around "the Stygian darkness of Nazi oppression."

Meyer's personal view of the war was expressed in an address to the graduates of Sarah Lawrence College on June 6, 1942:

> This war differs from all others in that it is truly universal. The battlefield is everywhere—and everywhere at once. . . . The battle-fields of this war also include every mind and every heart—every factory and every farm. The warriors are men and women, the old and the young. The war upon which we are engaged is a total war in every category of action and thought.

In mid-February 1942, the *Post* launched a determined drive for the conversion of government to a wartime footing. One editorial accused department heads of "running around town trying to grab this and that war activity to build up their own jobs, regardless of what is already being done." Another piece entitled "Stripping for War" argued: "If the Government is to be put on a war footing comparable to the transformation of industry, some of its peacetime activities must be completely abolished, some must be temporarily suspended and others curtailed." The editorial went on to list agencies that could be safely shrunk or deactivated. Stephen Early, secretary to the President, cited one of these editorials as having been the subject of discussion at the White House, and a few days later Roosevelt issued a series of executive orders at least partly responsive to the advice he had been getting from several newspapers. The *Post* was far from being satisfied with this mild retreat from "government as usual" and continued to call for the elimination of nonessentials and duplication of effort.

The contrast between military heroism and civilian laxity was often shocking. In April 1942, a *Post* editorial declared: "The tragic fact is that the heroes of Bataan were finally blasted out of their foxholes because we as a Nation have been painfully slow in disciplining ourselves for sacrifices that are insignificant compared to theirs." A few days later the paper called upon Congress to enact a national labor policy that would make "shipyards and armament factories . . . as much a part of the war effort as armed forces at the front." The editorial shrieked: "Wake up, Congress! We are at war."

The paper took a leading role in demanding longer working hours, the rationing of gasoline, the conservation of rubber, wider use of women and blacks in war work, control of inflation, and the adoption of a master supply plan geared to the month-to-month requirements of all the Allies. But occasionally its zeal was wasted in frivolous campaigns, as in the case of Casey Jones's tirades against "Mellett's Madhouse"—an epithet applied to the U.S. Information Office presided over by Lowell Mellett.

One controversy led to a physical encounter. Meyer returned from Berkeley, California, where he had received an honorary LLD, and found among the proofs of editorials scheduled to run the following day a piece entitled "Mr. Jones's Excuses." It assailed Secretary of Commerce Jesse H. Jones, a former colleague of Meyer's in the Reconstruction Finance Corporation, for failing to acquire an adequate rubber supply for wartime. The publisher sent for Anna P. Youngman, writer of the editorial, and after an extended discussion asked her to add a sentence saying: "The chief reason for his [Jones's] failure is a boundless ambition for power that has led to his taking on more jobs than he can successfully manage."

On the evening of the day that the editorial appeared, when Meyer went to the Willard Hotel to greet James F. Byrnes and other friends in the Alfalfa Club, which was meeting there, Jones approached him uttering threats and abuse. Several club members stepped between them. Meyer went over and spoke to Byrnes and was starting to leave when Jones, now accompanied by former Congressman John J. O'Connor, approached him again. Meyer thought his former colleague intended to apologize. Instead, Jones renewed his tongue-lashing, grabbed Meyer by the lapels of his coat and shook him. O'Connor also closed in with fists flying as he yelled, "Let me get at the son of a bitch." (O'Connor blamed the *Post* for his defeat in 1938.)

As Meyer struggled to free himself, his pince-nez glasses fell off and shattered on the floor. He swung at Jones's jaw and missed. Maneuvering to keep Jones between himself and O'Connor, Meyer swung again, trying desperately to remember what "Gentleman Jim" Corbett had taught him half a century ago, but again he missed. At this moment someone had the brilliant idea of playing "The Star-Spangled Banner," causing everyone to stand at attention until it was finished. By this time Meyer should have been at home dressing for an embassy dinner, but, feeling that he must not appear to be running away, he sat down with Fleming Newbold of the *Star* and several other newspaper men. They all agreed that the incident was a disgrace to the Alfalfa Club and that nothing should be printed about it. Meyer had little faith in that understanding, and, as it turned out, the *Post* was almost the only major daily paper in the country that did not carry the story. Though he understood the outraged feelings of *Post* editors, he remained inaccessible for comment because he did not want his newspaper to present his version of an incident involving himself. The disgruntled feelings at the *Post* were magnified when he confessed his Corbett connection to the *Star*.

The incident became the source of much amusement. Meyer wrote many joking letters about it. He insisted to Joe Louis that he had "scored a knockout" by two misses to the jaw—something Joe had never done. The press made much of the fact that Jones was some forty pounds heavier and much taller than Meyer, although his sixty-eight years topped Meyer's sixty-six. Roosevelt had several good laughs over it. Before leaving the hotel that night Meyer had asked Jim Wright of the Buffalo *News* to convey a message to F.D.R. through "Pa" Watson: ". . . if I could have stayed a little longer at the Alfalfa Club, I would have rid him of one of his fastest-growing liabilities." "Pa" delivered the message at a staff breakfast in F.D.R.'s bedroom the next morning, and someone (presumably the President) asked, amid a hilarious uproar: "Why didn't he hit him in the belly instead of reaching for his jaw?" At the next meeting of the Alfalfa Club, Watson appeared with an MP badge and a night stick and said the President had ordered him to "keep the peace between Jesse and Gene." The incident did not end the *Post's* criticism of Jones. A year later Meyer walked into an editorial conference carrying a critical piece about Jones, and commented: "I don't know whether you know it or not, but this happens to be the night of another Alfalfa Club dinner."

The *Post's* efforts to discourage large-scale drafting of men before quarters, uniforms, instructors, and weapons were available led to a clash with General Marshall. Meyer remembered the loss of morale that had followed the herding of men into unprepared camps during World War I and sounded a warning against repetition of that error. Marshall, then Chief of Staff, not only took vigorous exception to that view but also publicly assailed the *Post* in intemperate terms. Meyer called Secretary of War Stimson to lodge a protest. "You don't like our army," Stimson countered. "It's because I do like your army," Meyer retorted, "that I'd like to see you at your earliest convenience."

Obtaining an appointment for the following afternoon, Meyer told the Secretary that the *Post* was trying to promote public understanding of an important issue and that General Marshall's response had been both "unfair and improper." The conversation then ranged over other subjects for nearly an hour. On the same day Marshall wrote Meyer an apology, acknowledging that his comment had been "unfortunate and should not have been made." The publisher accepted the apology with good grace:

> Please accept my assurance that while we may and will make mistakes in the Post, our Americanism is unquestionable and complete and our willingness and anxiety to cooperate with the responsible officers of our government and the armed forces is without limit. At any time you think we need guidance, or correction in our position, you have only to send for me. You need have no hesitation and I will always consider it a privilege to hear from you about anything that you consider of interest.[1]

Meyer made good his pledge of close contact with the military by visiting Assistant Secretary of War John J. McCloy about twice a month for a quiet chat about the war, with maps pulled down and formalities laid aside. The information thus obtained was enormously helpful in guiding the *Post's* general policies. In return, the publisher alerted Mc-

[1] Eugene Meyer to General George C. Marshall, October 14, 1942.

Cloy to weak spots in the war effort before seeking corrective action through public opinion.

There was no apology for this cooperation with the government. Meyer believed that a constructive attitude—"a well-founded idealism, intelligently understood and persistently pursued"—was the best foundation for success in journalism no less than in business or banking. His "golden rule of opposition in wartime" was "to propose rather than oppose." Critics who were merely negative were not doing their job. The *Post* found much to commend in the constructive criticism that was emanating from Senator Harry Truman's committee investigating the war effort, but it was also quick to call the Truman Committee to account when it seemed to disregard its own rules of objectivity and fairness. "It is a war and not an argument," one editorial insisted, "that we must win."

While demanding sacrifices of many kinds, the *Post* had no sympathy with short-cuts in regard to civil liberties. It sharply assailed the administration's bill (in early 1942) that would have authorized heavy fines and imprisonment for disclosure of a record, file, or memorandum declared secret by a government agency. In the name of military security, the bill would have permitted any government agency to conceal its blunders from the public. When overzealous censors tried to excuse indiscriminate snooping on grounds of military necessity, the *Post* warned that "the American people will not condone Gestapo methods" even under the pressure of an emergency. While recognizing the need for vigilance on the home front, the paper also deplored the herding of Japanese-Americans into concentration camps on the West Coast.

Roosevelt's suggestion that curiosity-seekers and social butterflies should get out of Washington to make room for war workers was heartily re-echoed by the *Post*, but it also pleaded for more housing in the capital so that essential war workers would not be stranded. Another subject of much interest at the time was "Wartime Taxation." The *Post* published a series of twenty-four articles by economists and eminent citizens under that heading. Meyer's own view was that taxes should be raised to the point of "maximum returns" not only to defray a large portion of the cost of the war but also to absorb part of the country's greatly increased income that was putting pressure on prices. When the Treasury finally asked for $10.5 billion in new taxes, the *Post* said that the strongest criticism of the bill was "that it did not go far enough" and that citizens who were merely paying higher taxes to win the war were highly privileged.

Both Meyer and his editors were thinking beyond the war to a more secure peace. In his Sarah Lawrence speech the publisher called for United States participation in a postwar peace organization. Meanwhile the *Post* was urging a constitutional amendment so that a peace treaty could be ratified by the Senate without danger of repeating "the colossal blunder which followed World War I."

Meyer's influence on the war extended far beyond the operations of his paper. When it appeared that high officials were withholding information from the country because they could not speak freely at their news conferences without the enemy listening, he organized background sessions at his home where military men and other officials were invited to brief select groups of journalists off the record. These "backgrounders" proved to be of great value in understanding what was going on. On some occasions, however, closed sessions of this kind led to embarrassment. Managing Editor Jones was so exercised one night by General Marshall's report of the devastating effects of strikes on war production that he persuaded the general to let the story be written without attribution. Edward Folliard wrote a front-page story on the basis of Jones's notes and oral briefing and several other papers carried similar accounts of what the general had said. When the New York newspaper *P.M.* identified Marshall as the source of the comments, both the general and the papers quoting him anonymously came under criticism. The *Post* defended Marshall against the barbs of labor leaders and once more called for enactment of a national service law.

Meyer's keen interest in everything that was being done to win the war led him to the door of Henry J. Kaiser. On a trip to San Francisco, he had been favorably impressed by Kaiser's highly efficient cement-manufacturing operation. After Kaiser had agreed to build two hundred 10,000-ton Liberty ships for Britain, Meyer asked a mutual friend to arrange a meeting for him with this new industrial genius. That meeting led to the inspection of Kaiser's shipbuilding operation across the bay from San Francisco. Meyer went with Kaiser from plant to plant offering comments on the new venture in the mass-production of ships. It was obvious that this experiment could have an enormous impact on a war that was peculiarly dependent upon shipping. Later Kaiser received a large order for Liberty ships from the United States government.

On a visit to Washington, Kaiser lunched with Meyer and Wayne Coy, then assistant director of the Budget Bureau. With pleasantries out of the way, Meyer asked what brought the industrialist to Washington, and Kaiser replied: "I have an idea." He proceeded to scratch out on a piece of paper plans for a "baby aircraft carrier," which would be a modification of his Liberty ships. Though it would be built of thin steel and would carry no armament save machine guns and anti-aircraft guns, its deck would accommodate about fifty fighter planes and some torpedo planes; it could be built in a small fraction of the two or three years required for construction of a full-fledged aircraft carrier, and it would serve to ferry military planes to areas where they would be needed.

"What are you going to do about it?" Meyer asked. The industrialist replied that at 3 P.M. he and his staff were to present the idea to a committee of sixteen admirals. Meyer said he would be greatly interested in the outcome of the meeting. Within a couple of hours Kaiser was on the telephone. The admirals had spent fifteen minutes discussing the baby aircraft carrier, after Kaiser's staff had presented the idea, and said they wanted none of it. Only big, well-armed carriers would serve their purpose and scarce labor and materials could not be diverted to anything else. "I'm licked," Kaiser said, "and I'll take the five o'clock train home." Meyer urged him to "stick around for a couple of days" to see if something could be done.

Meyer had already given Wayne Coy an album of photographs showing the new Kaiser shipbuilding operation on the Columbia River where construction time had been greatly shortened by building superstructures in three units that were later welded together. Coy was going to see the President, and Meyer suggested that he be alerted to the Kaiser idea. Meanwhile the industrialist himself sought help from other Washington friends, and within two days he had an appointment at the White House. Admiral Emory Land, head of the shipping board, was with the President, but no navy men. Before the conference was over, it was agreed that Kaiser should go ahead with the construction of fifty "baby flat-tops."

When the operation got into full swing, Kaiser turned out one aircraft carrier a week and they proved to be enormously useful in the war in the Pacific. The part that Meyer had played in getting the program under way was fully recognized by Edgar Kaiser, Henry's son and collaborator, in a toast offered at a luncheon when the first baby carrier was launched. The industrialist himself later wrote Meyer that this contribution to the war could not have been made without "your encouragement and help." In the same letter he commented: "Truly and sincerely in the early days of the shipbuilding you were a great inspiration to me."[2] When the navy boasted that it had a hundred carriers, Meyer thought it was very ironic that half of them had been built by Kaiser against the navy's wishes, but he dismissed his own role in thus expanding the carrier fleet by saying: "There are many opportunities in journalism to put in a plug at the right time."

Archibald MacLeish of the Office of Facts and Figures asked Meyer

[2] Henry J. Kaiser to Eugene Meyer, January 18, 1947.

if he would be chairman of an advisory committee to that agency. Without much reflection, Meyer responded: "Advisory committees aren't worth a damn. If you want me, push a button and I'll come to see you without any formal status." As he mulled over MacLeish's problem, however, the publisher concluded that he had responded too cavalierly. The next morning he went to see MacLeish and said that the country's powerful advertising agencies were in the best possible position to promote the national interest in wartime. It should not be difficult to hitch them to public service in this period when the advertising of products was slack because so many big corporations had been diverted to war production. MacLeish asked the publisher further to explore the possibilities and to offer some concrete suggestions.

Having noted a Squibbs advertisement that suggested a feeling for the public interest, Meyer went to see Bertram B. Geyer whose agency was handling the Squibbs account. Geyer organized a lunch at which Meyer presented his ideas to Miller McClintock, director of the Advertising Research Foundation, and others. He assumed that the advertising agencies would be glad to help the country in wartime, that they would modify their charges because of the public nature of the causes they would be promoting, and that funds spent for such advertising would be tax deductible. But McClintock reported back that no one could figure out how to make public-interest campaigns tax deductible. The purpose of the organization would be, Meyer replied, "to promote the military power of the United States in time of war, for its government and people." That seemed to clinch the public nature of the undertaking.

The Advertising Council which grew out of these discussions mobilized the ablest promotional minds in the nation and was responsible for the spending of approximately $18 million by the big corporations to popularize the saving of food, the acceptance of quotas, and the observance of essential wartime restrictions. As a member of the council's advisory committee, Meyer used his influence to keep the council on the beam of the national welfare and to exclude the intrusion of commercial interests. After the war the council interested itself in reconversion, world trade, and many other causes. It was credited with pouring $150 million a year into public service information.

There were dividends for the *Post* as well as the nation in this kind of advertising. *Post* solicitors began to write public service copy and submit it to the big corporations, with the result that national advertising in the *Post* grew to a million lines a year, compared to 600,000 for the *Star*. That achievement attracted attention in New York, and both the *Times* and *Herald Tribune* called Meyer to ask how it had come about. Reflecting that they had never been inclined to share their secrets with him, he merely replied that in Washington you have to do things differently.

In Chicago one night in July 1943, Harold Anderson took Meyer to a display of military weapons sponsored by the *Tribune*. It stimulated Meyer's thinking that more should be done to keep the people informed about the progress of the war. Back in Washington, he suggested a series of army shows to Secretary of War Stimson, but the military had a war to fight and was not interested in mere demonstrations. When the Treasury launched its third war loan drive for $15 billion, however, Meyer tried again. "Why don't you show the public what it is getting for its money?" he asked Secretary Morgenthau. Together Morgenthau and Meyer succeeded in getting the army's cooperation, and the *Washington Post* sponsored a "Back the Attack" show on the grounds of the Washington Monument.

In opening the show on September 9, 1943, the publisher declared that the modern military equipment covering sixteen acres was an inspiring sight. "The enslaved populations answering the whiplashes of ruthless dictators have not been able to produce in a decade of preparations what this nation has brought into being in twenty-four short months," he said. "It will do your heart good to know that your son has the best that brains and money can furnish in hastening the day when we can live in peace." The show was a striking success and led to many similar exhibits in other cities. When the army moved its equipment, the *Post* spent $6,000 to clean up the Monument grounds, but Meyer was more interested in the warm congratulations that were forthcoming from the Secretary of War, the Secretary of the Treasury, military leaders, and the public in general.

The war brought Meyer face to face with another problem that had been dogging him for nearly half a century. At Yale he had acquired a keen interest in psychology and psychiatry and said he would like to delve into both if he "didn't have to be a damn banker." In later years he had dipped into Freud, and an assistant of Freud had spent two weeks with the Meyer family at Mount Kisco. In Washington, Meyer had become well acquainted with Dr. William Alanson White, superintendent of St. Elizabeth's Hospital, and White had tried to draw him into the National Committee for Mental Hygiene, but he had been too absorbed in his government work at the time. It was not until a close friend and neighbor near Mount Kisco, Dr. Marion E. Kenworthy, alerted him to the psychiatric casualties of wartime that he finally became active in this sphere.

At the suggestion of Dr. Kenworthy, Meyer accompanied her to Fort Monmouth, New Jersey, where a mental hygiene unit had been set up to deal with recruits who were under emotional stress because of homesickness, military discipline, or fear of war. Captain Harry L. Freedman, in charge of the camp, was reaching the roots of most of the problems and was sending about 75 percent of his patients back to their units after treatment. Meyer was much pleased by what he saw, and he and Dr. Kenworthy later went back to the camp, taking Edward Folliard, who wrote an understanding article on this new mental hygiene unit and the great improvement that had been made in treating the mistakenly called cases of "shell shock" since World War I. Its conclusion was that timely attention to emotional and psychiatric problems in the services would pay high dividends on the battlefields. Meyer made the article available without cost and some newspapers reprinted it. Brigadier General Edgar L. Clewell, who had ordered creation of the Fort Monmouth unit, wrote Meyer: ". . . this article demonstrates to me what journalism at its best can do."

After this baptism into psychiatry, Meyer was drawn into many related activities. He sent Folliard to cover the annual meetings of the American Psychiatric Association, and news of psychiatric developments received special attention in the *Post*. The publisher's lunch room became a center for many discussions with eminent practitioners in the field, including Dr. Frank Fremont-Smith, formerly of the Harvard Medical School. The doctors found that they could bring their nonprofessional problems to Meyer, and somehow he would find a way to be helpful. There were indications that he was especially zealous in this field because it frequently brought him into the company of Marion Kenworthy, but the results were nonetheless efficacious.

In December 1944, Meyer became the first lay president of the National Committee for Mental Hygiene, having consented to serve on condition that Dr. Fremont-Smith would become vice-chairman. His special interest at the time was the readjustment of returning veterans to civilian life. Neglect of that problem, he noted in a memorandum to Admiral Ross T. McIntyre, Surgeon General of the Navy, would be "cruelly destructive of the individual and fraught with danger to the nation's communities." Yet the trained personnel available to do the job was grossly inadequate. Meyer saw the mounting wartime neuroses, against this background of meager resources, as "the most important sociological problem this country has ever had to face."

There were, however, some bright spots. Noting that General Motors had employed some 15,000 veterans and was giving special attention to their problems, Meyer spent four days visiting GM plants. Some of them were "doing wonderful things"—finding jobs the returning veterans could do without exacerbation of their problems. For once, work situations were being tailored to human needs.

When the Committee for Economic Development asked Meyer to take charge of its postwar planning in the Washington area, he consented on condition that the welfare of veterans be given a special place in the program. Proper placement of veterans was more important, he said, than the reconversion of business. Largely through his influence, a center was organized where veterans could go for guidance in finding jobs, obtaining medical care, or being reoriented into civilian life. Within medical circles Meyer was given great credit for this work. Major General Howard McC. Snyder, who later was to become medical adviser at the White House, once introduced Meyer at a cocktail party at the home of General Eisenhower as "the man who advanced the psychiatric care of the veterans in this country by one year." The publisher was immensely pleased. "Nobody," he commented, "[has] said a nicer thing to me in all of my experience."

As chairman of the National Committee for Mental Hygiene, Meyer pushed for funds and legislation as well as for the training and placement of more psychiatric personnel. Dr. Thomas Parran, the Surgeon General, said that Meyer's testimony before House and Senate committees was "the single most important factor leading to the passage of the bill," which became the National Mental Health Act.[3] Bringing the energy and wisdom of a powerful layman to bear on the problems of psychiatry, Meyer played a significant role in the rescue of that profession from its traditional place as the stepchild of medicine.

The *Post* celebrated the tenth anniversary of the Meyer regime on June 13, 1943. Circulation in that decade had increased from 51,000 to about 165,000; advertising from about 4 million lines to 12 million. For the first time the paper was making a small profit because of the war boom. *Time* had described the *Post* as "one of the world's ten greatest newspapers," and *Fortune* had ranked it "among the first half-dozen newspapers in the United States." No one could be devoid of pride in having lifted a bankrupt newspaper to that status in ten years, but Meyer had expected faster progress. To one well-wisher he replied that he was thinking "how much better I should have done and how much better I must do in the future." To another he wrote: "We are not now at the end of the first ten years patting ourselves on the back and indulging in any smug self-satisfaction. . . . in the words of Churchill, 'this is the end of the beginning.' "

[3] Dr. Frank Fremont-Smith to Eugene Meyer, October 10, 1946.

The paper was still fighting pugnaciously for numerous causes. Two of its long-range campaigns were concerned with aid to education and Secretary Hull's reciprocal trade agreements, but there were more exciting contests. In July and August 1943, the *Post* printed a series of punchy front-page editorials demanding the appointment of a separate chief of staff for air. The first of these, "Give Air Power Its Wings," accused the President of trying to fight the air war of the forties with the obsolete organization of World War I:

> You are keeping air power in Cinderella's role. Even the tradi-tional British are not so hidebound.
>
> With all respect, Mr. President, we ask you to reexamine your own organization, and then look at Eisenhower's [General Dwight D. Eisenhower was supreme commander in Europe] and the conclusion will be inescapable. Give air power its wings in your counsels, Mr. President. Advance its status and you will advance the bombing to victory.

The next editorial on the subject was addressed to the Secretary of the Navy. Air power, it said, was caught in a tug-of-war between land and sea chiefs. Since Congress was not in session, Meyer had the editorial re-printed as an advertisement in twenty-one papers where it would most likely be seen by key members of Congress in their home districts. On August 16 the *Post* came out for a single Department of National Defense as a first essential of postwar planning and argued that meanwhile an approach to that objective should be made by naming an all-air staff with a chief ranking equally with General Marshall and Admiral Ernest J. King, Chief of Naval Operations. The editorial assailed the navy for continuing to put its primary faith in obsolete battleships.

Admiral King called on Meyer and asked what he had against the navy. "Nothing," the publisher replied. "Why are you attacking us?" the admiral persisted. After an extended discussion Meyer summed up by saying: "The difference between us is that the navy wants to beat the Japanese navy and the *Washington Post* wants to beat Japan."

If subsequent history is a reliable criterion, the contest was a complete victory for Casey Jones, who wrote the editorials, and Eugene Meyer, who encouraged and supported him. But use of the front page for editorial comment produced a ruckus within the *Post*'s own organization. Elliston resented Jones's encroachment upon the editorial field, and of course Meyer had violated his own rule of keeping editorial expressions out of the news columns. Front-page editorials became rather common in the war years and were a source of friction every time the basic rule was violated.

A few months later a campaign that began on the editorial page ended with a successful front-page splash. Radio Station WALB in Albany, Georgia, had paid Congressman Eugene E. Cox $2,500 for his help in obtaining a radio license, although the law forbade members of Congress to accept pay for appearing before a federal regulatory body. The Federal Communications Commission sent evidence of the pay-off, including a photostatic copy of the check, to the Department of Justice. In retaliation Cox got a resolution through the House and began a furious investigation of the FCC, with himself as the chief inquisitor. The *Post* launched a campaign against this gross abuse of the investigative power. Some other newspapers, magazines, and the Civil Liberties Union also made the case a *cause célèbre*.

FCC Commissioner Clifford J. Durr petitioned Speaker Sam Rayburn to disqualify Cox because of his obvious bias and personal interest. Rayburn referred the complaint to the chairman of the Judiciary Committee, and nothing was done. The investigation continued—"a mockery of basic American traditions of fair play." Meyer wrote a letter to Rayburn and printed it on the front page of the *Post*. The Cox investigation, he said, "has been a star chamber; it has been black with bias; it has sought to terrorize those who exposed the Chairman's own corrupt practices." The open letter laid the mess directly at the door of the Speaker:

> Mr. Speaker, you are known to us and to the country as a legislator of integrity and good will. . . . The Post calls upon you and your colleagues to arouse yourselves and to submerge whatever there may be of personal loyalty to Mr. Cox to the far higher compulsions which derive from your proven loyalty to the integrity of the American legislative process.

Rayburn had been quoted as saying two days earlier that the House would take no action in the matter, but when Meyer's open letter appeared on September 25, 1943, the atmosphere on Capitol Hill changed. Within a few days Cox resigned from the investigating committee because, as the *Post* explained it, his conduct "was bringing the entire House into disrepute." Rayburn demonstrated his personal feelings by rushing down from the rostrum and putting an arm around Cox when the resignation was announced, and there was some grousing among the cronies about the high-handed *Washington Post*. But the general reaction to the incident was praise for a "magnificent fight." Thurman Arnold of the United

States Court of Appeals wrote Meyer that his "fight on Cox was the most brilliant piece of crusading journalism of the past ten years."

About the same time Meyer lost a fight with Cissy Patterson. For some years Mrs. Patterson had been seeking membership for the *Times-Herald* in the Associated Press, the world's dominant cooperative news service, over the opposition of the *Post* and the *Star*. At that time the rules of the Associated Press permitted existing members to keep out new applicants who were in direct competition with them. In Chicago, Colonel McCormick was taking advantage of the same rule to deny Associated Press service to the Chicago *Sun* which had begun publishing in 1941. There was a spirited fight over these exclusions at the annual meeting of the Associated Press in 1942, and Meyer found himself in the uncomfortable position of supporting McCormick. They were successful within the organization itself, but an antitrust case went to the courts, and the Supreme Court knocked out the rule which had permitted existing members to bar competitors. Meyer's view of the Associated Press was shared by many others at the time, but it is hard to reconcile it with his usually liberal stance on public issues.

In the first years of the war the *Post* was chronically impatient over the slow progress in striking at Germany and Japan. As early as July 1942, Elliston was sympathetically supporting Moscow's call for a second front. The Allies, he thought, should take "calculated risks" and not wait for the Russian front to disintegrate "in fightless impotence." Meyer himself was more cautious on this point. In a radio speech long after the paper had begun pushing for a second front, he said that "the blow could not be struck until there was a good chance of success" and that "when it could best come was a military question," although he did not blame the Russians for complaining about the delay.

While final preparations were being made for the assault on Hitler's Europe, Meyer discussed the coming events with Douglas S. Freeman, editor of the Richmond *News-Leader*. Anticipating a landing of General Eisenhower's allied forces on the Normandy coast, Marshal Pétain was urging the French to treat them as invaders. Meyer commented that "invasion," with its connotation of hostility, was an unfortunate word to describe the operation. Freeman said that a much better word would be "liberation." Meyer passed that thought along to Elliston, who wrote an editorial, "What's in a Word?" suggesting a "word of the heart" to describe the great impending event: "Let us then call this invasion the Liberation —the end and not the means, the civilizing purpose and not the military mission, the war aim and not the battle operation."

Folliard was primed to lay the suggestion before the President at his next news conference, but before he was recognized, another reporter asked a question about some phase of the forthcoming "invasion." Roosevelt quoted the foregoing sentence from the editorial of May 13 and said that the word "invasion" had been discarded in favor of "liberation." The press associations carried the story and quoted the editorial. At this point Meyer was concerned because the *Post* had not given Freeman credit for the suggestion. He sent Steve Early a copy of *Editor and Publisher's* article about the incident and asked him to tell the President that the *Post* had inadvertently failed to give Freeman credit for the idea. The result was a letter from the President expressing his thanks to Freeman, but the Richmond editor insisted that Meyer "had sense enough to push" the idea, while he had not done so.

As the liberation got under way, with the momentous "D-Day" strike across the Channel, the *Post* was acutely aware of history in the making. Victorious Allied armies swept over France crushing the Nazi hordes that had conquered the country four years previously. The Russians were smashing their way to Berlin. In Germany the ferment of rebellion was gathering strength. Surveying these events on August 12, 1944, the *Post* concluded:

> We are living, then, in what may well prove to be the most momentous days of the twentieth century. The magnitude of these events is likely to leave us dizzy, but we think it is scarcely possible to overemphasize their long-range significance. We are witnessing the rising of humanity to the achievement of feats that seemed well-nigh impossible four years ago. We see the resurgence of greatness in this and other democratic lands. . . .

While the victorious United Nations forces moved through Europe, the *Post* repeatedly called for "the creation of an international agency that can give stability, order and continuity to world policies evolving from the present conflict." As plans for a peacetime United Nations began to take shape, the paper commended Roosevelt and Hull for their avoidance of the mistakes that followed World War I. The American proposal was worked out through consultation, not only with the British and Russians, but also with a bipartisan committee of Senators. Governor Dewey, the Republican presidential candidate in 1944, agreed with Hull to keep the peace organization entirely out of the campaign. Public opinion had turned completely around on this issue, and the *Post* had played a significant role in bringing about the change.

The paper was loath to see any disruption of the national unity that had been attained. When Senate Majority Leader Alben W. Barkley resigned in February 1944, an editorial commended him for thus asserting the independence of Congress in the face of cantankerous and arrogant demands from the White House. But it also warned against carrying the congressional revolt too far. "That . . . might easily be disastrous. It would leave us with a divided Government in the midst of the greatest war we have ever fought."

In this kind of atmosphere the election of 1944 was an unwelcome intrusion. The time was not ripe for any change of leadership. The *Post* was torn between its distrust of Roosevelt's domestic policies and its admiration for his sometimes superb direction of the war—between its dislike for a fourth term and its lack of enthusiasm for Dewey. The idea of a fourth term was especially abhorrent to Meyer, but not abhorrent enough for him to commit his paper against Roosevelt.

The publisher had attended the Republican National Convention of 1944 as usual. However, his chief activity there had been an attempt to persuade Governor Earl Warren of California to seek the vice-presidential nomination. He argued vehemently that a ticket headed by Dewey of New York, the largest state in the East, would be greatly strengthened by a running mate from the largest state in the West. But neither Warren's admiration for Meyer nor their common ties to California could jar the governor from his refusal, because he felt that it would be a breach of faith to leave the governorship after serving only two years. Senator John W. Bricker was chosen instead, and the *Post* frequently collided with him, and sometimes with Dewey, during the campaign.

A sizzling controversy between Meyer and Drew Pearson enlivened the campaign. The *Post* had taken on Pearson's column, "The Washington Merry-Go-Round," after his former mother-in-law, Cissy Patterson, had thrown it out of the *Times-Herald* in the course of a noisy row with Pearson and Robert Allen, then co-author, whom she denounced as "the headache boys." Meyer was pleased to have the column, but he and Casey Jones were often troubled by Pearson's reckless accusations without supporting facts. Columns of this sort were pruned or omitted. In September 1944, Pearson wrote a series of columns attempting to show that "John Foster Dulles, in the spring of 1939, was still defending dictator nations." It was assumed that Dulles would become Secretary of State if Dewey should win the election. The only tenuous threads of evidence cited by Pearson were that Dulles's firm, Sullivan and Cromwell, had had legal relations with Count René de Chambrun, Laval's son-in-law (a charge that Dulles flatly denied), and that a Dulles client had financed Hitler in 1933. But Pearson assumed that Hitler's friend, Baron Kurt von

Schroeder, was a member of the J. Henry Schroeder Banking Company, when in fact there was no connection between the two.[4]

Jones read the Pearson allegations to Meyer by telephone to Mount Kisco. The publisher said they were "false and libelous" and concurred in Jones's decision not to print them.[5] Ordinarily the omission might have attracted little notice, but Walter Winchell had told a radio audience two days before the column was scheduled to appear that it would "rock the nation" and that some timorous newspapers would censor or suppress it. Irate *Post* subscribers who looked for the column and could not find it swamped the newspaper's switchboard with calls. Why was the supposedly liberal *Post* afraid of fearless reporting? Pearson complained, in an angry telegram to Meyer, that his "free and fair reporting" had been sabotaged and accused Jones of frequently blue-penciling his columns because he was "nursing a personal grudge." He asked permission to print the column as an "ad" for which he would pay. When this request was denied, he read his telegram on the radio (Meyer had given him free time on the *Post*'s station WINX). The publisher replied to many critics with a front-page statement on September 17. Freedom of the press, he said, was not a guarantee that every irresponsible statement will be printed. "The editors of The Post are solely responsible for this newspaper and no outsider is going to dictate its policy." He was especially resentful about the Winchell broadcast, which he regarded as an attempt at intimidation.

The columnist's slap at Casey Jones stemmed from a broadcast in which Pearson had talked about young men in uniform who were assigned to soft jobs in Washington. One example he cited was a college man who was serving as an admiral's chauffeur when he would rather be out fighting. It was Jones's son. The editor called Pearson and singed his ears with "obscene and insulting language." Actually, young Jones had been assigned to Washington during a period of temporary disability for active duty, without advance knowledge on the part of his father, because the admiral wanted a driver who knew the city. Jones had informed Meyer of the tiff and insisted that it would make no difference in his handling of Pearson, but he was obviously edgy in regard to the columnist.

The ruckus was still in full swing when Luvie Pearson called on October 12 and invited the Meyers to dinner. Agnes made some excuse, but Eugene later called Mrs. Pearson and suggested that she come to tea at

[4] *The Christian Century* (October 25, 1944) investigated the Pearson charges and concluded they were "completely false." Dulles's biographers, Deane and David Heller, also fully discredit these charges made by Pearson and others—*John Foster Dulles* (New York: Holt, Rinehart and Winston; 1960), p. 99.
[5] Eugene Meyer's memorandum in his papers.

Crescent Place the following afternoon. She did so, and Meyer rehearsed the entire controversy with her. When she sought to excuse her husband's conduct by saying he had lost most of his help and was working under a strain, Meyer responded that the columnist was not the only one in that predicament. He continued to feel that Pearson had impugned the editorial integrity of the *Post* and that he owed Casey an apology in view of the facts about his son. "What do you want him to do?" Mrs. Pearson asked. Meyer replied that that was up to Pearson himself. The following day he received a letter of apology:

> I am afraid that in this headlong, sometimes thoughtless world in which we live I have been much too thoughtless and have seriously offended you. For this I am very, very sorry.
>
> . . . I expect just as we sometimes impose on our real friends, I was too hasty and inconsiderate during the events of the other week. I have been out of town almost continually except for week-ends, but I should have come to see you nevertheless. I appreciate so much your talking to Luvie, and I hope that I may have a talk also. You are a grand guy, even if we don't agree on everything; and it would be a hell of a world if everyone agreed.

Pearson completed the reconciliation with a personal call on Meyer and a somewhat less gracious letter of apology to Jones. No doubt the incident had a salutary effect on the columnist who, despite his great capacity for exposing skullduggery, was often careless with facts.

As soon as the votes giving Roosevelt a fourth term had been counted, the momentous events in Europe overshadowed everything else. For *Post* readers Walter Lippmann reviewed the nature and scope of "the vast battle now in progress along the German border" on December 10, 1944. His emphasis on the magnitude of the task was reechoed in an editorial which concluded: "Our understanding of the war can be best conveyed to the men in uniform by a fresh dedication at home to the fulfillment of all their vital needs."

Almost in the hour of victory came the stunning news of Roosevelt's death at Warm Springs. Because his physical deterioration and weariness had been concealed from the people, they were unprepared for the shock. In a black-bordered editorial on April 13, 1945, the *Post* spoke for many grieving citizens: ". . . the news comes like a bolt from Jove, and the thunder is still echoing and reechoing through the diameter of our planet . . . Franklin Delano Roosevelt has put a stamp upon history which may well be unique in recorded time." Despite all his reservations about Roosevelt, Meyer went on the air twice with generous tributes. He saw F.D.R. as

"the greatest of our war casualties"—a President who had exerted powerful leadership to save the world from catastrophe in a time of unparalleled
crisis. Fearing that the new President, Harry S. Truman, might be overwhelmed by the burden that had suddenly fallen upon him, Meyer offered
him unlimited support.

The climax in Europe came with relentless speed. Banners in the *Post*
of May 8 proclaimed:

GERMANY SURRENDERS UNCONDITIONALLY

The War in Europe Is Over

This is V-E Day [the lead story began], the day for which
millions throughout the Allied world have waited, prayed, fought,
hoped and died.

In an editorial the same day the *Post* rejoiced over the end of the
"bloodiest and costliest and most destructive conflict in the long and
troubled history of the human race. . . . Democracy has proved its strength.
Courage, persistence, unity and faith in our cause have triumphed."

Early in August came the shattering explosion of the atomic bomb. A
three-line banner in the *Post* of August 7 crisply summarized the story:

SINGLE ATOMIC BOMB SHAKES JAPAN
WITH FORCE MIGHTIER THAN 20,000 TONS
OF TNT TO LAUNCH NEW ERA OF POWER

Folliard's lead story began: "Mankind has entered a new age, the age
of atomic energy." An editorial viewed most Americans as receiving the
news "not with exultation but with a kind of bewildered awe." The *Post*
hoped that the bomb, which had wiped out Hiroshima with most of its
inhabitants, would frighten the Japanese into surrender. It recognized the
quintessential implication of the news—that "if the peoples of the world
cannot now live in unity and peace, they will presently not live at all." The
paper sought to justify the wholesale sacrifice of life in the demonstration
of the new weapon. In later years Elliston would keenly regret this failure
to protest against the callous initial use of the atomic bomb, a feeling that
was heightened by his belief that Japan was already beaten when Hiroshima
and Nagasaki were obliterated.[6]

For some months the *Post* had been involved in psychological warfare
against Japan. While the Allied armies were closing their grip on Germany
in the summer of 1944 Meyer had begun to ruminate on the cost of

[6] Interview with Elliston in The *Washington Post*, April 20, 1953.

subduing the Japanese. There were estimates that invasion of the Japanese mainland would cost up to 800,000 American casualties, to say nothing of the destruction upon Japan. Meyer conceived the idea of a direct appeal to Emperor Hirohito on the front page of the *Post* which could be transmitted to Japan by shortwave. It would warn the emperor that all American might would be transferred to the Pacific as soon as Hitler was beaten and it would appeal to him to save his people and his cities by surrendering before the final drive began.

When Meyer discussed his idea with Elmer Davis, head of the OWI, he got a cool response—the chiefs of staff were opposed to doing anything of that sort at that time. With the collapse of Germany, however, psychological pressure on Japan assumed enormous importance. Without consulting Davis or the military, Meyer began to work on his own editor, Herbert Elliston, who had previously been unresponsive to the idea. Meanwhile Admiral Chester W. Nimitz invited Meyer to be his guest in the last great naval attack on Japan. Meyer declined because he wanted personally to supervise the psychological assault he had been planning. On May 9, 1945, the *Post* printed an editorial directed at Tokyo which said that "unconditional surrender was never an ideal formula" and urged the President to let the Japanese know what they must do to stop the war. It produced some formidable protests from people who saw any deviation from "unconditional surrender" as a sign of weakness.

Elliston tried again on May 19, saying that the objective was "the destruction of Japanese militarism at the lowest possible cost in American lives." The terms imposed on Japan should be severe, but—"To insist that a war be continued, after its purposes have been realized is to make an end of the means, to make war for its own sake. This is militarism pure and simple, and it is a dangerous inversion of the racist superstition to suppose that only the Germans and the Japanese are biologically capable of militarism."

Truman joined in the game of telling the Japanese that only surrender could save their country from ruin, but he also reiterated the vague "unconditional surrender" demand of his predecessor. Again the *Post* pleaded for a more precise spelling out of terms. Premier Kantaro Suzuki· was goading his people to fight to the bitter end by telling them that unconditional surrender meant their destruction and abolition of the Japanese national structure. The navy was carrying on psychological warfare in Japan by shortwave radio, and it transmitted the *Post* editorials as a hint that American terms could be had for the asking.

Captain Ellis M. Zacharias of the navy, who had been working on the problem behind the scenes, joined the public argument on July 21 with a letter to the *Post* signed "A Constant Reader." In it he asserted that the conditions Japan would have to accept had been made clear by the Atlantic Charter, the Cairo Declaration, and Truman's statement of May 8. The *Post* insisted that a specific statement would hasten Japanese submission. When Truman, with the support of the British and Chiang Kai-shek, at last laid down terms for Japan in the Potsdam Proclamation, leaving the door open for preservation of the emperor's status, the *Post* hailed it as "a stroke of high statesmanship."

Meyer felt, as he wrote to President Truman, that the militarists in Japan should not be allowed to perpetuate their power by hiding behind the emperor and that Hirohito or his successor should retain only his spiritual prerogatives. The *Post* resisted the first Japanese offer to surrender for want of assurance on this point but favored leaving the fate of the emperor to the Japanese people after the country had been occupied.

Japan ultimately accepted the specific conditions spelled out by the victorious powers, and the assurance given that the "national structure" could survive appears to have been far more effective than the dropping of the atomic bomb. The lives of an inestimable number of Americans and Japanese were spared. After the war was over, Meyer received from Dennis McEvoy of the Office of Naval Intelligence a gratifying letter of thanks for the part he had played in bringing about the surrender of Japan. It said in part:

> Soon, throughout the country, other papers and magazines began to follow the Post's lead. I believe it is beyond question that this gradual ground swell of public opinion was to a large degree responsible for President Truman's ultimatum to the Japanese on VE-Day, in which the meaning of unconditional surrender was defined in part, and the Potsdam Proclamation, where it was defined in full. The Japanese accepted our terms and our war aims were achieved without our being called upon to pay the cost sure to have attended an invasion.
>
> That the atomic bomb, or the entry of Russia into the war, was not the deciding factor is clear from the fact that Japan offered to give up before either of these occurrences took place.
>
> The fact that the Post made no claim to these distinctions (the great contribution to capitulation of the enemy) is presumably due to editorial modesty. But that they are justified is beyond doubt of many of us who . . . were closely associated with the political aspects of the war against Japan.

Meyer's concept of journalistic public service probably reached its apex in this incident. Meanwhile statesmen from the victorious powers had met in San Francisco to create a peace-keeping organization after the pattern that had previously been worked out at the Dumbarton Oaks meetings. Meyer took three of his best men to the conference—Elliston, Albright, and Gilbert. It was a pleasant occasion because of his visits with his sister Rosalie Stern, then a widow, but before the conference attended to its principal business, adoption of a charter for the United Nations, the *Post* contingent was embroiled in a row with the new Secretary of State, Edward R. Stettinius. Elliston wrote a bristling editorial accusing the "bush-league diplomats of the State Department headed by Secretary Stettinius" of intrigue to get Argentina in the conference; ". . . this kind of blundering is worse than criminal," the editorial said, because it had prejudiced the United States' relations with the Soviet Union. Although the editorial was written by Elliston, it appears to have reflected Meyer's harsh judgment that the Secretary of State, son of an old friend, "had no brains." In any event, the piece threw Stettinius into a spluttering rage.

The following morning as the Secretary was holding a news conference at the Fairmont Hotel, with all of the American delegates and more than two hundred newsmen present, he spied Meyer far down in the audience and motioned to him. At first Meyer paid no attention. He was not accustomed to being ordered around, not even by a Secretary of State. But the gesturing continued, and it became obvious that he wanted Meyer to meet him in the hall. As soon as both were there, the Secretary began to yell: "Gene, you and your goddamn sheet! You and Walter Lippmann are trying to destroy me."[7]

Time's account of the incident noted that Meyer was accustomed to sparring with irate readers and that his "defensive equipment included a bland, impressive air, two years of boxing lessons from Heavyweight Champion James J. Corbett, and a one-round 1942 decision over Jesse Jones, who also once objected to a *Post* editorial. From this armory of possible defenses," the account continued, "Publisher Meyer chose the mildest. Said he: 'Mr. Secretary, I will be glad to discuss this with you after you have calmed down a little.' Having given the Secretary of State a lesson in diplomacy, he walked away."

To the press corps Meyer was suddenly a hero. Everyone who witnessed the incident or heard about it seemed to feel that he had responded to the Secretary's anger with the right finesse. "You were wonderful," he was told again and again, which led him to comment in later years: "I was wonderful for ten minutes."

Back in Washington, Meyer asked for an appointment with Truman.

[7] Dean Albertson's interviews with Eugene Meyer, April 10, 1953.

"Mr. President," he said, as soon as they were together, "I don't bother you very often, but I have three worries I would like to discuss with you. One is your Secretary of State."

"Don't worry," Truman said, with a gesture that indicated Stettinius's days were numbered.

"The next thing," Meyer said, "is that the Veterans Administration worries me." An order appointing a lackluster crony to that agency was said to be on the President's desk.

"Don't worry," Truman said again. "I'm going to appoint a four-star general."

Knowing this meant Omar Bradley, Meyer expressed his gratitude, mentioned his third worry, was once more satisfied, and took his leave.

At last the surrender of Japan was announced on August 14. While rejoicing over "a great task . . . finished in triumph," the *Post* turned philosophical. It saw mankind "in a transition between a world that has died and a world that is aborning." It saw that both enemies should be "brought back as soon as possible into the world's polity" and that the problems of winning the peace would make even the greatest military achievement seem like child's play. A momentous era had ended, and a very different but no less momentous era was about to begin.

29 /

Transitions Within the Family

The great international trauma quickened the evolution that was taking place within the Meyer family. Each of its members felt the disruptive consequences in one way or another. Yet war was only one of many complex forces that were straining family ties.

For some years Agnes had been discovering that inheritance and wealth do not necessarily produce a happy and well-adjusted family. As her children grew to maturity, they encountered many problems they were not prepared to cope with. Neither parent had made family-rearing a foremost concern. Eugene had been so preoccupied with his work that conversation within the home, especially when guests were present, tended to focus on government, politics, finance, business, and similar subjects of limited interest to the children. Florence had written him in 1931: "I wish we'd had time to talk more before we both went in opposite directions."

Agnes felt that, after many years of married life, she had escaped from her "adolescent narcissism" and her rebellion against motherhood,[1] but she continued to be so busy with her writing, recreational work, and social activities that she had little time for the children. They grew up without the day-by-day, hour-by-hour mothering that seemed essential to bind a family together in harmony and mutual understanding.

Florence, the eldest daughter, had tried to escape from the family by eloping at the age of sixteen. The chauffeur had stopped her. At Bryn Mawr and later Radcliffe her emotional problems were exacerbated when her mother broke up one romance after another. Having studied ballet techniques in Moscow and Paris, Florence became a professional dancer and made her debut in Max Reinhardt's stage spectacle, *The Eternal Road*. A reporter described the new starlet as a "tall, lithe-limbed girl with a sleek, dark, shingled head." She maintained a New York studio where she sometimes danced for her friends, but she was never able to find a comfortable

---

[1] Agnes E. Meyer's unpublished manuscript, "Life as Chance and Destiny," p. 89.

330

place in the turbulent world about her. On August 21, 1939, she married Oscar Homolka, an Austrian character actor in Hollywood. Concluding that he was "endlessly destructive," she divorced him in 1946. For nearly a decade thereafter Florence would exile herself and her two children from her parents, either in California or in Europe. Although she would occasionally write affectionate letters to her father, he would often not know where she could be found.

Elizabeth (Bis within the family) was more successful in coping with the frustrations she shared with her elder sister. On one occasion when she was at Vassar there was momentary fear that she was in serious trouble. While the family was eating dinner at Seven Springs Farm the butler came in and solemnly announced: "Sir, the police are here for Miss Elizabeth." But the alleged offense proved to be only an automobile accident she had not disclosed to her parents. A small car had emerged from a narrow lane as she sped by and ripped off one side of her mother's Packard.

After two years at Vassar, Bis spent a year at the University of Munich. She then went to Barnard, found it to be uninspiring, and shifted again to Columbia, meanwhile studying violin with Louis Persinger and playing in both the Columbia and Juilliard orchestras. The most out-in-the-open rebel in the family, Bis repeatedly challenged her father's rules of social and moral conduct, disagreeing with his concept of what *seemed* right as well as his ideas of what *was* right. But Agnes invariably intervened to prevent a showdown. It was never the right moment to burden her father with domestic worries. The result was a continuing intergeneration conflict.

For a brief period Bis tried to please her parents by becoming engaged to a young relative of one of their distinguished friends, but she quickly broke it off. Determined to escape the guilt she felt by taking money from her father while disregarding his counsel, she went to Hollywood and worked as a script writer for Selznick International Pictures and wrote occasional magazine articles. She was a member of the staff of *Reader's Digest* in 1943 when she married Major Pare Lorentz of the Army Air Force. Herbert Bayard Swope congratulated Meyer on the occasion in a telegram which read: "I hear the troublemaking daughter of a troublemaker has married a troublemaker." But Meyer declared a truce as the couple left on their honeymoon after a wedding in the garden at Seven Springs Farm. Leaning across Pare in the driver's seat, he whispered: "Even Father can be wrong." It was, Elizabeth said, a good wedding present.

As director of the United States Film Service, Lorentz had written, directed, and produced such memorable documentaries as *The Plow that Broke the Plains*, *The River* and *The Fight for Life*. During the war he was commanding officer of the Overseas Technical Unit, Air Transport Command, USAF, which produced serial motion pictures and stills used to brief pilots on navigation and flight lanes to all overseas bases. His service won him the rank of lieutenant colonel, a citation for saving lives, and both the Air Medal and the Legion of Merit.

Eugene Meyer III (Bill) followed his father to Yale but no further. His chief interests at the time were flying and diving. When he wanted to leave Yale and take up night flying in California, his father induced Colonel Edward V. Rickenbacker, an old friend of Maxwell Motor days, to counsel the young man at Mount Kisco. After his second year of coasting at Yale, Bill was sent to the London School of Economics, where he worked under Professor Harold J. Laski. Elizabeth had taken a job in England, and she and Bill lived together in a London flat, she serving as housekeeper and Bill as her chaperon.

As part of his education under Laski, Bill took a trip to the Soviet Union and so dazzled the Russians with his diving skill that he received a rare invitation to stay and teach that sport. Though tempted to accept it, he returned to Yale, convinced that the Russians were developing "a really constructive society," and took so much interest in the Spanish Civil War that he was accused (falsely) of recruiting for the Loyalists. A letter to his distressed father confessed that he thought of going to Spain if he could be of help in fighting fascism.

On his return to Yale, Bill had decided to go into medicine, and his marks were a succession of A's. Instead of telling his parents, he asked Dr. Kenworthy if she thought they would permit him to take up medicine instead of banking or journalism. She replied that she felt sure they would and reported to them what she had said to Bill. He entered Johns Hopkins Medical School, graduated with the class of 1941, and was about to begin his career in the Public Health Service when the Japanese attacked Pearl Harbor. He volunteered for military service, and the family followed his movements as a medical officer with the Sixty-fourth Fighter Wing which hit the beaches of North Africa and Italy along with the infantry; the unit was among the forces spearheading the drive into Sicily, Salerno, and Anzio. While still at Hopkins, Bill had married Mary Adelaide Bradley, daughter of the late Reverend Charles F. Bradley of Boston.

The Meyers' youngest daughter, Ruth, was also engaged in war-related work. Having graduated from Sarah Lawrence College in 1941, she served as a full-time nurses' aid at Bellevue Hospital in New York. On July 29, 1951, she married Dr. William A. Epstein, an obstetrician and gynecologist associated with Mount Sinai, who had been a major in the Army Medical Corps during the war.

The only one of the Meyer children to show any sustained interest in journalism was Katharine, number four. While a student at Vassar, she worked on a local paper at White Plains. Her father then let her go to the University of Chicago to broaden her intellectual horizon. In 1938 he helped to find her a $25-a-week job on the *San Francisco News,* but she was ready to quit within a week because she did not know the city or the job. Meyer induced her to stay for the experience. When she was given a rough assignment on the waterfront during a period of labor turmoil, her father was pleased because, as he wrote her, "That is where the hot news is." He asked for copies of her stories. Returning to Washington in 1939, she was given several different assignments on the *Post,* including a tour of duty on the editorial staff.

At this time Kay was undoubtedly an important factor in her father's thinking about the future of his paper. His basic hope was to keep management of the paper in the family. Though Kay was shy and unassuming, she seemed to share his interests and to possess an innate sagacity akin to his own. It was apparent to friends that Kate, as he usually called her, was the apple of his eye. The special affinity between them did not mean that she always agreed with him—far from it. Kay's San Francisco experience, which had taken her into close contact with union leaders and working-men, had strengthened her attachment to Roosevelt's New Deal—a view she shared with her sisters and brother. They all argued with their parents about political issues. If there had been any doubt that Kay had a mind of her own, her demeanor at the *Post* removed it. One day she and several others who were waiting to see her father heard him thundering, despite a closed door between them, over the telephone.

"Are you going in to see him when he's in that kind of mood?" she asked Raoul Blumberg.

"I have to see him," Raoul said.

"I don't," Kay replied and left the room.

Katharine's budding journalistic career was soon interrupted, however, when she fell in love with a brilliant, forthright young lawyer—Philip L. Graham. On their very first date Graham began a whirlwind courtship and found her responsive. Fearing he would clash with her father, Kay took advantage of an opportune moment—when Meyer was talking about his confidence in the younger generation—to remark that the greatest of the upcoming young men was Phil Graham. "I'd like to meet him," her father responded. A dinner was arranged with two other young men also invited so that it would not be too obvious that the host was looking over a prospective son-in-law. Since Graham was law clerk to Justice Stanley Reed of the Supreme Court, the after-dinner conversation drifted to the Court-packing fight, and Meyer showed his guests a favorite cartoon—Elderman's savage caricature of Justice Black's appointment, depicting a hooded Ku Klux Klan figure on the supreme bench. Graham said that Black was a hard worker and one of the ablest men on the court; a hot argument ensued. Kay was worried, but both Phil and her father took it in stride. The redoubtable publisher may have seemed ogre-like to the liberal young lawyer, but that did not restrain him from asking for the ogre's daughter. They were married June 5, 1940, with none of the fussing and obstruction that had plagued Kay's older sisters.

Graham brought a new element into the family. A native of South Dakota, he had grown up in Florida and graduated from the University of Florida. At Harvard Law School he had captured top honors as president of the *Harvard Law Review*. After leaving Justice Reed, he was law clerk to Justice Frankfurter and worked as an attorney in the Office of Emergency Management and the Lend-Lease Administration before joining the Army Air Force as a private. In the service he won a commission and special recognition for his work with General MacArthur's air intelligence staff during the Leyte and Luzon campaigns. He was awarded the Legion of Merit and emerged from the army with the rank of major.

Meanwhile he had established smooth and amiable relations with the Meyer family. Graham had an avid interest in the experiences and ideas that his father-in-law liked to talk about. Meyer was especially happy about the addition of this poised and dynamic young man to his family because of the possibility that it would relieve him of a dilemma that was beginning to assume large proportions in his mind. While he had been grooming Katharine for a larger role at the *Post*, she was still too young and inexperienced for a managerial assignment, and in any event it would be difficult to give a daughter responsibilities at the paper that he had denied to his wife. But if Graham would interest himself in the paper, with Kay at his side, that might well be the ideal solution.

Mrs. Meyer had played no part in the management of the *Post* and had no place in Meyer's thinking about its future. Though she was legally a partner in the firm, he had scrupulously kept the reins in his own hands. It was not a question of thwarting her or of denigrating her ability, which he generously recognized, but a desire on his part to shield the paper from her occasional indiscretions. The news department had orders not to print anything written by a member of the Meyer family, or anything about the family, without his approval.

This curb on the most energetic and talented writer in the family became a source of friction between them. After all, it was she who had a journalistic background, brief though it had been. Agnes nursed the feeling that she knew more about newspapers than he did. Ever since their court-ship she had asserted her right to a career of her own. As long as he was in business and government her competitive impulse had found other outlets, but now that he had entered *her* field she wanted to participate.

At first Agnes tried to circumvent his curbs. She wrote articles and, without showing them to Eugene, asked family friends to recommend them as ideal pieces for the *Post,* but this proved to be a losing game. Some of her stories were printed, with Meyer's approval, and occasionally they attracted wide attention. Her ambition demanded a much broader outlet for her ideas, however, and she increasingly turned to speeches, magazine articles, and books. When her frustrations multiplied, she also sought relief from another source—alcohol. This, too, increased the bickering in the family because Eugene kept the liquor locked up and, although Agnes had the income from a $22-million trust, she refrained from buying a liquor supply of her own.

Agnes's indulgence was indirectly related to a new adventure in romanticism. In 1936 while the family was at their Red Rock Ranch in Wyoming's Jackson Hole country, Agnes was frightened by a horse that ran away with her in the saddle. She was rescued by Ruth and a cowboy; the horse did not throw her but the whiskey which she drank to soothe her nerves did. For some days she would not speak to Eugene or he to her. Agnes isolated herself on a high mountainside and delved into Thomas Mann's novel, *Joseph in Egypt.* Some members of the family followed her there, and helped to patch up the marital rift, but it was the intensity of Mann's writing that captivated her and brought a new zest for life.

A short time later when Agnes was lunching at *The New York Times* she heard J. Donald Adams, the book review editor, remark that he could find no one capable of reviewing *Joseph in Egypt.* Although she had never written a literary review, Agnes volunteered for the assignment and got a skeptical commission to "go ahead and try." She produced a remarkable essay (some critics insisted it was not a review) that was pages, not columns, long. It ran in both *The Times* and the *Post* and brought so much com-ment that Mann was delighted to grant her an interview. There followed what Agnes would describe many years later as "a friendship of so high quality, so passionate and yet so dispassionate, that its repercussions have only just begun to make themselves felt."[2]

The two kindred spirits began to exchange letters in German—often at the rate of one every day. Agnes took a house in New York and Mann visited her there every day for a week. When they parted, she felt she had

---

[2] "Life as Chance and Destiny," Chapter X.

suddenly descended "from the top of Mt. Everest to its base." In her view two "god-seekers" had gone "their way together, for a little while." Agnes later translated Mann's *The Coming Victory of Democracy* into English with a view to awakening the country to the growing menace of Nazism. The novelist and his wife were often at Mount Kisco and Crescent Place, and they entertained the Meyers at Princeton. Two years after her first encounter with Mann, Agnes wrote to her daughter Katharine in San Francisco that she and Eugene were taking Dr. and Mrs. Mann to hear *Tristan and Isolde*. The letter continued:

> He still awes me, but I surprise him a little too, with the result that I adore him openly and he returns it diffidently. I have the feeling I am one of the few people and one of the very few women he has ever liked.

Meyer's reactions to the new friendship were very different. After he and Agnes had spent a Sunday with the Manns at Princeton, he wrote to Kay: "It was a bit grim, but I am always ready to sacrifice myself in a good cause"—the good cause in this instance being Mann's denunciation of the Hitler regime in Germany.

There is some evidence that Meyer understood the hero-worship complex that engulfed his wife from time to time. She fell in love only with luminaries, and her passion was in the nature of a girlish crush which she expected other members of the family to share. Her conduct might have provoked a more jealous-minded husband to separation, but Meyer did not permit his irritation to extend beyond the family circle. Fortunately, both had a sense of humor and a faculty for laughter in the face of tension. Agnes once remarked that "desperation always turns to mirth *chez moi*." Eugene could taunt her with a humorous thrust that would leave little sting. On one occasion she chided him for not sending out enough copies of one of his speeches. "The trouble with you, Euge," she said, "is that you don't have any ego." "That's all right, Ag," he replied, "because you have enough for both of us."

During the war Agnes found new outlets for her boundless energy. Son Bill and son-in-law Phil took her into the library one night and said that the book she was writing—a comparison of the work of Mann with that of Tolstoy and Dostoevsky—was not as important as beating Hitler and that, while they were away at the front, they would like to feel that she was doing her special kind of job at home. Their challenge induced her to fly to Britain in September 1942, taking an old friend, Ruth Taylor, Commissioner of Public Welfare of Westchester County, and to write a

A photograph of Agnes Meyer used on her lecture tours.

Meyer and his great friend, the photographer Edward Steichen.

A Herblock cartoon while Meyer was president of the World Bank.

"$1,999,999,998 — $1,999,999,999 — TWO BILLION —
AND HOW ABOUT A SUBSCRIPTION TO THE WASHINGTON POST?"

Truman parade in Washington, November 5, 1948, after his upset election victory.

Meyer and Winston Churchill.

Meyer celebrates a Washington Post *anniversary with a group of employees. Left to right: Jerry Kluttz, Charles Paradise, Molly Parker, Mary Haworth, Meyer, DeVee Fisher, Edward T. Folliard, William V. Nessly, William Maben, Oliver Goodman, Jack Sacks, Louis Janoff, and George Hartford.*

A family gathering on Eugene Meyer's 75th birthday. Seated with the Meyers is Mary Bradley Meyer. Standing, left to right: Pare Lorentz, Ruth Epstein, Florence Homolka, Bill Meyer, Katharine Graham, Elizabeth Lorentz, and Philip Graham. Assorted grandchildren sit beside the Meyers or on the floor.

The executive staff of the Post *in January 1951. Left to right: R. Brandon Marsh, Harry Gladstein, Raoul Blumberg, Herbert Elliston, John W. Sweeterman, Philip Graham, Meyer, J. R. Wiggins, G. S. Phillips, Donald M. Bernard, John Hayes, and T. J. Weir.*

Meyer is made an honorary member of the International Printing Pressman's Union at the dedication of the new Washington Post *building in 1951. General George C. Marshall is at left and Philip Graham at right.*

At his desk in the Washington Post *building.*

The final purchase of the Times-Herald, *after many disappointments, was a joyous occasion for the Meyers and Grahams.*

Meyer displays the first edition of the Washington Post and Times-Herald *as it came off the press, March 17, 1954.*

Philip L. Graham, publisher of the Post, *explaining the Meyers' stock gift to the paper's employees, June 19, 1955.*

The Meyers in his study at Mount Kisco.

series of articles for the Associated Press on the heroic efforts of the British people to save their homes and themselves. Some critics thought she gave the best description of Britain's "social mobilization" that appeared in the United States. The success of the venture led to a herculean survey of "America's Home Front" from February to June 1943. Working day and night in one city after another all across the country, she produced twenty-nine articles that were published in the *Post* and later collected in a pamphlet, giving a vivid picture of failures and deficiencies as well as triumphs in the struggle to put the country on a war footing. Her observations were later expanded into a book, *Journey Through Chaos*, which the *Saturday Review* said was "the best, most nearly comprehensive report on social conditions in wartime America." Other series followed on the plight of migratory workers, the riots in Columbia (Tennessee), conditions in the coal mines, and numerous crises in the schools, which became the favorite subject of her writing and lecturing.

Meyer heartily applauded these achievements. Feats of human endurance in the public interest always commanded his admiration. He and Agnes had common interests, moreover, in many benefactions and acts of kindness. One of these was the Clovercroft School. While the bombing of Britain was at its worst, Meyer assumed responsibility for a group of sixteen English children who were brought to this country with three adult guardians. A leased estate near Warrenton, Virginia, was converted into a school for them. The Meyers visited the children with some degree of regularity, corresponded with them, sent them birthday presents, provided vacations, and continued to send some of them food and other presents years after they had returned to Britain.

Another project in which they had a common interest was a beautiful estate on the Potomac River downstream from Great Falls. Mrs. Meyer had bought 130 acres next to the Madeira School, with a picturesque view from high palisades, and Meyer had engaged Waldron Faulkner to build a house on the site. It was a favorite retreat for the family and their guests. Agnes also used it as a retreat where she could write—and sometimes drink—without interruption. The property was ultimately given to Madeira, from which all four of the Meyer daughters had been graduated.

In December 1944, they jointly set up the Eugene and Agnes E. Meyer Foundation with funds for donation to community service and development, to the arts and humanities, and to projects concerned with health, mental health, and education. At first their gifts to the foundation were relatively small, but in subsequent years they boosted the total; the foundation's assets were valued at approximately $25 million in 1972. It is one of the largest charitable institutions in Washington. More than a decade after

Meyer's death it was funneling about $1 million a year into projects designed to enrich community life in the city.

Selection of the first board for the foundation brought Meyer into collision with his son. When he asked Bill to be a member of the board, he expressed the hope that the foundation would carry on some of the philanthropies that he had supported personally in the past. Bill replied that a self-respecting, independent board could not enter into any such understanding; he would not agree to serve if the freedom of the board were to be so circumscribed. Few men had ever talked so bluntly to Meyer. In the end he backed down and gave the board a completely free hand in managing the funds of the foundation.

Despite the intensity of their activities, the Meyers continued to enjoy numerous amenities of life. Occasionally Eugene took Agnes to Saratoga Springs for a period of relaxation. During part of the winters they would find relief from Washington's weather in Nassau, Florida, Bermuda, or some other enticing spot. On several occasions he was a guest of Milton Esberg and Herman Phleger at the Bohemian Club Grove in California's redwoods. These encampments were made memorable by good fellowship, theatricals, musicals, speeches, relaxation, and endless talk involving Irvin S. Cobb, Gene Buck, Samuel Blythe, George Armstrong, and others.

Phleger experienced a striking demonstration of his friend's continued mental alertness when he called Meyer by telephone in New York and asked him to look up something in Washington and call back. "I suppose you will be at your country place," Meyer said. "Yes," his friend replied. "The telephone number there is Woodside 298." "You must have changed it since I was out there last year," Meyer challenged. "My God," Phleger confessed, "you're right and I'm wrong." The number was 289.

The severe losses at the *Washington Post* did not substantially alter the family's standard of living. The home at 1624 Crescent Place as well as Seven Springs Farm was a distinctive combination of luxury and comfort. There was not always harmony, however, when Agnes moved most of the household to Mount Kisco for the summer while Eugene remained on the job in Washington. On one occasion he complained that she was taking most of the staff with her. "I've left you the butler, the cook, and a housekeeper," Agnes replied. "But you know," he protested, "that I can't stand camping out."

Life at Mount Kisco continued to be a complex round of sports, entertainment, relaxation, argument, and Meyer's incurable teasing. On one hectic weekend, when Agnes was dividing her time between her guests and one of her huge county music festivals, an "army" came out of the woods and approached the house. It was the Scarsdale Walking Club responding to an invitation she had forgotten. There was a scramble to find refreshments, and the new guests seemed not to realize that their reception was entirely impromptu. Shortly after they had left, a violent thunderstorm swept over the area, and Meyer, with a mischievous gleam in his eye, sent the butler to tell the harried hostess that the Scarsdale Walking Club had returned.

Thomas Mann, who loved comfort, used to tell the Meyers that they ran the best hotels on two continents, but other guests remembered Seven Springs Farm as a sizzling gridiron. There was one occasion when everyone present pounced on Justice Felix Frankfurter for a dissenting opinion he had written. Far more discomfiting was the experience of Spyros P. Skouras, the movie magnate, who had worked with Meyer to relieve hunger in Europe and had sought an invitation to Mount Kisco to set Mrs. Meyer straight about the motion picture industry. She had made a speech blasting motion pictures featuring drugs. A furious battle of wits began as soon as Skouras raised the subject. Mrs. Meyer seized the offensive with the cutting remark that "the Greeks used to be noted for their taste." Meyer kept out of the battle as it raged on with mounting intensity, but he expressed sympathy for the beleaguered male protagonist by repeatedly supplying him with cigars.

Meyer's penchant for teasing and banter was also well known at the Metropolitan Club in Washington. He was one of about two dozen men who assembled for lunch, with some degree of regularity, at "the Table" where stimulating debate and amusing stories were part of the fare. Included in this group were such raconteurs and fascinating conversationalists as John Lord O'Brian, Charles Warren, Judge J. Harry Covington, Swagar Sherley, Arthur Krock, Judge Harold M. Stephens, Frank Kent, Walter Lippmann, Edward B. Burling, and others. Meyers was also fond of bridge and often played at home or with his fellow club members, who named him "the Champ" after an extraordinary run of luck in which he "cleaned out the crowd."

One evening Meyer was standing near the door of the Metropolitan Club when a man rushed in and tried to buy a special delivery stamp. Since he was not a member of the club, the clerk refused to sell him one. Trying to be accommodating, Meyer bought a stamp and handed it to the man, who offered a quarter to pay for it. As Meyer reached into his pocket for ten cents in change, the fellow said: "Thank you very much. Keep the change and buy yourself a good cigar." Meyer retorted: "That will cost you forty-five cents more." At this point the intruder fled and left the smoker of fifty-five-cent Havanas enriched by ten cents. He jokingly tried to pass the dime on to the club, but without success.

Meyer was also in a playful mood when he was asked to speak at the fiftieth anniversary of his graduating class at Yale. He began his speech by reading a discussion of old age by Plato and Cicero in the original Greek and Latin. With mock solemnity, he said he knew his fellow graduates of the Class of '95 would be delighted to refresh their memories of the classics. "But in case any of you have gotten a little rusty," he added, "I'll make some hasty translations." He then proceeded to read the best classical English translations as if they were his own. Actually, he had had Joe Lalley of the *Post* editorial staff dig up both the quotations and the translations. As soon as his speech was finished he skipped out and went home before his hoax could be exposed.

As age crept up on him, he became more and more concerned about the future of the *Post*. "I've got to know what will happen to this paper when I'm no longer around," he told a friend in 1942. Since he wanted to keep management of the paper in the family, every survey of the outlook brought him back to Philip Graham as his logical successor. It would be a long shot to rely upon a young man who had been in the family only two years and who was a lawyer rather than a journalist. Yet Graham had already proved to be a kindred spirit—a man of high ideals with a sensitive conscience, a disposition to face realities, a capacity for hard work, and a genius for getting along with people. The publisher decided to sound out his son-in-law.

First, however, there was the question of his own son. Bill had worked as a police reporter on the *Post* for one summer, but, having gone into medicine before entering the army, he was then studying tropical diseases at Walter Reed Hospital. His father called him in and asked if he would be interested in "the job at the *Post*." Aghast at the idea of such a drastic turn in his career, Bill asked for three days to think it over and walked the floor at Crescent Place trying to make up his mind. It is indicative of their relationship that Meyer sent Wayne Coy to discuss the big decision with his son, but there was no pressure on Bill one way or the other. In the end he decided to stay in medicine because he was already in it and because he feared, without saying so, that he might not get along with his father in a business relationship.

That left a clear track for Phil Graham if he were interested. Meyer went to see his son-in-law at the Army Air Force Intelligence School in Harrisburg. "I'm sixty-seven," he said. "I've got to know if you are interested in coming to the paper." The publisher made clear that he was not proposing to dump a bonanza into Phil's lap. The *Post* was still losing money; it was still in fierce competition with the *Star*, the *News* and the *Times-Herald*. All that Meyer could offer was an opportunity to join the fight to build a great newspaper, with the prospect of succeeding to its management and ownership.

It was a new idea for Graham, who had planned to return to Florida after the war and go into politics. The burden of succeeding the formidable Eugene Meyer in a venture that was peculiarly his may also have given him pause. For a long time he mulled over his problem, in consultation with Kay, but without any urging on her part. Ultimately he decided to take the plunge. It would cost him a good deal in terms of personal reorientation, but it opened new vistas that were in some respects more alluring than a legal or political career.

Several years would pass before Graham could join the *Post* organization, but each one brought confirmation of Meyer's conviction that he had found the right man. Reports from Manila, where he served as air information aide to General George C. Kenney, were to the effect that both officers and men regarded him as a "wonderful guy." Meyer took Wayne Coy into the *Post* in order to make the position that Phil would occupy more comfortable for him. The old order was passing and a new era was about to begin.

The end of the war and the promise of new blood in the *Post* organization made Meyer's seventieth birthday, October 31, 1945, an especially happy occasion. Friends and associates gave a luncheon in his honor at the Statler Hotel, with six members of the Cabinet, four justices of the Supreme Court, and eight ambassadors present. A greeting from President Truman expressed the view: "You simply haven't time to grow old." Within the family, the birthday was a very special occasion. Florence and her sons came from Hollywood. Elizabeth and Pare as well as Ruth were down from New York. Bill and Mary and their two children were spending a month with his parents after his release from the army. Phil, Kay, and their two children attended the party before leaving for a vacation in Arizona. Oscar Homolka was absent—a portent of his break-up with Flo. The children and their spouses joined in presenting a biographical skit of verse and song written by Elizabeth. Banter and ribbing were mingled with admiration as they followed his career from his youth to the *Washington Post*, with the Meyer-Jones fight and other lighter moments sandwiched in between:

> And that is one of his characteristics,
> A wild man—backed by sound statistics.

Meyer himself was philosophical about the occasion. At first he had viewed the attainment of threescore years and ten with apprehension, but as soon as the "dreaded day" passed he consoled himself with the thought that "eighty is so far off that I am not worrying yet." He was content that the new era should belong largely to the younger generation. When Graham came to the paper as assistant publisher on January 1, 1946, Meyer felt that he had acquired a new right arm. He would later describe Phil as "the greatest godsend I ever had."[3] The latter would come to occupy a place in Meyer's trust and affection comparable only to that attained by his brother Edgar and Gerald Henderson.

[3] Author's interview with Sidney Hyman, June 4, 1971.

30 /

President of the World Bank

WITH THE WAR ENDED, MEYER'S FOREMOST INTEREST WAS to prevent a recurrence. Peace was too elusive and too vital to be left wholly to the statesmen. Long experience had taught him that it was closely related to the aspirations and well-being of men and women everywhere. World War II had been a direct result of the failure to heal the wounds of World War I, and he was loathe to see that happen again.

As the winter of 1945–46 came on, millions of people in the war-torn lands were in danger of starvation. Yet Congress had cut off funds for the United Nations Relief and Rehabilitation Administration which had tried to alleviate the worst of the suffering by civilians in some countries during the war. The *Post* charged that Congress had withheld $550 million due to UNRRA. The result could be only misery, death for many innocent victims of war, and hatred for the rich and powerful United States—the only source from which aid could come. In a series of editorials the *Post* argued that such undermining of the great victory so recently won was "unthinkable."

Obviously trying to win newspaper support, the House of Representatives approved an amendment to the UNRRA appropriations bill withholding relief funds from countries denying freedom of the press. The *Post* vigorously opposed it: "When people are suffering from hunger we can no more ask them to embrace freedom of the press in return for food than we can buy a change of politics or religion by domestic food grants. It is an outrageous misconception of democratic principles to suppose that they can be fostered by this means."

Meyer went before the House Committee on Foreign Affairs on November 19 with a personal plea for continued support of UNRRA. "We know what are the munitions of war," he said. "The measure you are considering concerns the front-line munitions of peace. The failure to supply that first line adequately would threaten the achievement of the kind of peace for which we fought and sacrificed so much in blood."

343

Another aspect of the problem assumed formidable proportions when President Truman asked the Advertising Council to meet with himself and the Cabinet on February 12, 1946. Drought in Europe had worsened the shortages of food. Greece was ravaged by starvation; Italy, Yugoslavia, and Poland were plagued by acute hunger, and food supplies in many other countries amounted to less than half of what was necessary for health. In the face of these conditions Meyer was shocked to hear both Herbert Lehman, head of UNRRA, and Secretary of Agriculture Clinton P. Anderson say that the United States would have to default on its commitment to send a million tons of wheat per month abroad because the grain was not available. There would also be a default, they acknowledged, in the shipment of fats to Europe.

Meyer's impulse was to challenge the assumption that these shortfalls could not be avoided. In the United States food consumption had increased by about 500 calories per capita daily over prewar standards. Most Americans were eating too much and some were shamefully wasting food. Meyer restrained his inclination to cry out against the apparent official acceptance of this appalling maladjustment, but he was convinced that the American people would do something about it if they knew the facts.

That night he vented his vexation at a dinner he and Agnes gave for Bishop Bernard J. Sheil of Chicago, head of the Catholic Youth Organization. Philip and Katharine Graham were also present. The dinner turned into an indignation meeting with everyone present convinced that something should be done to check overindulgence and waste so that starving people might live. Meyer indicated that the *Post* would go to work on the problem, and Bishop Sheil summed up the arguments for an anti-hunger campaign so eloquently that the publisher welcomed him as a formidable ally.

"What are you doing tomorrow morning?" the publisher asked, and before the bishop had a chance to reply he was placed under virtual command to write out what he had said. The bishop responded favorably, and the *Post* printed his "Message to America" on March 10. His appeal was starkly simple: "This is a time for greatness. It is not a time for vengeance. . . . If America does not feed the hungry, the hungry will die."

Meanwhile Meyer had visited both Lehman and Anderson to see if they could be spurred into a food-saving campaign. Both welcomed any help that Meyer might give, but neither seemed to have much faith in a voluntary campaign. With the consent of Anderson and the White House, Meyer then wired former President Hoover in Florida and enlisted his help in the venture. Relations between Meyer and Hoover had been strained by their controversy over the bank holiday and by Meyer's opposition to a

Hoover candidacy in 1936, but the specter of starvation in Europe overrode those estrangements. Hoover became honorary chairman of the venture; for the active chairmanship Meyer called upon Chester Davis, who had been wartime food administrator and was then president of the federal reserve bank in St. Louis. Davis was reluctant but consented when Meyer agreed to be vice-chairman and to carry the burden in Washington when Davis could not be present. The Famine Emergency Committee was formally announced after a session at the White House on March 1 which Truman said was the most important meeting he had presided over since becoming President. It presented a rare spectacle—a President and a former President of a different party sitting down together to work on a common problem. Meyer's simple and direct statement of the aims of the committee was adopted by the conference. When the session broke up, the Famine Emergency Committee had official standing, but it had really been brought into being by a persistent and energetic publisher who was determined to tighten enough belts in America to save Europe from starvation and demoralization.

The other members of the committee included Henry R. Luce, editor of *Time* and *Life*; Mrs. Anna Lord Strauss, president of the League of Women Voters; Assistant Secretary of State William R. Clayton, Lehman, Anderson, and Dr. George Gallup. Hoover was sent abroad to survey the extent of the food deficiency. At home the campaign got off to a whirlwind start. On the very day of the White House meeting, DeWitt Wallace, editor of *Reader's Digest*, and a neighbor of the Meyers in Mount Kisco, lunched with Meyer and was touched by the moving quality of Bishop Sheil's message. If he had had the message a day earlier, Wallace said, he could have laid it before a potential 40 million readers by printing it on the back page of *Reader's Digest*. "But isn't there yet time if you telephoned this to Pleasantville?" Meyer pressed. Wallace went to the telephone and ordered his magazine to carry the message.

The Advertising Council, numerous advertising agencies, the press, and most of the radio stations in the country were mobilized to broadcast the committee's plea for self-rationing. The free advertising in newspapers and magazines and the radio time devoted to saving food were estimated to be worth $18 million. Dozens of organizations were brought into the campaign, and a National Famine Emergency Council was organized to extend the food-saving efforts throughout the country.

Not content with extensive coverage of the campaign and editorial support, the *Post* assembled hunger stories and cartoons on clip sheets that were sent to newspapers throughout the country. Probably the most pointed commentary of all was to be found in the cartoons of Pulitzer Prize winner

Herbert L. Block, who had joined the *Post*'s staff soon after his release from the army. One Herblock cartoon that was widely reprinted, "Bread Upon the Waters," had a hand extending a loaf of bread across the sea to starving Europe. Another pictured a fat hog wallowing in feed and saying to a starving child who looked on: "How much are you worth?"

At first it was difficult to persuade the restaurants and hotels to join in the food-saving venture. But committees of leading citizens were organized in Washington and other cities to police the restaurants and induce them to serve no rolls or bread unless requested. In general the public response was gratifying. A survey conducted by the *Post* in Washington indicated that three of every four residents were making some effort to save food. Secretary Anderson thanked the *Post* for launching the program and carrying it through. "On occasion," he wrote, "some of us thought you were pushing us a little hard. But . . . we did meet our relief commitments which is surely a vivid testimony of the working together of a free government and a free press."[1]

As summer approached, the larger problems of economic recovery came to the fore. Meyer felt that economic stability in Europe had to be restored, but it was not yet clear what help the various countries would need. When the Meyers gave a lunch in honor of the British ambassador, Lord Inverchapel, early in June 1946, Eugene took Secretary of State James F. Byrnes into the library and urged him to send a commission to Europe to investigate economic conditions and recommend a course of action. Meyer did not wish to be chairman of the commission but volunteered his services as a member because of his broad experience in Europe and his ability to speak French and to understand German.

"Well now," Byrnes said, "I've listened to you. Will you listen to me?"

"Why certainly," Meyer responded, with obvious surprise.

"I don't want you to go to Europe on a committee," the Secretary continued. "We can get other people to do that. I want you to be president of the World Bank. In that job," he added, "you could do something about the problems of economic recovery."[2]

It was a stunning surprise. Meyer had long since ceased to think of himself in any other role than that of publisher, and he was trying to shed some of his responsibilities in even that sphere. In his seventy-first year, he had thought himself immune to demands of this kind. Stalling for time to think, he told Byrnes: "The President of the United States is the only man who can decide who is to be president of the World Bank."

"I think he will take a recommendation from me," Byrnes replied.

[1] Clinton P. Anderson to Philip L. Graham, January 6, 1947.
[2] Dean Albertson's interviews with Eugene Meyer, April 13, 1953.

The Secretary assured Meyer that he could handle the assignment without giving up his position at the *Post*. When Meyer protested that he was too old to assume such a burden, Byrnes said he was asking him only to launch the bank. The President was eager to get the organization going because nearly a year had passed since the charter of the bank had been adopted at the Bretton Woods Conference. Several potential candidates, including Lewis Douglas, had turned down the job. At the end of the conversation Meyer was still noncommittal, but Byrnes left no doubt about what his advice to the President would be.

That night Meyer brooded over his problem with the Grahams and Bishop Sheil, who was a guest at Crescent Place. "I don't want to be president of the World Bank," he said. "I want to run the *Post* and fight for what I think is right." After sleeping on the unwelcome bid for his services, he consoled himself with the illusion that since he had not really been asked he would not have to refuse. He went to the office and spent the day as usual. As he was putting on his hat to leave, the call from the White House came.

"I want you to be president of the World Bank," the President said abruptly, without any invitation to the White House to talk it over.

"You don't want me to make up my mind overnight, do you?" Meyer replied. "I have to think about it a little."

"This ought to be acted on as promptly as possible," Truman said. "I hope you will say yes and let me know as soon as you can."[3]

The following morning Meyer's visceral reaction was still negative, but his innate sense of public duty was beginning to stiffen. It was vital that this International Bank for Reconstruction and Development be launched by an experienced financier in accord with sound banking practices. Wall Street was looking askance at the bank. In Meyer's view it was a disgrace that everyone was running away from "the outstanding banking opportunity for world service in world history."[4] If properly operated, this institution would hasten economic recovery and buttress the precarious peace that had followed World War II. When he candidly faced the President's request from this point of view, he could not bring himself to join the ranks of those who were running away from the job. He telephoned his acceptance.

The first step was to relinquish his responsibilities at the *Post*. At no time did Meyer share Byrnes's illusion that he could hold both jobs at the same time. The bank presidency would put heavy demands upon him, and in any event it would be highly improper for him to run a newspaper

---

[3] *Ibid.*
[4] Eugene Meyer to Frank R. Kent, December 30, 1946.

347

with one hand and the International Bank with the other. Fortunately, the question of succession at the *Post* had already been decided when Phil Graham became assistant publisher. Although Graham was only thirty years of age and had been on the job less than six months, he had won the full confidence of his father-in-law. Meyer's chief regret on this score was that he would unload upon the young man the unsolved problems that had accumulated during the war. Even though the *Post* was then operating in the black, it was desperately in need of a new building, its staff had been depleted by the draft, paper was still in short supply, and the competition for both advertising and circulation was fierce. Meyer was relieved to learn that Graham did not shrink from facing these burdens, and this was probably the conclusive element in his decision.

On June 18 the *Post* announced that Meyer was withdrawing from active direction of its affairs, while retaining his ownership interest. The paper would go forward, the announcement said, with Philip L. Graham as publisher; Herbert Elliston, editor; Alexander F. Jones, managing editor; Charles C. Boysen, business manager; Donald M. Bernard, advertising director; Wayne Coy, assistant to the publisher.

Meyer's first contact with the executive directors of the bank was not reassuring. A young lawyer came in with a contract that he was asked to sign—a duplicate of that signed by Camille Gutt, the distinguished Belgian statesman who was head of the International Monetary Fund. The contract could not be altered, Meyer was told, without an affront to Gutt. Noting that the agreement called for a salary of $30,000 a year, plus enough to make it free of taxes, Meyer said he had no desire to take the bank's money and would prefer to work for a dollar a year. The directors, who had authority to confirm or reject Meyer's appointment, insisted that the contract would have to be signed in its original form.

During this controversy, the United States executive director for the bank, Emilio G. Collado of the State Department, informed Meyer that the presidency of the World Bank was not a part-time job. Meyer said he was well aware of that fact; if elected by the board of executive directors, he would sever every tie that made any substantial claim upon his time or might affect his point of view. Collado seemed disappointed, as if he were hoping that Meyer would withdraw when he knew that he could not continue as publisher of the *Post* at the same time.

Collado was soon back again, asking Meyer to meet with the board before a vote was taken and stressing the importance of speed in getting the bank fully organized. The president-designate said he could see the board the following day and would arrange to report for duty in perhaps two weeks. He talked to the board about the need for cooperation and friendly relations in an international agency and was unanimously elected on June 4, 1946. The board had previously fixed June 25 as the date on which the bank would formally begin its operations. The question of salary was easily resolved after Meyer talked to Gutt, an old friend, and found he had no interest in keeping the contracts uniform. The five-year contract that Meyer finally signed gave him $30,000 a year, without any tax bonus, and this was mostly absorbed by taxes because of the high bracket he was in by reason of income from investments.

Three major tasks awaited the new president. First, it was necessary to assemble a competent staff. Second, the bank had to demonstrate the ability to obtain capital by selling its securities in the market. Third, the president had to work out smooth working relations between himself and the board of twelve executive directors who represented the governors (one from every member state) in the day-to-day operations of the bank.

Meyer first addressed himself to building an organization. The staff should be assembled from many different countries, he told the board, but he would like the privilege of naming an American vice-president, who would act for him in case of absence, and an American general counsel who would be important in setting up the organization. The board agreed to this. For vice-president he chose Harold D. Smith, Truman's director of the budget, largely on the advice of Wayne Coy, a former deputy director under Smith. It was soon evident, however, that Smith, despite a favorable reputation in government, was a misfit at the bank. Meyer felt he was bureaucratic and more interested in his holidays and his farm than in building a great institution that could contribute to international stability and peace.

In seeking a general counsel there were also disappointments. Meyer's first choice was John J. McCloy, an eminent lawyer who had been Assistant Secretary of War. Then he called on his friend Herman Phleger, one of the top lawyers appearing before the Supreme Court. Also on his list were John Lord O'Brian, Laird Bell of Chicago, and others. But in each case there seemed to be good reasons why the man he wanted could not serve. Through McCloy, he finally enlisted the services of Chester A. McLain, an able member of the Cravath firm in New York who had broad experience in international finance. McLain assembled an excellent legal staff, which played a large part in getting the bank off to a good start.

The position of treasurer went to D. Crena de Iongh, president of a large bank in the Netherlands. Leonard B. Rist, a French economist and son of the eminent financier Charles Rist, was named director of the bank's research department. Morton M. Mendels, a lawyer from Montreal, became secretary, and Simon Aldewereld of the Netherlands was assigned to the investigation of projects. Meyer's immediate office was in charge of Richard H. Demuth and John H. Ferguson. The new president felt that the British should provide a director of the loan department because of their banking experience in all parts of the world, but he got no cooperation from Sir James Grigg, the disgruntled executive director from London.

When the bank and the fund held their first meeting in Washington in September 1946, Britain was represented by Chancellor of the Exchequer Hugh Dalton and the head of the Bank of England. Meyer exacted of them a promise of three recommendations of English bankers qualified to head the vital loan department. Hearing nothing from them, Meyer bombarded Cameron Cobbold, then deputy governor of the Bank of England, with telephone calls until he recommended a partner in Lazard Brothers, but after the young man visited Washington and consented to take the job, his partners pressured him into changing his mind. At last the position went to Charles C. Pineo of Canada, with heavy reliance on the second man in the department, Arthur S. Hoare of Britain. For engineering talent, relations were established with Colonel Carlton S. Proctor, head of the United States Engineering Council. Through an old friend, Per Jacobsson of Sweden, Meyer obtained for the World Bank all the economic data assembled by the Bank of International Settlements.

Within a few months the bank had the nucleus of a sound organization. Meyer had laid, in the words of McCloy who was to be his successor at the bank, "a very good base in terms of a highly competent staff on which to build the bank."[5] Most of the key men he hired would still be running the bank a quarter of a century later.

Meyer met with leading bankers and life insurance executives on August 19 in New York to assure the financial community that the bank would not provide "lend-lease under disguise." All loans would be made on a sound basis, he said, with only a "calculated risk." Nor was there any danger that the bank would use up its capital of $7.5 billion provided by the member governments and then call for more. Rather, he said, the bank would work largely with funds obtained from the security market. The sale of World Bank bonds was complicated, however, by the fact that state laws did not permit savings banks and insurance companies to buy these previously unknown securities. Such state laws would have to be modified before the World Bank could operate successfully on a large scale.

Almost before his chair was warm, Meyer was in conflict with the bank's directors. The founders at Bretton Woods had given the bank a

[5] John J. McCloy to the author, July 6, 1971.

full-time board of executive directors to match the organization of the International Fund. That board was in operation long before the bank had a president, and some of the directors felt that they should run the bank with the president functioning as their handyman. Sir James Grigg seemed determined to keep control of the bank in the hands of the directors so as to limit American influence in its operations. Meyer had different ideas.

The aggressive and quarrelsome British director reserved his most scornful barbs for Dr. Vavaresso Kyriakos of Greece, one of the hardest workers in the bank. One day a paper the Greek had prepared for the board provoked Sir James to an especially intemperate outburst. When Meyer could stand it no longer, he accorded the hot-headed Englishman his slow-puncture treatment. In dulcet tones he expressed interest in what Sir James was saying and conceded that there might be some errors of detail in the report, but "if you don't mind my saying so," he added, "the report is otherwise thorough and I don't think its author has really committed any crime of a serious character." The meeting broke up after Meyer told a story on himself. Sir James had been deflated almost painlessly.

Meyer felt that the French representative, Pierre Mendes-France, was the best man on the board, but he did not stay in Washington. The directors who did had been sitting as a sort of international convention, with long hours devoted to drawing up documents to guide the bank in all possible contingencies. Some of them were also making embarrassing speeches about what the bank was going to do. Johann Beyen of Holland agreed to speak in Canada as a substitute for Meyer and submitted his text for clearance, but after he had delivered the written version he talked so recklessly about what the bank was going to borrow and what interest it would pay that Meyer repudiated his comments and attributed them to misunderstanding.

By far the most serious collision involved the United States director, Emilio Collado, a brilliant and ambitious man who seemed to think that the World Bank should function as an adjunct of the State Department. Long before Meyer had assembled his staff, Collado pressed for action on loans through ad hoc committees of the board of directors, with himself as the key member. On July 19 he submitted a memorandum arguing for such a committee to consider loans to France and Czechoslovakia. Meyer was determined that no loans should be made until he could submit recommendations to the board on the basis of a thorough staff investigation in each case. A proposed multiple-purpose loan to Chile became a controversial issue because Meyer refused to accept Collado's personal assurance that it would be a proper loan for the bank. Collado pounded the table and called for action, but Meyer insisted a bank that would soon be in the market for large sums of capital could not act as a relief agency.

The new president was shocked by the brashness and persistence of the State Department's director who, he thought, should be supporting him in his efforts to build the bank on a solid foundation. When he complained about Collado's conduct to Assistant Secretary of State Clayton, the latter responded: "Why don't you tell him to get out of your room and shut up?"

"He isn't my man," Meyer said. "It's your business to keep him in order, not mine."

The tug-of-war continued, and Meyer asked Under Secretary of State Dean Acheson to discuss the problem with himself and Clayton. The latter did not show up until the meeting with Acheson was nearly ended, but Meyer did have a chance to alert these officials to the fact that the department's own representative was making his task at the bank almost intolerable. Meyer suspected that Collado, on top of his other mischief, was "leaking" slanted reports to the press. While fully recognizing the right of the State Department and the Treasury to be represented in the bank's organization—the United States was providing about 40 percent of the bank's capital—Meyer thought that he, as president of the bank, was entitled to some degree of cooperation from the government which, in effect, had twisted his arm to induce him to take the job.

Except for his official complaints and long discussions of his troubles with Phil Graham, Meyer smoldered in silence. He was not disposed to jeopardize this promising international agency by airing an internal struggle for power at its very beginning. His disillusionment was reflected, however, in a comment he made to E. D. Coblentz, publisher of the San Francisco *Call-Bulletin*, in response to a letter noting the parallelism in their careers. "We both were in the newspaper business," Meyer wrote, "but you have had sense enough to stick to it."

There was a respite from the contention when the World Bank and International Monetary Fund held their first meeting in Washington at the end of September 1946. The chief financial officials from · many countries were present. At the final dinner at the Statler Hotel, Gutt and Meyer presided jointly, and the latter took advantage of the occasion to proclaim his idealism in regard to the bank. "The whole world is one community," he said. ". . . Prosperity, like peace, must therefore be viewed as indivisible.

"So, in the large sense, our task is nothing less than to play a part in the creation of conditions upon which an enduring peace may rest. . . . We are engaged in the first large-scale, practical implementation of the United Nations' spirit, in an area which cannot fail to shape decisively the whole pattern of international relations."

After the meeting, Meyer finally hired a temporary director in the loan department and tried to get down to business. Five or six countries had requested loans, although no formal applications had yet been received. As Meyer turned his attention to broad, long-range policies, he was "in quite a stew" about how the bank could best contribute to reconstruction and higher standards of living.[6] Again he consulted freely with Phil Graham. Then suddenly he concluded that he was violating his own principle because he was planning a ten-year program he would not be able to carry out. At seventy-one, he had no thought of remaining at the bank indefinitely, and it was foolish to suppose that his plans would be taken over by his successor. After all, Byrnes had asked him only to launch the bank. That he had done, or almost done, and the next steps should be taken by a president who would be on the job for a longer period.

When Meyer discussed this trend of thinking with members of his family, he was advised to stay at the bank. He had scarcely made a beginning. But he could see no good reason for prolonging his agony. If he intended to stay indefinitely, he felt that he could force the dismissal of Collado, through either Secretary Byrnes or the President, and a word to the Chancellor of the Exchequer would remove his other nemesis, Sir James Grigg, but such a course might create a moral commitment to stay longer than he wished. After a few weeks of soul-searching, he told Byrnes of his intention to quit and then talked to the President and the bank's board of executive directors. The reason given was the same in all cases—that he had finished the job Byrnes had asked him to do and that the long-range planning could best be undertaken by a younger man.

Meyer held fast to this explanation in his letter of resignation submitted on December 4, 1946, just six months after his election, and in many letters to friends. Writing to James H. McGraw, Jr., he went so far as to say: "There was one reason and only one why I got out of the World Bank." In a long explanation to Russell Leffingwell, he emphasized his distrust of advancing years "as a solid basis for hard work and important public responsibilities." But all this rationalization cannot obscure the fact that he was engaged in a power struggle at the bank that finally became intolerable. Meyer told his secretary: "I could stay and fight these bastards, and probably win in the end, but I'm too old for that."

[6] Albertson interview, April 13, 1953.

It is evident, moreover, that if Meyer had been thinking only of the long-range interests of the bank in securing a permanent head before its loan operations began, he would not have pulled out with only two weeks notice. His abrupt departure left the bank in turmoil that could have been avoided if he had remained until his successor could take over.

For a time the Meyer-Collado impasse even thwarted the naming of a successor. Meyer was delighted when the Truman administration offered the job to McCloy, whom he had once introduced to the directors with the unexpressed thought he might well become president of the bank someday. But when McCloy sought advice from Meyer and McLain, the general counsel, both warned him to lay down conditions that would enable him to function as president of the bank and not just a lackey for the State Department and Treasury. McCloy's conditions were rejected, and the administration began to look elsewhere for a president. Meanwhile the bank was marking time.

McLain reported to Meyer that the two departments had vetoed McCloy because he insisted that they approve in advance any course he might take. "That's ridiculous," Meyer commented as he called McCloy to get his version of the impasse. McCloy said that what he really asked for was a chance to present his views before the National Advisory Council on International Financial and Monetary Problems before any final decision affecting the bank was taken. "They can't object to that," Meyer observed. "They must misunderstand what you have in mind." Meyer asked if he could repeat to Clayton at the State Department and Secretary of the Treasury John Snyder what McCloy had just said. To avoid any further misunderstanding Meyer repeated McCloy's condition and made a written note of it.

Within minutes Meyer called Snyder: "Will you let me tell you what McCloy has in mind?" Snyder seemed disgruntled about the whole business, but after hearing McCloy's statement, he withdrew his objections and, at Meyer's request, called Clayton for an immediate appointment with the peacemaker. Meyer repeated his mediation efforts. The ultimate outcome was installation of McCloy as president of the bank and replacement of Collado as executive director for the United States by a man of McCloy's choice, Eugene R. Black, who was to become president after McCloy.

The controversy over who would run the bank in its day-to-day operations was thus resolved in favor of the president, without any change in the bank charter. The bank began its operations with the staff investigating loan applications and the president submitting approved projects to the board of directors. The principle for which Meyer had fought was thus established as a by-product of his resignation. That outcome was far more important to the bank than his continued presence for a few more months would have been. It is strange that he sought to conceal his part in this fight that was so essential to successful operation of the bank as a great international institution.

His brief tenure at the World Bank completed Meyer's career as a public official. He had served in seven major assignments from six different Presidents. It is indicative of his independence in public office that four of these assignments came from Democratic Presidents and three from Presidents of his own party.

31 /

Back to the Post

THE LURE OF RETURNING TO THE PUBLISHING FIELD WAS AN unacknowledged but nonetheless significant factor in Meyer's departure from the World Bank. He had no thought of retiring to a life of ease. His first concern was to get back into harness at the *Post*.

A less sensitive man might have reclaimed the position of publisher which he had left only six months ago. Meyer was content to leave Graham in charge of the paper and to assume an advisory role as chairman of the board. Graham was pleased to welcome his father-in-law in that role. The paper was still plagued by critical problems. Meyer's advice and assistance on a day-to-day basis would contribute much to the objectives in which both men were interested. So the builder of the new *Washington Post* was installed in a modified version of the position he liked best.

He made a special point of disabusing those who assumed that he was back at the wheel. "Mr. Graham has full authority and responsibility for the conduct of the paper," he wrote. Often he described himself as "merely the old man called chairman of the board." It was a pleasure to watch Graham's talents and confidence unfold as he gained experience. To one friend Meyer wrote: ". . . maybe the best thing I have done in connection with The Post was to succeed in interesting him [Graham] in making it his occupation." Graham in turn exuded respect and goodwill toward his father-in-law, making a special point of including him in the most important events concerning the *Post*.

There were, of course, collisions. Meyer was troubled by Graham's spending on gimmickry to promote circulation and sometimes felt that his son-in-law made major decisions without consulting him. On rare occasions the new publisher described his father-in-law as "an irascible old man," and at one point he dictated a letter indicating that he intended either to run the paper or return to the practice of law. The mere presence of Meyer, with his vast experience, prestige, resources, and dominating personality, was a formidable challenge to the young publisher. But Graham's genius for getting along with people kept the friction at a low level, and the chairman followed a policy of supporting his son-in-law's decisions and of defending him against criticism from any source.

Expansion and upgrading of the *Post* staff had begun before Meyer went to the World Bank. A friend who was aware of his long search for an editorial cartoonist sent him samples of the work of Herbert Lawrence Block, a graduate of the Chicago Art Institute who had won distinction for his work with the Chicago *Daily News* and the Newspaper Enterprise Association before going into the army. After surveying all other possibilities and submitting sample cartoons to numerous friends, Meyer invited the tall, meticulous artist to meet him at the Yale Club in New York, with the result that Herblock joined the staff at the beginning of 1946.

The most significant change came in 1947 when Graham induced James Russell Wiggins to become managing editor of the *Post* in place of Casey Jones. Wiggins and Alfred Friendly, a former *Post* reporter, had been instructors at an Army Air Force intelligence school where Graham was a student. Wiggins had later returned to the St. Paul *Dispatch-Pioneer-Press* where he was editor in 1945–46. The *Post*'s first bid for his services did not interest him because he was shifting to *The New York Times* as assistant to the publisher. When both Graham and Meyer importuned him a year later, however, Wiggins accepted. "Do you want to see a financial statement?" Meyer asked by way of clinching the agreement. "No, Mr. Meyer," Wiggins replied, "you are enough of a financial statement for me."

To soften the blow for Jones, he was made assistant publisher. In that role he was unhappy and ultimately left to become executive editor of the Syracuse *Herald-Journal*. Jones's brusque manner was out of key with Graham's suavity, but the change also reflected the new publisher's determination to broaden the horizon of the paper, especially in the international field. Meyer went along with his son-in-law's ambition because it reflected his own hopes, but it is doubtful that he would have removed the managing editor who had piloted the *Post* through its most difficult years. Clearly Graham was in the driver's seat.

Wiggins's flair was in the direction of complete, unbiased reporting of the news. In a series of seminars for the staff he warned against what he called the "Jehovah complex"—the tendency of journalists to decide what was good or bad for the public to read. The people, he said in effect, are tough enough to endure news of all sorts, however dismaying, discouraging, shocking, or alarming it might be. One of his early reforms was to eliminate racial identification from news stories, except where it was part of a pertinent description or essential to make a story understandable.

Although the *Post* was attracting high praise from many sources,

Graham was concerned about its weaknesses. Keenly aware of the fact that the paper had sent its general-assignments reporter, Edward T. Folliard, to cover the last months of the war in Europe and its sports editor, Shirley Povich, to report the war in the Pacific, Graham was determined to build up a strong staff of foreign correspondents. At home there must be constant improvement in news coverage and in editorial perception. In a remarkably short period the new publisher was pulling the staff up to higher levels of performance. He brought into the paper a sensitivity to personnel problems that Meyer, with all his generosity in some cases, had never attained. Graham worried about reporters' low salaries and about means of holding the new writing and executive talent he was assembling.

Among the promising writers who joined the staff in the early postwar years were Ferdinand Kuhn, Jr., international affairs reporter; Chalmers M. Roberts, who was to become head of the national news bureau; and Murrey Marder, who specialized in foreign affairs. Friendly returned to the staff and was later to become managing editor. Folliard became White House reporter, and Robert C. Albright covered Capitol Hill. Ben Gilbert was city editor; John J. Riseling, night city editor; Aubrey Graves, assistant managing editor; Luther D. (Bus) Ham, sports editor; William V. Nessly, chief of the national bureau; and James Cutlip, news editor. Bill Gold switched to the *Post* from radio station WINX and began a popular column, "The District Line."

The editorial staff was not disturbed. Elliston was at the peak of his distinguished career and would add a Pulitzer Prize to his laurels in 1949. Other members of the staff during the early postwar period were Pusey (then associate editor), Anna Youngman, Lalley, Alan Barth, Robert H. Estabrook, and Thomas K. Ford. Meyer had hired Barth, an avowed New Dealer, from the Office of War Information in 1943 because he wanted a variety of viewpoints represented on the staff making editorial policy. Before joining the OWI, Barth had been editorial writer for the Beaumont (Texas) *Journal* and had written for the McClure Syndicate in Washington. Estabrook had earned his journalistic spurs on the Cedar Rapids *Gazette* and came to the *Post* after a stint in the army.

On the business side Meyer pushed for the acquisition of new talent. "You've got to have a business head for the paper," he told Graham. Boysen was ill and lacked both the strength and the initiative to project the paper into new dimensions. The search for a new business manager went on until Graham was convinced that John W. Sweeterman, vice-president and general manager of the Dayton *Journal-Herald*, was the right man. But Sweeterman refused to risk a move to Washington for a $30,000 salary—the maximum that Graham was prepared to offer because that was what he was making. In the end the publisher increased his own salary to $35,000 and signed a contract with Sweeterman at the same figure. The latter proved to be a highly competent, hard-working, and resourceful executive, with an amiable disposition and a special talent for multiplying newspaper profits. He was later to become publisher of the *Post*.

On the mechanical side, Harry Eybers, a transplant from the Salt Lake City *Tribune*, brought new vigor into the organization, beginning in 1951, as production manager. The game of musical chairs in the circulation department was ended with the hiring of Harry Gladstein in November 1949. After graduating from Indiana University, Gladstein had worked for newspapers in Louisville, Des Moines, and Rochester. He was in the army for four years and came to the *Post* from the Los Angeles *Examiner*. Though he was the thirteenth director of circulation since 1933, this genial expert settled into the office for a stay of more than twenty years in which time the circulation of the *Post* would be tripled. Later he became vice-president and business manager.

One of the areas in which Meyer and Graham did not see eye to eye was the *Post*'s relation to broadcasting. The chairman's interest was centered in the newspaper. He viewed broadcasting as a problem industry that sooner or later would run into complications from government control of the air waves. Graham, on the other hand, saw broadcasting as a lucrative, expanding industry that would help to carry the press through years of hardship. A serious clash might have evolved, except for the fact that the *Post* was already operating a small radio station, WINX, which Wayne Coy had talked Meyer into buying in 1944. When Meyer discovered that numbers racketeers used WINX's race broadcasts to calculate their daily winning number, he asked what the result would be if WINX substituted classical music for race results. It might cut revenue by as much as $200,000, he was told.

"Let's do it anyway," he said.

Thereafter WINX operated in the red, and its losses helped to convince Meyer that the best way out of an unfortunate venture was to acquire a big network station. Graham entered into negotiations with the Columbia Broadcasting System for the purchase of WTOP. The network showed little interest in the *Post*'s offers, however, until Meyer came up with the idea of buying only 55 percent of WTOP so as to leave CBS a strong minority interest. That arrangement became effective in February 1949, and the *Post* acquired sole ownership of WTOP five years later.

In anticipation of expanded operations in this sphere, the *Post* had hired John S. Hayes as broadcast manager in 1947. During the war Hayes had commanded the American Forces Network of radio stations in Europe, and later he was manager of *The New York Times* station. With WTOP (radio) well integrated into the *Post* family, Graham authorized Hayes to look for a television station. The quest was disappointing. Meyer used to comfort Hayes by saying: "Someday you'll be able to buy Jack Straus's station," meaning WOIC owned by General Teleradio, Inc., a subsidiary of R. H. Macy and Company, of which Straus was president. Months passed, however, and no progress was in sight.

Then one day Meyer asked Hayes if he were aware of the relationship between Gimbel's and Macy's. "Straus's balance sheet is not going to be as good this year as Gimbel's," he continued. "It may be time to buy WOIC."[1] Negotiations were begun, and the *Post* announced on July 23, 1950, its ownership of WOIC, Channel 9. The call letters of the station were changed to WTOP-TV.

As Graham had foreseen, profits from the broadcasting division helped to carry the paper through three lean years—1949 to 1951. Profits were especially vital now that the Grahams were in control and the Meyer millions were no longer on tap. Graham and Hayes saw another opportunity to strengthen the company's broadcasting branch by purchasing radio and television stations (WMBR) in Jacksonville, Florida, but for some time Meyer proved to be a stone wall of opposition. After exhausting his own persuasive powers, Graham asked Hayes to talk to the chairman of the board.

Meyer felt that the purchase of broadcasting stations in Jacksonville would be going too far afield. His opposition seemed to be adamant up to the point where Hayes gave up and said: "Okay. We'll drop it."

"I thought you wanted to buy it," Meyer came back.

"I do," Hayes said. "It's a promising investment."

"Who else wants to buy it?" Meyer asked.

"Phil," Hayes replied, "and the bank thinks well of it."

"Who opposes it?"

"You."

"Well, let's buy it then," the chairman surrendered. "I think it's very important to Phil."[2]

The purchase was made in 1953. Glenn Marshall, one of the former owners, became business manager and the stations proved to be highly profitable. After the company sold WMBR radio in 1958, the call letters of the television station were changed to WJXT-TV. Later the *Post* would acquire Station WPLG-TV in Miami and WCKY-AM in Cincinnati.

[1] Author's interview with John S. Hayes, October 31, 1972.
[2] *Ibid.*

Meyer's general practice of working through the publisher did not preclude personal contacts with department heads and individual employees. For many years he had carried on a one-man campaign against excessive erudition on the editorial page, and when Joseph Lalley's use of the word "avatar" in a scholarly piece sent him to the dictionary he dictated a memorandum to Elliston. Many readers among "the common people," he said, would regard the use of such unfamiliar words as "an attack upon their ignorance." But when his old friend Carl Sandburg complained that *Post* editorial writers "go to their goddam dictionaries so often that they lose their Man in the street," he vigorously defended the staff for writing pieces that would appeal to congressmen, statesmen, and people of learning.

Printers' ink did not blind him to the crimes or follies sometimes committed in the scramble to be first with a story. Scoops were all right if they came in the regular course of reporting, he told Wiggins, but a frenzied struggle for scoops could not take the place of day-by-day reporting with accuracy and fairness.

Meyer maintained a close watch on what the paper and broadcasting stations were doing, and department heads learned not to reply to his questions with generalities. If they did so, they got a brusque: "I want facts and figures, not adjectives." One day he asked Hayes what his statement for the next month would show. "About $5,000 in the red," Hayes replied. "Mr. Hayes," came the response, "considering the fact that we spent five months looking for a man of your caliber, I think you could answer a question a little more precisely than 'about $5,000.'" Hayes was soon on the telephone again with the exact figure.

The chairman also continued his personal involvement in the business operations of the paper. Taking advantage of his broad contacts, he approached friends in person and wrote hundreds of letters about the advantages of advertising in the *Post*. Sometimes he got a laugh without an ad. After attending a party for India's Prime Minister Nehru at White Sulphur Springs, he found in his pocket a pen he had borrowed from Roger Lapham. He wired Lapham that if he would advertise his loss in the *Washington Post*, he (Meyer) would guarantee that the fountain pen would be returned.

Every time Meyer rode in a cab he gave a tip "with the compliments of the *Washington Post*" and often left with the driver's subscription in his pocket. He found special delight in sending these subscriptions to Gladstein, along with a good-natured prod. "What do you personally do," he would ask, "in order to get subscriptions, not by telling others to get them?"

There were other demonstrations of the chairman's usefulness. When Joseph Paull, a new reporter, was assigned to a job at the courthouse, Meyer offered to give a reception in his honor and suggested that he submit the names of about sixty people to be invited. Paull loaded his list with the names of judges, Supreme Court justices, government officials, and the like—many of whom he did not know but wished to meet. All of them were invited and most of them came, affording an enormous boost to a young reporter.

Businessman Frank Jelleff took a delegation from the National Symphony Orchestra to ask Meyer for a donation and to suggest that he fire Paul Hume, the *Post*'s new music critic, because of something he had written about the orchestra. "Gentlemen," Meyer replied, "your trouble is not Paul Hume." As soon as the delegation had gone, he called Hume in and asked what was wrong with the orchestra. Hume supplied particulars. "Should I continue to give them a contribution?" Meyer asked. "How much do you usually give?" Hume responded. The answer was $750. "That's not enough for you, Mr. Meyer," Hume advised. Meyer picked up the telephone and called Jelleff. "Paul Hume is here in my office," he said, "and on his recommendation I am raising my contribution to the orchestra to $1,500." But there was no interference with Hume's criticism.

The chairman celebrated his new freedom by going to Europe in the summer of 1947, taking Friendly as his traveling companion. In London he reported a crisis brewing. After visiting Paris, Berlin, Frankfurt, and Rome, he concluded, in a dispatch to the *Post* on September 13, that hunger and cold were still grim realities in Europe and that American aid would have to be forthcoming if the peace were to be saved.

While in Rome, Meyer had an interview with Pope Pius XII and found him keenly interested in Europe's hunger problem. Most of the quarter hour with the Pope was given, however, to another project in which Meyer was interested—universal military training. Since the Catholic Church in America was divided on the issue, Meyer lobbied shamelessly for the Pope's support of Bishop Sheil and the faction that was supporting UMT. Quoting General George C. Marshall to the effect that UMT was an essential tool for maintenance of American military strength, he argued that only American power could cope with the rising menace of communism. The Pope heartily agreed, but he gave no assurance of support for the American Catholic leaders who were working for UMT. As Meyer arose to leave he apologized for speaking so pointedly but said it reflected his interest in peace and came from the bottom of his heart. "*Ça vient aussi de la tête*," the Pope replied.

Meanwhile the *Post* had deeply involved itself in the struggle against hunger in Europe and the aggressive ventures emanating from Moscow. Secretary of State Marshall had advanced his historic proposal for massive American aid to build new economic strength in Europe on June 5, 1947. The *Post* called for an extraordinary session of Congress to give the President the authority and the money he would need for that purpose. The postwar hope for recovery had given way to fear, frustration, and uncertainty. Only heroic measures in Washington could save Europe from its slide toward communism, chaos, and the threat of another war. On November 23 the *Post* published its Marshall Plan Supplement, with articles by Meyer, Elliston, Folliard, and others. From many different angles the great scheme for revival of European civilization was hailed as "this generation's chance for peace." The USIA sent copies of the supplement to libraries throughout the world and heavy demands for it continued at home and abroad for months after its publication. In expressing its thanks to Philip Graham, the State Department reported that the supplement had become source material for thousands of articles, editorials, radio broadcasts, and pamphlets on every continent. It brought the *Post* the National Headliner's Club award, citing the contributions of Meyer and six other writers.

The plight of Europe had been worsened by the Soviet Union's pressures on Greece and Turkey. The President went to the rescue with his Truman Doctrine pledging aid to free nations endangered by aggressive communism. The *Post* heartily applauded the doctrine, while urging that aid to Greece and Turkey be tied to the United Nations. In the cold war that followed, Meyer and his colleagues were consistently on the side of resistance to the spread of communism by force, violence, and treachery. "Spinelessness," an editorial admonished, "is no way to cope with sabotage."

When the Soviet Union cut off the flow of supplies from West Germany to West Berlin in 1948, the *Post* saw that action as a testing of American intentions rather than a bid for open warfare. Instead of trying to reopen the obstructed rail line and highway to Berlin by force, the United States responded with a heroic airlift, which kept West Berlin functioning until the Russians lifted the blockade. Ferdinand Kuhn, Jr., wrote a series of articles to convey the substance of a 25,000-word State Department report on the Berlin crisis to rank-and-file readers. Meyer printed the articles in booklet form and sent out a great number of copies.

The Communist coup in Czechoslovakia brought new awareness that Europe was in danger of subversion or open aggression. In March 1948, the *Post* began arguing for a defensive alliance in western Europe, and a few months later Senator Arthur H. Vandenberg induced the Senate to pass a resolution encouraging the establishment of regional arrangements for collective defense adhering to the principles of the United Nations but free of the veto in the Security Council. The way was thus paved for approval of the North Atlantic Treaty Organization which brought twelve nations together in what was to become the most formidable and successful peacetime alliance in history. As described by the *Post*, "The pact is an 'all-for-one' and 'one-for-all' treaty providing for a common defense in organized form." If the treaty is used to hasten a closer union of the countries involved, an editorial predicted on April 27, 1949, "its ratification can be a turning point in world affairs."

The need for NATO was further demonstrated when the Soviet Union achieved its first atomic explosion in September—an event that was no surprise in Washington. It set in motion a long campaign for international control of nuclear power in which the *Post* would play an active part.

In dealing with the relatively puny menace of communism in the United States, the *Post* was less forthright. One faction of the editorial staff was deeply concerned by the subversive activities of the Communists who had infiltrated many organizations and some governmental units. Another faction was so worried about infringements on civil rights that it tended to fight every investigation of alleged Communists, thus creating an impression of sympathy for the ruthless elements that were trying to destroy both freedom and representative government. Elliston not only tolerated the various arguments; he sometimes accepted editorials from different writers which looked in opposite directions.

Though troubled by this schizophrenia, both Meyer and Graham took pride in the *Post*'s emancipation from labels. Its day-to-day reaction to events could not be predicted in terms of liberalism or conservatism. The paper fought the State Department's denial of passports on ideological grounds. It assailed the wartime exclusion of 120,000 persons of Japanese ancestry from the West Coast. It campaigned for ratification of the Genocide Treaty and for confirmation of David E. Lilienthal as chairman of the Atomic Energy Commission. On the other hand, it supported the Taft-Hartley Act (with some reservations) to curtail abuses of organized labor. It ridiculed the Morgenthau plan to convert postwar Germany into a rural pasture, and it favored the constitutional amendment limiting future Presidents to two terms.

The paper's persistent crusade against crime led to a feud with the Washington police. A conscientious policeman informed a friend at the *Post* that Robert J. Barrett, then chief of detectives, had concealed six hundred cards carrying details of crimes reported to the police about which they had done nothing. These hidden complaints did not get into the crime statistics, thus distorting reports on law enforcement. One night when Barrett was away from his office the disgruntled policeman removed the cards from Barrett's desk and allowed *Post* men to photocopy them. Wiggins, city editor Gilbert, chief photographer Hugh Miller, and police reporter Al Lewis worked most of the night over the cards. The *Post* broke the story shortly before Barrett was scheduled to become chief of police in July 1947, but the appointment was allowed to stand.

For more than four years after this event the *Post* was especially vigilant in exposing irregularities and corruption in the police department, and Barrett struck back by investigating *Post* editors and reporters, by harassing *Post* delivery trucks, and by urging businessmen not to advertise in the *Post*. In the fall of 1951 Gilbert supplied all the evidence the paper had collected against Barrett to a congressional investigating committee, and the chief was forced to retire under charges that remained nebulous because he invoked the Fifth Amendment.

Protection of the rights of Negroes had been a major facet of *Post* policy from the beginning of the Meyer regime. The paper had scolded the Daughters of the American Revolution in 1939 for denying the use of Constitution Hall for a concert by Marian Anderson. After the war the paper was an active participant in the fight for desegregation in the theaters, restaurants, and schools. It was also partly responsible for reviving the "lost law" of 1873 requiring equal service in Washington restaurants, hotels, and barber shops.

In June 1948, the *Post* celebrated its fifteenth anniversary under Eugene Meyer, with elaborate reviews of "Fifteen Exciting Years" by Elliston, Kuhn, Folliard, and others. It had been a momentous period marked by the world's worst depression, its greatest war, and the advent of the atomic age. As a consequence, Washington had become the world capital. The *Post* reviewed that turbulent era in depth as if to suggest that it had indeed given its readers a first version of history. While the editors looked backward, publisher Graham looked forward and pledged the *Post* to remain independent, to pursue truth, to correct errors promptly, to function as the conscience of the community, and to keep editorial opinions on the editorial page.

Less than a month after this event Meyer transferred the voting stock of the Washington Post Company to Graham and his wife, Katharine Meyer Graham. The publisher had used a $75,000 gift from his father-in-law and additional resources to purchase *Post* stock at a reasonable price; his family was living on Kay's income. For a time the Meyers continued to hold the nonvoting stock, but it was soon transferred to the Eugene and Agnes Meyer Foundation. While divesting himself of ownership, Meyer remained chairman of the board.

At the same time an advisory committee was set up to preclude any future sale of the paper that might undercut "its principles of independence and public service." Meyer was confident that the orientation of the paper toward public service would continue under the Grahams, but he was not content with safeguards that might last for only one generation. "It is our purpose," he said, "that control of the *Post* shall never be transferred to the highest bidder without regard to other considerations." The advisory committee, appointed for life with authority to fill vacancies, was given "absolute discretion" to approve or disapprove any proposed transfer of the voting shares with the object of keeping the paper married to the public interest. The company's articles of incorporation were amended so as to leave no doubt about its intention to publish "an independent newspaper dedicated to the welfare of the community and the Nation, in keeping with the principles of a free press."

The idea of thus insulating the paper against opportunism was Graham's, and one of the models he held up before his father-in-law was the committee established by the *Times* of London in 1924, with the Lord Chief Justice of England as its most eminent member. Meyer was delighted with the idea, but he raised strenuous objection to giving Chief Justice Fred M. Vinson any role in a committee that might decide the future of the *Post*. In the end there was agreement on the membership of the committee as follows: Chester I. Barnard, president of the Rockefeller Foundation; James B. Conant, president of Harvard University; Colgate W. Darden, Jr., president of the University of Virginia; Chief Judge Bolitha J. Laws of the United States District Court for the District of Columbia; and Mrs. Millicent C. McIntosh, dean of Barnard College. When Judge Laws died a few years later, however, the United States had a new Chief Justice, Earl Warren, and he was asked to fill the vacancy on the committee. The arrangement still stands as a sincere and thoughtful attempt to prevent the sale of a newspaper solely for commercial reasons.

A dramatic turn in Washington's journalistic struggle came only a day after the Grahams had acquired control of the *Post*. With the death of Eleanor Medill Patterson, from a heart attack at the age of sixty-three, ownership of the *Times-Herald* passed to its seven top executives. Hearing this news at the Meyer estate in Mount Kisco, Graham immediately flew to Washington to tell William C. Shelton, the *Times-Herald* business manager and one of the new owners, that the *Post* would make a bid for the now rudderless enterprise.

Cissy Patterson had piloted her rambunctious journal into a strong position. With ten editions daily, morning and afternoon, it had a larger circulation than any other Washington newspaper, and it was reported to be prosperous. Yet it was under constant pressure from the rising popularity of the *Post*. With newspapers disappearing from the national scene at an alarming rate and with Washington admittedly overcrowded with papers, the disappearance of one or the other of the morning journals was generally taken for granted. So the Grahams saw a potentially great opportunity in the sudden shift of their rival to committee ownership. There was little feeling of cohesiveness among the new owners of the *Times-Herald*, and they were soon working at cross purposes.

Talk of a sale was interrupted, however, when Mrs. Patterson's daughter, Felicia Gizycka, went to court in an effort to break her mother's will because she was not satisfied with the $25,000 a year for life (tax free) bequeathed to her. Five months were required to settle this dispute out of court, and the negotiations for a sale were resumed in the spring of 1949. By this time other publishers were bidding for the *Times-Herald*, including William Randolph Hearst, Jr., Samuel Newhouse, and the Scripps-Howard chain which published the Washington *Daily News*.

One evening in mid-July Graham invited two of the heirs, Frank C. Waldrop, the executive editor, and Shelton, to his Georgetown home for an intensive review of the complications that had been encountered. While the conference was in progress, Meyer dropped in to give the *Times-Herald* men full assurance that Graham could speak for him, not only in bidding for the paper, but also in regard to financing any deal that might be made. In effect, the Meyer millions were put on tap.

It was not, however, simply a matter of agreeing on a price for the paper. Mrs. Patterson had owned the *Times-Herald* personally, as if it had been a house or a necklace. It thus became an integral part of her estate, and since she had left it to the paper's executives tax free, the huge estate tax, estimated at more than $10 million, would have to come out of other assets in the estate, the total being valued at $16.5 million. These other assets consisted largely of Mrs. Patterson's interest in the Robert R. McCormick-Joseph Medill Patterson trust, which represented stock in the Chicago *Tribune*. The trust units would have to be sold before the end of the tax year. The heirs decided to tie the sale of the trust units to the sale of the paper.

Meyer did not want stock in the Chicago *Tribune*, but he was willing to go along with this arrangement up to a point. On July 18, 1949, he and Graham submitted a written offer to the seven executives. They would pay $4.5 million for the *Times-Herald*, including its building and parking lot, and assume its liabilities. In a separate letter Meyer offered to buy thirty units of the McCormick-Patterson trust for $1,050,000 and to assist in the disposal of the other trust units that Mrs. Patterson had held. Counsel for the seven heirs had assured Meyer that the trust units could be transferred to him, although it later appeared that this might require the consent of Colonel McCormick.

Meanwhile rumors of what was in the wind had reached McCormick in Canada. The shocking prospect that Eugene Meyer or any other outside buyer might acquire stock in his newspaper sent him hurrying back to Chicago. While the seven heirs were in session at the Statler Hotel discussing the bids they had received, McCormick's lawyer telephoned an offer to buy Mrs. Patterson's trust units as well as the *Times-Herald*. According to Raymond F. Garrity, Shelton's attorney, the seven were "preparing to sign a document"[3] approving the Meyer-Graham offers when the telephone call from Chicago came. Some members of the group later insisted that they had no intention of accepting the *Post*'s offer, feeling that absorption of their paper by the *Post* would be a "betrayal and surrender." In any event, the Colonel's intervention proved to be decisive.

McCormick merely duplicated the Meyer-Graham offer of $4.5 million for the *Times-Herald*, but his other bait was irresistible. Publication of the paper, with its round-the-clock editions, would continue. Its marriage to the ultraconservative *Tribune* seemed to carry assurance of lusty battle with the liberal *Post*—a war in which at least some of the seven had a deep ideological interest. No less important was the fact that the Colonel's offer would solve the estate problem—Waldrop and Shelton were executors under the will and Waldrop was also a trustee—and permit the heirs to buy a limited portion of the lucrative trust units.

In the Meyer and Graham households this sudden turn of events had the impact of a bombshell. Up to that last moment McCormick had shown no interest in the *Times-Herald* or even in the trust units. Both Meyer and Graham had thought the prize was virtually within their grasp. The exhausted young publisher had joined his family at Narragansett, R.I., where they were vacationing, with a report that "it looks too good to be true." If the deal did not go through after all the effort he had spent on it, he told Kay, he would "just die for a week." When word of the Colonel's coup came, however, Graham rushed back to Washington and began a frantic scramble to pick up the pieces. Mrs. Meyer was summoned from Mount Kisco because some of her assets might be needed. Always heroic in such moments, her response to the crisis was: "Throw in everything, including the house in Crescent Place. I don't need to live so elaborately."

Working all night with their lawyers, Graham and Meyer put together another offer, but the seven heirs had gone into hiding and could not be found. Finally, attorney Fontaine C. Bradley succeeded in delivering the

[3] Floyd Harrison's affidavit of July 29, 1949, quoting Garrity.

offer to Joseph W. Brooks, an executor of the Patterson estate. One letter said the *Post* was prepared to increase the purchase price previously offered and sought an interview for this purpose; another offered to buy 202½ of Mrs. Patterson's 272½ units of the McCormick-Patterson trust for $7,-687,000. But it was of no avail. The now happy heirs concluded that a price-boosting contest for the paper would raise the valuation of the estate (and the amount of the tax) to a point where some of Mrs. Patterson's residual bequests would be wiped out. So the transaction with McCormick was closed without any renewal of negotiations with the *Post*.

Notified by telephone, Kay Graham wept as if the end were at hand. At Phil's request, she left their children at Narragansett and joined him in Washington for his "week of dying." His spirits began to revive, however, after he had spent most of one night reading a book on the careers of Colonel McCormick and Captain Joseph Patterson, who had been publisher of the New York *Daily News*. Heartened by the fact that they had launched their great journalistic enterprises at an age younger than he then was, Graham went back to work with the comment: "I do think we are going to make it." The journalistic battle on the Potomac was resumed with a powerful new protagonist who hated much of what the *Post* stood for and who looked upon his Washington paper as a sort of "Fort Necessity" from which he could "introduce the United States to the 'burocrats.'"

32 /

The Great Merger

NOVEMBER 1948 BROUGHT ANOTHER HUMILIATION OF A DIFFER-
ent kind. Throughout the presidential campaign of that year the *Post* had
held fast to its policy of nonendorsement, while commenting independently
on both the candidates, President Truman and Governor Dewey. Meyer had
exerted his influence at the Republican National Convention to get Governor Earl Warren of California on the Dewey ticket, but neither he nor
Graham saw any momentous national issue in the Truman-Dewey contest. It was not partisanship but journalistic thumb-sucking that led the
Post, along with many other papers, to assume that Dewey was going to
win.

The last Gallup Poll before the election gave Dewey 49.5 percent of
the vote and Truman 44.5. Folliard's election-day story said: "Gov. Thomas
E. Dewey of New York, the Republican nominee, is regarded as a certain
winner over President Truman." An editorial the same day took note of
the "general agreement" that Dewey would win. But the following morning
the President had 304 electoral votes and Dewey only 189. Journalistic
faces were red all over the land.

Graham rose to the occasion with a telegram to the President which
the *Post* printed on its front page on November 3. It invited Truman to a
"crow banquet" at which political reporters, editors, pollsters, and columnists, including the *Post*'s own, would eat "tough old crow en glace" while
the President would dine on turkey. The guest of honor was asked to wear
a white tie; the others would be in sackcloth. The President magnani-
mously declined the invitation and took advantage of the occasion to call
for national unity. On his triumphant return to the city, however, he was
much amused by the sign in the *Post*'s window overlooking Pennsylvania
Avenue: "Welcome Home, from the Crow Eaters."

Within the *Post* family, the glaring miscalculation of voter opinion
caused a good deal of commotion. Wiggins sought to drop the Gallup Poll.
By his own admission, Gallup was so full of emotion that he "couldn't

even finish a sentence" on election night. But the next day he wrote Graham a letter saying that "Mr. Meyer . . . has been such a great and good friend through all the years that I would literally crawl through hell over ground glass for him." Gallup revised his methods, and Meyer insisted that the *Post* continue using the poll.

As for relations between the President and the *Post*, no lances were broken until the night of December 5, 1950, when Margaret Truman sang at a concert at Constitution Hall. Trying to be compassionate as well as honest, music critic Paul Hume noted that Miss Truman was "extremely attractive on the stage" but also reported that she could not sing very well and that she was "flat a good deal of the time." When the President read the review the next morning, his passion for revenge took the form of a letter to Hume that was to become internationally famous.

"I've just read your lousy review of Margaret's concert," the President fumed. "I've come to the conclusion that you are an 'eight-ulcer man on four-ulcer pay.'

"Some day I hope to meet you. When that happens you'll need a new nose and a lot of beefsteak for blackeyes, and perhaps a supporter below."

Incredulous, Hume asked White House reporter Folliard to check the script, and, when the letter was found to be authentic, the news department ordered a Truman-Hume art display to accompany a story about the sensation. But the layout was never completed. Wiggins said the letter made him sick; Graham told Hume that he had similar letters from Truman that would never be published; Meyer's reaction: "The President will not be embarrassed by the *Washington Post*." But Hume talked about the letter and naïvely showed it to Milton Berliner of the *Daily News*, who memorized key passages and wrote a story that was picked up and amplified by the wire services. After notifying the White House that the *Post* had not intended to publish the letter, Graham permitted his editors to reproduce the version that had appeared in the *News*. The President's crude threat of physical violence produced a furor because it was the second time in recent weeks that his temper had flared.

The fanaticism of the early 1950's quickened the pace of the journalistic struggle in Washington. With aggressive communism on the march in many parts of the world, fear of subversion at home mounted to the point of hysteria. The *Post* assigned itself a role of reason, but occasionally it added fuel to the fire by ignoring the nature of the Communist menace. In April 1950, the *Post* editorially commended Earl Browder, former general secretary of the Communist Party, for defying a Senate committee that was trying to compel him to disclose the names of his former companions in conspiracy against the United States. In defending the right of privacy, the editorial evidenced less concern for the right of a nation to protect itself against subversion, and it deeply offended many readers by associating Browder with "fundamental American decencies." Meyer, Graham, Wiggins, and many members of the *Post's* own staff were shocked by the editorial, and the paper's enemies had a field day. The *Times-Herald* repeatedly assailed the *Post* as "Browder's organ," and the Chicago *Tribune* alternated between calling the *Post* a "defender of the Reds" and a spokesman for the Truman administration. Other *Post* editorials were distorted in an effort to justify the epithets hurled.

Smarting under continued references to "the Red *Post*," Graham sought to clarify the paper's position in an editorial on May 22, 1950, entitled "The Road Back to America." With due regard for the facts that a "cancerous evil of totalitarianism" was abroad in the world and that fifth columns were at work in the United States, he warned against "the rising distrust, the roaring bitterness, the ranging of Americans against Americans, the assault on freedom of inquiry, the intolerance of opposition . . ." The "mad-dog quality of McCarthyism," he wrote, was "sowing confusion and suspicion." His plea was for a bipartisan commission on national security that could substitute fact and rationality for hysteria and the big lie. The editorial brought a hearty response, and bills to create such a commission were introduced in Congress.

In December 1950, Senator Bourke B. Hickenlooper made a critical speech on the Senate floor about a book review that had appeared in the *Post*. In reporting the speech the *Times-Herald* referred to the *Post* as "sometimes labeled the Washington edition of the Communist Daily Worker," although there was no such language in Hickenlooper's remarks as they appeared in the *Congressional Record*. Graham sent a memorandum to Meyer recommending that "we . . . hit them and hit them strongly" with a libel suit. "I believe we have got to the point where we must strike back in some effective way," he wrote, "and this seems the most effective one."

By this time, however, the United States was again at war and nothing came of the proposed libel suit or the idea of a commission on national security. North Korea had invaded South Korea on June 25. The *Post* concluded: "This country is committed to repel the aggressor by every reason of prestige in Asia and of moral obligation to the Koreans." There was no equivocation in its response to Communist conquest in the international sphere. The *Post* was ahead of the President in calling for American action; it consistently supported the war and refrained from criticizing the President for acting without congressional authorization.

When it appeared that Communist China was about to enter the

Korean struggle, the *Post* addressed an editorial directly to the Chinese, reminding them that the United States had been an ally of China, "always a friend, never an enemy," and had defended the integrity of China for fifty years. Americans were in Korea, the editorial said, only to resist the aggression supported by the Soviet Union; China could not serve its basic interests by becoming Russia's pawn. The piece was broadcast by the Voice of America and drew a reply from the official newspaper in Peking.

Leaving crises to younger men, Meyer went to Europe in the fall of 1950, but he had not dropped his journalistic role. On the return voyage aboard the French liner *Liberté* he picked up an amusing story about a fellow passenger, Perle Mesta, the famous Washington party-giver who was then American minister to Luxembourg, and reported it to the *Post* by radio telephone. *Time* took note of the article and the fact that the "alert shipboard correspondent" had won a by-line: "Eugene Meyer, *Post* Reporter."

The 1950 congressional campaigns were coming to a close, highlighted by wild charges. Meyer complained to Wiggins about a headline which read: "Truman Set to Embrace Chinese Reds," without identifying the source of the charge. Meyer's own Republican moorings were subordinate to his desire to keep the *Post*'s news coverage fair and objective.

A few days before the election he celebrated his seventy-fifth birthday. It brought a note from the President, an editorial in *The New York Times*, and an outpouring of praise for his life of public service. Under the caption "Young at 75," *The Times* congratulated him for crowding "three careers into one lifetime" and for being "successful in all three." Publisher Arthur Hays Sulzberger sent Meyer the type of the editorial as a memento. Birthday eulogies abounded with superlatives: ". . . one of the twentieth century's great men"; ". . . thanks to Almighty God for what you are and for what you have done." At the birthday dinner Joseph Pulitzer Jr. of the St. Louis *Post-Dispatch* said that, among the many bankers and industrialists who had owned newspapers, Eugene Meyer was the first who turned out to be a natural newspaperman. Phil Graham arranged a series of group meetings of *Post* employees to honor his father-in-law, and the grandchildren gave a party in the afternoon. The staff presented Meyer with a plaque which read:

TO EUGENE MEYER
NEWSPAPERMAN OF CONSCIENCE
ON HIS 75TH BIRTHDAY
A MARK OF ESTEEM FOR
DEDICATING TO THE PUBLIC SERVICE
THE NEWSPAPER HE BUILT

The plaque was given a prominent place in the new building into which the *Post* moved in November 1950. For many years after he bought the paper Meyer had resisted the pleas for a new building. "I want to build a newspaper first," he would say. In the late forties, however, the *Post's* eight hundred employees were dispersed in four buildings. Since the ancient structure on E Street where the paper had been published for fifty-seven years could not be further expanded, the *Post* built a new, seven-story, gray-limestone newspaper plant at 1515 L Street at a cost of $6 million. Meyer paid for the building by selling stock.

Secretary of Defense Marshall dedicated the building on January 28, 1951, hailing the *Post* as a worthy example of the independent and free press. Graham rededicated the paper to "a determination to keep alive the forces of light." In a happy finale Meyer pushed a button which started the big Scott presses rolling. The International Pressmen's Union had made him an honorary member, and Emory Mayhew initiated him by placing on his head a square-shaped newsprint hat bearing the nickname "Butch" in large red letters. It was a gesture of camaraderie that tells us much about Meyer's journalistic career. Even the glowing tributes to the *Post*— ". . . little short of a miracle," John Cowles; ". . . the magnificent institution you have created," John A. Danaher; and many others—seemed less significant than that paper hat.

A year later the *Post* took another step designed, in part, to toughen its sinews for the continued battle with McCormick—a stock-option plan under which eighteen executives of the paper and WTOP were permitted to buy nonvoting shares in the company over a ten-year period. The partnership which had owned the paper for many years had been succeeded by a new Washington Post Company in 1947, but the stock had been closely held. Under the new plan, key employees were permitted to share in the company's anticipated profits and growth as an incentive for continuity of service. Graham and Meyer felt it was imperative to insulate its managerial talent against raiding.

The arrangement was to yield handsome rewards as the price of the stock advanced under a formula adjusted yearly by Price Waterhouse and Company. Shares purchased at $47.50 under the option plan were valued at $1,173 in 1970, and after the company went public in 1971 there was further appreciation. An executive purchasing 200 shares of stock for $9,500 over a period of ten years could have sold them in 1972 for more than $420,000.

The stock-option plan was followed, in 1953, by a profit-sharing arrangement. Ten percent of the company's earnings before taxes—25 percent of the amount left after taxes—was put into a trust fund for the benefit of employees with five years or more of service. Units of the fund credited to each individual, on the basis of salary, could be drawn in full in case of death or disability or on retirement after age sixty or retirement at fifty with ten years of service. At the time there was little profit to share, and a unit of the fund was worth only $1. As profits increased, however, the fund, invested largely in Washington Post Company stock, grew phenomenally, along with the price of the stock. A unit of the fund was worth $23.31 in 1972, and representative employees in the composing room who had been in the fund from the beginning had to their credit about $62,000.

The approaching contest for the presidency in 1952 brought a new test for Meyer and his colleagues. Disgusted with Truman and the corruption that had developed in his administration, Meyer was eager for new national leadership, and he was increasingly convinced that General Dwight D. Eisenhower was the right man. Eisenhower had charmed Meyer and some of his editors at a *Post* luncheon after his triumphal 1945 homecoming. It was not his stature as a hero that made the great appeal but his lack of pretensions, his keen understanding of humanitarian problems and democratic processes, and his dedication to the public interest without either self-righteousness or stuffiness. Several who attended the luncheon left with the impression that this man ought to be President of the United States.

In November 1951, Meyer and Wiggins joined the parade of Eisenhower supporters to Paris where the General was struggling to weld the NATO alliance into an effective defense system. At that point Eisenhower was resisting any association with politics because he was in uniform and was devoting all his energies to NATO and the cause of European union. Unlike many others who visited the general, Meyer did not urge him to declare his availability for the White House but said the *Post* regarded him as a national asset and was eager to safeguard that asset in the most effective way. The general laughed and said that everything he had seen in France bolstered his belief that the military must be kept separate from politics. But he agreed with Meyer's assertion that a background of military service should not disqualify a man for elective office.

Eisenhower seemed much interested in Meyer's suggestion that his dilemma was similar to that of Justice Charles Evans Hughes, who became the Republican presidential candidate in 1916 despite his aloofness from the preconvention campaigns. The interview ended without any change in the general's determination to stick to his international knitting for the time being, but it may have pushed him a few steps closer to an active candidacy. Meyer went home convinced that Eisenhower "has the one thing that we have been looking for in recent years . . . It is generally described as character."[1]

Despite the general's reiteration on January 7, 1952, that he "would not seek nomination to political office," Meyer continued to send him the Gallup Poll and other data, while carrying on a quiet campaign among friends. These activities were temporarily interrupted when Meyer took a train for California on February 17. Dressed in pajamas in his bedroom, he was trying to fill a paper cup with water when the train hit a curve at high speed and sent him tumbling against a steel projection. He spent the next two weeks in a Chicago hospital nursing a broken rib and then went to Florida to recuperate. While he was still there, the Post came out for Eisenhower on March 24.

It was the first time the Post had endorsed a presidential candidate under the Meyer regime. "This declaration of preference," the editorial read, "is an exercise of our independence, not an abandonment of it." The momentous issue of 1952 called for extraordinary measures. The time for a change was overdue. The Democrats in power had become "blind to error and obtuse about wrongdoing." Out of power for twenty years, the Republicans had become irresponsible and reckless in opposition. "Eisenhower would be the dynamic force to rejuvenate our politics."

Herbert Brownell, who would be Eisenhower's Attorney General, said it was the most effective journalistic blow that had been struck for Ike. At the time there was general agreement in the Post hierarchy on the course taken. Graham wrote to Joseph Pulitzer on March 28: ". . . we all of us came to agree that the question of competent leadership was preeminent, and that it would probably be determined at convention time." The choice was between Eisenhower and Senator Robert Taft, and Taft's foreign policy would be a reversal of all that Meyer and the Post stood for.

At one point there was fear that Mrs. Meyer was inadvertently undermining the cause. She made a speech in Detroit that ripped into the Catholics in a way that seemed likely to turn some against Eisenhower. Meyer had tried various methods of curbing Agnes's unrestrained outbursts, but she managed to evade them in one way or another. On this occasion he criticized his secretary for not letting him know in advance what was in the speech. The Post was engaged in a bitter fight with Senator Joseph McCarthy over his crusade against imaginary Communists

[1] Eugene Meyer to Herman Phleger, January 12, 1952.

in government, and Meyer was loath to antagonize McCarthy's Catholic supporters unnecessarily. Wiggins called Alfred H. Kirchhofer of the Buffalo *Evening News* and induced him to intercept the train on which Mrs. Meyer was returning home and present her with a statement prepared by Graham, saying that in some cases, including this one, her views differed from those of the *Washington Post*. The mother-in-law of the publisher accepted the statement, and the *Post* carried it the next morning. As a further offset to repercussions from the speech Meyer managed to have his picture taken with Eisenhower and a Catholic bishop.

When Eisenhower at last plunged into the contest with Taft, the *Post* supported him and rejoiced over his victory at the Chicago convention. In some measure, however, the enthusiasm for Eisenhower had mounted on the assumption that the alternative would be Taft or Truman. When the President bowed out of the race and the Democratic Party turned to Adlai Stevenson, the choice was less obvious. Graham and Meyer took a delegation of *Post* people to the Democratic National Convention, and Graham helped to push the Illinois governor into the race. While Stevenson was still wavering over the nomination, Graham told him it would be an "act of arrogance" to turn it down.[2] Stevenson agreed, and on this basis Folliard wrote an exclusive story saying that Stevenson would accept a draft from the convention. His nomination put an obvious strain on the *Post*'s endorsement of Eisenhower.

The problem was further complicated by Eisenhower's failure to denounce Senators McCarthy and William Jenner for their wild charges that the State Department was overrun by card-carrying Communists. Eisenhower had made clear his abhorrence of witch-hunting, but, as a newcomer in politics, he refused to fight any Republican in the midst of the campaign. With the *Post* deeply involved in the fight against McCarthyism, there was a strong temptation to switch over to the Democratic candidate who was fighting the same battle.

Still another complication was the illness of Herbert Elliston. For some months he had been recuperating from a heart attack at his summer home in New Hampshire. As the campaign warmed up, he concluded that the *Post* ought to switch its allegiance to Stevenson, a view he shared with several other members of the editorial staff. Graham, Meyer, and Pusey, acting editor of the editorial page in Elliston's absence, held steadfastly to the Eisenhower endorsement, and the editorials reflected their view despite the telephonic bombardment from New Hampshire and the com-

[2] *Time*, April 16, 1956, p. 65.

plaints from some staff members. Elliston returned to his office before the campaign was over, but he was still ailing and would not again become the dominant influence on editorial policy that he had been in the past.

In the final days of the campaign the *Post* dropped Herblock's cartoons from the editorial page to avoid the appearance of schizophrenia. Graham complained to Elliston in a memorandum dated October 24 about Herblock's partisanship and said he should "stay away from political subjects." But the preliminary sketches submitted by Herblock continued to jab at Ike or to extol Adlai. The editors rejected so many of them that a temporary holiday for Herblock was agreed upon, although he continued to draw for his syndicate.

There was no wavering in Meyer's view. Though he respected Stevenson, he felt that the Democratic candidate would be handicapped by the problems he would inherit from Truman and that, in any event, a change was necessary to preserve the two-party system. His response to Stevenson's witty thrusts was that "a little wisecracking and repartee is good but too much is repartedious." When Truman accused Eisenhower of "moral blindness" and of willingness to "accept the very practices that identified the so-called master race," Meyer called on the President, in a front-page statement, to withdraw his "slanderous charge."

After voting at Mount Kisco, Meyer went to bed with an attack of virus pneumonia. As the returns came in, he nevertheless described himself as singing silently "God Bless America" because the decision at the polls had been so strong and overwhelming. To another friend he wrote: "Yesterday was a glorious day in the history of America." His hopes for the future were high, as indicated by a letter to a friend, C. W. Halbert, on November 8: "I am hopeful that Ike may again make in his new position a reputation for ability to unify allies. The allies now are the good Americans of any and every party who want a strong, honest, competent government for our country."

The new President's performance, however, fell substantially below campaign hopes. One of the sharpest disappointments for the *Post* was the intensification of Senator McCarthy's rampage. Instead of subsiding, as the *Post* had predicted he would under a Republican administration, the Wisconsin demagogue smeared Eisenhower's appointees as recklessly as he had smeared Truman's. The *Post* repeatedly exposed his chicanery, and the Senator directed some of his most virulent barbs at the paper, persistently calling it the "Washington Daily Worker."

In February 1953 Agnes Meyer struck a powerful blow at the "shameless" investigative methods of McCarthy and other witch hunters in a speech before the American Association of School Administrators at Atlantic City, and it resounded throughout the country. The nature of the *Post's* comments, during this and previous periods, is indicated by the captions over some of its McCarthy editorials: "Mucking," "Manufactured News," "Sentence Before Trial," "Sewer Politics," "Guilt by Reiteration," "Piltdown Man," "Demagogue." In August 1953, the Senator asked the American Society of Newspaper Editors to set up a committee to investigate the editorial and news policies of the *Washington Post*, but was rebuffed. McCarthy's clash with Secretary of the Army Robert T. Stevens brought his rampage to a climax. Fearing that its own prestige had been tarnished, the Senate launched an investigation, which led to a 67–22 vote to censure him in December 1954. The Senate's rebuke broke his power, and he died two and a half years later, leaving as his monument a new word in the language —"McCarthyism"—which, as the *Post* noted at the time, had become a "synonym for reckless slander."

On December 7, 1952, the *Post* celebrated its seventy-fifth anniversary, with a look backward to the days when Stilson Hutchins had founded the paper and achieved a circulation of 11,875 in its first year. Yet the emphasis was on the more recent past during which Eugene Meyer and his associates had quadrupled the circulation of the paper. The staff presented him with a plaque which claimed for the *Post* a place among the foremost newspapers of the world—"a monument to the integrity of his purposes, the soundness of his policies, the firmness of his resolution." In response Meyer said: "It's fun to work in the field of ideas," and reiterated his belief that Washington offers the greatest opportunity in the world for a group of people to work together in this sphere.

One feature of the celebration was a display of the awards won by *Post* people, including Pulitzer Prizes for Felix Morley, Herbert Elliston, Edward T. Folliard, Merlo J. Pusey (for biography), and two Pulitzers for Herblock; Heywood Broun Awards for Alan Barth, Alfred Friendly, and Raymond Clapper; a Sigma Delta Chi Award for Barth; the Cosmopolitan Club Medal for public service and the Council of Social Agencies Award for Meyer; the National Headliners Club award for outstanding public service to Meyer and six other members of the staff. Other awards had been won by Jerry Kluttz, Sam Stavisky, Elsie Carper, dramatic editor Richard Coe, Shirley Povich, Malvina Lindsay, Phil Austensen, Mary Haworth, Agnes Meyer, Robert Estabrook, and photographers Arthur Ellis, Harry E. Goodwin, Charles Del Vecchio, and Thomas Kelley.

Having suffered a paralytic stroke subsequent to his heart attack, Elliston was no longer able to carry the burden of editor. His transfer to the relatively relaxed role of "contributing editor" in the spring of 1953 brought praise for the prestige the editorial page had acquired under his direction

379

through thirteen turbulent years. Walter Lippmann said of him: "He had —like Cobb of *The World*, like Parsons of *The Herald Tribune*, like C. P. Scott of *The Manchester Guardian*—the true genius of the editor." Though he wrote only in longhand and was often careless in editing copy, he was a prodigious writer and an observer of rare insight. Recognizing that it would be difficult to fill Elliston's shoes, Graham first offered the job to James B. Reston of *The New York Times*'s Washington bureau and, that failing, elevated the youngest member of the editorial staff, Robert H. Estabrook, thirty-four, to the position of editor of the editorial page.

The twentieth anniversary of the Meyer regime in June 1953 brought another round of celebration and warm congratulations. The paper was steadily gaining in circulation and its advertising lineage had grown from 5,847,537 to 24,484,016 lines in two decades. The *Post* seemed to be winning the long struggle for survival. Edward L. Bernay's poll among eminent national leaders placed the *Post* fifth on the list of the country's best newspapers. Yet it was under almost daily attack from the formidable McCormick press.

Relations between the *Post* and the *Evening Star* remained placid and cordial. Meyer often chided associates who manifested antagonism toward the *Star*. "We don't want anything to happen to the *Star*," he would say. "Washington deserves two good newspapers." This friendly feeling did not, however, interfere with the banter that was often exchanged between himself and executives of the *Star*. One evening at the National Press Club when Fleming Newbold, vice-president of the *Star*, complained that he suffered from insomnia, Meyer said in his most cooperative manner, "I think I can help you."

"How?" the incredulous executive asked.

"Don't read your paper until you go to bed," Meyer quipped.

The outlook for the *Times-Herald* went from bad to worse. In 1949 McCormick had made his niece, Ruth (Bazy) McCormick Miller, publisher of his Washington paper, and it became a weak imitation of the fiercely right-wing Chicago *Tribune*. A succession of journalistic blunders and Bazy's marriage to her city editor, Garvin E. Tankersley, after she had divorced Peter Miller, convinced the Colonel that he had better assume personal responsibility for running the *Times-Herald*. He became editor and publisher in April 1951, but the journalistic style that had brought him millions in Chicago aroused no comparable response in Washington. *Times-Herald* losses were estimated from half a million to a million dollars a year.

Well aware of the bitter fruit McCormick was harvesting, Phil Graham planted a seed that was to bear abundantly for the *Post*. Sitting next to Alicia Patterson, editor and publisher of *Newsday*, at a press dinner, he asked why the Colonel insisted on spreading himself so thin. She replied that Meyer's attempt to buy Cissy Patterson's trust units had convinced McCormick that he was trying to horn in on the *Tribune*. Graham assured her that Meyer had never wanted the *Tribune* stock; he had bid for it only because that was necessary to get the *Times-Herald*.

Soon after this conversation Meyer received a confidential letter from an old friend, Kent Cooper, who had been general manager of the Associated Press for many years and was then living in retirement at Palm Beach. The letter to "Dear Eugene" was dated January 23, 1954:

> I am wondering whether you expect to be in Palm Beach any time soon for I would like very much to talk to you about a business matter of importance to you. Please let me know.

Scenting a hint that the *Times-Herald* might again be for sale, Meyer showed the letter to John Sweeterman and asked: "What do you think?"

"I'm probably thinking the same thing you are," Sweeterman replied. "Mr. Cooper is a good friend of Colonel McCormick, lives near him in Florida, and he could be talking about the *Times-Herald*."

Meyer placed a telephone call. "Kent," he queried, "this business matter to which you refer, is it in the field of journalism?"

"Yes," came the reply.

"Is it in Washington?"

"Yes."

Meyer said he had been thinking of going to Florida in the next couple of days, and Cooper asked him to call on his arrival. The next step was to telephone Graham, who was in Jacksonville, and ask him to be in Palm Beach for the meeting with Cooper. As soon as Meyer, Graham, and Sweeterman were ensconced at the Brazilian Court Hotel, Cooper was invited to join them. The gist of his message was that Colonel McCormick was ill and, being fed up with the *Times-Herald*, was disposed to sell it to Eugene Meyer if he were interested.

"Yes I am," Meyer said, smothering his inward exultation. "How much does the Colonel want for it?"

Cooper replied that McCormick wanted to recoup the $4.5 million he had paid for the paper, plus the cost of new presses and an addition to the building—a total of $8.5 million.

"That's all right with me," was Meyer's decisive response.[3]

---

[3] Edward T. Folliard's manuscript history of the *Washington Post*, p. 101.

When Cooper reported back to McCormick that evening, January 28, the latter was equally decisive. "It's a deal," he said. Cooper telephoned that reply to the *Post* men the next morning, and Meyer suggested that lawyers representing the two sides be summoned to Palm Beach to draw up an agreement that could be signed. But the Colonel did not think that was necessary; Meyer's word was enough. Through Cooper, he informed the eager buyers that he or one of his associates would be in touch with them in March.

In some respects it was an amazing transaction. Ideologically, the *Washington Post* and the Chicago *Tribune* were at opposite poles. Competition between the *Post* and the *Times-Herald* had been fierce and unrelenting. Yet the two chief protagonists arranged the transfer of a major journalistic enterprise from one to the other without a word of haggling, disagreement, or recrimination. McCormick's biographer explains his strange behavior by saying that he was grateful to Meyer for his support in the Associated Press case and that he respected Meyer as a fellow Yale man and a successful journalist.[4] It is also clear that Cooper's services as a friendly broker eased McCormick's surrender on the Washington front. McCormick later wrote Cooper: "I told Eugene Meyer emphatically that it was due to you that I sold him the paper . . ."[5] Cooper explained his interest in the transaction, not only as an accommodation to two old friends, but also as insurance for sound and effective news coverage in the national capital. Loath though he was to see any newspaper die, he felt that Washington could not long support two newspapers in the morning field.

There was no mystery, of course, in the attitude of Meyer and Graham. The *Post* had been eager to buy the *Times-Herald* ever since 1937. Nor was it strange that Meyer did not haggle when the great prize was about to fall into his lap. His business operations were usually bold and decisive, and now at the age of seventy-eight his greatest interest in life was to provide a secure future for his journalistic enterprise.

The wait required by the Colonel was tantalizing. For six weeks nothing was heard from him. The Meyers reluctantly went on the vacation they had planned in Jamaica after arranging with Graham to call them back on short notice if necessary. At last Cooper notified Graham on March 13 that a *Tribune* representative would visit him shortly, and he wired his father-in-law: "You have to come home." That same evening Chesser M. Campbell, vice-president of the Tribune Company, phoned Graham at his

---

[4] Frank C. Waldrop: *McCormick of Chicago* (Englewood Cliffs: Prentice-Hall; 1966), pp. 278–9.

[5] Kent Cooper to Philip L. Graham, March 28, 1954.

Georgetown home and arranged for a meeting the following day, Sunday, in the office of the *Tribune* law firm, Kirkland, Fleming, Green, Martin and Ellis.

Flying home on Saturday night, Meyer joined Graham and Sweeterman in laying plans for the big event. Floyd Harrison, then treasurer of the Washington Post company, and Frederick S. (Fitz) Beebe of Cravath, Swaine, and Moore were summoned from New York for a meeting at 10 A.M. Sunday. Beebe met with Fontaine Bradley and other lawyers of the Covington and Burling firm to draw up a written offer for presentation to the *Times-Herald* board of directors at its meeting on Monday. Meanwhile Graham and his associates conferred with the *Tribune* men, and they went to lunch at Graham's home, where the discussions continued. Graham then picked up Meyer at Crescent Place, gave the lawyers downtown a fill-in on the day's negotiations, and asked the *Post*'s top executives to meet him at home. Sweeterman, Wiggins, Bernard, Gladstein, Eybers, and Hayes responded to his calls, and as soon as Graham and Meyer had disclosed the good news they began to lay plans for a 100 percent expansion of the *Post*'s operations in three days. It was a monumental task to be accomplished under the handicap of absolute secrecy. Graham asked the executives not to tell even their wives. McCormick was worried about the effect of any premature disclosure on morale at the *Times-Herald*, and the lawyers wanted to discourage any possible antitrust action at the Department of Justice by announcing the merger as a *fait accompli*.

When the *Times-Herald* board met Monday at noon, the text of the proposed agreement was not ready. Last-minute changes had been made at the suggestion of the *Tribune* executives. Graham delivered the documents while the meeting was in session, however, and McCormick secured approval of the sale despite the protests of his niece, Bazy Tankersley, who gave the impression of having been "struck by a thunderbolt." The only concession the Colonel would make was that she might have forty-five hours to seek money to buy the paper on condition that she would not disclose what she was trying to do. McCormick then flew home for a meeting of the *Tribune* board on Wednesday.

Another period of waiting ensued, although this time it was to be mercifully short. Meyer and Graham could not help reflecting on how close they had come to buying the *Times-Herald* in 1949 only to have it snatched out of their hands at the last minute. This time the basis for their hopes seemed more secure, but the contract had not been signed and no money had changed hands. Graham talked again with Chesser Campbell at the Carlton Hotel and then, one at a time, with four *Times-Herald* executives who had just been informed of the impending sale by a *Tribune* spokesman. While this was going on, the tension was lifted by a humorous sight. Campbell came into the room with a worried expression and began looking under the furniture. "What's missing?" Graham asked. "To tell you the truth," Campbell replied, "it's the letter of transmittal from you and Mr. Meyer." The search proved futile, but Campbell checked with his lawyers and discovered they had the "missing" document.

John Hayes and Stanley L. Temko of Covington and Burling were sent to Chicago to wind up the details of the deal. Graham gave them final instructions in a state of high excitement. Hayes was to take a copy of the sale agreement and a cashier's check drawn to himself for $1.5 million. The check could not be made payable to the Tribune Company, he was told, without starting rumors. Hayes said he would call the airport immediately for reservations. "The hell you will," Graham retorted. "You'll go by train. You can return by plane if you wish, but I don't want to hear that a plane has crashed carrying a *Washington Post* check for $1.5 million."

Hayes and Temko were at Colonel McCormick's office in the Chicago Tribune Tower early on Wednesday. A private telephone line had been installed so that they could report completion of the transaction at the earliest possible moment, but pesky details remained to be disposed of. Clarence E. Manion, a prominent right-wing Republican, was running in and out of McCormick's office in a desperate effort to stop the sale. Bazy Tankersley was pleading for more time in which to raise money. According to *Time*, she had pledges of about $4 million from interested millionaires but was not within striking distance of the Meyer offer. McCormick turned her down, and his board approved the sale to the *Post*. Meanwhile Hayes and the lawyers were still struggling with minor problems. What about the Colonel's house in Washington? The newsprint in transit? The *Times-Herald* trucks? Hayes agreed to take everything in a frantic effort to speed up the signing.

In Washington, the Meyers and Grahams had assembled in Phil's office. With them was Charles Moore, former promotion manager of the *Post* and then a vice-president of the Ford Motor Company, who had been summoned by Meyer so that he might share a moment of triumph. Members of this impatient group took turns keeping the line to Chicago open. Hayes made periodic reports of his progress. Graham told him to stop haggling over trifles. At last about noon on March 17 the agreement was signed, and the check to Hayes was endorsed to the *Tribune* as a down payment. Hayes rushed to the telephone.

"Okay. You've got it," he told the exuberant publisher on the other end of the wire.

Graham cut off any further talk with an excited: "Good-bye. We're off. Come on home."[6]

Coming after so many tries and disappointments, the final triumph was electrifying. While Kay Graham screamed in ecstasy, her husband flashed the signal that the next paper on the street would be the *Washington Post and Times-Herald*. For both the Grahams it was a dream come true. Throughout the difficult negotiations Phil had acquitted himself with skill and resourcefulness. The future of the great journalistic venture that had been initiated by his father-in-law and piloted by him for the last eight years now appeared to be secure. For Meyer the *Post*'s sudden leap into full command of the morning field was the capstone of his career, but the veteran of many battles was not looking backward. "The real significance of this event," he told Sidney Hyman, "is that it makes the paper safe for Donnie," meaning his bright-eyed and serious-minded grandson, Donald Edward Graham, then only eight years old.

The honor of pushing the button that started the presses rolling for the first edition of the new *Washington Post and Times-Herald* put Meyer in his most exuberant mood. Wearing a pressman's paper hat and a grin that covered his face, he displayed the first paper of the new era with a sense of deep satisfaction. His inner glow was not diminished when he walked into the *Post*'s snack bar for a cup of coffee and discovered that his money pocket was empty.

"Could someone lend me a nickel?" he asked the line-up at the food counter. "I just bought a newspaper."

Although the lawyers had threshed out many troublesome details, the transaction had been carried out within the spirit of the initial agreement between Meyer and McCormick. In addition to payment of $1.5 million down and $7 million more within a year for the *Times-Herald*, the *Post* also paid nearly $1 million in severance pay and set up an employment office to find jobs for personnel not absorbed into the consolidated organization. Among the five hundred *Times-Herald* employees taken over by the enlarged paper were W. Frank Gatewood, who eventually became advertising director and a vice-president of the *Post*; William Brady, who succeeded John J. Riseling as night city editor; Harry Gabbett, a brilliant rewrite man; and Bob Addie, baseball reporter. In later years Meyer would make a practice of saying that he had paid more than $8 million to get Gatewood.

There were, however, other assets in the transaction. The *Times-Herald* had reported a circulation of more than 250,000 before the sale, compared to about 204,000 for the *Post*. On the first Sunday after the consolidation

---

[6] Author's interview with John S. Hayes, October 31, 1972.

the paper printed nearly 500,000 copies of the largest edition it had ever issued—a 228-page monster weighing two pounds and five ounces. It was a herculean feat for a merged staff that had been working together for only three days. At the end of its first year the *Washington Post and Times-Herald* had a circulation of 395,000, which meant that it had kept most of the unduplicated subscriptions of both papers.

Despite the laments that always accompany the death of a newspaper, the triumph of the *Post* in Washington's fierce journalistic contest brought a shower of congratulations. Lord Beaverbrook commented: "You now have the strongest newspaper position in the world and perhaps the most important." Robert Lincoln O'Brien said it was "The most glorious news I have heard in years." Walter Lippmann wired: "Hooray for the canary that swallowed the cat."

The consolidated paper retained many *Times-Herald* features and operated with a keen awareness of "its enlarged obligations to the community and to the Nation . . ." But it remained independent, and there was no change in its liberal editorial policy oriented toward international cooperation, democratic government, and personal freedom. It was the *Post*'s identity that prevailed.

Media Records published soon after the merger showed the *Washington Post and Times-Herald* fifth among all morning and Sunday newspapers in the United States in total advertising lineage and twelfth among all seven-day papers. More important was the foundation for growth that had been laid. Events of the next two decades would clearly demonstrate that Eugene Meyer's fondest dream had indeed been realized. He had put no limit on either his spending or his efforts to build a great newspaper, and his all-out strategy had won.

33 /

The Meyer Legacy

THE PURCHASE OF THE *Times-Herald* WAS ONLY AN INTERLUDE in Meyer's twilight period. After his seventy-fifth birthday he had begun deliberately and systematically to heed his own advice—that old men should not get in the way of the rising generation. His usual reply to comments about the *Post* was that he was only "an approving onlooker and sympathizer" with those who were doing the work. When Stanford University asked him to make its commencement address in June 1951, he used the occasion for a sort of swan song.

"I have always preached—on the basis of experience," he said, "that old men are dangerous—dangerous, that is, when they give advice or hold on too long to positions of authority." He proceeded to demonstrate, however, that old men can be both salty and profound.

Worries of the present generation about being born too late, he said, were as unfounded as his youthful pessimism because the price of land in the city of Los Angeles had increased from $2 to $20 an acre. ". . . my whole life experience has been marked by a series of national crises, one seemingly more alarming than the last—crises of all kinds, military, economic, political, social, that appeared to threaten our very existence as a nation. Yet by intelligent cooperative action, by self-confidence, foresight, and hard work, our people emerged from every one of these well-nigh catastrophic events stronger, wiser, and more conscious of the latent power of free men."

Reviewing the four great depressions that he had known intimately, he declared that they were all man-made—the result of human ignorance and mismanagement. ". . . it follows," he added, "that it is possible for wiser men to avoid much of this in the future." Discounting the possibility that he or anyone else of another generation could spell out the answers for the present generation, he nevertheless suggested "a broad and challenging avenue of approach." It lay in a continuous, persistent, and sincere "search for truth." The great challenge of the twentieth century was "to maintain the proposition that knowledge and reason offer the true pathway for man."

"It is this widening of knowledge," he said, "that permits me to come to you as a colleague. For if institutions of higher learning such as Stanford are the root source of knowledge, it is also true that journalism represents the medium whereby knowledge may be associated with day-to-day existence." Both were dependent, of course, on freedom and on the concept that every man "has an awesome importance because he is put here in God's image." The most valuable contribution of his generation, he concluded, was its faith in, and its exemplification of, "the as yet unfathomed power of free men wholeheartedly committed to the preservation of their freedom." The address was at once a summary of his philosophy and an explanation of the great interest he had found in journalism. He saw the newspaper he had built as a medium of enlightenment closely associated with the great objective of human progress.

Another significant demonstration of his interest in that profession came on June 19, 1955, when he and Mrs. Meyer gave half a million dollars worth of nonvoting stock in the Washington Post Company to 711 employees and circulation contractors. It was a princely gift designed to reward those who had stood with him. The presentation was made at a luncheon celebrating the twenty-second anniversary of the Meyer regime at the *Post*, with all the beneficiaries as guests. Meyer briefly announced the gifts—from four to twenty shares to each employee with five years or more of service, the shares being apportioned in accord with responsibility and tenure. Graham explained the details of the gift in a happy mood, and Edward Folliard responded for the fortunate employees. "Well, you never know," he began. "You come downtown a wage earner and you go home a capitalist." At the time his appraisal of the gifts seemed an exaggeration, but some employees who received the maximum of twenty shares would sell them two decades later for more than $43,000.

On October 31, 1955, seven hundred friends assembled at the Willard Hotel to honor Meyer on his eightieth birthday. The luncheon had been organized by Arthur Hays Sulzberger, publisher of *The New York Times*; Robert V. Fleming, president of Riggs National Bank; and the Right Reverend Maurice S. Sheehy of Catholic University. Vice-President Nixon and members of the Cabinet were present. Greetings were read from President Eisenhower and Adlai Stevenson. Chief Justice Earl Warren delivered the principal tribute, and former Ambassador George A. Garrett presented a surprise. Meyer's family, friends, and associates had contributed $300,-000 to create a chair of medicine in his honor at the George Washington University, and Dr. Thomas McPherson Brown had been designated as the first occupant of the chair. Meyer was overwhelmed. "In all my eighty years," he said, "no single act has meant so much to me."

Once more *The New York Times* saluted Meyer as "one of the nation's leading citizens." There was much banter about his indestructibility, and Meyer joined in the fun with a general invitation to his ninetieth birthday party. But in the quiet of his office or study he was more philosophical. To Drew Dudley he wrote that after attainment of eighty years "you would be foolish to expect, and I think foolish to want to number too many years in the future. Death is as natural as birth. The only thing that is important is that the life between the beginning and the end is spent in a decent way."

The chair of medicine in his honor was especially touching because it reversed the usual flow of benefactions. Meyer had been generous with his money all his life, and as old age crept upon him he had multiplied his gifts. In addition to the funds distributed through the Eugene and Agnes Meyer Foundation, he gave generous contributions to Yale, the Harvard Law School, Barnard, the University of California, Children's Hospital, the Washington School of Psychiatry, the National Gallery of Art, and many other institutions. He financed a new wing for the Jewish Community Center and gave smaller sums to a great variety of useful community projects. In 1953 Yale belatedly established the Eugene Meyer Public Service Fund which brought together Meyer's gifts totaling $250,-000.

The relentless march of time was further evidenced by the death of his sister Rosalie on February 8, 1956. Despite her use of the cat-o'-nine-tails to make him behave in his youth, Rosalie was his most cherished tie with the past. On one occasion when she gave a party for Admiral and Mrs. Chester Nimitz, Meyer had ordered orchid leis and corsages from Honolulu for his sister and all her feminine guests. When San Francisco paid homage to the great lady on her eighty-fifth birthday, the *Post* had put out a special edition with pictures and a story about the event. For many years she had been president of San Francisco's Recreation and Park Commission; she had given the city a natural amphitheater for musical events—the Sigmund Stern Grove—in honor of her husband; she had donated Stern Hall to the University of California. Meyer's expression of affection for her took the form of a scholarship in her honor at Stanford University; in addition he set up the Rosalie Meyer Stern Fund at the University of California as a reward to women graduates for outstanding community work. San Francisco honored her with flags at half-mast.

Less shattering was the death of his only remaining brother, Walter

E. Meyer, in January 1957. Walter had given most of his life to the practice of law. In World War I he had served on the staff of the Council of National Defense and had been a director of the Palestine Economic Corporation for twenty years. His most notable achievement was a courageous and protracted fight to save the St. Louis Southwestern Railway (commonly called the Cotton Belt) from a ruthless group of looters. As chairman of the Protective Committee of Cotton Belt Stockholders, he succeeded in thwarting one of the most aggressively powerful combinations in American business.

Eugene and Walter had taken very different paths. From the beginning their personalities had clashed, and even in their old age Eugene's domination and Walter's sensitivity had left each uncomfortable in the other's presence. With Walter's passing, only three of the eight Meyer children were left, and Eugene's two surviving sisters, Mrs. Charles J. Liebman and Mrs. Alfred A. Cook, were not well.

The most painful problem in Meyer's own family was his daughter Florence. Not only had Florence exiled herself and her two boys from the family for many years; after the *Post* had purchased the *Times-Herald* she had written her father from Zurich: "I feel myself at the moment punished and punished in my boys for having failed to be around Washington and to exert any influence I may have had for the purpose of establishing good worth for my children." Though she acknowledged that her children would be well off after her death, she complained that they would be excluded from the "wonderful opportunities" she associated with the *Post*. The Grahams would be in control.

Meyer wrote Florence a patient and thoughtful letter explaining that Phil Graham had been chosen as his successor at the *Post* after Bill had decided to stay in medicine; that the Grahams had thereafter purchased the controlling "A" stock; that most of the nonvoting stock had been given to the Eugene and Agnes Meyer Foundation; that purchase of the *Times-Herald* had been accomplished mostly with borrowed funds and proceeds from the sale of stock to Bill, Kay, Phil, and some of the executives at the paper; that his "estate situation" would not be changed one iota by the transaction. The estrangement of Florence and her sense of grievance in the face of his generosity left wounds that even time could not completely heal. The unhappy daughter had only a few years to live, although she would briefly survive her father.

There was no doubt in Meyer's mind that he had taken the right course as far as the future of the *Post* was concerned. "I don't feel old," he wrote in 1957, "because my ambitions have been realized by the fine organization in the *Post*." Nor was there any sourness for him in the fact that his son had chosen medicine over journalism. Bill made a practice of checking his father's physical condition in his old age, and Meyer often expressed pride in Bill's "good name in his profession" and in his work at the Johns Hopkins University and Hospital, where he became professor of both psychiatry and internal medicine.

Numerous amenities brightened the days of the chairman of the board. In November 1956, Prince Bernhard of the Netherlands presented him with the William the Silent Award for excellence in the presentation of international news. One day the postman brought a gratifying letter from Clarence C. Dill apologizing for having voted against Meyer's confirmation for several federal offices when he (Dill) was a member of the Senate. Dill acknowledged that he was suffering "a little twinge of conscience" and he wanted Meyer to know that "liberals all over the country glory in your independence and broad-minded attitude in presenting news and opinion . . . through the medium of your great newspaper in the national capital." Meyer responded graciously, giving Graham full credit for the current performance of the paper.

The *Post* executives jokingly called the Tuesday Morning Club voted unanimously to reward the chairman of the board in this fashion:

> The Chairman really ought to get
> Three times his present pay.
> How fortunate the Chairman is
> (We hope that he relaxes)
> Three times as much as nothing
> Will not cost him any taxes.

Much of his time was given to unpaid tasks. He was a member of President Eisenhower's Committee on Purchases of Blind-Made Products and honorary chairman of the Washington Criminal Justice Association. He was a trustee of the Boys Club of Washington, the Committee for Economic Development, and the National Industrial Conference Board. The American Society of Newspaper Editors and the Advertising Council claimed some of his time, and he continued to be a director of the Allied Chemical Company. In 1955 he was chairman of the "brotherhood dinner" of the National Conference of Christians and Jews in Washington.

The election year of 1956 brought a rerun of the 1952 contest between Eisenhower and Stevenson. Meyer noted long before the campaigns began that the issues would be less momentous than they had been four years earlier. The *Post* reverted to its traditional policy of nonendorsement. While expressing some disappointment in Eisenhower's performance, an editorial on October 28 concluded that "voters will be in the happy position . . . of being able to select between two high-minded men, both of them conciliatory in their approach to problems and neither of them addicted to extreme remedies."

The Meyers attended a rally for Stevenson in White Plains, N.Y., organized by their son-in-law, Pare Lorentz. After the rally they went to a party for the candidate at the Lorentz home. When Meyer greeted Stevenson, the latter said he had thought of mentioning him at the meeting but he had not done so because "I thought maybe you would rather have it otherwise." Meyer telephoned the *Post* that the great enthusiasm for Stevenson in the Republican stronghold of Westchester County suggested "quite a good showing" for the Democrats. Mrs. Meyer had openly endorsed Stevenson; for her he was not only a political idol but also the object of a new romantic fixation. Stevenson told a friend he had great respect for Meyer's financial judgment and experience but could scarcely get a word with him in Agnes's presence. Even Meyer seemed surprised by the second Eisenhower landslide.

Despite his numerous connections, Meyer was sometimes restless for want of something to do. How dull it was to "rust unburnished, not to shine in use." He seemed to welcome complaints from subscribers to which he could give personal attention. He made a habit of visiting William McChesney Martin, Jr., chairman of the Federal Reserve Board, as he had done with Martin's predecessor, Thomas B. McCabe, for extended discussion of monetary policy. He loved to reminisce and to play bridge or gin rummy. But observation and coaching from the sidelines were less interesting than active combat in the real world. One day he asked Wiggins what he would rather do if he had his choice of all occupations.

"I think I'd rather write history," Wiggins confessed.

"I wouldn't," Meyer retorted. "I'd rather make it."

For several years Meyer had been spending a good deal of time on a book about himself. Sometimes it appeared to be visualized as an autobiography, although the writing was done by a professional, Sidney Hyman. Other parts of the manuscript were written in the third person, with Meyer supplying most of the data. It grew into a mountainous document but was never completed.

Long vacations in Nassau, interludes at Saratoga Springs, and summers at Mount Kisco helped to brighten the last years. In regard to Saratoga he wrote: "It does us both good to drink the water, take the baths, stop smoking, stop drinking and lose a little weight." Agnes spent seemingly endless hours playing cards with him. While he was in Nassau, *Post* executives kept him aware of the paper's progress. A note from Joseph

Paull said that *Post* profits had exceeded those of the *Star* every year since 1955.

Meyer's deteriorating health led to an operation in which doctors removed a cancerous polyp from his intestines, but not before the malignancy had impaired his mental alertness and memory. Despite the cheerful front that he presented to his friends, he fretted over the approach of the inevitable. Coming down the stairs one day, he said he resented every tick of the grandfather clock.

Agnes wrote Kay on August 5, 1957, that her father had suddenly fallen into a mood "of deep dissatisfaction with everything" and that she (Agnes) had become "the target of his inner turmoil." Meyer had been highly gratified when the University of Kentucky had offered Agnes a degree of doctor of laws. But his pride in her achievements did not eliminate the friction between them. "I actually get frightened about the future," Agnes's letter continued. "When he was strong, I could fight back. That is out of the question now. He conquers through weakness and I am helpless. The only people who can help me, therefore, are you and let's admit it, especially Phil who can say anything because he is the one person who can do no wrong."

A still more formidable cloud began to shadow the future. The son-in-law by whom Meyer laid so much store was showing signs of mental illness. Not since the tragic death of his brother Edgar in the *Titanic* disaster had Meyer invested so much trust and affection in a young man as he had in Phil Graham. Phil had become not only an integral part of the family; he was also a source of intellectual strength, a genial companion—a man whose potential seemed to match that of Meyer himself. In family squabbles Graham had even become an effective mediator between his father-in-law and mother-in-law.

For some years Meyer had worried about Graham's health. "Phil is too skinny and too high-powered," he would say. His concern was whether Phil had the physical toughness to withstand the increasing pressures upon him. The image of unlimited strength that Graham liked to project was deceptive. Though tall and active, he was frail and highly sensitive. As a means of easing the pressures on his son-in-law, Meyer induced him to hire an administrative assistant. Graham thought a law clerk would be most useful to him, but Meyer insisted that journalistic experience was important in such an assignment. The compromise was to hire Joseph Paull who had previously left the paper to become administrative assistant to Chief Judge Bolitha Laws of the United States District Court in Washington.

393

In the fall of 1957 Graham suffered a siege of acute depression. Members of the family induced him to seek psychiatric treatment, and the doctors prescribed temporary detachment from the responsibilities he had been carrying at the *Post* and elsewhere. Designating Sweeterman and Wiggins to run the paper in his absence, he and Kay retired to Glen Welby, their Virginia farm, where he could relax and seek recuperation.

Knowing that her father himself was ill, Kay shielded him from any detailed knowledge of her husband's troubles. Meyer knew that Phil was sick, but he could only guess as to the seriousness or nature of his illness. There was great relief within the family when Phil notably improved after some months at Glen Welby and was able to resume his activities. For a time he would play a meteoric role, which would include the purchase of *Newsweek* by the *Post* and the exertion of a strong influence on the formation of the Kennedy–Johnson ticket that would win the presidential election in 1960. But his very success seemed to contribute to his undoing.

In the first decade of their association, the relations between Meyer and Graham had been singularly free from any son-in-law or father-in-law complex. On one occasion Graham had taken special note of the tendency of fathers-in-law to be wary of their daughters' husbands, and had proudly asserted that his was an exception. He assuredly had the full confidence and backing of his father-in-law. During his illness, however, an unsuspected sensitivity over his son-in-law role came to the surface. He began to tell intimates that, without Meyer's wealth and influence, he "would have made it" on his own. "If I had gone back to Florida to practice law," he would say, "I might be in the Senate now." The sudden rise of his friend and contemporary, Senator John F. Kennedy, in the political world stimulated his thinking in this vein and accentuated his mental agitation. His former affection for his father-in-law gave way to bitterness.

Driven by a feeling that there was nothing he could not do—hypermania, the doctors called it—Graham found it impossible to relax for any length of time. A friend met him in Chicago one night after he had made three speeches in a single day and was en route to Detroit to deliver another. Under pressure from President Kennedy, he became chairman of the Board of Incorporators for the Communications Satellite Corporation—an assignment that multiplied his burdens. His drinking and dissipation increased. Ultimately his whirl from one wild exploit to another would land him in Chestnut Lodge, a psychiatric hospital in Rockville, Maryland. After six weeks of treatment he would plead for a day at home, using all his extraordinary powers of persuasion that had contributed so much to his success. Soon after reaching Glen Welby, on August 3, 1963, he would take his life with a shotgun blast.

Meyer would be spared this tragedy, which would not come until four years after his death. Fate seemed to shield him from that cruel blow. Yet he had never allowed his hopes for the future to rest solely upon any individual. In the background was his resourceful, energetic, and journalistically inclined daughter Kay, who would in fact fill the void left by the death of her husband. Kay, he once said, was like a Chinese doll: no matter how many times she might be knocked down, she always came up straight. She was quite capable of projecting his great enterprise into a new era within the Meyer tradition.

In his last year Meyer reaped a number of additional rewards for his public service. Georgetown University presented him with an honorary LLD and the Public Relations Society of America gave him its 1958 "Community Service Award" as he passed his quarter-century milestone in journalism. Floyd G. Blair described the *Post* as Meyer's "shining halo," and Mark Ethridge wired that Meyer's acquisition of that paper in 1933 had been "a blessed day for American journalism."

At the *Post* the celebration of this twenty-fifth anniversary took a somewhat different turn. Meyer's associates gave a dinner for Mrs. Meyer and himself at the Statler Hotel, featuring a "This Is Your Life" presentation. While Bill Nessly, introduced as "the Masked Boswell," recited a spoofing biographical sketch, Bill Gold flashed on the screen a series of historical pictures generously interspersed by views of Meyer being caressed by glamorous actresses and other well-known beauties. The show made such a hit that it was repeated at the party the Grahams gave at Glen Welby, and Meyer asked the wigged "Boswell" if he would go to Mount Kisco and repeat the performance every night.

But these lighter moments were only interludes. Awareness of his shrunken role came as a shock to Meyer one night as he prepared to dress and go downstairs for a party Agnes was giving. One of his daughters asked why he wanted to make the effort in his weakened condition.

"You're ashamed of me," he said accusingly, but accepted the hint and kept out of the hubbub below.

Long before the end came, Meyer had prepared for it by arranging his estate with meticulous care. Yet he repeatedly asked Harrison and his lawyers if he had done everything he should do. As his condition worsened in the summer of 1959 from both cancer and cardiovascular disease, he was taken to George Washington Hospital where he was under the care of Dr. Brown, the first occupant of the Eugene Meyer memorial chair. For a time he was troubled by the absence of Kay and Phil, who were in Europe seeking much-needed relaxation, but they returned before he lapsed into his final coma. One highlight in his twilight period was a discussion with Graham on what it was really like to be publisher of a great paper. Circulation Manager Gladstein called to pay his respects and was warned not to tax the sick man by talking business. But the first question Meyer threw at him was: "Have you reached 450,000 Sunday yet?" Gladstein's comments on what the Post was doing were so optimistic that Meyer begged him to stay. "You're so good for my morale," he said.

Agnes and Elizabeth engaged in a bantering flirtation with the patient until Agnes offered to have the chauffeur take Elizabeth home—presumably so that she could be alone with her husband. Stormy though their marriage had been at times, they had lived together for half a century with mutual respect, admiration, and unflagging interest in each other. In place of high romance they had achieved an enduring partnership that yielded abundant satisfactions. As the hour of parting approached, it brought an appalling sense of loss.

Meyer went into shock after choking on orange juice. Late that night he went into a coma, and the family was called in the early morning hours. Edward Steichen, who was a visitor at Crescent Place, and Al Phillips, the chauffeur, joined the long vigil in a hospital corridor. On the afternoon of July 17, 1959, the California lad who had barnstormed through Wall Street, through the United States government, and through the press yielded at last to death. He was eighty-three.

The country seemed to resound with praise for the life he had lived. President Eisenhower lamented that "the Nation and the news profession have lost an outstanding newspaper executive." Secretary of the Treasury Robert B. Anderson called the deceased "one of the Nation's ablest leaders." Carl Sandburg had kind words for Meyer "as a financier, scholar and patron—friend of all the arts." Through hundreds of comments friends of high and low station recalled his integrity, his keen sense of justice, his repect for human values, his dedication to the public good, and his generosity to friends and worthy causes. Recognizing the fullness of his life, Walter Hagen commented that Meyer had been able "to smell the flowers along the way." Steichen was content to say: "Good-bye, sweet noble friend."

An editorial in the Baltimore Sun was typical of the journalistic comment. While recognizing Meyer's first two careers, in Wall Street and in the government, the Sun went on to say: "Yet the monument by which he is most likely to be remembered is the newspaper, the Washington Post and Times-Herald, which he built. . . . Mr. Meyer died knowing that he had not failed in his purpose."

Private funeral services were held at the family home in Crescent Place, and internment was in Kensico Cemetery near Mount Kisco. On the following Tuesday eight hundred friends gathered at the All Souls Unitarian Church for a memorial service at which Chief Justice Warren eulogized Meyer as "a distinguished mind, an artist in many metiers, a rare friend, a giver of good counsel, a patriotic spirit, a source of humor, and a graphic model of how a citizen in our democracy ought to bear himself if he means to bear himself well."

Everywhere the emphasis was on Meyer the man—not on Meyer the millionaire. His skill in accumulating money had been matched by his foresight and generosity in distributing it. Yet his material resources were a minor element in the contribution he had made to the era in which he lived. His real legacy lay in the pattern he had followed: know everything about your task, work harder than anyone else, and be absolutely honest. It lay too in the respect he had shown for "the power and glory of truth." These imperishable ideas and the newspaper that he re-created are the most meaningful measure of the man.

INDEX

i

Index

Index

Index

Index

Index

Index

xii

A NOTE ABOUT THE AUTHOR

MERLO J. PUSEY was born in Woodruff, Utah, in 1902 and was graduated from the University of Utah. He has worked for two newspapers: the Salt Lake City *Deseret News*, from 1922 to 1928, and the *Washington Post*, from 1928 until his retirement, as an associate editor, in 1971. He is the author of six other books, including a biography of Charles Evans Hughes, which won both the Pulitzer and Bancroft prizes in 1952. Mr. Pusey is also the author of *The Supreme Court Crisis* (1937), *Big Government: Can We Control It* (1945), *Eisenhower the President* (1956), *The Way We Go to War* (1969), and *The U.S.A. Astride the Globe* (1971). He lives with his wife in Dickerson, Maryland.

A NOTE ON THE TYPE

THE TEXT OF THIS BOOK WAS SET IN ELECTRA, a Linotype face designed by W. A. Dwiggins (1880-1956), who was responsible for so much that is good in contemporary book design. Although much of his early work was in advertising and he was the author of the standard volume *Layout in Advertising*, Mr. Dwiggins later devoted his prolific talents to book typography and type design and worked with great distinction in both fields. In addition to his designs for Electra, he created the Metro, Caledonia, and Eldorado series of type faces, as well as a number of experimental cuttings that have never been issued commercially.

Electra cannot be classified as either modern or old-style. It is not based on any historical model, nor does it echo a particular period or style. It avoids the extreme contrast between thick and thin elements that marks most modern faces and attempts to give a feeling of fluidity, power, and speed.

This book was composed, printed and bound by The Haddon Craftsmen, Scranton, Pennsylvania. Typography and binding design by Guy Fleming.